NEGOTIATING THE INTERSECTIONS OF WRITING AND WRITING INSTRUCTION

INTERNATIONAL EXCHANGES ON THE STUDY OF WRITING

Series Editors: Joan Mullin, Magnus Gustafsson, Terry Myers Zawacki, and Federico Navarro

Series Associate Editors: Anna S. Habib and Karen P. Peirce

The International Exchanges on the Study of Writing Series publishes books that address worldwide perspectives on writing, writers, teaching with writing, and scholarly writing practices, specifically those that draw on scholarship across national and disciplinary borders to challenge parochial understandings of all of the above. The Latin America Section of the International Exchanges on the Study of Writing book series publishes peer-reviewed books about writing, writers, teaching with writing, and scholarly writing practices from Latin American perspectives. It also offers re-editions of recognized peer-reviewed books originally published in the region.

The WAC Clearinghouse and University Press of Colorado are collaborating so that these books will be widely available through free digital distribution and low-cost print editions. The publishers and the series editors are committed to the principle that knowledge should freely circulate and have embraced the use of technology to support open access to scholarly work.

Recent Books in the Series

L. Ashley Squires (Ed.), *Emerging Wrioting Research from the Russian Federation* (2021)

Natalia Ávila Reyes (Ed.), *Multilingual Contributions to Writing Research: Toward an Equal Academic Exchange* (2021)

Cecile Badenhorst, Brittany Amell, and James Burford (Eds.), *Re-imagining Doctoral Writing* (2021)

Bruce Morrison, Julia Chen, Linda Lin, and Alan Urmston (Eds.), *English Across the Curriculum: Voices from Around the World* (2021)

Alanna Frost, Julia Kiernan, and Suzanne Blum Malley (Eds.), *Translingual Dispositions: Globalized Approaches to the Teaching of Writing* (2020)

Charles Bazerman et al. (Eds.), *Knowing Writing: Writing Research across Borders* (2019)

Sylvie Plane et al. (Eds.), *Research on Writing: Multiple Perspectives* (2017)

Lisa R. Arnold, Anne Nebel, and Lynne Ronesi (Eds.), *Emerging Writing Research from the Middle East-North Africa Region* (2017)

NEGOTIATING THE INTERSECTIONS OF WRITING AND WRITING INSTRUCTION

Edited by Magnus Gustafsson and Andreas Eriksson

The WAC Clearinghouse
wac.colostate.edu
Fort Collins, Colorado

University Press of Colorado
upcolorado.com
Louisville, Colorado

The WAC Clearinghouse, Fort Collins, Colorado 80523

University Press of Colorado, Louisville, Colorado 80027

© 2022 by Magnus Gustafsson and Andreas Eriksson. This work is licensed under a Creative Commons Attribution-NonCommercial-NoDerivatives 4.0 International License.

ISBN 978-1-64215-146-6 (PDF) | 978-1-64215-147-3 (ePub) | 978-1-64642-313-2 (pbk.)

DOI 10.37514/INT-B.2022.1466

Library of Congress Cataloging-in-Publication Data

Names: Gustafsson, Magnus, 1965– editor. | Eriksson, Andreas, 1973- editor. | Conference of the European Association for the Teaching of Academic Writing (10th : 2019 : Chalmers tekniska högskola, Göteborg, Sweden) Title: Negotiating the intersections of writing and writing instruction / edited by Magnus Gustafsson and Andreas Eriksson.
Description: Fort Collins, Colorado : The WAC Clearinghouse ; Louisville, Colorado : University Press of Colorado, [2021] | Series: International exchanges on the study of writing | Includes bibliographical references.
Identifiers: LCCN 2022000569 (print) | LCCN 2022000570 (ebook) | ISBN 9781646423132 (paperback) | ISBN 9781642151466 (pdf) | ISBN 9781642151473 (epub)
Subjects: LCSH: European Association for the Teaching of Academic Writing—History. | Academic writing. | Academic writing—Study and teaching (Higher)—Europe. | Rhetoric—Study and teaching (Higher)—Europe.
Classification: LCC P301.5.A27 N44 2021 (print) | LCC P301.5.A27 (ebook) | DDC 808.06/6378071—dc23/eng/20220215
LC record available at https://lccn.loc.gov/2022000569
LC ebook record available at https://lccn.loc.gov/2022000570

Copyeditor: Don Donahue
Design and Production: Mike Palmquist
Cover Photo: "Kuggen" [Cog Wheel, campus building], Chalmers University of Technology.
Series Editors: Joan Mullin, Magnus Gustafsson, Terry Myers Zawacki, and Federico Navarro
Series Associate Editors: Anna S. Habib and Karen P. Peirce

The WAC Clearinghouse supports teachers of writing across the disciplines. Hosted by Colorado State University, it brings together scholarly journals and book series as well as resources for teachers who use writing in their courses. This book is available in digital formats for free download at wac.colostate.edu.

Founded in 1965, the University Press of Colorado is a nonprofit cooperative publishing enterprise supported, in part, by Adams State University, Colorado State University, Fort Lewis College, Metropolitan State University of Denver, University of Alaska Fairbanks, University of Colorado, University of Denver, University of Northern Colorado, University of Wyoming, Utah State University, and Western Colorado University. For more information, visit upcolorado.com.

§ Contents

Introduction 3
    Magnus Gustafsson and Andreas Eriksson

PART ONE. SELECTED PAPERS 11

1. Voices from EATAW: A Narrative of the Organization's First
20 Years 13
    Erin Zimmerman

2. Two Experiments in Technologically Mediated Education: 2012
and 2020 41
    Karen J. Head

3. A Heuristic Approach to Selecting Technological Tools for Writing
Instruction and Support 63
    Chris M. Anson

4. Research Writing, What Do We Know and How to Move Forward ... 89
    Montserrat Castelló

5. Fostering Multilingual Academic Writing Knowledge in
Interdisciplinary EMI Degree Programs 123
    Ina Alexandra Machura

6. Considering Individual and Situational Variation in Modeling
Writing Processes 165
    Sabine Dengscherz

7. Conform, Transform, Resist: The Scandinavian Way of Master's
Thesis Supervision and Its Contribution to Acquiring Research
Literacy and Practice 195
    Vibeke Ankersborg and Karl-Heinz Pogner

8. The Challenges of Professional Development in the European
Higher Education Area: Targeting Success in Writing, Research,
Learning and Teaching 233
    Erika Melonashi, Paul Donovan, Basak Ercan,
    Alison Farrell, and Sonia Oliver

9. Moments of Intersection, Rupture, Tension: Writing and Academic
Disciplines in the Semiperiphery 259
    Amy Zenger and John Pill

Contents

PART TWO. REFLECTIONS ON AN EATAW OUTLOOK: OBSERVATIONS FROM COLLEAGUES WITH OVERLAPPING INTERESTS 283

10. EATAW as a First-Year College Composition Course 285
    Djuddah Leijen

11. A Reflective Post-Script of Academic Writing in Times of Internationalization, Interdisciplinarity and Multilingualism 289
    Emma Dafouz

12. A Reflection on Academic Writing: The Perspective of a Group of European Writing Researchers 293
    Nina Vandermeulen, Catherine Meulemans, Lise Paesen, and Teresa Limpo

13. Reflections: An Evolving Academic Writer 301
    Robert Wilkinson

14. Intersection and Challenges in the Teaching of Academic Writing: Voices from Europe and Latin America 307
    Elaine Espindola

Contributors 313

NEGOTIATING THE INTERSECTIONS OF WRITING AND WRITING INSTRUCTION

Introduction

Magnus Gustafsson
Andreas Eriksson
CHALMERS UNIVERSITY OF TECHNOLOGY

Teachers of academic writing across European languages meet every two years for a conference to share research findings, pedagogical approaches, and to discuss new and old challenges. Having access to such a community is of course an asset. This collection grows out of the 10th conference of the European Association for the Teaching of Academic Writing (EATAW) in 2019. The EATAW conferences and the publications from them, exemplify how drawing on, and contributing to, the collective wisdom of colleagues is essential to our professionalism. Given the range and quality of the research presented at the conference, the call for papers was a joint one with the *Journal of Academic Writing* (*JoAW*), and the special issue from the conference (https://publications.coventry.ac.uk/index.php/joaw/index) was published in December 2020.

There is a natural overlap in topics and research approaches between the two publications but the contribution of a collection like this is the extended studies it allows. Chapters are twice as long or more than the article-length publications available in the special issue. The research areas and interests are very similar but the scope possible in the collection chapters is simply not an option in the special issue. There is also, possibly, a slight change of character between the *JoAW* articles and the collection chapters. Since the collection is a much slower publication, the findings, conclusions, and recommendations communicated in the collection chapters are slightly less time sensitive. One shared denominator in the chapters is the element of discussing models, approaches, and frameworks more than individual results. Needless to say, this is a difference of degree only.

The 2019 conference explored the theme "Academic writing at intersections—Interdisciplinarity, genre hybridization, multilingualism, digitalization, and interculturality," and the contributions to this collection focus on the sorts of choices we face as teachers of academic writing and, indeed, as writers who seek publication as we stand at various intersections. Intersections explored in the chapters include our use of technology. It is true most of us increased the use of technology in the 2019/2020 and 2020/2021 academic years, and we got better at using different platforms and applications. We also, however, need to continue questioning each choice and application of technology. What are the effects on learning with its use and what are the, possibly conflicting, assumptions about learning with a specific technology? Another recurring intersection we tend to face very often is that of choosing supervision approaches. We need to be able to assess what the respective student learning profiles expect and need at any given point during a learning process. While that requires situational awareness, such choices are also informed by our own experiences and fundamental assumptions about learning. A third intersection comes with our needing to scaffold writing processes. We continuously negotiate what we know about writing and publication process variations and contextual challenges. Without such negotiation, optimizing supervision and writing development is even more challenging. A fourth category of intersections occur within and across our shifting contexts. Most EATAW members find themselves in translingual conditions addressing multiple languages and often facilitating learning in English-medium education. The translation or adaption of approaches between different international higher education systems and publication traditions constantly require us to explore and expand our positions as teacher-researchers in relation to traditions and canons—the center. The individual chapters in this collection address these recurring topics and offer an entry into the shared conversation of the EATAW community.

As expected in EATAW work, most chapters negotiate pedagogical intersections in one way or another. One of those concerns, as expected in EATAW with its multilingual contexts, is that several chapters address, directly or indirectly, the negotiation of language use and translanguaging. On the one hand, EATAW members obviously need to promote writing development in the respective first languages of their many higher education systems. This often involves relying both on the tradition and history of the local or regional context as well as on translating or adapting what might be done in international contexts. As we move from first cycle levels (bachelor level) into the second and third cycles (master and Ph.D. levels) promoting student mobility, language diversification increases and any one writing process or supervision approach needs testing and adjusting to an ever more heterogeneous student body. So, language use, educational backgrounds, and interdisciplinary contexts prompt added attention to writing processes and supervision practices.

It is obviously true that the emergency remote teaching we have all experienced since spring 2020 has accentuated the need to also navigate and negotiate technology and the challenges and affordances it comes with. This pedagogical focus is implicit in some chapters and explicitly addressed in two chapters. There is a need for us to be well-informed about the assumptions and limitations of any tool or platform we choose to use. Therefore, beginning to discuss how to assess the tools and applications we consider is a critical step for the community.

The EATAW context is also one characterized by significant organizational variation. Coming out of these different contexts and traditions, the chapters emphasize the constant negotiation of theory, frameworks, and approaches that may have been initially articulated in other contexts or for different conditions in the past. The strength of much EATAW work is precisely this negotiation of the situated character of our respective contexts and our use of "theory" as these affect decisions about writing assignments, supervision approaches, research designs, as well as institutional and support for teachers, students, and researchers.

Chapter Outlines

The first part of the collection has work from Europe and beyond and includes three chapters elaborating on two of the keynotes from the conference. In addition to the empirical data-driven work in the studies conducted, the collection also provides three additional and important overviews. One is an interview-based history of the 20-year-old association. The second is an impressive summary of the many ways writing instruction, research support and support for teaching and learning is organized across the many different higher education systems in Europe including a vision for steps forward. The third overview is an important discussion of the constant negotiation of centre—periphery including positions of the semi-periphery in issues and discussions concerning writing studies, writing instruction, and writing for publication in English as a second or foreign language.

The collection opens with a look at 20 years of the association. We believe readers who are new to the community might benefit from this background as they later take on the following chapters with elaborations on the studies that informed two of the keynotes and five additional studies conducted based on presentations delivered at the conference. In this sense, the nine chapters we offer from the 2019 conference in the first part of the collection exemplify a sample of the issues of interest in the community. The production process of the collection coincided with the COVID-19 pandemic and while authors have had an opportunity to add comments about the pandemic where relevant, this collection does not focus on the impact COVID-19 has had on our research, processes, and pedagogies. That topic might receive more coverage in the publications from the EATAW2021 conference. This 2019 collection emphasizes the continual negotiations, the flexibility and tenuousness of our positions as writing researchers and teachers in EATAW.

Zimmerman offers a 20-year history of the association. While the history of EATAW can likely be traced in additional ways, this interview study is the first of its kind and very important as a way of documenting the evolution of EATAW over 20 years, a history often lacking in associations and one that provides necessary reflection on our values and purposes as a field within our contexts. Zimmerman summarizes the recurring themes of the association's development from interviewing a number of colleagues with connections to the history of EATAW. Current and past board members get to articulate reasons for establishing EATAW and what has driven them to maintain or help develop the association. Overseas colleagues get to point at what a European community means to them and how it has affected scenes outside Europe. The chapter also accounts for the work that went and goes into the *Journal of Academic Writing* as well as the various phases of the work the EATAW board has been involved in.

Chris Anson and Karen Head gave a joint keynote at the 2019 conference. Here, **Head** describes and discusses two parallel processes of exploring the roles and conditions for technology in our learning environments. Her account of the MOOCs trend and the work of designing and developing one for academic writing provides an insightful view and a set of issues with assumptions of learning in MOOCs. Similarly, our respective learning platforms, accentuated by the pandemic in 2020 and 2021, also come with at times troublesome assumptions and learning philosophies that do not necessarily promote the processes and the learning activities we would prefer for teaching academic writing. And, so, we find ourselves needing to share workarounds.

Anson's chapter from the joint keynote first elaborates on the assumptions and affordances of the various tools we might consider using. He presents us with a brief history of how our belief and trust in instructional technology has evolved from what may have been a naïve quasi-Skinnerian philosophy to more recent tools with additional affordances. But no tool is perfect or even suitable for all situations. Therefore, Anson offers a heuristic for helping colleagues decide whether or not to use a particular tool. Does it, in fact, hold the potential we need, and does it meet the requirements of inclusive support that facilitates disciplinary writing development as well as writing to learn? The tool Anson offers helps readers make more informed decisions based on a critical analysis of the tools and platforms available to us and our students.

Castelló, who offered the second keynote at the conference, takes a close longitudinal look at the writing processes of Ph.D. students. She follows the drafting and revision of articles, and we get to see how arduous the transition to writing for publication can be, even if we provide the support of something like an eight-week writing workshop. We believe many colleagues will recognize the challenges and the long processes; in this chapter, however, we also get additional perspectives for further understanding the processes. Castelló provides information also on the networking of the students and their self-assessed journeys of development. As we get to see connections between revision impact and the simultaneous aspects of the students' development, we begin to see a more systemic or holistic picture of graduate and professional writing development.

Machura studies an increasingly important challenge in education globally—what are the effects of studying in English medium education (EME) contexts and how can we help students and faculty reap the benefits of EME while also coping with the challenges? The research context is one of close collaboration between content specialists and English-specific-purposes (ESP) specialists on a multilingual interdisciplinary management degree program. Such integration of language or communication development into subject courses, rather than treating communication and language as stand-alone competences to be practiced, appeals since language is the carrier for learning and since, therefore, distinguishing between *language* and *content* is not really possible. Together, the team developed writing intensive assignments to promote learning and a shared discourse. While the study is set in Germany, it emphasizes the translingual affordances of English medium education and English as a lingua franca. The study shows how students' writing and self-assessment indeed improve along some dimensions and how faculty become more aware of the importance of a shared approach to writing development. An additional and important insight from the study is how our educational contexts limit the research designs available to us and how our interpretation of results is heavily situated and contextualized. This challenge of evaluating interventions and student learning in them is further accentuated for EATAW members as we try to adapt studies and interventions between our various higher education sites.

Dengscherz presents a case study of Austrian translation studies students' writing processes and argues that focusing exclusively on activities risks missing crucial aspects of writing processes. She continues to outline a model that also includes a number of factorial conditions. By specifying functions and effects of the challenges students face with heuristic and rhetorical requirements and by allowing room for the specifics of any one writing situation, Dengscherz arrives at a rich dynamic description of writing processes based on her cases. Her account of previous descriptions of writing processes and her addition of translingual dimensions of writing processes provide a good example of how the EATAW community and its conversation can enrich the research and development in writing studies through its negotiation of central concepts in view of the numerous situated contexts it draws from.

Ankersborg and Pogner exemplify another closer look at the way in which our different educational contexts and traditions influence our negotiation of EATAW concerns. They describe and analyze supervisory roles and models and argue that a shift in responsibility can be detected in their Danish problem-oriented learning context compared to some models and roles described in the literature from contexts where English is a dominant language. Based on interviews with students, the study arrives at a matrix for supervisor roles and models based on student preferences at the master's level and finds that the partnership model is the one that students prefer. This partnership model enables a supervisor multiple roles including being a knowledge expert, a methods supervisor, and a process supervisor. It is also a model that allows the student far more room to negotiate a way forward with the supervisor.

Melonashi et al. account for a large sub-study in a five-year European COST project (https://www.werelate.eu/) exploring the shared dimensions and values across the many different ways of organizing support for writing, research, and teaching and learning at European universities. With data collected from 252 colleagues from universities across 31 European countries, they show first the degree of variation in support and the management assumptions that might explain the decisions for formats and levels of ambition in supporting these overlapping facets of university activity and academic writing. They also account for the suggestions resulting from the voices in the data; one recurring dimension of these visions, again, is the situated character of each context and the constant negotiation of core and periphery. They ask a question and provide a way to reflect on what we all must continually revisit: Is the model that grew out of the core really applicable in the specific context?

Zenger and Pill present a study that in many ways is pivotal to the EATAW scene. Interestingly, they do this from a site outside Europe as they account for and offer an analytical framework for the publishing work of Lebanese researchers and suggest that these researchers can be considered to be located in the semi-periphery. The study is important precisely because in a discussion of negotiating our respective contexts and conditions. As can be seen in the complex context of Lebanon, our relative geographical, political, linguistic, disciplinary, and conceptual locations and conditions problematize the mere concept of center-periphery. Situating and positioning our work in relation to a sense of core, a peripheral, and a semi-peripheral position becomes a recurring challenge for EATAW researchers as well as for the students whose writing development we aim to empower. Being successful in such an endeavor requires the kind of creative adjustments the researchers in the chapter exemplify. Building models for understanding such challenging knowledge production dynamics is a necessary task for the EATAW and other writing studies communities.

The second part of the collection provides reflections on the collection chapters and the image they generate of EATAW work. We asked the EATAW chair **Leijen** to comment on the content and we similarly asked **Dafouz**, who gave a keynote at the conference, to add her perspective. Beyond the conference and the association, we asked our colleagues in two other European communities to reflect on the studies presented. **Vandermeulen, Meulemans, Paesen,** and **Limpo** relate the nine chapters to the work that is done is the EARLI Sig Writing sphere (https://earli.org/SIG12) and **Wilkinson** offers his view of the work in the collection from the point of view of Integrating Content and Language in Higher Education (ICLHE, https://iclhe.org) and our work supporting writing. The fifth reflection takes us outside Europe for a glimpse of writing studies in Latin America. **Espindola** reflects on the research in the collection from the point of view of the Latin American Association of Writing Studies in Higher Education and Professional Contexts (ALES, https://www.estudiosdelaescritura.org).

Trying to Get a Sense of EATAW

As expressed multiple times in keynotes, presentations, and workshops during the EATAW2021 conference "The residence of writing and writing support" (https://www.eataw2021.org/), describing something like an *EATAW profile* would be worthwhile. As an association, we are continuously at work on that rewarding task. The contributions in this collection are part of that rewarding long-term project of understanding our EATAW context.

In short, the collection does not provide an overview nor really a profile or state-of-the-art account of the research and development in the EATAW community. What we believe it offers is an account of the multidimensional and situated environment facing the community. It picks up some of the issues in an ongoing process of negotiating choices at intersections. Our respective situated contexts often prompt different responses, interpretations, and reaction to the themes, frameworks, languages, and philosophies we face. The collection, therefore, provides an insight into our negotiations and models on which colleagues might base their own decisions in a tangent situation.

However, we also need to distinguish between something vaguely thought of as *European writing studies* and *EATAW work*. EATAW publications definitely form a subgroup of European writing studies but there are multiple organizations, associations, and research programs with all their individual researchers that are similarly dedicated to promoting the shared field of writing studies in Europe. We have captured a limited representation of that dimension of the tangent communities in the closing reflections, which we hope add further insights to the chapters.

Needless to say, one of the main and lasting motivation factors for the association was, has been, and is to provide a lively forum for discussing these many negotiations. These chapters contribute to that discussion, and we know the suggestions, conclusions, and recommendations brought to the table by these authors will spur continued conversation and future publications. In this way, we continue to develop our 20-year-old association such that it remains dynamic, progressive, and inclusive in the eyes of new and veteran members.

Part One. Selected Papers

1 Voices from EATAW: A Narrative of the Organization's First 20 Years

Erin Zimmerman
UNIVERSITY OF NEVADA, LAS VEGAS

July 2019 marked the 10th conference and 20th anniversary of the European Association for the Teaching of Academic Writing (EATAW). EATAW's mission, most visible through its biannual conference, is to support members as they teach, tutor, research, administer, and develop academic writing and writing programs across Europe. For more than 20 years, EATAW has offered its members a space for support, conversation, and collaboration, which is precisely why the original founders sought to create the organization. Few written records of EATAW's history exist beyond what is found on the EATAW website, in the biennial conference proceedings, and in the special issues of the *Journal of Academic Writing*. Even with these archives, little has been documented about how the organization came into being, who took the lead in various endeavors, and what that work has entailed. This chapter relates the history of the organization through interviews of the stakeholders who played key roles in the creation and continuation of EATAW. Through these conversations, the history of EATAW's early steps, development, and future trajectories are traced as a way to archive the work that has gone before so that we might inform the work that is yet to come.

As the European Association for the Teaching of Academic Writing celebrated its 10th biennial conference at Chalmers University of Technology in Gothenburg, Sweden in July of 2019, many new faces could be seen in the crowd alongside members who have been a part of the organization since its inception. One of the beautiful things about EATAW has been the growth that has occurred while still remaining small enough that attendees get to know a lot of people. In many ways, this balance has allowed the organization to move forward while maintaining close ties to its history. Founding members and members of the board throughout EATAW's years can still be called upon to gain, store, and retrieve organizational memory. Previous conference

DOI: https://doi.org/10.37514/INT-B.2022.1466.2.01

websites, edited collections, and issues of the *Journal of Academic Writing* (*JoAW*), among publications elsewhere, house a wide range of information about the work done at EATAW and by its members in the past 20 years.

However, as EATAW moves into its third decade, as more and more new members join, as central figures such as Gabriela Ruhmann pass away, as databases are lost, and as websites disappear, it becomes more necessary for the members of EATAW to actively keep track of its history. This is necessary for its members to know where it came from, why it exists in the form it does, and what its challenges and successes have been so that future decisions and changes may be grounded in the knowledge, visions and actions of those that came before. Plus, as the premier international organization for the teaching of academic writing in higher education in Europe, EATAW's history is filled with a wealth of knowledge and resources useful for all teachers and researchers of academic writing.

This chapter is a humble attempt at providing a narrative that traces the development of writing teaching and research in Europe over the past twenty years and how the organization has provided a network to support those efforts. Because EATAW, like any organization, is an organism made up of a wide variety of people, locations, perspectives, memories, documents, actions, and decisions, it is impossible to craft a completely whole and unbiased picture. However, my goal is to share the voices of members who have been integral during the first 20 years of the organization in order to preserve pieces of its history, identity, and evolution that others may not know about. I also have included a handful of tables throughout the chapter that identify books, websites, and other information denoting key scholarship or moments of EATAW's past.

To create such a history, I conducted interviews with twelve individuals who were founding members, long-time members, board members, and conference organizers, all of whom having served more than one of these roles. The voices that tell this story of EATAW are those of Lawrence Cleary (University of Limerick), Lisa Ganobcsik-Williams (Coventry University), Katrin Girgensohn (SRH Berlin University of Applied Sciences), Magnus Gustafsson (Chalmers University of Technology), John Harbord (Maastricht University), Otto Kruse (Zurich University of Applied Sciences), Djuddah Leijen (University of Tartu), Joan Mullin (University of North Carolina at Charlotte), Lotte Rienecker (University of Copenhagen), David Russell (Iowa State University), Jacqueline van Kruiningen (University of Groningen), and Stuart Wrigley (Royal Holloway, University of London).

This tracing of EATAW's history archives the rich teaching and research exchanges that have taken place as well as the ways and speed to which

EATAW's members have tackled challenges that researchers, teachers, and writers have faced over the past two decades. Equally important, is the recognition of how the organization developed alongside the members' work while simultaneously supporting those networks within and across institutional and national borders. My hope is that this chapter can be a step for more historical and archival work to be done to ensure the memories of EATAW and its members are not lost. There has been and continues to be the need for collaboration across borders, and attention to the early steps and trajectories perhaps helps readers find instances where the work that has gone before can now inform the work that is yet to come.

In addition, having joined EATAW in 2013 as a doctoral student from the United States who was interested in learning more about writing across all contexts, I knew little about writing practices and instruction outside of the U.S. educational system. I was overwhelmed and excited by the work being done across Europe and the array of systems, teaching practices, and challenges that existed and were all being talked about in one place. Because I wanted to learn more about this work, I decided to run for the EATAW board in 2017. What I did not realize until my first meeting with other board members was that I actually knew almost nothing about the organization itself. So, a personal hope is that members, like me, who have joined EATAW not fully grasping its context and significance, and possibly having wondered how to contribute to the organization, might become better oriented by finding some of those details in this piece.

The Beginnings

> We needed a wider, European perspective on the teaching side of academic writing.
>
> — *Otto Kruse*

When I asked two historians of writing instruction about the founding of EATAW, Otto Kruse, one of the founding members, and David Russell, a member since 2001, both commented that the decisions in 1999 to create EATAW were impacted by nearly two centuries of history of writing instruction across European educational systems. These scholars recount that beginning in the early 1800s, more empirically based language studies began to replace the position that rhetoric had held within universities through much of Europe. The most significant teaching methods that continued to impact Europe and the United States and introduced writing as a means of teaching and learning were the German seminar method and the British tutorial model. In German seminars, students were expected to write one paper, which essentially could act as a semester-long writing-to-learn activity but during which students were typically receiving very little writing instruction. In some British universities, students would meet one-on-one, or in small groups, with teaching staff, called tutors, to read and discuss their writing and receive feedback. David reflects that both models could be considered near-ideal instructional processes. And perhaps, at times, they were.

But as the twentieth century progressed, and more and more students began to go to university, meaningful instructional practices within these models could not be sustained. Plus, with more students came more diversity in the challenges they faced with writing. Researchers began to look beyond problems narrowly limited to language. And unlike in the United States, where most students were required to take first-year composition courses, in Europe, students had few places dedicated to teaching about and offering practice for writing skills that they could turn to. Teachers were reading about and were inspired by the American writing across the curriculum movement and writing centers but were having to import and adapt those practices and theories to often very different European contexts. Thus, teachers often struggled to locate useful resources for enacting the support they realized their students needed.

A handful of national movements, international organizations, and networks began to carve out a niche for examining writing and language in higher education. During the late 1980s and 1990s, several organizations were bringing a variety of individuals together to explore issues related to academic writing: for instance, the British Association of Lecturers in English for Academic Purposes (BALEAP), Writing Development in Higher Education (WDHE), EARLI SIG Writing, the International Writing Centers Association (IWCA), and its counterpart, the European Writing Centers Association (EWCA). There was also a well-established academic writing community in Germany that was hosting their own conferences for teachers of academic writing in German. In 1999, Gabriela Ruhmann hosted a writing conference at her home university in Bochum, Germany, and co-edited a book of presentations from that conference. (See Table 1.1). Many of the participants at the conference were Germans interested in academic writing instruction, though a handful of people from across Europe attended. While there, she, Lennart Björk, Lotte Rienecker, Otto Kruse, and Peter Stray Jörgensen came together to create the European Association for the Teaching of Academic Writing.

Table 1.1. The Published Collection of Presentations from the 1999 Conference in Bochum where EATAW was Founded

Title and Publication Information	Editors
Schlüsselkompetenz Schreiben: Konzepte, Methoden, Projekte für Schreibberatung und Schreibdidaktik an der Hochschule. Luchterhand. 1999.	Otto Kruse, Eva-Maria Jakobs & Gabriela Ruhmann

Lotte remembers conversations with Otto about how such a conference should be held in English and should be made more international. She was traveling from Denmark to various academic writing conferences in England, Germany, Scandinavia, and the United States and noticed so much overlap in conversations being had, yet there was no centralized forum to bring them together. During such conversations, Otto remembers wide agreement on the perspective that there was a need for a Europe-wide organization dedicated to the European perspective of teaching academic writing. Lotte vividly remembers watching a plenary speech about text types in academic writing given by Lennart Björk, a then professor of English Literature at Gothenburg University, Sweden, and an influential figure in the field. Then moments after he finished, she noticed him walking up to several people and whispering to them. He soon approached her and whispered, "In just a second, I am announcing a new organization and I want you to chair it. Please don't say no." And she agreed. Though most attendees of the conference were surprised by the announcement because there had not been a visible movement for such an organization, it also felt like a logical step to highlight the important work that was going on in Europe.

Lennart recognized the importance of establishing a democratic process for elections, but to get the organization off the ground he simply appointed those he thought best positioned to do so. Lotte realized that she was not the most obvious selection for the role of chair. Yet, Lennart's rationale was political: She held the most permanent position within an actual writing program, the writing center in Copenhagen. And Jacqueline van Kruiningen, though not a member of the board, quickly agreed to organize the first conference at her university in Groningen, Netherlands, which was scheduled for two years from then as a joint conference between EATAW and the European Writing Centers Association, which had been created in 1998 by Anna Challenger and Tracy Santa.

Jacqueline recalls being very interested in the idea of organizing the conference because she was doing a significant amount of work at the University of Groningen, running a project designed to create more attention for communicative skills at the university. She and her team were holding workshops and meeting with teachers to help with writing assignment design, creating writing intensive courses and writing tasks, and giving feedback on and assessing writing. Because they felt they were a unique program isolated from others doing the same sorts of work elsewhere, they recognized the need for exchange with colleagues, especially with those in Europe and not as far away as the United States.

Jacqueline remembers being in regular contact with Lotte and Peter, making plans for the conference. To publicize the conference, they created an email list based on personal contacts they had both inside and outside Europe, and Lotte made announcements about it at other teaching and writing-related conferences. Everything was done in an informal way and with only a little money coming from sources such as the hosting university and the Hans Böckler Foundation. And yet, 200–250 people attended, and the feedback was overwhelmingly positive: Attendees were pleased to finally have a place to exchange ideas and learn from others, to network with so many people from across Europe, as well as from the United States, for the first time.

Table 1.2. The Published Collection of Presentations from the 2001 EATAW Conference

Title and Publication Information	Editors
Teaching academic writing in European higher education. Springer Science & Business Media, 2003. https://doi.org/10.1007/0-306-48195-2	Lennart Björk, Gerd Bräuer, Lotte Rienecker & Peter Stray Jörgensen

Lotte remembered that everyone involved expected the conference to be big but also professional, and the organizers took a lot of care to create requirements and review abstracts to ensure the presentations in this new and growing field would be as scholarly as those in other fields. From these presentations, an edited collection was published two years later. (See Table 1.2). The board also wanted to maintain the organization's European identity. To honor that theme, Olga Dysthe was invited to be a keynote speaker, whom Lisa Ganobcsik-Williams clearly remembers placing writing within the rhetorical tradition of ancient Greece. Concurrently, the board decided that because they were heavily inspired by writings from the US, they would bring only one American keynote speaker. John Bean, invited to be the sole American keynote speaker at this first conference, spoke about the connection between writing and critical thinking, something different than the purely cognitive approach that was dominating many discussions about academic writing. Many, like Otto and Lotte, recall his talk as one of their fondest

Voices from EATAW

memories of EATAW because it provided a strong theoretical basis through which to teach writing and it reinforced the decision to build connections with teachers and researchers in the United States.

Since 2001, the EATAW conference has been held every two years. (See Table 1.3 for conference hosts and locations and Table 1.4 for conference themes and websites). Recent conferences have seen more than 300 attendees. Comments made by EATAW conference attendees all have similar things to say about their experiences. Lisa found it "exciting for me to finally, after many months, find a community of people who were interested in writing development." And, Djuddah Leijen says, "because we were just starting to get involved with the topic at the university, it was more or less a 'wow factor' that so many people are really working on this and have answers to it."

Table 1.3. EATAW Conference Hosts and Locations

Date	Host University	Location
2001	University of Groningen	Groningen, Netherlands
2003	Central European University	Budapest, Hungary
2005	Hellenic American Union	Athens, Greece
2007	Ruhr Universität	Bochum, Germany
2009	Coventry University	Coventry, England
2011	University of Limerick	Limerick, Ireland
2013	Central European University	Budapest, Hungary
2015	Tallinn University of Technology	Tallinn, Estonia
2017	Royal Holloway, University of London	Egham, England
2019	Chalmers University of Technology	Göteborg, Sweden
2021	VSB-Technical University of Ostrava	Online

Table 1.4. EATAW Conference Themes and Websites

Date	Conference Theme	Conference Website
2001	"Teaching Academic Writing Across Europe" (with EWCA)	none
2003	"Tutoring and Teaching Academic Writing" (with EWCA)	http://web.ceu.hu/eataw/about.htm
2005	"Teaching Writing on Line and Face to Face"	https://eataw2005.hau.gr/index.htm
2007	"Teaching Academic Writing across and in the Disciplines"	http://www.schreibzentrum.de/eataw2007/index.html

Date	Conference Theme	Conference Website
2009	"The Roles of Writing Development in Higher Education and Beyond"	http://www.coventry.ac.uk/eataw2009
2011	"The Role of the Student Experience in Shaping Academic Writing Development in Higher Education"	https://ulsites.ul.ie/eataw2011/mlc/
2013	"Teaching Writing across Languages and Cultures"	https://asszisztencia.hu/eataw2013/
2015	"Academic Writing in Multiple Scholarly, Socio-Cultural, Instructional and Disciplinary Contexts: Challenges and Perspectives"	https://issuu.com/eataw2015/stacks/
2017	"Academic Writing Now: Policy, Pedagogy and Practice"	http://eataw2017.org/
2019	"Academic writing at intersections: Interdisciplinarity, genre hybridization, multilingualism, digitalization, and interculturality"	https://2019.eataw.eu/
2021	"The residence of writing and writing support"	https://www.eataw2021.org/

In the first few years, the board members spent a lot of time and energy constructing the missions and structures of EATAW. Otto remembers a lot of conversations about how the organization should work because there was no model for having a European-wide organization. Specifically, they understood the need for academic writing to be professionalized as its own discipline and recognized that the organization must play a central role in that development. As difficult as that is for any field of study, the diversity of the different cultures and languages, writing traditions, and educational systems was a central facet of conversations for EATAW board members. Unlike American scholars who were used to dealing primarily with English language writers, EATAW wanted to assert that writing instruction in all European languages was important. Lotte in particular noted the emphasis on members "contextualizing, not just emulating, but contextualizing what would be possible to do in very, very different contexts from what we can read about in the WAC journals or the [WAC] Clearinghouse."

In attempting to carve out its own domain, there was, and continues to be, overlap with writing center practice and scholarship coming out of the EWCA. The first two EATAW conferences were titled as joint conferences with EWCA, but there soon existed concern about the imbalance of support coming from each organization. In addition, EWCA was born directly out of the American writing center movement, with the first affiliates being American universities in Europe. Many felt that in the early years, EWCA was a home for Americans exporting their model of writing center work; meanwhile, EATAW leaders were searching for formats that fit or could be adapted to European educational systems, and which could very well be inspired by the U.S.-models. Thus, after the 2003 conference, the board members decided that the organizations should run their own conferences. In 2005, both conferences were in Greece a week apart, and later EWCA switched to holding its conferences in even years so that there would be a writing conference offered every year.

While the two organizations did not officially collaborate much over subsequent years, Katrin Girgensohn observed that many of the same individuals were showing up at both conferences and have sometimes been known to serve on both organizations' boards. In fact, she recalls that EATAW had a peer writing tutor panel and a peer tutor keynote before the EWCA did, and Lawrence Cleary recalls specific conversations with scholars in TESOL, EAP, first-language writing, genre studies, and more that impacted how members of his writing center team conceptualized their center's work. Thus, even in separation the two organizations were developing in ways that were often parallel to one another and relevant to each other's members.

Inclusivity was also a major topic of discussion during the first few years. Several early board members remember John Harbord, who was working at the Central European University at the time, as especially vocal about making decisions that allowed individuals from every European nation to have access to all aspects of EATAW. A favorable idea with persuasive arguments established EATAW as an open organization: no member would have to pay fees, and no university hosting a biannual conference should make any profit from the event. Scholarships were created for scholars in need of financial support to attend conferences, and decisions on the conference locations have at times included discussion of ease and cost of travel. As a result, founding and long-time members of EATAW have observed a growth in participation from southern and eastern European nations that were not initially represented at conferences.

The Only Major Conflict

> A stormy two years.
>
> —*John Harbord*

In 2005, a surprising turn of events at the Athens conference caused members to reconsider the status of Europe and European languages within EATAW.

Some members and conference attendees voiced their concern that EATAW in name was excluding people from the Americas, Africa, the Middle East, and Asia, and that because academic writing in English dominated real-life practice, it should likewise be at the center of the organization. Others, however, were concerned that a focus on one language would reduce the support EATAW could offer to writing teachers of other European languages. In addition, the argument was made that EATAW needed a permanent home, with a recommendation to locate it in Athens. Some board members remember receiving phone calls a few days before the conference requesting support on these issues, and others later found that they were left out of the loop. Then when the general assembly was set to vote at the end of the conference, attendees who were not technically members were casting votes in order to sway the outcome of the board elections.

By the end of the conference, this newly elected board found themselves split almost down the middle between the two sides of the issue. John recalls eight of the nine board members being evenly split, and one more neutral individual who at the end of the debate told John that she initially was not partisan and after weighing both sides carefully, came down on the side of the European group. And the general membership was often just as divided. Joan Mullin witnessed a number of nationalistic and territorial opinions presented during general meetings and conversations at meals that at times gave the impression that many were ready to give up on any kind of enterprise for working together and moving forward. Otto remembers some pointing out that they were not prepared to have an international organization: Researching writing in Europe was already a large enough task.

Perhaps surprisingly for an association that is 20 years old, this instance was the only major divisive conflict in EATAW's history. While several of the individuals on the side of expanding borders to become a world-wide organization and centralizing EATAW in Athens are no longer affiliated with EATAW, this event resulted in an organization that remains primarily European, with a shared focus on language other than English, and also open to everyone. Yet, more neutral and positive perspectives also exist. For instance, from hindsight, Otto finds that the event was not important for the overall development of EATAW. Joan thinks of it positively because she witnessed how the debates could have destroyed the organization and permanently split apart many more people than it did, and as a result, the experience forced everyone to look at the bylaws and constitution and think about what the organization is.

Though perhaps this incident did not alter the vision and missions of EATAW, it did significantly impact the structures of the organization. There was a push to ensure that EATAW would exist as a fully-fledged, legally recognized organization. A handful of clauses were voted into the constitution; for instance, the clarification of procedures for adding items to the agenda of the general assembly, a decrease of board size from nine to seven members, and limitations on how many members could be elected from a certain country as well as from countries outside of Europe. John comments on these types of "peculiar clauses" that were there simply because the board elected in 2007 wanted to prevent any future faction from gaining control of EATAW.

Language used to describe the "chaos" of the potential "takeover" in Athens range from "exciting" to "hostile" to "suspicious." Such negative perspectives were influential to the work that continued over the next few years, as Magnus Gustafsson reflects that the fear of a recurrence of such an event meant that the constitution was still being revised as far into the future as 2014. Joan considers EATAW a stronger organization because of the work done during and following this event: "It did make them look at their bylaws. It did make them look at their constitution. It did make them think about what the organization is." And John recognizes that fifteen years after the Athens conference, EATAW has matured enough as an organization that threats like these are no longer concerning.

A Journal is Launched

> [This journal] should provide a platform, a venue for people all over to be able to access academic writing scholarship.
> — *Lisa Ganobcsik-Williams*

Another act that many interviewees claim has helped to strengthen the organization is the *Journal of Academic Writing*. For many years, the conference and the listserv were the only methods for EATAW members to interact. And though two edited collections had come out of the organization—one in German, *Schlüsselkompetenz Schreiben: Konzepte, Methoden, Projekte für Schreibberatung und Schreibdidaktik an der Hochschule*, and one in English, *Teaching Academic Writing in European Higher Education*—research contributions were mainly only occurring at the conferences themselves.

The board had continuously talked about creating a journal, though Otto states that they never had a discussion about the need for such a journal; they all knew it was essential. Lisa remembers that initially the conversations were centered on the idea of publishing a print journal; but as online, open-source journals started becoming more mainstream, that discussion shifted. John and others felt strongly that the journal should be easily accessible to anyone, especially since so many EATAW members were at institutions that might not have the funding to purchase a subscription to a paper-based journal. With that in mind, board members Esther van der Voort and Lisa researched a variety of publishers, but they soon realized that without EATAW collecting membership fees, paying a publisher was not feasible. Thus, they turned their attention to the Open Journal Systems (OJS) software, a free journal platform developed by the Public Knowledge Project and housed at Simon Fraser University.

Lotte contacted Gert Rijlaarsdam, an editor of *Journal of Writing Research*, to learn about the roles of the staff as well as the workflow and production process of such a journal. Meanwhile, Lisa began a collaboration with Joanne Marsh at Coventry University's Lanchester Library who had worked with OJS previously and could share her expertise. Over time, with the support of the IT team and the Centre for Academic Writing at Coventry, Lisa was able to set up OJS to have the first issue of *JoAW* released in 2011 with submissions from the 2009 conference on "the Roles of Writing Development in Higher Education and Beyond" in Coventry. During these nine years, there have been ten issues completed with a further two in the pipeline. Five of these have been guest-edited issues containing scholarly articles, presentations, and other pieces from the bi-annual conferences, as well as one issue exploring topics related to an integrating content and language in higher education colloquium held in Gothenburg in 2012. (See Table 1.5 for the full list of special issues). Lisa particularly credits Magnus Gustafsson who has contributed greatly as a Guest Editor on a number of issues. Other Guest Editors include Lawrence Cleary, John Harbord, Stuart Wrigley, Íde O'Sullivan, Bojana Petrič, Laryssa Whittaker, and Andreas Eriksson. Lisa has sourced support with statistics-checking, proofreading, copy-editing, and layout largely from her own university and occasionally from Guest Editors' universities, while the EATAW board and a growing database of EATAW colleagues have served as Peer Reviewers.

Lisa Ganobcsik-Williams, the founding Editor of *JoAW*, affirms that the journal has provided a platform for people to access academic writing scholarship, and to make contributions that will be widely read. As such, nearly every person interviewed commented on the impact the journal has had on helping to establish EATAW and the discipline of academic writing within Europe as a legitimate field of study and practice. In keeping with the value of the organization's founders to encourage research in one's own language, *JoAW* accepts submissions written in English, French, Spanish, and other European languages. Additionally, Stuart Wrigley commented on debates his editorial team with Laryssa Whittaker had in 2017 about maintaining high levels of academic rigor while simultaneously trying to open up venues for all voices to contribute. Though they primarily accepted traditional research papers, he remembers a couple of the articles were more polemical or ideas-led rather than evidence-led, and three short lightning talk submissions designed to allow writers to contribute short learning interventions. Lisa notes that what she is most proud of is assisting in setting up a journal that helps EATAW members and beyond "engage in dialogue with other writing teachers and researchers and make contributions themselves—for their contributions to be read by the wider world and to have value." She, Stuart, and Magnus all observed the significance that papers coming in for review often cite other people's papers from previous issues, and they would be interested to find out how widely *JoAW* articles are being cited elsewhere too.

Table 1.5. *Journal of Academic Writing* Special Issues

Publication Information	Volume Title
Vol. 1 No. 1 2011	The Roles of Writing Development in Higher Education and Beyond
Vol. 2 No. 1 2012	The Role of the Student Experience in Shaping Academic Writing Development in Higher Education
Vol. 3 No. 1 2013	Student Learning and ICLHE—Frameworks and Contexts
Vol. 5 No. 1 2015	EATAW 2013: Teaching Writing across Languages and Cultures—The Wealth of Diversity in European Context
Vol. 6 No. 1 2016	Selected Papers from the 8th Conference of the European Association for the Teaching of Academic Writing, Tallinn University of Technology, Estonia, June 2015
Vol. 8 No. 2 2018	Selected Papers from the 9th Conference of the European Association for the Teaching of Academic Writing, Royal Holloway, University of London, UK, June 2017
Vol. 10 No. 1 2020	Selected papers from the 10th Conference of the European Association for the Teaching of Academic Writing, Chalmers University of Technology, Gothenburg, Sweden, July, 2019

Since the start of the journal, OJS has been updated, and Coventry University has continued to upgrade their systems and add IT support to ensure the success of *JoAW* and the other journals housed there. Lisa has been able to slowly grow the staff, bringing on George Ttoouli as managing editor and Niall Curry as an assistant editor from Coventry, Jonathan Potter as an assistant editor from Birmingham City University, and initially Íde O'Sullivan from the University of Limerick and then Mark Carver from the University of St. Andrews as book reviews editor. Together, they are working to expand the editorial board further, and aim to work with the EATAW board towards *JoAW* having its own domain or moving its hosting to the EATAW website. And EATAW members are interested to see how that growth will occur and contribute to it. Magnus imagines that as technology continues to change, additional publication venues might emerge. Stuart wonders how scholarly genres might be pushed even further to allow for both empirical research projects, as well as teaching interventions or practical submissions. And Jacqueline hopes for a larger journal staff so that with increased time and energy could come more frequent publication.

The Importance of a Network

> People are exchanging information, links, resources, and that's exactly what we've always wanted with it: this exchange of resources.
>
> — *Lotte Rienecker*

At the end of the first conference in Groningen, Jacqueline remembers good evaluations and a lot of enthusiastic people. She says, "I realized what I needed was what all those people needed: They needed a network, a place to exchange and to learn from each other." This theme of gathering, talking, and learning is the one that came up most often in the interviews as individuals reminisced on conversations, keynotes, workshops, and presentations that impacted their work and ways of thinking. Writing center growth in Germany, assessing the effectivity of writing retreats, processes for teaching proofreading, and working with students with disabilities are just a few topics that the individuals interviewed expressed as ones that left them with tangible inspiration for their own work.

John recalls his fascination at suddenly being in a room with people from various disciplinary backgrounds who were all talking about academic writing. He mentions learning so much from people with backgrounds in psychology and communication studies:

> If somebody is suffering from depression and stress and writer's block, then the first thought was "Who do we need to help somebody who has psychological problems with writing? A psychologist." So those people were bringing the tools of psychology in a very professional way to the teaching of writing.

Magnus also notes, "We are not always good at describing what it is in our context and history when doing things the way we do." So conference attendees identify this sharing of various approaches as essential for informing their own work.

Stuart and Lisa share similar feelings of awe and excitement being at their first EATAW conference because they were meeting people who were interested in academic writing and writing development. Magnus recognizes that

EATAW is a significant venue for introducing people. He has seen many teachers, writing developers, and academic support faculty who feel isolated in their workplaces and are frustrated at having to reinvent the wheel arrive at an EATAW conference and receive help or evidence that what they are doing is meaningful. Also, he has gotten to know several colleagues from his home country of Sweden at EATAW. He finds it a shame that nationally they are doing a poor job of setting up networks, but he accedes that for that reason, EATAW is an asset.

At the same time EATAW succeeds in bringing teachers and researchers together to share perspectives, large numbers and diverse populations also bring challenges. One broad shift that occurred over time was that John saw the contingent of presentations and conversations about writing in English increasing at the conferences. With so much scholarship on academic writing coming from the United States, Britain, and Australia, and with more universities in Scandinavia and elsewhere in Europe creating English-language programs, he observes that it would be impossible to prevent English from dominating.

However, EATAW has always tried hard to keep a space for those who have things to say about teaching writing in Dutch or Swedish or other languages. As someone teaching in the United States, Joan recalls a moment when a Dutch colleague told her, "I publish in Dutch. Who's going to read Dutch? Nobody cares about what I say." And Joan immediately had to disagree. She sees that as a crucial component of EATAW: Others need to know that there are rich research traditions and practices in languages beyond English, and EATAW is one of few organizations that is trying to make these accessible and promote them. In fact, John notes that because the conference moves locations,

> we can go to different parts of Europe and involve new people and find that we can have similar conversations and that we have similar interests, and yet there are also different problems and different concerns in different places—that not every place is the same.

Yet another central challenge that Jacqueline has observed is how EATAW can establish academic writing as a discipline, to combine good practices with research and empirical evidence. This is not always a simple task because of the diversity of cultures, writing traditions, and educational systems in Europe. Additionally, as Stuart recognizes, many of those who are teaching or tutoring academic writing are not always in faculty positions where that research is supported or contributes to an individual's promotion. Yet, EATAW provides a forum for members to learn about what others are doing in various institutional and national contexts. Stuart appreciates the range of perspectives, being exposed to realities that he did not know existed, but that broaden his horizons and influence his work. Some individuals even attribute specific moments at EATAW conferences as impacting their professional trajectories. For instance, Djuddah identifies Christian Schunn's keynote address at the 2009 conference in Coventry as giving him direction for conducting his own research. Katrin notes that after her keynote at the 2017 Royal Holloway conference, a colleague from Sweden approached her, and that one informal conversation led to an ongoing collaborative research project.

The topics covered at the conferences also signal changes over time within teaching, writing, and the research being done on these issues. Lotte has seen conversations over topics such as the rise of e-learning transform and become a more central subject. Founding members could not have imagined this when preparing for the 2001 conference, and yet e-learning has become so prominent that it has warranted keynote addresses, most recently, Karen Head and Chris Anson's presentation, "Technological Gains and Losses" in Gothenburg. With this adjustment in the instructional landscape comes the question of how to maximize e-learning as a tool for teaching academic writing without falling into the trap of teaching more popular or journalistic genres. Yet even that question leads to others, such as Lawrence arguing that the term "academic writing" needs to be un-simplified, that even academic writing is context-specific with diverse conventions, languages, and situations that impact ways of online and paper-based thinking and communicating.

Despite these competing approaches to new questions and through the majority of its history, Lotte explains, "people are not trying to find hairs in the soup." Instead, she and the others interviewed agree that EATAW's atmosphere is exceedingly positive and supportive. David agrees that he has never seen posturing or a competitive ethic; he muses, "People don't really have time for that at EATAW because you're making connections, and people might be really helpful to you and the future of what you're doing." Lotte is proud of this, identifying that "this intention was shared by the first board; this is what we should do, share resources."

An American Perspective

> They have this incredible research going on in Europe that we are not even accessing in the US.
>
> —*Joan Mullin*

Otto recalls three main issues that the founding members wanted the first conference as well as the organization to consider: The relationship among teaching, research, and writing; the relationship between teaching writing in classrooms and tutoring writing in writing centers; and how cultural or intercultural writing is. Because the discipline of rhetoric and composition was burgeoning in the United States, all these issues were being studied within the American national context, but many were not looking abroad. For EATAW, however, the international context was always a central factor. Otto recalls how much David Russell's and David Foster's book, *Writing and Learning in Cross-national Perspective,* was an important eye opener, tying the differences in writing not only to cultures and languages but to the traditions in higher education and the uses of writing for such issues as learning, selection, disciplinary specialization and the transition from secondary to tertiary education. So, he specifically posed the questions "Do we all write in the same way in Europe? And what's the American way of writing? And what is the best way of writing?" as ones that EATAW was designed to explore. And because of this, Americans were necessary to add those perspectives to the conversation.

In fact, a handful of Americans were very much considering these types of intercultural questions, which is what brought many of them to EATAW. Of course, as both American and European interviewees joke, for many Americans the locations of the EATAW conferences was enough to be a draw. Yet some, like David Russell, were already conducting research on international writing traditions or working on both continents. And others, like Joan Mullin, learned about EATAW through colleagues and their work through other international organizations in which they were involved. David observed the ethic of research that permeated EATAW from the beginning and believed this combination of research and teaching was a direction that he and others from the US wanted to go. Thus, these two Americans, as well as many others, have returned year after year.

On the whole, EATAW members have valued the exchange between Europe and the US. Otto clarifies, "Even if the United States had started much earlier with explicit writing pedagogy, it's a two-way conversation. There are some things that go back to the US, and on the other hand, we got a lot of help from American colleagues." These conversations are also useful on more individual levels, as Lisa explains, "I transplanted from one country where there is a long history of writing development to a place where there wasn't a formal tradition of writing development. And I have had to seek it out and try to understand." Lotte, when recalling a variety of collaborations that have occurred, even between Americans and Europeans, states, "This is how ideas travel. This is where they come from. This is where they go. This is how they come back again. And this is how they get transformed. [EATAW] is a long-lasting community for those who want to take home elements and transform them into what is useful there."

Yet, comments were made that some Americans came to EATAW with false notions about what is occurring with writing instruction in Europe. Joan and David agree. David recalls witnessing an American colleague approach a European one and ask, "Do your senior faculty teach first-year composition?" David laughs, saying, "Those seven words are just full of so many disconnects. It would take a long time to untangle it." But what he noticed in the first decade of EATAW was that Americans were bringing to Europe ideas for programmatic initiatives, such as writing strategies and heuristics, technical communication instructional practices, or staff development activities. Meanwhile, they were learning from Europeans a strong ethic of research. He comments that at the Conference on College Composition and Communication (CCCC), there were a lot of "what I did Monday" types of presentations; whereas, at EATAW, even individuals studying their own programs or teaching were expected to do that work in systematic, empirical, and theoretical ways. And he regrets that since the 1980s the United States has not had any large government-funded research projects devoted to writing as has been the case in Europe.

Joan recalls how conversations had at EATAW conferences surpassed those at CCCC in the US, especially how writing was first imagined back in the 1970s by James Britton. In fact, after a few years, the research coming out of European writing centers was very much ahead of what was being done in American spaces; she tried to get other US-based researchers to pay attention, arguing that "it could infuse how we are thinking about language in ways we can't even imagine because we aren't even paying attention." And even now, she sees that many presenters at CCCC focus on writing as if it is separate from everything else, and they are largely concentrating on genre, activity theory, and first-year composition courses as a gateway to university-level writing. David sees EATAW as much more of a disciplinary melting pot, where he is excited, like Otto and Lawrence, to be able to learn from individuals thinking about writing and writing instruction through psychological, programmatic, rhetorical, sociological, linguistic, and so many other lenses.

Now, Joan considers everyone she sees at EATAW family. She says, "I go to those conferences as much as possible because it's so intellectually rich. Plus, I have known these people for 20 years." In similar ways, some of their fondest memories have been more social than intellectual. "It's personal. No question," Joan immediately answers. "A lot of it is centered on the meals and bars," David says, only half-jokingly. Joan recalls a conversation she had about the role of English in academic writing instruction and research as she was walking up a hill in Athens. She says, "That's what I mean about physically being there where people have these conversations. I would have never realized all those layers of colonialism and ethnocentrism that exist in our academic and scholarly traditions." And all of those interviewed have noted that they look forward to the biennial conferences to see people and reconnect after two long years because this is where they learn and exchange ideas on very specific issues.

Challenges of the Board

> The running of the organization is a challenge, absolutely, for everyone who is in the board.
>
> — *Djuddah Leijen*

Over the years, the size, make-up, duties, and challenges of the board have evolved. The board members during the two years leading up to the 2001 conference were nominated in order to get the association running. At the Groningen conference, the first board election took place; however, so few individuals agreed to be nominated that the process essentially comprised one vote either for or against the five members who put themselves forward. Lotte agreed to stand again to keep continuity, but everyone else were new members.

John Harbord was one of those elected, and during the initial board meetings, a discussion of where to hold the second conference came up. John and his colleague, Bojana Petrič, left the conference so impressed that they quickly met with their team at the Central European University (CEU) and offered to host the second conference in Budapest, Hungary. The CEU has since become the only university to host the EATAW conference twice, in 2003 and 2013. John very clearly is pleased at having been able to host the conference two times, noting the importance of that endeavor by quoting someone else who once said to him, "EATAW *is* the conference."

Yet, over the years, the board has at times had difficulty securing host universities for the conference. John recollects that in 2015 four bids came in, the most that had ever happened. Having options allowed the board to reflect on rationales and processes for selecting a host. In 2015, the board opted to hold the conference in Tallinn because it was relatively inexpensive and accessible, and they felt it was a good time to bring stimulus to a place where people were starting to come together to really work on academic writing issues. John discloses that one of the benefits of hosting the conference is that people within the host university, country, and surrounding countries get to learn a lot about EATAW and the teaching and research of academic writing. In fact, when looking at the numbers at the 2019 Gothenburg conference, the country with the highest number of attendees was Sweden. It is likely that some of those individuals had not previously known about EATAW and were now able to come into contact with it.

In other years, though, members of the board had to rally to find a host location. At times, weak or no proposals came in, so board members themselves had to undertake the task of hosting the conference in order for it to happen. This was actually the case at the most recent conference in Gothenburg. Magnus admits that his university has been the plan B for a few years, and while he would have preferred to wait another conference or two, without any other option it needed to happen in 2019. Even though the timing was not ideal, he concurs that hosting the conference was something the department wanted to do and could learn from. At the same time, it offered a possibility of setting an agenda as well as placing the department on the EATAW map. Between hosting the conference and editing the 2019 conference edition of the *Journal of Academic Writing* as well as a WAC Clearinghouse collection, he believes that will be achieved.

While organizing the conferences is a large undertaking that every iteration of the board must manage, there are a variety of other behind-the-scenes tasks that make up the running of an international organization. Several boards have drafted and revised documentation for the organization, such as the constitution and a code of ethics. Determining where to locate and how to access and move the organization's funds has been a challenge for some boards, a rather difficult task since EATAW is not permanently housed in any one European nation. Still other board members' knowledge, skills, and patience have been tested as they attempt to manage technologies, such as the website, the membership database, and the listserv. For an organization that does not collect fees, the lack of financial resources can limit this work despite good ideas.

Djuddah Leijen, the current board Chair, mentions spending a lot of time over the course of his three years on the board deliberating how to maintain member engagement in between conferences. Many potential opportunities have been discussed, including creating committees, national chapters, and special interest groups. EATAW members like Magnus, Stuart, and David agree that these sorts of activities might help people stay active and connected during the many months from one conference to the next. Djuddah and Stuart have also observed that even though topics researched and presented at the conferences and in *JoAW* have changed over time, some questions and considerations that were discussed a decade or more ago are still relevant for certain individuals. Djuddah believes that the board needs to contemplate the organization's accommodation of new members who might have basic questions about teaching writing alongside long-standing members who are looking for ways to move forward or dig in deeper. More specifically, Stuart wonders whether there might be ways of creating official channels for inviting communication and support among members in between conferences.

In Djuddah's mind, though, the question is how to balance engagement with guarding individuals' time and energy. Because all of the board members are volunteers, Djuddah finds simply that "the running of the organization is a challenge, absolutely, for everyone who is in the board." Djuddah sees a need for the organization members to know that there is a board standing for them and supporting their needs; but at the same time, the work being done should not be overly demanding. So even when good ideas arise, anyone asked to plan or oversee a new activity would also have to volunteer their time. This reality makes adding opportunities a challenge.

The size of the board has fluctuated at times, with there being five, nine, and now seven members. Those elected to the board have ranged in their demographics: years of experience with EATAW, national and institutional locales, linguistic backgrounds, research interests, and more. Many interviewed would agree with David who has seen how with each iteration of the EATAW board, a balance has been struck between returning and new members. And even with the wide range of wishes, duties and challenges, current and previous board members who were interviewed all agreed that by being on the board they have had the opportunity to work with outstanding people.

Because there have been moments in EATAW's history when nominees were not lining up to join the board, it is worth mentioning that several of those interviewed ran for the board because they were encouraged to by others. As a Ph.D. student, Katrin thought joining the board might be interesting, but felt unqualified and uncertain of her ability to contribute until Werner Fiedler from the Hans Böckler Foundation pushed her to run. Djuddah also recalls both Magnus and Lisa suggesting to him that he should put his name forward, and he was at a stage in his career where he wanted to be involved in more activities outside his university. The need for such encouragement is significant because it highlights that some members might feel unsure about what being a board member entails, question whether they have the qualifications necessary to join the board, or are even uncertain if they are eligible to run for the board. As the board continues to strategize and improve communication, it might look to ways for new leaders to find systems for contributing.

Looking toward the Future

> We must continue because EATAW is needed.
>
> — *Magnus Gustafsson*

Though not strictly a part of the organization's history, because my interviewees have participated in central ways to the first 20 years of EATAW, I asked all twelve what their hopes are for the next 20 years of EATAW. While the responses stem out of each individual's areas of expertise and interests, both within EATAW and out in their home institutions and lives, everyone interviewed had thoughts on why the organization is vital: Some comments overlap with others' remarks, and many reflect original goals or sustained missions and visions of the organization, its board, and its members.

Some individuals want to see EATAW continue in the ways it has been running. For instance, several of those interviewed commented how they have seen EATAW become more professional over the years, in terms of having more formalized documents and procedures and drawing high quality contributions to the conferences and journal. Joan hopes that the organization will continue to invite new scholars in and not create, as she observes, what "has happened in so many places, a cadre of stars that lead everything. Because that's what is exciting about EATAW: So many exciting new voices." John, likewise, hopes that EATAW "can continue to be a platform for anyone who wants to explore issues of academic writing practices, whether on a personal level or an institutional policy level, can do so."

Meanwhile some would like to see EATAW extend its activities and involvement. At the most basic level, Magnus says, "First of all, we must continue because EATAW is needed . . . and second, [we must] find more appropriate ways to communicate with the community." Building on that, Djuddah has witnessed people who attend the conferences, get inspired, but then return to their home institutions and run up against hurdles. He worries that they then have to either try to solve the problem on their own or wait until the next conference to locate support. He sees this difficulty of sustained interaction between conferences as a "missing link." And some have ideas for how to fill that gap. For instance, David would like to see an ongoing, active committee structure that helps recruit members and set goals. Magnus agrees, imagining the possibility of national EATAW chapters. And Stuart envisions the possibility of special interest groups that could continue to meet after conferences.

Though many networks and initiatives have tangentially grown out of EATAW work or through the work of EATAW members, some would like to see EATAW itself getting involved on external issues. Specifically, Stuart would like to see the organization working alongside European institutions to better professionalize the staff who teach and tutor academic writing, potentially helping to create more academic lines and promotion opportunities for members of the field. Lotte sees this as important too, articulating that many EATAW members are in small facilities that are often threatened with funding cuts or even closure. Additionally, in light of Brexit and the removal of the Central European University from Hungary, David would be interested in seeing EATAW work toward creating position papers to identify its stances within these changing political contexts. Likewise, Katrin would like to see EATAW join conversations occurring about EU curriculum decisions to consider how to make teaching and facilitating academic writing a more central component of those mandates.

Others spoke to specific research topics and types of publications they hope to see broadened. For example, Otto would like to see continued work on the digitalization of educational and writing technologies. He is glad to see that it is a topic already being discussed, but with the acceleration of technological advancement, it is difficult for individual teachers and researchers to gain more than a limited view of what is happening. So he hopes for more collaboration in order to broaden that scope. Along those lines, Stuart would be interested to see a wider variety of genres appearing in publications about academic writing. He sees EATAW as an ideal space where Western-centric traditions have already been and may continue to be challenged.

And still others spoke to goals that have been harder to achieve as fully as some would have liked. Even though EATAW has been marketing itself in a way that has promoted growth, Djuddah would like to see EATAW's outreach expand to the point that it becomes the first place anyone who is teaching academic writing would think to turn to for support. Many of those interviewed commented that the majority of the organization's members come out of Northern European countries. So there is the desire for more participation from individuals further east and south. And with that comes the objective to keep expanding awareness of the role of writing within educational systems in various national contexts.

Attention to context will always be of significance to EATAW members. Lotte expresses that she would like to see presenters at the conferences better considering their international audiences: Speaking more slowly, defining terms, and using fewer abbreviations. Not everyone has the same amount and types of experience, and attendees have a wide range of disciplinary backgrounds. So inclusivity even at this level is important. And when it comes to the variety of languages present in EATAW, John remains hopeful that writing will continue to be supported in languages other than English, and that more conference presentations and *Journal of Academic Writing* articles will be produced in other languages. Likewise, because writing in English or writing in English as a Second Language are such prominent topics of research, Jacqueline would like to see more publications on students writing in their mother language and the instruction related to that.

Some would like to see the maintaining of a strong reconnection to conversations about teaching. Lotte observes that in many scholarly contexts, the focus on research methodology has become a central topic of discussion, and she would like EATAW to remain firmly connected with teaching methodology, praxis, and pedagogical implications instead. Djuddah agrees, stating, "EATAW should not become a research conference, but we should be using research, putting it into practice and to make clear that [pedagogies] are not just based in observations, but they are grounded in research and theory." He hopes EATAW can continue to be a central hub for that work.

More specifically, Katrin would like to see more conversations, and perhaps even conference collaboration, between EATAW and EWCA to bring together discussions of teaching and tutoring, perhaps focusing on the potentials of and the power that writing gives to European citizens. Joan and Lawrence hope for EATAW to create more conversations among all types of writing teachers and tutors at universities, primary and secondary schools, and other consultancies. Lawrence points to a need for collaborative learning, for members of EWCA and EATAW, teachers at all education levels, and anyone else interested in writing instruction need to keep holding conversations on writing because "we have a lot of the same agendas, and we have to recognize that. And whatever the separate things are, I think we are going to learn from each other."

Magnus, Lisa, and Djuddah would like to see the board better able to locate and adapt to sustainable communication methods. In practical terms, there should be a dynamic and easily-searchable membership database. And, even though Magnus views the conference as a secure venue for teachers of academic writing in the short term, he poses the questions, "How will academics involved in writing development in Europe know of each other and connect in 20 years? Is the conference still the most important element? What additional publication venues will be available to EATAW members, and should EATAW be proactive and a part of that?" And Djuddah wants to see the members come together to think about "Who are we as an organization, and where do we want to grow to? Does growth mean getting more members to attend conferences, or how else should we define growth?" These questions, along with the other hopes are crucial for the organization's membership considering how to move forward so that EATAW can continue to meet the needs of teachers of academic writing as the educational landscape in Europe alters and flourishes.

Twenty Years Young

> EATAW is a scholarly forum which seeks to promote the scholarship and practice of teaching and learning in higher education by bringing together those involved or interested in the teaching, tutoring, research, administration and development of academic writing in higher education in Europe.
>
> — *EATAW Constitution*

Inevitably, over the course of twenty years, much of EATAW has changed; however, much of the original goals and guiding ideals have remained the same. The 2001 conference set many of the expectations that still exist in EATAW today. Otto mentioned the organizers' desire from the start to have a good mix between research, teaching, and conceptualizations. Lotte describes the conversations the original board members had as they labored to create the first conference. She recalls everyone being in agreement that the utmost goal should be to bring people together to exchange ideas that help to answer the questions, "How do we teach? How do we research? What are our possible practices? How can we inspire each other?"

The exchange of good teaching practices was the main focus of that first conference because the organizers recognized that not a lot of research was being done yet on the teaching of academic writing in Europe. While teaching tools, technology, and practices have changed significantly since 2001, members today still come to the conferences to discuss what they do in their classrooms. Most recently, the 2019 conference included Teaching practice presentations, which, according to the conference website, were "10-minute presentations on teaching-related designs, development or experience." And between the conferences and *JoAW*, members today are getting clearer glimpses into research being done on teaching and writing across Europe. We continue to see researchers examining topics related to language, assessment, and supporting writers at all levels and across disciplines, alongside scholarship discussing methods to acclimate to changes in institutional and national policies and identifying how new and adapted technologies can support and expand teaching and research.

JoAW, in particular, has made access to this work available to all. According to the interviewees, the challenges that EATAW will likely continue to face center on continuing to broaden access and maintain diversity: How can EATAW ensure that its conferences are not only available to those at the best funded universities? How can EATAW encourage researchers who are not confident in their English-language presentation skills? How can new opportunities be created for members to get involved and sustained connections be made with other organizations when EATAW has limited funding and staff? How can EATAW support individuals and institutions that might want to host a future conference? None of these questions are new, but they have perhaps shifted to the forefront as other concerns, such as revising the constitution, overhauling the website, and establishing an academic journal for research output have been resolved over time.

In hearing the interviewees' stories, it becomes clear that the challenges that EATAW has faced, whether ones created by external forces, like the debate in Athens over a focus on English-language writing instruction, or ones agreed up by members to improve the organization's efficacy, such as constructing *JoAW* to be freely available to everyone, have helped to form the EATAW we now are a part of. The difficulties in certain years of finding a host location for the conference, of addressing some of the technological issues with the website and member database, and of finding venues that engage members in valuable ways have, at times, stymied board members and taken a lot of effort to settle. Yet, long-time members, like Joan and John, see that EATAW is stronger and more mature because of the time and energy put in to overcome those difficulties: Inevitably, a host institution is always found because the conference is the lynch pin of the organization; a new website exists to inform and promote the organization while also storing portions of its history; a newsletter for keeping members engaged has had seven issues over four years. And, the board and other members continue to bring new ideas that will push EATAW forward into the next 20 years.

The founders saw the need for this forum that would bring diverse teachers and researchers of academic writing together for a long time into the future. We should all be grateful that they took the opportunity to begin that work. The fact that most of those original members contributed for many years after the 2001 conference—some even in attendance at our most recent conferences—speaks to their devotion to EATAW and its members, and also to the sustained significance of this space for teachers and researchers of academic writing in Europe. Additionally, many others over the past 20 years have joined the organization, coming back to the conferences every two years and voicing their hopes and plans for EATAW at the general assemblies. The conference in Gothenburg boasted 229 presenters and attendees from 41 countries. The need for this venue is obvious, and the original goals still sit at the core of the organization even as it moves into its third decade. John possibly said it best when he identified that those who have been attending the conference since 2001 are pleased to find that one thing has sustained over the past 20 years: Attendees get "to see and exchange ideas again with colleagues that you haven't seen in two years, and to see that those colleagues are still active in the profession and have done new things that they have to share with you."

Acknowledgments

I would like to thank all twelve of the EATAW members interviewed for this project: Lawrence Cleary, Lisa Ganobcsik-Williams, Katrin Girgensohn, Magnus Gustafsson, John Harbord, Otto Kruse, Djuddah Leijen, Joan Mullin, Lotte Rienecker, David Russell, Jacqueline van Kruiningen, and Stuart Wrigley. They graciously gave me their time, knowledge, and perspectives on EATAW and the contexts in which European teachers and researchers of academic writing work.

And though the interviewees named several people who impacted EATAW and their growth as academic writing teachers and researchers than could be acknowledged in one chapter, the name that came up most often was Gabriela Ruhmann. She is remembered as "the person best at connecting writing and thinking," as someone who gave unforgettable presentations, and as a teacher who all of her colleagues learned from. She was important not only in the development of EATAW but also of writing centers in Germany as well as across Europe. She was a founding member of EATAW, a member of the board for many years, and an advocate for inclusivity within the organization. I wish I had had the chance to meet her.

Where to Find EATAW Online

To learn more about EATAW, its members, and their research, Table 1.6 identifies the online spaces with digitally archived organization business, scholarship, ongoing conversations, announcements, and events.

Table 1.6. EATAW's Online Resources

Resource	Website
EATAW official website	https://eataw.eu
EATAW Wikipedia page	https://en.wikipedia.org/wiki/European_Association_for_the_Teaching_of_Academic_Writing
EATAW listserv	https://www.jiscmail.ac.uk/cgi-bin/webadmin?Ao=EATAW
Journal of Academic Writing	https://publications.coventry.ac.uk/index.php/joaw/index

2 Two Experiments in Technologically Mediated Education: 2012 and 2020

Karen J. Head[1]
GEORGIA INSTITUTE OF TECHNOLOGY

Writing technology is a tool for writing pedagogy, not its master. Nevertheless, proponents of technology often promote an implicit theory that technology impels us to teach differently, even in ways that are circularly defined and valorized by what the technology is capable of. In the process, much that is of value is neglected or underplayed, and we are encouraged to compromise, or adopt what is merely good enough and compromise on excellence. These two tendencies—submission to the technology imperative/inexorability and compromise—combine with situational urgency to create what I refer to as ICU (Inexorability, Compromise, and Urgency). I share and analyze two episodes of technology intrusion into the teaching of writing that illustrate ICU: the technology compromises required by "MOOC[2] mania" in 2012, where the urgency arose from an academic arms race; and the over-reliance on a grammar checker (and other compliance technologies) in urgent reaction to the pivot to distance education during the COVID-19 pandemic of 2020. In the first case, the promises of technology were interrogated and proved to be hyperbolic; in the recent case it is too early to tell whether the compromises we have made will define a "new normal."

Teachers of academic writing, writing program directors, and writing center directors are process-oriented scholars and practitioners who have long understood the affordances and challenges of incorporating new technologies into their pedagogical practices—and, most importantly, the critical need for

---

1 Karen J. Head https://orcid.org/0000-0003-1953-3475. I have no conflicts of interest to disclose. Correspondence concerning this article should be addressed to Karen J. Head, School of Literature, Media, and Communication, Georgia Tech, Atlanta, GA 30332-0165. Email: khead@gatech.edu

2 Massive open online course.

discourse surrounding the assessment of these tools and practices. We must continue to place ourselves at the center of these interrogations.

Considerations of technologies into pedagogical practice is at the heart of the work we do in my lab, the Naugle Communication Center at Georgia Tech. Because the space functions as both my research lab and as a site for pedagogical intervention via student consultations, I pause for a moment each day to reflect on what my earliest teaching and tutoring experiences were like. As a student, I began tutoring just before my seventh birthday, when I was recruited to go to summer school with some of the last wave of Vietnamese refugee children who were brought to the United States in 1974. It was educational intervention in its purest form—children playing and studying together in an immersive language acquisition program. Mostly this was the pedagogy of human connection. Classroom "technology" was limited to chalkboards—with occasional access to shared projectors and televisions usually housed in the school library.

In my lab and my instructional spaces today, I am surrounded by touch-screens, video-conferencing equipment, studio-quality green screens, and sundry other technologies too numerous to name. These technologies support but do not supplant the attitude that I started to develop when I was still a young peer tutor. While technologies often open pedagogical pathways, at the heart of what we do the critical process remains simple and direct: one person having a conversation with another.

Writing this in late 2020, the relationship between writing pedagogy and writing technology is more relevant than ever. In March 2020, my lab, along with the rest of my university closed its physical spaces in response to the COVID-19 pandemic. It was clear that a bricolage of technology hastily assembled to react to a health situation that had not been foreseen or planned for, would have to suffice. Fortunately, because technology is our tool, not our master, and because I had participated in an earlier episode in which technology was widely promoted as a savior—the MOOC mania of 2012—I was confident our primary mission (tutoring) could be served. Perhaps my confidence was misplaced. As I explain below, the solicitations from technology companies promising panaceas soon started to arrive, and just as in 2012, many administrators and colleagues developed unrealistic expectations that tools designed to support an essential but minor component of the writing process would be the answer to most of their problems.

But before telling the two parables of 2012 and 2020, I will explain their genre: ICU. ICU stands for Inexorability, Compromise, and Urgency (I acknowledge that this acronym is most associated with Intensive Care Units in hospitals—the association is intentional).

Writing Technology and ICU

ICU is the confluence of two factors: a faith in the efficacy of technology to support a human process (here the teaching of writing) with the satisficing compromises that this entails, in conjunction with a sense of urgency to react that undermines critical analysis of technology adoption decision making.

Affordances and the Anthropomorphic Ascription of Values to Technology

Scholars in the fields of human-computer interaction, human factors engineering, and interaction design use the concept of affordances to explain a technology's ease and convenience of use. Originally defined by the ecological psychologist, J. J. Gibson (1986), an affordance is an alignment between a human performance characteristic for a specified task and the characteristics of the environment that make the task feasible. Gibson, who was researching human and animal vision, had in mind generic tasks such as scanning the environment, but applied psychologists later adapted the concept of the affordance to more specific and purposeful actions, such as opening a door. Famously, Norman (1988) fulminated against designers who attach door handles that "ask" to be pulled, onto the side of doors that open away from the user. The affordance of a successful door handle in the case of the user pulling the door handle toward them is the alignment between a graspable and turnable door handle and the grasping gesture of the human hand. The affordance for opening a door away from the user is the alignment between a flat plate (for example) and the gesture of pushing with the open palm.[3]

Affordances can be extended from the sensori-motor interactions to the cultural realm. According to Brey (2010), a system or app discloses to us ethical assumptions that are embedded in the way it presents itself to users (Brey does not draw the parallel between disclosed values and affordances, but we see them as direct analogs.) For example, a chalkboard and its associated organization of the classroom embeds the value that teaching is defined as listening to didactic presentations. This carries with it a power difference between teacher and students: teachers are authority figures who command

---

3   From these modest sensorimotor examples, the idea of the affordance has blossomed into a way of conceptualizing the alignment between more complex technologies and their socio-cultural use contexts. I will leave it to others to debate whether it is a metaphorical overextension or a valid use of the term, and I will use the term to refer to any compatibility between a technology's presentation to its users and those users' cultural needs and expectations.

attention, and students have a duty to listen, watch, and take notes. This is not to say that designers of chalkboards have these values in mind or that they would espouse those values if asked. It is merely that the technology exhibits these values, fits into contexts best where those assumptions are accepted, and is most convenient and usable to users who share these values. Conversely, in a democratic and highly interactive teaching context, chalkboards have a more peripheral role or must be reinvented (not very effectively) as shared workspaces. They can still be used effectively, but there is an awkwardness to their use. They are the cultural equivalent of Norman's door handles that ask to be pulled when they need to be pushed.

Similarly, Hsi and Potts (2000) analyze desktop apps to reveal their underlying ontology, the centrality or peripherality of concepts in that ontology, and how they evolve over generations of releases. For example, in a calendar app weekends may be distinguished visually from work days, working hours may be distinguished from leisure time, and even Sunday may be marked off as a day of rest. Essentially, the app is acting as if it is making claims about its users' cultural practices, claims that the users may assent to or disagree with. The app will be usable and useful to the extent that those users share these cultural assumptions or can be encouraged to shift their practices so that they fit the technology they are using. Similar cultural assumptions are built into learning management systems (LMS) like Blackboard, Moodle, and Canvas. Each LMS has its own ecosystem, privileging different interactions over others. For example, Blackboard and Moodle tend to prioritize communication and collaboration. Canvas places more emphasis on content and assignments. Blackboard and Canvas are commercial platforms with robust 24/7 technical support systems; Moodle is an open-source system which allows institutions to customize it for their particular uses, but there is no corporate support—meaning that students and instructors sometimes cannot find "just in time" support. Again, there is no claim that the designers were intending to impose assumptions (learning is completing assignments or learning is communicating with other students, as two examples), on their users, or even that they would defend them if challenged, merely that the platforms present themselves to users in ways that privilege certain approaches over others.

One COVID-19-related example of this was the scandal caused by the United Kingdom government's decision to use machine learning algorithms to predict A-Levels (standard national university entrance exams) in the United Kingdom. These exams are taken simultaneously by students all over the country. Because schools had been closed for safety reasons, the exams had to be canceled, and predictions were used instead to sort candidates into their preferred universities. Despite expert warnings that the predictive algorithms discriminated against students from less well-financed and state-run schools, it was these predictions that were used to calculate students' results. When the results were published, many students found their algorithmically predicted results differed by more than two grades from the estimates their teachers had provided (which originally were to be the basis for the entrance decisions). Soon after that, the UK government changed course and reverted to teachers' estimates. It is possible that the teachers' estimates were affected by wishful thinking and that the algorithmic predictions, which normed estimates by taking into account aggregate school performance in recent years, were more objective. However, a teacher's estimate can be justified by a narrative about the student, whereas the algorithm's "justification" was an inscrutable chain of statistical approximations that clarified nothing to a non-specialist. In an atmosphere of distrust, it is no surprise that members of the public felt aggrieved.

The controversy over the UK's A-Level prediction algorithm can be seen as a failure in the affordances of the decision-making technology. Within the web of decisions that significantly affect people's lives, such as which university to attend, it is important that the decision-making approach adopted, and any technology that makes or supports decisions, should not only lead to the making of effective and fair decisions, but also to the explaining and defending of the decision being made so that the people affected understand and can live with the outcome. A teacher's narrative explanation of a student's outcome can be related to shared knowledge of the student's previous performance on practice exams or continually assessed coursework. A statistical algorithm, in contrast, merely performs one of the tasks associated with decisions: making them.

These extensions of the notion of the affordance are anthropomorphic, but the anthropomorphism is figurative. The technology is not intelligent enough to *have* values or ideas, but it presents itself *as if* it does, and it is a useful technology to the extent that those values and ideas align with those of its users. More fancifully, the popular technology writer and pioneer in the hacker movement, Kelly (2010) in his controversial book *What Technology Wants* appears to claim quite literally that technology is a force in social evolution that has its own intentions.

Kelly is an extreme example of a long line of writers who propose that future trends will follow technological developments inexorably. In the context of higher education, some writers have recently argued that technology developments will propel higher education in "disruptive" new directions. Not only is there an inevitability to this forthcoming (or perhaps ongoing) disruption, but also those in higher education with a vested interest in preserving the status quo will not see these inexorable trends at work until it is too late. The inevitable consequences are that these dinosaurs will be displaced by more nimble, non-traditional higher education providers. Christensen and Eyring (2011) build on Christensen's (1997) now controversial theory of disruptive innovation to explain and defend the innovations in one institution of higher education. Painting a broader brush, DeMillo (2011) makes similar arguments, about institutions of higher education in general. The major universities that escape DeMillo's negative judgment are few in number, and none of them are in Europe. Anything old is to be swept away. In my book (Head, 2017), I analyzed at length these authors' rhetoric and their appeal to cherry-picked case studies. But they are just recent examples of a long tradition of writers who argue that technology in all spheres of life, not just higher education, has a telos of its own.

Compromise: When Technology is Good Enough

Ceding pedagogical authority to an algorithm is inadvisable when machine evaluation mechanisms have repeatedly been proven inadequate (Perelman, 2016). As with all automated writing evaluation systems, the notion of "good enough" is always a factor. If "good enough" is what you are willing to settle for (and pay for because these platforms are usually not free), then perhaps that is acceptable. However, as I have noted in previous research:

> [There is a] more obvious difficulty with machine grading of writing. It can't be done. How can someone program a computer to check whether a complex thesis statement is complete and supportable? How can it assess whether the appropriate disciplinary sense of has been achieved in a piece of writing? How can it evaluate whether the evidence presented is valid for the thesis at hand? The problem is that algorithms cannot yet substitute for human evaluation where higher order concerns are in question. . . . (Head, 2017, p. 99)

Academic writing scholars and instructors should not be willing to accept a "good enough" model of student support because it serves us in a crisis. For example, would the costs for such platforms be better used to expand existing programs that can address more complex writing assessment? While the supplemental aspects of online writing correction tools might be helpful to some, there is a danger that students could misinterpret the capabilities of these programs—resulting in poorer than expected evaluations of their work. Additionally, we should work with IT professionals to assess issues of privacy and text ownership.

Urgency: "The Train is Leaving the Station"

One of the most enduring metaphors from the MOOC year was that of the train—as in "We need to be on this train—preferably driving it," a call to arms that Georgia Tech's Provost, Rafael Bras, frequently issued. The problem for most institutions (and, I continue to argue that Georgia Tech was one of those institutions) is that they had no idea where the train was going, and, perhaps worse, they had no idea what to do once it arrived at the unknown destination. An auxiliary metaphor was the "tsunami"—the wave of disaster that would destroy universities that did not "get on the train." The urgency in 2012 was the result of complaints about the rising costs of higher education, and delivering content at scale was Silicon Valley's innovative answer—an answer quickly embraced by the media and by legislators who were eager to cut more spending on public universities.

Similarly, in a crisis, like the pandemic, the momentum behind technology adoption can be unstoppable. There can be a strong temptation toward embracing tools and practices that offset increased workloads at the expense of providing students with the necessary skills and habits of mind to be truly successful.

Whether the sense of urgency arises from organizational enthusiasm, as was the case in 2012 MOOC episode, or an exogenous agent, as in the 2020 pandemic, the outcome is similar: there is not or appears not to be enough time to analyze the evolving situation critically, and as a result bandwagon effects, arms races, FOMO (fear of missing out), public safety concerns, and political pressure to deny or downplay any disruption of operations all contribute to a rush to technology adoption and compromise.

Two ICU Episodes in Writing Technology

The following case studies share the aforementioned qualities of ICU: a faith in the efficacy of technology (with satisficing compromises); and a sense of urgency that undermines usual protocols through an insistence that rapid decision-making is the only reasonable approach to technology adoption because some crises outweigh the need for critical analysis. The first example, which focuses on the 2012 "tsunami" of Massive Open Online Courses, discusses how many elite universities rushed to win a kind of "moon shot" race, only to produce, in some cases, poorly designed and now obsolete courses. The second example discusses the same kind of reactionary arguments for expediency that resulted from the sudden need in 2020 to pivot courses online—a legitimate need given the COVID-19 pandemic—but a need that shifted quickly from providing the critical tools to facilitate online learning to more problematic technology adoptions that were not critical to the moment and that were sometimes more about convenience than about well-designed pedagogical tools.

2012: The Year of the MOOCS

Because the first MOOCs were products of elite universities, many of which did not have large distance learning programs, quality of instruction seemed more dependent on reputation than on actual pedagogy. However, reputation mattered because elite universities had the luxury of failing: "Elite schools . . . can afford to play in the most disruptive sandboxes with minimal risk, pitching any failures as important research—and whatever happens in the aftermath of these failures will register as little more than a toy tossed aside for some new plaything" (Head, 2017, p. 133). And, in fact, that is precisely what happened with MOOCs. Georgia Tech has created several graduate programs, like the Online Master's of Science in Computer Science, and while those programs are scaled-up versions of programs we offer locally, they are neither massive nor open (that is, free).

In other parts of the world, the desire to implement MOOCS tended to focus more on social inclusion and educational access, with a strong focus on a general audience rather than full-time students. In a report from the European Association of Distance Teaching Universities that surveyed 89 institutions from 24 (mostly European) countries, Ubachs and Konings (2018) found that the top four reasons for offering MOOCs were as follows: 1) flexible learning opportunities; 2) increase institution visibility; 3) reach new students; and 4) innovative pedagogy. The report also reflected a declining interest in MOOCs, with some institutions concerned about quality issues and access. Also, respondents repeatedly mentioned the need for reliable online student proctoring and assessment.

Many of the original arguments about providing open access education were based on notions of altruism and public good. However, too little attention was given to how access would be fully realized. Another long-term problem has been maintenance and management of the MOOC courses—the fact that MOOCs were "free" for students does not correspond to the necessary and ongoing operational costs of keeping those courses pedagogically sound. The result has been that some MOOC offerings, which may not have been particularly well-designed in the first place, are now no longer updated. The idea that MOOCs could be "good enough" because they were free and open has, in some cases, created a database of courses that are the equivalent of moldy and outdated textbooks—some of the information might still be useful, but the overall experience is lacking.

2020: The Plague Year

Like regular course meetings, academic support services like the Naugle Communication Center had to close as a result of the COVID-19 pandemic. In the pre-pandemic world, my work as a course instructor benefitted from the tools all instructors had access to at my university, but I also enjoyed access to tools I had in my communication tutoring lab. And, of course, the staff in my lab was also accustomed to the same access for the work they needed to do. Suddenly access to many of the technologies located in the lab or in classroom spaces was gone, and I found myself, along with my colleagues, investigating the availability of tools we might use for the pivot to remote instruction. Simultaneously, I began to be bombarded with solicitations about platforms claiming to make instruction more expedient. Some of the platforms being marketed focus on test proctoring, some focus on enabling connections (asynchronous and synchronous) between instructors and students or between student groups, and some promise to keep students "honest" by preventing cheating through different kinds of surveillance. As a teacher of academic writing, I was particularly concerned about the platforms related to the writing process. One of these platforms, Grammarly, a grammar-checking interface, was representative of platforms that address expediency over pedagogy; I will examine that platform as a case study later in this chapter.

Prior to the COVID-19 pandemic, the word "pivot" was, for many people, made famous on the American television show *Friends* (Varinaitis et al., 1999) when the characters try to move a large couch up a narrow and winding staircase. After shouting, "Pivot" several times, one of the characters finds his new couch wedged between floors. However, the punchline comes at the end of the scene when another asks, "What did you mean when you said 'pivot'?" Similarly, in 2020 faculty found themselves trying to answer the call to pivot their courses to remote delivery without a complete understanding of what that meant, and like the characters in *Friends* they found themselves stuck between where they came from and where they thought they were heading. Staff in university centers for teaching and learning, along with distance education support teams (where such centers or teams existed) rushed to help faculty but were quickly overwhelmed with the volume of assistance needed.

Along with an increase in use of learning management systems like Blackboard and Canvas, video-conferencing platforms like Zoom, Microsoft Teams, and WebEx rushed to accommodate the surge of users. Suddenly, however, there was an issue of scale akin to MOOCs. While instructors were not attempting to reach thousands of users (or in the case of many MOOCs tens of thousands), the challenges for synchronous interactions with students did involve adjusting for scale. Instructors may have used video-conferencing for one-to-one meetings with individual students, but now they needed to reach their entire class at once. One of the biggest complaints at my institution is that our main video-conferencing platform only allows users to see nine participants at a time. Once the issues of creating classroom interaction substitutes were solved, instructors began to face other challenges. How would students take their exams? How could students get supplemental assistance with projects? How would students work in small groups? Developing new course materials and reconfiguring for remote course delivery to achieve the best student outcomes are labor intensive tasks. For some instructors, the sudden and unwished-for move to remote learning represented a significant and unwelcome new workload. Tools that might alleviate that workload are positioned to be embraced in the current crisis because instructors have so many additional demands on their time. It is easy to understand how extraordinary stressful situations can lead instructors (and administrators) to make decisions that are more about expediency than striving for pedagogical excellence.

As the months of the pandemic have passed, qualitative assignments, like essays and research papers, have been suggested as alternatives for exams. Consequently, companies that provide automated writing analysis have become a focal point. Automating the difficult work of providing feedback and evaluating writing has long been a point of contention with writing scholars. The questions surrounding the capabilities of machine-learning to provide a platform that might replace the time-intensive work doing by writing instructors (or instructors in any discipline that favors writing assignments that require qualitative assessment) are not new. As was the case with MOOCs, the arguments for machine-grading, test proctoring, plagiarism checking, are unsurprising. Companies like Grammarly (a grammar checking service), Honorlock (a proctoring service), and Turnitin (a plagiarism detection service) have increased their marketing efforts in an attempt to leverage the current crisis to increase customer base. From the first hours of universities shifting to remote instruction, email boxes began to fill with advertisements for platforms that claimed to make teaching more efficient. Concurrently, many instructors reacted first about the shift to remote teaching by expressing concerns about academic dishonesty (Head, 2020). The task of suddenly moving courses online, along with the shift to more qualitative assessments, left faculty stressed in ways that were novel for some of them. Even academic writing faculty, who are generally acclimated to the time-consuming nature of qualitative assessment of student writing, were finding preparation for class online a burden. Therefore, it is not surprising that companies offering "easy" answers for taking away some of the faculty workload might be more enticing than ever.

Having said that, the year 2020 promises to initiate a disruption far more significant than anything discussed or even imagined in 2011. Had MOOCs not been developed during the preceding decade, many colleges and universities would have been incapable of pivoting to remote teaching with such urgency during the spring of 2020 when the COVID-19 pandemic created new or expanded remote learning approaches. In the United States, most colleges and universities managed surprisingly well to move online during the late spring and summer. (In the United States, most institutions scaled down operations during the summer months when most students are on vacation or working in internships.) In Europe, the closing of many institutions happened between terms, giving instructors a few weeks to prepare classes for online delivery. However, nobody was under any illusion that this was a planned experiment. In any case, there was little time to plan, and the pedagogical adaptations that needed to be made were compounded by domestic circumstances that affected the interactions among students, faculty, and staff. Because most students in large, high-status universities in the United States live on campus or rent accommodation near campus, as opposed to commuting to classes from their family homes, and because their college years are widely accepted to be a transitional period between adolescence and adulthood during which they form enduring social bonds with future friends and associations, and because so many of these students come to their institution of choice from other states or countries, the evacuation of campuses caused severe personal disruption in their lives and the prospect of a yearlong void in their personal and professional development.

While campus life is sometimes different in other parts of the world, students still felt a new kind of disconnect with their usual academic communities, and some students had to relocate for health or financial reasons in addition to shifting to online lectures for their course. I was scheduled to be in Germany teaching a seminar at TU-Dortmund in summer 2020. Our team of eight instructors quickly reformatted the seminar as a synchronous online course, but throughout the term students and instructors struggled to connect (literally and figuratively) and had to manage our interactions alongside other people in our personal spaces.

For these two reasons—the suddenness and unplanned character of the shift to remote teaching, and the personal displacement and stress experienced by so many students—the technological innovations that many higher education pundits and politicians had argued for so vehemently in 2012 are now under attack. The broader social context, in which going to college is seen as the first flight from the family nest, meant that students and families were divided in whether the health risks of returning to campus at the beginning of the 2020-21 academic year offset the diminished quality of learning and personal growth that continuing to learn remotely would imply. This, coupled with a widespread minority opinion among members of the American public that the COVID-19 pandemic was a hoax or exaggerated, the belief early in the pandemic that the disease affected college-age people only mildly, and the desire of state and local governments to restart local economies by reopening campuses and businesses, led to pressure to bring students back in person. Many students experienced only a partial return, however. Although they moved back to campus, some of their courses were still taught in a remote or hybrid mode, where hybrid learning often was little more than remote learning with a few in-person experiences peppered throughout the term. Many colleges and universities in the United States decided not to reopen for in-person teaching in August or September, 2020. Some large universities, under pressure from state governments to reopen, remained open for in-person teaching only for a few weeks before the levels of COVID-19 infection required them to send students home. Others temporarily suspended in-person teaching for a few weeks to assess the situation. As I write this in fall 2020, some universities have already announced that they will continue remote teaching throughout the academic year, with in-person classes not returning until the summer or fall of 2021, at the earliest. My own institution has invested $13 million so far in health infrastructure (e.g., surveillance testing, contact tracing, extra isolation and quarantine accommodation locations) even though state appropriations have been reduced, and the levels of transmission on our campus are under control. Many students remain dismayed that they are not enjoying the full college experience, including in-person classes or hybrid classes with authentic in-person experiences, and like all universities and colleges that continue to teach students who are on campus, we have contingency plans to evacuate if necessary.

This is all a far cry from higher education's "business as normal." Not long ago, little could excite more passion among faculty than their diverging views on students using computers and smartphones in class. Some faculty viewed student-owned devices as engines of distraction and barred them from the classroom. Others incorporated their use into in-class discussions and discovery activities. As Thorp and Goldstein (2010) observe, "Classroom discussions are more incisive when laptops are present as fact-checking and information-gathering tools. The phrase, 'go home and look it up,' has been replaced by 'someone look it up, now'" (p. 16). With memories of COVID-19 lockdowns still fresh in our minds (or ongoing), and with many students still experiencing remote teaching, we can see that this controversy has become moot. When the world is a classroom and interactions among students and teachers is virtual, we cannot control engagement by preventing the use of technology: it is a given.

The affordances of technology for innovative pedagogy are many. However, those qualities and properties can create positive or negative experiences and outcomes for both students and instructors. Technology is also adopted not just because it has the right affordances (sometimes it does not) but also because of other issues of the moment. Those issues may be genuine or hyped. In the case of the pandemic, the need to shift to untested or less desirable technologies was imperative; however, a short-term compromise should not lead to long-term adoption—an argument that must be made because when the dangers recede there may be a ratchet effect, and the state-of-emergency assumptions are not walked back.

ICU in Writing MOOCs

In the group of four universities (Georgia Tech, Ohio State, Duke, and Mt. San Jacinto, which formed a loose consortium to discuss our MOOC design and implementation) teaching writing MOOCs in 2012, only one developed a course on basic writing: Mt. San Jacinto. Those colleagues who taught that MOOC reported machine-grading was useful to students who needed a great deal of help with basic grammar and mechanics, an unsurprising result when research has shown that many local errors can be assessed through automated writing evaluation platforms. Yang et al. (2002) found that such platforms focus on surface features such as word, sentence, and essay length, rather than on the content of the text or the creativity and style of the writer. Additionally, these platforms are unable to assess idioms, metaphors, humor, and words or phrases from different dialects (Graesser & McNamara, 2012).

Getting local-level feedback from faculty, especially from faculty who are from disciplines other than academic writing, may be inefficient and cause tensions between students and faculty. As Cavaleri and Dianati (2016) summarize in their aptly named article, "You Want Me to Check Your Grammar Again?" instructors "may feel that it is not their responsibility to provide detailed grammatical feedback on students' papers, or they may not feel confident that they have the 'know-how' to explain complex grammatical rules (Jones et al., 2013)" (A223). Likewise, O'Neill and Russell (2019) emphasize the writing and communication centers often focus on high level concerns and have less time in sessions to spend on grammar/mechanics (43).

As we learned when designing our MOOC, evaluation mechanisms are only as good as the algorithms that drive them. In our experience, those algorithms were implemented by coders at the vendor organization, Coursera, who had no experience teaching writing. The evaluation code built into the platform used superficial textual pattern matching algorithms, which constrained the feedback we could give to students. For example, any student response that consisted of a personal pronoun followed by a noun or verb would suffice for the algorithm to mark it as "complete." This became known as the "I Trout" problem (based on the arbitrary word combination a member of our instructional-design team used to test the system), after a particularly absurd "correct" answer that came to our attention.

Once I decided to take on the challenge of teaching a MOOC, I was committed to our mission: Investigate how this new technological approach might help students learn to be better communicators. At the end of the experiment, I had made two overarching discoveries: 1) platforms are built for teaching subject matters where there are clear right and wrong answers, which is why they do not adapt to academic writing; and 2) a thorough consideration of how to integrate any technology into a course is an imperative in the modern higher education landscape.

MOOCs have sometimes inspired professors to incorporate more technology into their teaching practices. Ignoring technological innovation in the context of higher education is a move that any instructor, or administrator, does at their peril given the public push for universities to add more learning environment options. And, the political arguments aside, any instructor who genuinely cares about their students should be investigating the ways that technology can help students be more successful. As Chris Anson noted in our shared 2019 European Association of Teachers of Academic Writing (EATAW) keynote, *Technological Gains and Losses: A Heuristic Approach to Analyzing Affordances for Classroom Instruction and Support for Writing* (which was the genesis of this chapter), technology can make it possible for skilled teachers to focus on higher touch interactions (like engaging with students in a collaborative writing exercise, e.g.) if they are not wasting time on routine tasks that can be handled more efficiently through technological interventions (like providing basic lectures or discussing course administration).

Post-MOOC, many faculty members imagined short-term scenarios in which they might need to shift a class online. Bad weather, travel to conferences, are two examples. However, this definition of hybrid was limited. COVID-19 created a scenario in which faculty were forced to shift online and, for many of them, that is where they wish to remain until the crisis has ended. But, in the same way that MOOCs changed education (even if not in the ways that disruptors imagined), the post-COVID-19 landscape will be different.

Grammarly: A Case Study in ICU[4]

One program for improving writing that has been highly advertised to students writing in English is Grammarly.[5] At my institution, a wide range of constituencies have been approached about an institutional subscription to Grammarly, a web plugin service that purports to offer users "Great Writing. Simplified." From solicitations to student government to student affairs to the library to individual faculty members, Grammarly has been working hard to get my university to sign up for an institutional subscription to their platform. Interestingly, their marketing efforts have not been directed, at least not without a redirect, to our writing center or writing program faculty, the very experts who are best positioned to judge its appropriateness as a tool for teaching academic writing. Grammarly is not unique in this cross-marketing approach. Each day since the pandemic began, I have received solicitations for technological interventions promising to make teaching easier and more efficient.

Grammarly advertises its product as more than just a grammar checker, explaining that they help writers create texts that are stylistically better, which raises the immediate question: which style is improved? For teachers of academic writing, a great deal of attention is given to questions of style—especially discipline-specific style. However, students often conflate proofreading with revision, and are, therefore unlikely to understand exactly what a platform like Grammarly can realistically promise. Grammarly is good at evaluating the rules of grammar and word usage but cannot pick up on subtleties of meaning and context in the way that a person can (Nova, 2018). Therefore, students need to understand that Grammarly can only assist them in identifying and fixing a portion of their composition errors. They must employ alternative methods to fully address potential problems in a text.

Despite this greater sophistication in communicative competence, today's students do not excel in writing for the sake of writing. They want

---

4   The author acknowledges the research contributions for some of the information in this case study from an internal report about Grammarly written by her with members of her lab: Brandy Ball Blake, Maria Chappell, Aaron Colton, Leah Misemer, Rob Griffin, Jeff Howard, and Kendra Slayton.

5   Programs like Grammarly exist in other in other languages. For example, Rechtschreibpruefung24, a grammar checking and readability analysis service for German texts.

to make a difference in the world and are therefore only motivated to learn to communicate information they care about. In contrast, "[i]n the typical five-paragraph essay, for example, the writer employs a prescribed method, almost a formula, to shape each section of the essay, and you don't deviate from that structure even if your audience changes. Nor do you need to because, in the traditional five-paragraph essay, the audience is unchanging: it's the professor" (Davidson, 2017, p. 93). Grammarly might "improve" the writing if the professor in question understands "good writing" as grammatically correct sentences, but teaching students actual writing competencies requires more sophisticated approaches. Warner (2018), a higher education journalist makes similar points in a recent book, arguing that writing courses should operationalize their learning objectives through experiences, rather than assignments or proficiencies. His reasoning is similar to Davidson's: students develop general competencies best when they are engaged in meaningful content-driven work, not when they are forced to concentrate on form and technique.

At best, Grammarly appears capable of improving the quality of a given document without promoting language acquisition or active learning. Students may be tempted to accept Grammarly's corrections without reviewing and evaluating them, especially if a student believes that proofreading at the local level is what matters most. This is particularly an issue for students whose first language is not English. For confident and experienced writers who are capable of considering the suggestions made by the program, Grammarly does offer some affordances for improving a text. At worst, Grammarly may overwhelm more inexperienced writers with comments and suggestions, including erroneous or unnecessary changes, that they do not understand. In this way, Grammarly does not help writers become better writers because it does not teach writers how to make decisions about what is correct in a given discourse scenario. This is analogous to how the plagiarism platform Turnitin analyzes documents against known sources, and while identifying matches for students to consider, does not teach them how to use source materials or help them understand when a matched passage might be acceptable. In all these cases, just as with the UK A-level prediction algorithm, the decision-*making* aspect of a situation is prioritized at the expense of decision *explanation.*

Many of the authors seem to agree that using Grammarly is better than nothing. Grammatical and other proofreading errors in professional writing can be frustrating, embarrassing, and undercut author credibility, even if the errors do not affect understandability at all. If Grammarly is only being used to fix these "superficial" non-critical errors, then it is immensely helpful in saving the student time and, in some cases, the cost of employing a copy editor.

One of the fundamental questions is how might a program like Grammarly cause harm that outweighs its benefits. Dembsey (2017) identifies several shortcomings in Grammarly, including repetitive comments, "incorrect use of terms, incorrect explanations, false positives, [and] insertion of errors" (p. 83). Such responses can cause confusion for students. Dembsey also notes that while Grammarly does offer explanations for its suggestions, it cannot clarify those explanations. The fact that some of Grammarly's suggestions are flawed, and that students may be unable to discern what suggestions to take up, indicates that Grammarly may benefit more able writers but harm less competent ones. Like the Mt. San Jacinto experience discussed earlier, this supports the findings of Jones and her colleagues (2013) who found that their grammar intervention benefited stronger writers more than weaker writers, and suggested that this was because more able writers "have clearer communicative and rhetorical intentions for their writing than less able writers, enabling [stronger writers] to make more appropriate use of their grammatical understanding to shape text appropriately" (p. 1256).

O'Neill and Russell (2019) argue that Grammarly sometimes provides inaccurate suggestions because of a lack of context, explaining that previous studies show that automated checkers may be better suited for more advanced writers who "have sufficient grammatical understanding to be able to filter suggestions that are incorrect," whereas "automated feedback can overwhelm students with low English proficiency" (p. 43). Cavaleri and Dianati (2016) noticed that "students felt some of the recommendations were flawed or hard to understand" (A233), making student usage problematic. Similarly, Gain et al. (2019) conclude that there is a great deal of user/student decision-making necessary for using Grammarly.

Overall, O'Neill and Russell (2019) caution that Grammarly is best used in a context where experts can "manag[e] students' expectations about the feedback by making them explicitly aware that it was not infallible" and can point out incorrect suggestions from Grammarly (p. 52). They argue that "the program is currently not accurate enough for independent use to be justified" (p. 42), which is to say, students need more expert guidance than the platform provides.

Grammarly may be useful if corrections pertaining to grammar, punctuation, and spelling are helpful to the revising process; however, such a program does not assist with the content and organizational needs that EFL/ESL/ELL students have when dealing with their specific writing requirements. The emphasis on grammatical and lexical analysis, if the corrections are applicable can be useful for word/sentence-level errors (Ghufron & Rosyida, 2018), but they can be a crutch that English language learners rely on without considering other issues of language fluency.

Chen and Cheng (2008) offer an excellent overview of automated writing evaluation and its effectiveness for EFL learners. The implementation of platforms like Grammarly were perceived somewhat favorably when used for early drafting and revising followed by human feedback from the teacher and peers during later writing stages. However, it is important to note the autonomous use of tools such as Grammarly with limited human intervention was frustrating to EFL/ESL/ELL users and limited their acquisition of writing processes. The researchers recommended that instructors need clear pedagogical plans for an automated writing evaluation platform's relevance to the learning of writing.

Ranalli (2018) was concerned with the use of automated written corrective feedback among EFL/ESL/ELL students in low and high-level writing courses. Ranalli's findings showed that the 82 ESL students receiving generic automated written corrective feedback had fewer successful error corrections compared to when receiving specific feedback. The students also indicated lower ratings of clarity and helpfulness from such programs.

Nova (2018) evaluated the strengths and weaknesses of Grammarly, which are presented in a case study analysis of three Indonesian graduate students' perceptions of the program. Strengths included the provision of useful color-coded feedback, ease of use and a high rate of evaluation speed. The drawbacks focused on misleading feedback, weaknesses in detecting errors pertaining to differing types of English usage and the lack of context and content evaluation. While correction leading to short-term writing improvement was considered a positive among the three students, misleading feedback was cited as frequent, often leading to changes in intentional meanings. In keeping with some of the other studies, this study supports the idea that Grammarly, while helpful for basic correction, may subvert the intended meaning by providing generic feedback that a confused EFL/ESL/ELL user may not be able to evaluate and implement.

Grammarly touts its privacy policy as being "trusted by millions of users" and is one of their primary selling points. However, many users have found that Grammarly is problematic in the same way that the plagiarism detection platform TurnItIn is—while you retain rights to your work, that work is no longer private. Grammarly's terms of service and license agreement (n.d.) state that "You retain all right, title, and interest in and to your User Content," but it also says: 'By uploading or entering any User Content, you give Grammarly (and those it works with) a nonexclusive, worldwide, royalty-free and fully-paid, transferable and sublicensable, perpetual, and irrevocable license to copy, store and use your User Content (and, if you are an Authorized User, your Enterprise Subscriber's User Content) in connection with the provision of the Software and the Services and to improve the algorithms underlying the Software and the Services. [Emphasis added]" Students within the European Economic Area can exercise their rights under GDPR, which, at least, allows them to request that their personal information be deleted after using the program, but there is no reference in the Privacy Policy about user content—only personal details. Therefore, encouraging students to use a program like Grammarly should only be done with a clear disclosure about what using the service means for their content ownership and personal privacy.

While questions of privacy for Grammarly are limited to a student exposing personal information and sharing texts, all technologies represent different levels of privacy concerns. Users make decisions to cede some of their privacy (usually by accepting user agreements they never read) because they decide the benefit of the program is worth the exchange of the information they are expected to share. However, the pivot to remote instruction created a situation in which students felt compelled to use certain technologies.

Students have grown up with the internet surrounding them, which is not an experience shared by their older teachers. As a consequence, students and faculty may differ in their expectations about what amount of personal disclosure by a student is appropriate, although, arguably instructors in countries with stricter privacy laws than we have in the US are likely more attentive to these issues. Many writers have documented how this tendency manifests itself in young people's use of social networks (e.g., Palfrey & Gasser, 2015). This liberality with personal information persists into the college years. So, it is interesting how the demands of COVID-19-era remote teaching technologies clash with students' desire to manage their identities with their classmates and teachers. Although students may be freer in their sharing of personal information on social networks, and may even curate this image through video, using tools like YouTube, they are more reticent to reveal their living circumstances through live video in a classroom setting, whereas they would be content to cede privacy for the perceived convenience of programs like Grammarly. I observed greater reticence when working with my students in Germany, many of whom were unwilling to turn on video cameras and expose their personal environments. American students, however, especially those who are living in university housing have been more willing to expose their residential environments.

Certainly, a program like Grammarly is more sophisticated because, unlike Coursera, writing evaluation functionality is central to their service. However, the shortcomings indicate a lack of awareness of the moves that matter most in academic writing (or their business model does not require it). As Grabill notes in his keynote address at the 2016 Computers & Writing annual conference, "In the [American] marketplace right now, there are at least eight serious products that promise to improve writing via some sort of robot. And there are many more robots running around out there embedded in other things. Almost none of them were developed by teams with anything close to a fraction of the writing expertise assembled in this room."

More specifically, Carbone's (2012) analysis of three grammar checkers found that Grammarly misdiagnosed or poorly explained 21% of the 52 errors it tagged in his experimental document, and Carbone did not do an analysis of issues that were missed. Another concerning observation about Carbone's data is that most errors identified by Grammarly were for the use of passive voice (14 tags). Writing instructors will understand why this is a problem: students must learn to write in their disciplines and passive voice is the expected discourse convention for some scholarly communities.

Conclusions

Whatever the "new normal" looks like as we move past the pandemic, it seems certain that educational practices will forever be changed. Just as I was, in the beginning, an unwilling participant in the MOOC experiment, many of my colleagues now find themselves grudging participants in a vast experiment. In many ways, the pandemic has become the catalyst for the greatest pedagogical experiment in history, and as such, educators must be vigilant about analyzing and evaluating its early results.

While MOOCs and the COVID-19 pandemic are two examples of reactive pedagogy, it is important to acknowledge that in the case of academic writing, technological interventions have always been susceptible to ICU thinking. As digital literacy has taken hold, teachers of academic writing have sometimes struggled to balance the changing contexts of traditional writing and multimodal composition, and non-academic companies will continue to entice students (and some faculty) into believing that there can be a quicker and easier ways to negotiate the changing academic communication landscape.

As scholars and teachers of academic writing, we have a responsibility to question the affordances presented by automated writing evaluation platforms. We must not allow ourselves, in the current crisis, to be tempted to abdicate parts of our workload, although that would be understandable given the current demands.

References

Anson, C. M. & Head, K. J. (2019, July 2). *Technological gains and losses: A heuristic approach to analyzing affordances for classroom instruction and support for writing*

[Keynote address]. European Association of Teachers of Academic Writing annual conference. Gothenburg, Sweden. https://2019.eataw.eu/video-recordings-and-session-material/.

Axelrod, A. (2019, August 11). A century later: The Treaty of Versailles and its rejection of racial equality [Radio series episode]. *Code Sw!tch*. NPR. https://www.npr.org/sections/codeswitch/2019/08/11/742293305/a-century-later-the-treaty-of-versailles-and-its-rejection-of-racial-equality.

Brey, P. (2010). Values in technology and disclosive computer ethics. In L. Floridi (Ed.), *The Cambridge handbook of information and computer ethics* (pp. 41–58). Cambridge University Press.

Carbone, N. (2012, October 31) An experiment with grammar checkers. *Seeing and learning: Making visible what students think and apply*, Blogger. http://ncce112carbone.blogspot.com/2012/10/an-experiment-with-grammar-checkers.html.

Cavaleri, M. & Dianati, S. (2016). You want me to check your grammar again? The usefulness of online grammar checkers as perceived by students. *Journal of Academic Language & Learning, 10*(1), A223–A236.

Chen, C.-F. E. & Cheng, W.-Y. E. (2008). Beyond the design of automated writing evaluation: pedagogical practices and perceived learning effectiveness in EFL writing classes. *Language, Learning & Technology, 12*(2), 94.

Christensen, C. M. (1997) *The innovator's dilemma: When new technologies cause great firms to fail*. Harvard Business School Press.

Christensen C. M. & Eyring, H. J. (2011). *The innovative university: Changing the DNA of higher education from the inside out*. Jossey-Bass.

Davidson, D. N. (2017). *The new education: How to revolutionize the university to prepare students for a world in flux*. Basic Books.

Dembsey, J. M. (2017). Closing the Grammarly gaps: A study of claims and feedback from an online Grammarly program. *The Writing Center Journal, 36*(1), 63–100.

DeMillo, R. A. (2011). *Abelard to Apple: The fate of American colleges and universities*. MIT Press.

Gain, A., Rao, M. & Bhat, S. K. (2019) Usage of Grammarly—online grammar and spelling checker tool at the health science library, Manipal Academy of Higher Education, Manipal: A study. *Library Philosophy, and Practice*, 1–14. https://eprints.manipal.edu/154019/.

Ghufron, M. A. & Rosyida, F. (2018). The role of Grammarly in assessing English as a foreign language writing. *Lingua Cultura, 12*(4), 395–403.

Gibson, J. J. (1986). *The ecological approach to visual perception*. Erlbaum.

Grabill, J. (2016, May 20). *Do we learn best together or alone?: Your life with robots* [Keynote address]. Computers & Writing annual conference, Rochester, NY, United States. https://www.youtube.com/watch?v=LHatYx8ziEs.

Graesser, A. C. & McNamara, D. S. (2012). Automated analysis of essays and open-ended verbal responses. In H. Cooper, P. M. Camic, D. L. Long, A. T. Panter, D. Rindskopf & K. J. Sher (Eds.), *APA handbook of research methods in psychology, Vol 1: Foundations, planning, measures, and psychometrics* (pp. 307–325). American Psychological Association.

Grammarly. (n.d.). Terms of service and license agreement. Retrieved December 2, 2021, from https://www.grammarly.com/terms.

Head, K. J. (2017). *Disrupt this!: MOOCs and the promises of technology*. University Press of New England.

Head, K. J. (2020). Let's add compassion to our online curriculum. Coping with Coronavirus: How faculty members can support students in traumatic times. *The Chronicle of Higher Education*, 13–14. https://icc.edu/faculty-staff/files/CopingWithCoronavirus.pdf.

Hsi, I. & Potts, C. (2000). Studying the evolution and enhancement of software features. *Proceedings of the International Conference on Software Maintenance*, 143–151. https://doi.org/10.1109/ICSM.2000.883033.

Jones, S., Myhill, D. & Bailey, T. (2013). Grammar for writing? An investigation of the effects of contextualized grammar teaching on students' writing. *Reading and Writing*, 26(8), 1241–1263.

Kelly, Kevin. (2010). *What technology wants*. Viking.

Norman, D. (1988). *The design of everyday things*. Basic Books.

Nova, M. (2018). Utilizing Grammarly in evaluating academic writing: A narrative research on EFL students' experience. *Premise Journal*, 7(1), 80–97.

O'Neill, R. & Russell, A. (2019). Stop! Grammar time: University students' perceptions of the automated feedback program Grammarly. *Australasian Journal of Educational Technology*, 35(1), 42–56.

Palfrey, J. & Gasser, U. (2015). *Born digital: How children grow up in a digital age*. Basic Books.

Perelman, L. (2016). Perelman-grammar checkers do not work. *WLN: A journal of writing center scholarship*, 40(7–8), 11–20.

Ranalli, J. (2018). Automated written corrective feedback: How well can students make use of it? *Computer-Assisted Language Learning*, 31(7), 653–674.

Thorp, H. & Goldstein, B. (2010). *Engines of innovation: The entrepreneurial university in the twenty-first century*. University of North Carolina Press.

Ubachs, G. & Konings, L. (2018). *MOOC strategies in European universities. Status report based on a mapping survey conducted in December 2017–May 2018*. EADTU. https://tinyurl.com/MOOC-Strategies.

Varinaitis, A. S., McCreery, G. & Rein, P. (Writers) & Tsao, A. (Director). (1999, February 25). The One with the cop (Season 5, Episode 16) [TV series episode]. In D. Crane, M Kauffman, K. S. Bright & M. Curtis (Executive Producers), *Friends*. NBC.

Warner, J. (2018). *Why they can't write: Killing the five-paragraph essay and other necessities*. Johns Hopkins University Press.

Yang, Y., Buckendhal, C. W., Juszkiewicz, P. J. & Bhola, D. S. (2002). A review of strategies for validating computer-automated scoring. *Applied Measurement in Education*. 15(4), 391–412.

3

A Heuristic Approach to Selecting Technological Tools for Writing Instruction and Support

Chris M. Anson
NORTH CAROLINA STATE UNIVERSITY

As new digital tools for use in writing instruction continue to burgeon, it has become increasingly urgent to forestall the rushed and unconsidered adoption of tools that do little to enhance conventional methods or even work against them. Although some selection criteria exist, they are generalized and lack reference to principled instructional methods and current best practices. This chapter proposes a set of theory-based perspectives, or lenses, to determine the instructional effectiveness of digital writing and learning tools. These perspectives include the informational, intellectual or cognitive, social and interpersonal, and rhetorical potential of the tool, along with the extent to which it places the student in an active-learning role and the extent to which the use of the tool is fair and ethical. After describing this set of perspectives, the chapter then tests them on three relatively simple tools that encourage writing of different kinds and purposes: Padlet (a classroom tool that facilitates active thinking and discussion); Fakebook (a platform that, emulating Facebook, invites students to create profiles of characters or famous historical figures and populate them with interactive posts, exchanges with "friends," videos, and other media), and the use of screencasting to facilitate student peer review. The perspectives are admittedly incomplete, designed heuristically to foster consideration of and dialogue around principled choice of digital tools on a small scale, such as Padlet, or a broader and more complex scale, such as the choice of an LMS for a course of study or entire department or program.

In 1957, noted scientist and engineer Simon Ramo sketched a dramatic vision of the classroom of the future: a technologically advanced system that "makes possible more education for more people with fewer skilled teachers being wasted in the more routine tasks that a machine should do for them" (Ramo,

DOI: https://doi.org/10.37514/INT-B.2022.1466.2.03

1957, p. 22). For this system, Ramo imagined a cash-register-like "memory machine" that would give preprogrammed encouragement to students when they submitted correct answers. Incorrect answers would trigger a red light with a sign that, like the warning that comes from jiggling a pinball machine, said "TILT!" (Andrews, 2019).

Ramo's ideas were soon picked up in the popular press. Cartoonist Arthur Radebaugh, illustrator of the syndicated newspaper comic "Closer Than We Think" (Novak, 2012), drew a version of Ramo's classroom that depicted students sitting at pushbutton terminals (with tiny, embedded cameras), watching a video monitor of a lecturing teacher (see Figure 3.1).

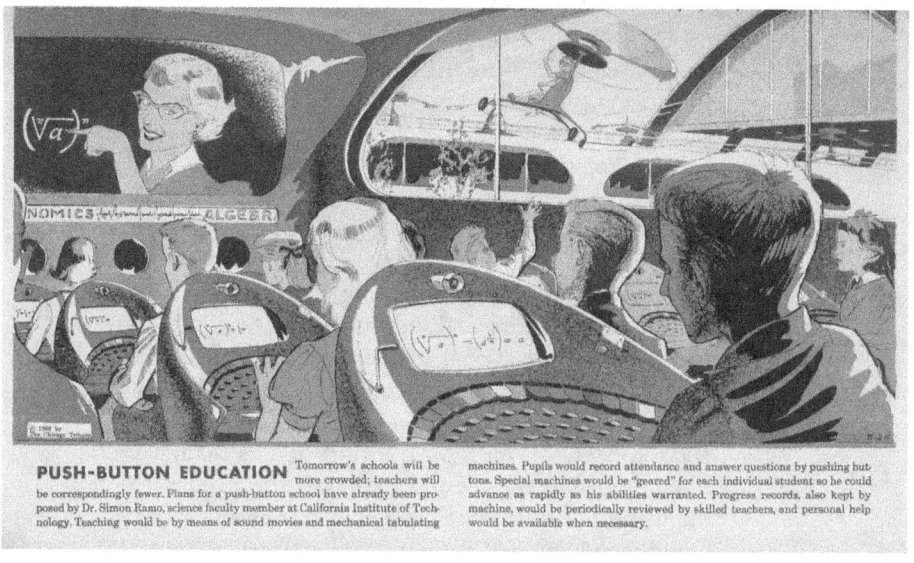

Figure 3.1. Push-button education (1958).

The description below the image reads, in part:

> Tomorrow's schools will be more crowded; teachers will be correspondingly fewer. Plans for a push-button school have already been proposed by Dr. Simon Ramo. . . . Teaching would be by means of sound movies and mechanical tabulating machines. Pupils would record attendance and answer questions by pushing buttons. . . . Progress records, also kept by machine, would be periodically reviewed by skilled teachers, and personal help would be available when necessary. (Novak, 2012)

Today, this Skinnerian vision of technology-assisted learning, driven by the psychology of operant conditioning, seems hopelessly uninformed. But it represented an attractive fantasy at the time: in the US and elsewhere, postwar school enrollments were soaring and a baby boom predicted overcrowded classes and overburdened teachers. Automation had been implemented successfully in the factory; now it promised equal "efficiency" in the classroom.

As Ramo's and similar initiatives remind us, ideas for the mediation of technology in the classroom do not always guarantee that the technology will enact the principles of effective learning as these are informed by educational theory and research. Personal accounts abound of well-intentioned administrators finding that an adopted technology does little to improve learning, or ends up being unfair, or traps schools and universities in unreasonable contracts with for-profit companies. The annals of educational commentary are filled with stories about dozens of computers provided free to schools by companies hoping to create the next generation of consumers, only to have the devices sit in closets—even in their own shipping boxes—for lack of teacher expertise (or support) to integrate them into the classroom. Researchers Cuban et al. (2001) studied technological adoption in two U.S. high schools located in the epicenter of digital technology—Silicon Valley, California. Over a period of seven months, they conducted observations, interviews, surveys, and reviews of documents in the two schools, which had significantly above-average access to technology. Yet they found that most teachers were "occasional users or nonusers" (Cuban et al., 2001, p. 813) of the abundant technology, and when they did use it, they did not do so to enhance their teaching practices.

In the context of present and future pandemics that force tens of millions of teachers and students to work online rather than risk viral transmission in physical classrooms and other spaces, choices of educational technology are no longer optional. The development of new perspectives for such choices has become increasingly urgent. After most primary and secondary schools and universities worldwide transitioned to distance learning during the COVID-19 pandemic, it was no longer a choice of *whether* to use synchronous or asynchronous communication technologies to "supplement" face-to-face instruction, but which ones to use for all interaction. As many teachers lacking experience with online instruction adapted to its necessity and became familiar with online conferencing systems such as Zoom, Skype, and MS Teams, additional tools presented opportunities to do more than lecture into a screen full of unresponsive faces.

What principles, then, should guide the adoption of new digital tools for writing instruction, beyond simple trial and (frequent) error? What kinds of analysis can forestall the eager but unconsidered attraction to tools that end up failing to improve student learning or enhance instruction? How can we forestall the adoption of tools that are not "subject to critical interrogation" (Borrowman, 2012, p. ix)?[1]

The purpose of this chapter is first to propose a set of perspectives, based on educational theory, research, and best practices in teaching and learning, to analyze digital tools for their potential adoption or adaptation in support of writing. Then the perspectives will be applied heuristically to three simple digital tools that can be used to enhance classroom interaction and writing instruction.

Current Perspectives for Digital Tool Choice

Across the landscape of education, the most common guiding principle for the adoption of digital tools focuses on the learning goal(s), or "defined educational rationales" (Wyatt, 2017, Step 2, para. 1) that the tool will support. Hughes (2004) suggests turning teachers into "technology integrationists" by encouraging them to "choose to use technologies *only* when they uniquely enhance the curriculum, instruction, and students' learning" (para. 3). In its position statement on technology integration, the (U.S.-based) National Council of Teachers of English (2018) proposes that "new technologies should be considered only when it is clear how they can enhance, expand, and/or deepen engaging and sound practices related to literacy instruction" (para. 11). An article in the *Chronicle for Higher Education* points out that "in choosing technology, people naturally gravitate toward tools that seem fun or easy, even if they're not the most useful," and suggests instead that teachers ask the "magic wand question" (what one skill, misconception, or task is most in need of attention?) and then choose a tool that will address it (Miller, 2019, para. 4). And Harris and Hofer (2009) recommend an approach to digital tool choice that "focuses on students' standards-based learning needs rather than the specific features of particular tech tools and resources" (p. 23).

A more extensive focus on goal-driven adoption appears in a model proposed by literacy scholars Hutchison and Woodard (2013), as shown in Figure 3.2.

---

[1] In this chapter, the term "tool" will refer not to generalized technologies such as computers, which are widely available to students in spite of a persistent digital divide (see Croft & Moore, 2019, for the U.S. and Chen & Wellman, 2004, for the world), but to all specific technologically-mediated programs, apps, and platforms—anything designed or used to facilitate instruction with, for purposes of this volume, a focus on written communication. However, because other authors often use "technology" to refer to specific digital tools, "technology" may appear when referring to these authors' works and ideas.

Selecting Technological Tools

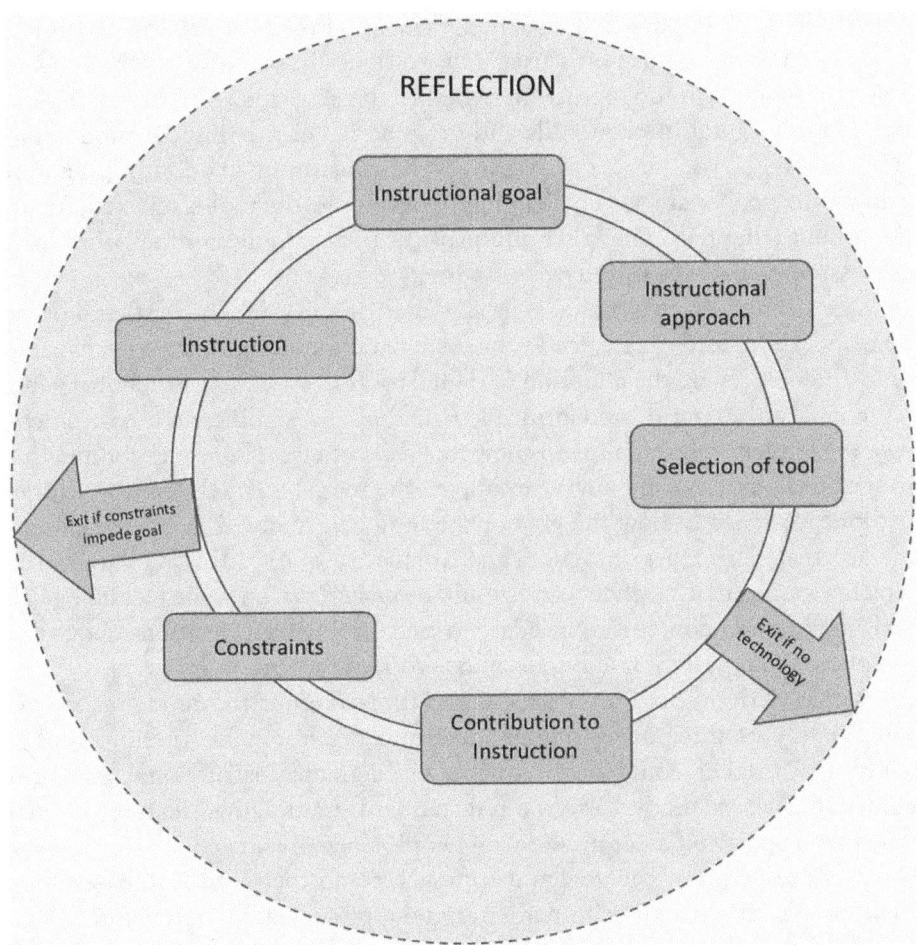

Figure 3.2. One model of technological adoption (Hutchison & Woodward, 2013).

In this model, the adoption of a digital tool is not the first consideration; rather, the process begins with the articulation of learning goals. The goals lead to the development of an instructional approach, which refers to "the method used to meet the objectives laid out in the instructional goal" (Hutchison & Woodard, 2013, p. 460). Several decision points inform the approach, including how teacher- or student-centered it is and whether the approach involves individual or group learning. These considerations inform the selection of a tool, with an analysis of the prior experiences students have with the tool, how the tool contributes to instruction, and what constraints might push against the realization of the goals. Because pencil and paper are not "technologies" (but see Baron, 1999), choosing them makes the rest of the model irrelevant because it focuses only on digital tools. Among the considerations involved in tool choice are whether the students will learn both digital and nondigital literacy skills and get practice in multimodal production (Hutchison & Woodard, 2013, p. 461). If the constraints in adopting the tool subvert the goal or are too challenging to overcome, the tool is rejected; if not, then the teacher reflects further on the use of the tool, envisioning issues such as classroom space and student work time.

One strength of this model is its advocacy of what Schön (1983) and other scholars call "reflective practice"—the systematic inquiry into the effectiveness of instruction. Tying the adoption of digital tools to specific instructional goals represents an attractive and principled method—a significant improvement over the tendency to reach for any new tool just because it looks new or fun. But in spite of helpful accompanying examples, the model is largely theory-neutral, without reference to how the goal or the tool are grounded in scholarship on literacy. Instead, it relies on Mishra and Koehler's (2006) "TPACK" framework, which assumes that teachers can "simultaneously draw on their technological, pedagogical, and content knowledge" to make principled decisions about the use of technological tools (Hutchison & Woodward, 2013, p. 457).

Acknowledging its limitations, the authors present the model as a procedural way of integrating digital tools into classroom instruction. But as a result, a teacher could begin with a problematic instructional goal and approach, such as eradicating the nonstandard grammatical features of students who speak a dialect by showing people's negative reactions to speakers' use of those features. The goal and approach could then lead to the development or selection of a discriminatory digital tool, such as an online interactive "quiz" requiring students to watch cartoon versions of people using standard or nonstandard dialect features and then selecting "correct" or "incorrect" options, with corresponding animations of booing or applauding audiences. Missing from the model is a finer-grained set of considerations based on educational principles—in this case, anti-racist approaches to language in the classroom (see Young, 2011) brought to bear on tool selection and integration.

Also missing from the model are the broader processes of tool development, which precede its adoption. If tool developers do not have access to current scholarship on literacy development, their tool's design may reflect outmoded or discredited pedagogical practices or, as Selfe and Selfe (1994) showed in an analysis of computer desktops, particular ideologies of "work" or "school." For this reason, the heuristic approach described in this chapter could be helpful beyond the educational community as technology companies continue to develop and/or market digital tools for use in classroom instruction.

Perspectives for Determining Choice

Choice of digital tools is often driven by cognitive goals that, as Vossoughi and Gutiérrez (2016) have argued, dominate our thinking about education. For example, a web-based grammar puzzle might attract a teacher as a learning tool, but lack consideration of the tool's rhetorical, social, interpersonal, or affective value. From the perspective of activity theory, written communication involves multiple social, contextual, and affective dimensions in addition to purely cognitive ones. As Russell (1995) puts it, "one acquires the genres (typified semiotic means) used by some activity field, as one interacts with people involved in the activity field and the material objects and signs those people use (including those marks on a surface that we call writing)" (p. 56). This social theory of communication reorients literacy as always involving interaction among human beings in context (Kress et al., 2001; Street, 2013). But this orientation has not been sufficiently used to analyze the adoption of digital tools for teaching and learning (see Zylka et al., 2015). A more appropriate focus for our purposes brings together the cognitive, informational, social and interpersonal, and rhetorical dimensions of literate work, as well as the extent to which the tool involves active participation and the extent to which it is ethical. As a heuristic for analyzing available tools and making informed choices, this model prompts us to ask the following operative questions (see Figure 3.3):

- What is the tool's informational potential?
- What is the tool's intellectual/cognitive potential?
- What is the tool's rhetorical potential?
- What is the tool's social/interpersonal potential?
- How *active* is the student in the learning process?
- How *fair and ethical* is the tool?

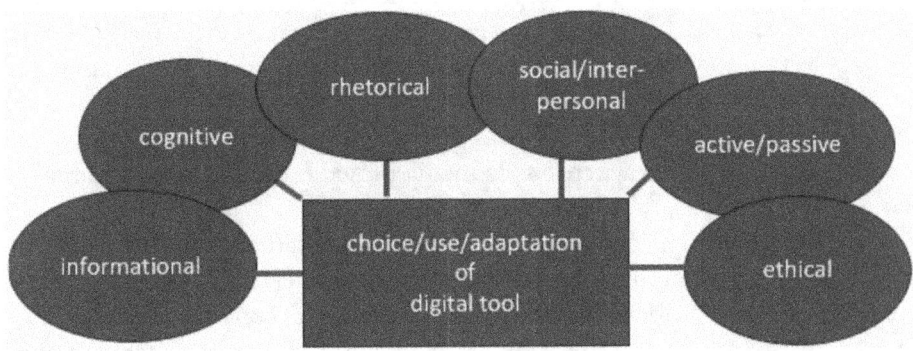

Figure 3.3. Dimensions of choice in the selection of digital tools.

In the analysis of any educational content, the informational perspective would normally refer to the nature and sophistication of the material and intertextual connections to other information (Bazerman, 2004); demands on the learner's information processing (e.g., Torrance & Galbraith, 2006); and the relationship of the information to the goals and outcomes of the course. This perspective is highly contingent on the quality and nature of the material itself because many digital tools simply provide an interface between content matter and the learner. However, some considerations remain and take us into the domain of universal design (see Rose et al., 2006; Rose & Meyer, 2002). The tool could render the information difficult to process, or provide no alternative access for those who need it, an issue we will return to in the context of the ethical perspective. When presented multimodally, the information also could be affected by the relationship between the modalities. For example, using eye-tracking equipment, Slykhuis et al. (2005) found that learners pay more attention to accompanying visuals onscreen when the visuals are "complimentary"—most highly integrated with the text. When included, audio narration of the text assists in students' processing of complimentary material but becomes superfluous when students are considering material not well integrated with the text. Other research has shown that students read certain kinds of texts more thoroughly and with better recall in print than onscreen (Clinton, 2019). For these reasons, informational potential will refer to the *informational interface* of the tool—how the tool presents the information—rather than to the quality of the information itself, which requires a separate analysis.

The cognitive/intellectual perspective refers to the nature of the reasoning required to use or interact with the tool (e.g., Applebee, 1984); the extent to which the tool activates critical thinking and evaluation (e.g., Bean, 2011; Condon & Kelly-Riley, 2004; Pearlman & Carillo, 2018), and, especially in the context of this collection, the relationship between the writing activity, as assigned, and the kinds of cognitive or intellectual processes, or "structure of activity," that students must engage in (Anson, 2017, p. 23; see also Melzer, 2014). Certain tools or digital media are better suited to the engagement of cognitive activity than others. For example, as Hewett and DePew (2015) point out, asynchronous digital tools and platforms support stronger cognitive engagement while synchronous media provide interpersonal advantages because of higher levels of social engagement.

The rhetorical perspective refers to the potential of the tool to help students develop discursive abilities such as using persuasive strategies (e.g., Selzer, 2004); decentering, identifying with audiences, and conceding to alternate perspectives (e.g., Flower, 1979; Kroll, 1978); and building awareness of rhetorical genres, in both their forms and structures and in their relationship to social and communicative contexts (e.g., Bawarshi & Reiff, 2010). McKorkle (2012), for example, analyzed the relationship of emerging technologies to the classical rhetorical concept of *delivery*, arguing that "delivery's scope can be widened to accommodate the practices of graphic design, digital editing, or the manipulation of formal elements within a medium (p. 3; see also Delagrange, 2011, and Rice, 2012, for further analyses of the relationships between digital tools and rhetorical understanding).

The social and interpersonal perspective refers to the way that the tool encourages interaction through language and the development of skills of collaboration and exchange, and how people negotiate their social positions, especially in situations that involve evaluation. It includes how sophisticated the tool is for supporting relational aspects of learning and performance (e.g., Kerssen-Griep et al., 2008; Kluger & DeNisi, 1996); the demands the tool places on negotiating "face work" (e.g., Goffman, 1955; Lim & Bowers, 1991); how effectively the tool fosters social awareness (e.g., Bazerman, 2017; Portanova et al., 2017); how fully it helps students to develop skills of teamwork (e.g., Wolfe, 2010); and the extent to which it encourages the development of "passionate affinity spaces"—"loosely organized social and cultural settings in which the work of teaching tends to be shared by many people, in many locations, who are connected by a shared interest or passion" (Gee, 2018, p. 8; see also Gee, 2005; 2007).

In addition to these perspectives, the active/passive continuum is a broader dimension of learning that draws from scholarship on the need for novice writers to be engaged in the processes of writing and the active construction and reconstruction of knowledge and understanding, rather than being passive recipients of information (Biggs & Tang, 2007). A synchronous chat places the learner in an active role that involves social and interpersonal interaction, compared, for example, to pure lecture. But while a self-guided online tutorial may appear to place students in an active role by virtue of their interaction with the screen, keyboard, and mouse, a more careful analysis will show that "activity" depends on and varies with a number of factors, such as how much work a program is doing *for* the user.

Finally—and perhaps most importantly—the ethical perspective refers to the fairness of the tool. Does the tool place anyone at a disadvantage on the basis of access, accessibility, prior experience, cost, or certain processing concerns (such as strongly favoring oral over visual information)? Is it discriminatory? Does it rely on prior knowledge or experience in ways that exclude some from full engagement? Do all learners have equal access to the tool, or is access new to some and not others? Who bears the cost of the tool? For example, a course that requires students to download an application that levies a substantial monthly subscription fee may unfairly place some at a financial disadvantage (see Anderson & Perrin, 2018). And, of importance to contexts in which the tool is created or programmed for the use of one language (such as English) but the users are L2 speakers of that language, does the tool place learners at a linguistic disadvantage or require accommodations to use effectively?

Of course, the tool itself may not fail the fairness criterion, but how it is used. This concern takes us beyond tool selection and into a complex world of instructional ideology and preparation, assumptions about learners and their experiences, and the presence of curricular mandates or guidelines that teachers must follow. Selfe and Selfe (1994), for example, consider the ways that computer interfaces—neutral when taken by themselves—are spaces that enact ideological and material legacies. Citing previous scholars, they point out that minority schools often use software for decontextualized drill and practice (driven by unfair assessments imposed from without) while schools populated by mainstream students may use the software to foster higher-order literacies.

It is also beyond the scope of this chapter, but essential in the analysis of digital tools for instruction, to consider deeper questions of usability, universal design, and fairness, as previously mentioned. Instructors rarely have the time and resources to fully test a tool to determine whether it poses challenges to particular students or groups of students. Concerns include physical differences (is the tool more difficult to use for students with limited hand function, for example); visual differences; hearing differences; learning differences; attention differences; and communication differences (see Burgstahler, 2008). For example, when students choose—or, such as during a pandemic, are compelled—to take courses online, it may be necessary to offer asynchronous options to accommodate differences in the pace at which students can learn. At the same time, advantages may also accrue from digital tool use, such as the ability for a distance learner to watch a video lecture multiple times, or stop and replay sections of it, which would be impossible in a face-to-face situation. But even in less thorough analyses of a tool for possible adoption, considerations of fairness are essential.

Together, these perspectives make up important theoretical orientations for the choice of digital tools in support of writing development. Each can be used to evaluate the possible affordances of the tool. Of course, a number of concessions are called for. First, the perspectives are not meant to provide answers automatically, because so much depends. For example, the ethical perspective has led many writing programs to reject Turnitin, the plagiarism detection tool, because it takes ownership of students' work to grow its database, because it invokes a distrust of students before a course begins and implies that they are guilty until proven innocent, and because it creates false positives and also misses legitimate cases of plagiarism (see Morris & Stommel, 2017; Schorn, 2015). Educators who believe students own the copyright to their academic work will find Turnitin to be problematic; those who believe the institution (or, when subscribed, Turnitin) owns students' work may find it less ethically questionable. Like the other perspectives, the ethical is contingent; its application is designed to create discussion and critical analysis, not to auto-generate decisions.

Second, although Figure 3.3 implies that all the perspectives should operate simultaneously when the tool is chosen, for various instructional reasons it may be desirable to consider them selectively. Sometimes watching online videos can provide learners with valuable information even though they are relatively passive. An analysis of the tool by itself will fail the active/passive test and rate low from the social/interpersonal perspective. But considering the model in the larger context of a course could lead to enhancements in students' learning. For example, students could watch a video passively, then engage in an asynchronous forum with other students to respond to teacher-generated prompts, or subsequently work in small groups to discuss specific aspects of the video after writing informally about their reactions. The tool must therefore be seen in the full context of *activity*.

Application: Three Cases

An analysis of the potential adoption of several digital tools can help us to determine the heuristic value of the perspectives in Figure 3.3 for writing instruction or support. The first case applies to the domain of classroom interaction using writing; the second to a writing assignment; and the third to a method of facilitating peer response to writing in progress.

The first case is a simple cloud-based app, called Padlet, that facilitates classroom discussion of content. After creating an account, the instructor designs a page using the provided templates. When the blank page is finished, the instructor gives a URL to students so that they can access the page on their devices. Each student can double-click on the page, which opens a text box. As they write in these boxes, their brief comments populate the page (which can also be projected in the classroom). Comments can then generate further written responses. After a period of time, the instructor can ask students to reflect on and discuss what everyone has written. Padlet is often used in physical classrooms, but it can also be used during synchronous online sessions. Several similar apps are also readily available, such as Poll Anywhere, Popplet, and iBrainstorm.

Figure 3.4 shows a sample Padlet screen from an undergraduate course in the US for prospective teachers focusing on literacy theory and instruction. Students have read a brief scenario describing an isolated farming community that has been highly successful for generations, passing on its farming techniques to its children, but it has no written literacy. Students have also read opposing articles about the cognitive consequences of literacy and literacy as a socially determined practice. They are asked to reflect on whether literacy would be useful to the farming community. Notice that in some cases, the students have responded to each other's posts.

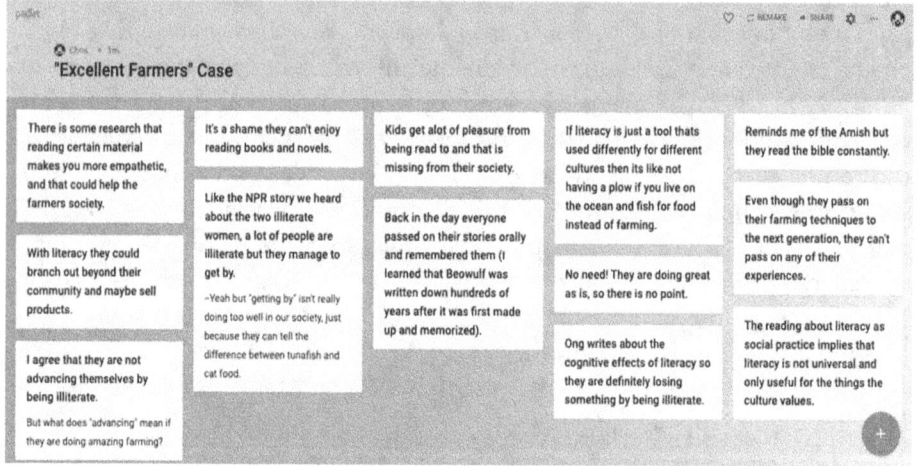

Figure 3.4. Sample Padlet screen from a college course in the US on literacy.

As shown in the analysis in Table 3.1, the informational interface is mostly positive (a simple display of text with colorful background options), limited only because the screen can become crowded, forcing students to scroll up and down to read the posts and making it difficult to project all the posts at once in the classroom. The cognitive potential of the app depends on the nature and quality of the material, and therefore cannot be judged apart from a specific use. In this case, however, it is strongly realized: students must apply their interpretation of the readings to a specific context and consider the implications, at the same time negotiating their reasoning with the reasoning of others. The app offers some rhetorical potential because students frame responses in the context of other responses, creating mini-arguments that can be expanded during discussion or more extensive written reflection. The app facilitates some degree of social interaction by making thinking visible and allowing students to read and compare their responses, and also respond to each other's posts. It places students in a highly active role, and its additional affordances include the possibility for anonymity, which can draw out students who otherwise might not contribute to a discussion. The app is generally fair because it is free and easy to use, gives students time to formulate ideas before posting them (and helps those who need more time to process the others' ideas and formulate their own), and provides instructional controls such as filters on profanity. However, it can also disadvantage the visually impaired, depending on whether proximity is a concern (students can see the Padlet on their own devices; if a blind student has a text-to-speech system, the posts can be read).

Table 3.1. Analysis of the Potential Adoption of Padlet

Perspective	Much	Some	Little/No	Depends
Informational Interface		✓		
Cognitive				✓
Rhetorical		✓		
Ethical		✓		
Social/Interpersonal		✓		
Active	✓			
Additional Affordances	✓*			

Potential for anonymity; visible thought; increased participation

The second case is an educational tool, Fakebook (https://www.classtools.net/FB/home-page), that can be used to create assignments with the goal of researching and writing about a historical figure or literary character, or practicing other languages through multilingual exchanges. Fakebook closely mirrors Facebook in its design and basic functionalities. As students research their chosen figure, they create a profile based on historical information, or background material if the person is a character in a literary text. They then add "friends" who interact with the figure, and populate the site with video clips, photos, and other material.

Figure 3.5 shows the first page of a Fakebook project on James Baldwin. At the top of the screen are photos of Baldwin and to the left is a bullet list of biographical details and a list (with photos) of "friends" that include singer-songwriter Nina Simone, Malcolm X, and Richard Wright. The most recent post by Baldwin is a statement about injustice, dated August 28, 1963, to which Martin Luther King, Jr., responds in agreement. Earlier "posts" contain images of Baldwin's books, a link to a song by Bessie Smith, and interactions with a number of people in a mix of formal, vernacular, and social-media-style writing, as well as "likes" by many others.

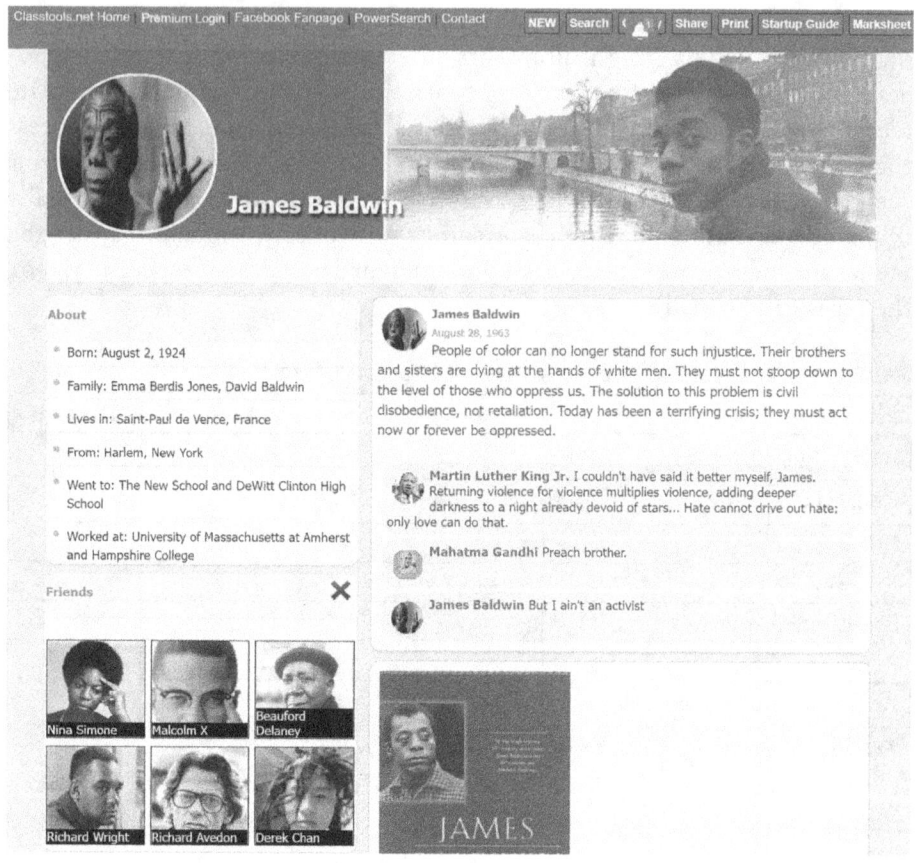

Figure 3.5. Screenshot of a Fakebook profile.

As shown in Table 3.2, this tool realizes multiple cognitive and rhetorical goals related to writing and information literacy. Students must find information and judge its accuracy, then translate it rhetorically to conform to the usual style and other features of Facebook discourse. They must create realistic written interactions with interlocutors (who take the role of "friends"), framing their remarks in ways that tap into and enhance their understanding of written interaction. The social and interpersonal perspective is realized through those invented interactions, but even more so if students visit each other's sites and share their responses. Students are highly active in their productions, the site is easy to use, free, and multimodal, and the emulation of social media motivates and engages students. The informational interface is attractive because of its familiarity, but also suffers from the inclusion of ads that intrude on and in some cases interrupt the other material. Like Padlet, visually impaired students may have difficulty obtaining all the information in a Fakebook page even with a text-to-speech program unless every image is described according to universal design principles. If audio clips are included, some deaf or hard-of-hearing students may also be disadvantaged. Students with limited computer skills may need additional coaching, although the basic functions are relatively intuitive.

Table 3.2. Analysis of the Potential Adoption of Fakebook

Perspective	Much	Some	Little/No	Depends
Informational Interface		✓		
Cognitive	✓			
Rhetorical	✓			
Ethical		✓		
Social/Interpersonal	✓			
Active	✓			
Additional Affordances	✓*			

Dynamic character roles; emulation of social media

The third example focuses on a widely available tool, screencasting, that can be used to facilitate student peer review. The goal for this use of the tool is to help students provide response to their peers' drafts to encourage revision, but also to facilitate the responder's own learning as they identify rhetorical, linguistic, and content-related issues. The screencasting program allows the peer reviewer to create a video as they work through and discuss their peer's draft, which the writer can then play (and re-play) as they continue to revise and shape their draft. Of course, one-way peer responses are generally not as effective as face-to-face group discussions of drafts, which allow for a conversation and real-time negotiation of ideas for revision instead of a monologue. But screencasting can still be a useful tool for peer review, especially in online courses, or in situations when it is problematic to devote entire class sessions to revision workshops (as in content-focused courses in the disciplines), or during pandemics or other emergencies when campuses must close. The screencast program considered here is Jing (produced by TechSmith), which provides a maximum of five minutes of audio-visual response. The student reads and optionally annotates a draft, activates the program, and then talks through it, scrolling and highlighting words, sentences, or broader textual units. The video is then saved and uploaded so the writer can play it.

Figure 3.6 shows one moment of a screencast peer review. The writer has begun her paper too generally, "writing her way in," as is the practice of many novice writers, with some statements that readers already know. Notice that the peer reviewer has utilized the more conventional tool in Word that enables marginal annotations to be inserted at various points in the paper. Now, as the student scrolls through the paper, she is able to discuss and elaborate on those responses orally, which serve as placeholders for elements of the paper that struck her as she read through it the first time. In addition, the running commentary can be useful for discussing the use of graphics or other visuals, as well as broader structural matters that are difficult to write about with comments inserted only at specific locations. At this point in the video, the peer reviewer is calling attention to the overly general introduction, moving her cursor around to show the area of the paper she is referring to.

> So here, I wrote that it feels like you're starting out really general, I mean, "computer use is increasing," and like we're affected by technology and stuff. I don't think you need to say this because your readers, like, already know it and want to know what you're going to talk about specifically. I really like the wiki Hawai'i thing so maybe you could start with that for your introduction and then say more about the wiki before saying what the paper will do.

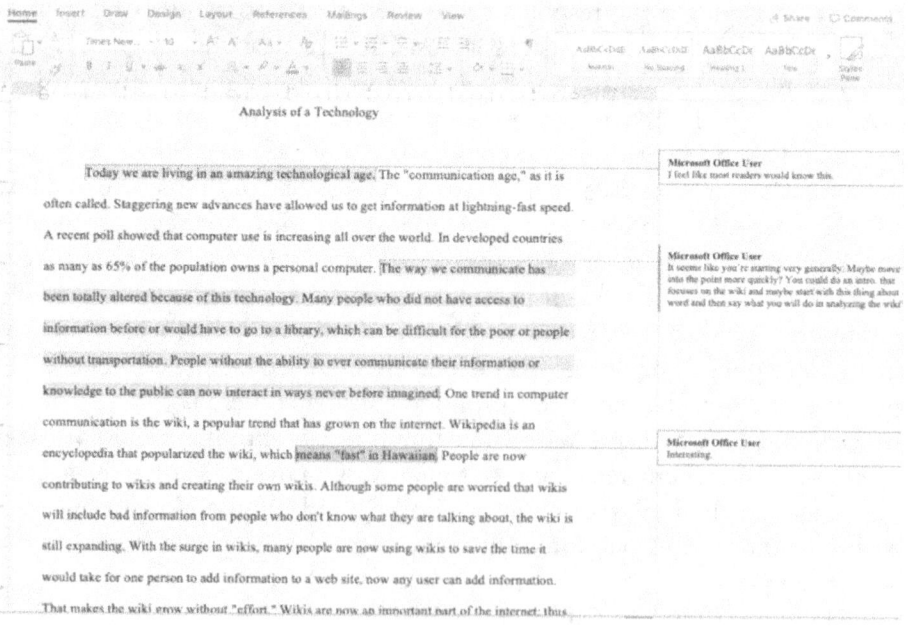

Figure 3.6. One moment of a Screencast peer review video.

As shown in Table 3.3, creating a screencast places the student in a highly active role. The app facilitates the processes of discursive evaluation and critique and is highly interpersonal, enabling the practice of diplomatic and helpful response provided vocally. Fairness may depend on the security of the screencast program; how challenging it is to record, save, and upload the file; and how students process oral vs. written information. Additional affordances are mixed: face to face interaction is preferable for negotiation, but the screencasts can also be replayed multiple times.

Table 3.3. Analysis of the Potential Adoption of Screencasting for Peer Review

Perspective	Much	Some	Little/No	Depends
Informational Interface	✓			
Cognitive	✓			
Rhetorical	✓			
Ethical				✓
Social/Interpersonal	✓			
Active	✓			
Additional Affordances		✓*		

Can be replayed; supports more extensive response

Applying the perspectives in Figure 3.3 to these three technologies shows that each can realize multiple goals related to support for students' writing development. In each case, the tool's affordances enhance an assignment or activity that would ordinarily use conventional teaching tools and methods. In the case of Padlet, the non-digital alternative is a classroom discussion, but without additional intervention, some students can remain passive, there may be no opportunity for the display of students' thoughts, it is challenging to remember all the points raised or to respond to them outside the flow of conversation, some students may be reluctant to speak, and they get no practice articulating their ideas in writing. In the case of Fakebook, the non-digital alternative is a print version of a biographical research paper; but without carefully scripted allowances for genre manipulation, the paper loses its social-media style (and the associated motivation) and creates difficulties to show the figure's historical or imagined interaction with others. In the case of screencasting, the non-digital asynchronous alternative is monologic written responses swapped in class or exchanged online, but these clearly lack the social dynamism of vocal commentary and the much more specific references to parts of the text and live explanations thereof. Research has also shown that in five minutes, screencast response usually provides seven to eight times more text (when transcribed) than conventional written response (Anson et al., 2016); however, as noted, a 15-minute face-to-face conversation in a standard in-class peer review session would far exceed the volume of response compared with a 5-minute screencast.

Enhancing the Selection Model

Ideally, the selection heuristic in Figure 3.3 needs to be placed in the context of the goal-based model developed by Hutchison and Woodward. With some small modifications to the model, the test of relevant dimensions is placed after the articulation of instructional goals and approach as part of the process of digital tool selection. If the tool fails one or more of the desired perspectives, there may be possibilities for its adaptation (cf. Figure 3.7). An apt example is the use of Turnitin, which has been heavily critiqued as a gatekeeping plagiarism-detection tool. However, Turnitin might be used formatively to good effect: students submit a draft of a writing project to the system, receive an analysis, and then study their draft against the results. If the system produces a false positive, the student can explore the reasons for the flag and then justify the use of correctly cited material (or some common phrases or boilerplate that do not require attribution) while they continue to work on their use of sources. Parallel reflections on their processes can provide instructors with useful information about students' learning. Note, however, that if a teacher considers Turnitin's archiving and ownership of student drafts to be unethical, then the tool could be rejected out of hand without the possibility of adaptation.

The enhanced model has the advantage of a strong focus on teacher reflection, goal-setting, planning, implementing, and assessing, but adds significant tests, based on scholarship on writing, learning, and literacy development, of the valuable developmental and performance-based perspectives in Figure 3.3. Two further points, however, are important in the context of how this model can be used effectively.

The Need for Faculty Development and Research

The enhanced model in Figure 3.7 can be used by individual instructors or administrators as they select digital tools for student learning. For example, instructors could use the model to think through the use of a specific tool in their instruction, or to develop a proposal for the adoption of a particular tool (especially one that may require funding). However, ideally the model should be used collaboratively. For example, in a centralized writing program such as those administered under the banner of "first-year composition" at U.S. universities, or several offerings of a single writing-focused course common in many other countries, a group of teachers and/or program directors could work through the model when deciding whether to adopt a particular digital tool. Applied heuristically, the model generates the kind of thoughtful discussion and negotiation that can provide a strong rationale for accepting or rejecting particular tools or finding ways to supplement or adapt them so that they become educationally useful and enhance instruction. The model can also be used in instructional development programs or in graduate courses to give teachers and students practice in the thoughtful integration of digital tools into instruction.

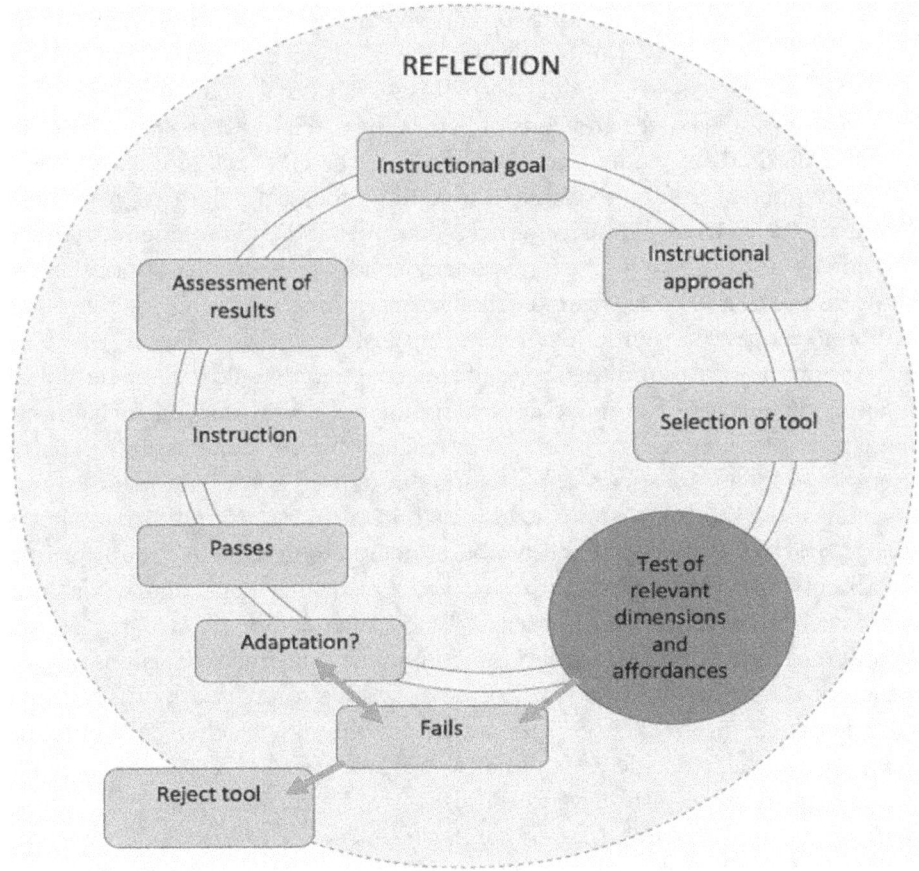

Figure 3.7. Enhanced goal-based selection model.

Finally, the generally positive results of the three case examples are based on projected uses of the tools in typical writing-enhanced classrooms, as seen through the lenses of the perspectives in Figure 3.3. Importantly, the enhanced model ends with implementation and assessment, which takes us into the realm of reflective practice (Schön, 1983) or, on a larger scale, program assessment. Reflective practitioners constantly measure the results of instructional interventions and practices against their learning goals, which makes them researchers of their own classrooms. Program directors constantly assess the effects of an intervention on the quality of instructional delivery and student success. In this way, a digital tool adopted because it meets the criteria of the perspectives in Figure 3.3 might present unanticipated problems or complexities in actual use, which leads to further modifications of the tool or even its eventual rejection. For example, when I first used screencasting to respond to students' writing projects, I administered student surveys across several courses over a period of two years to gauge their effectiveness and tap into students' opinions. The highly positive results eventually led me (alone and with colleagues) to conduct formal research on screencast response in first-year writing courses and courses across the disciplines, and then eventually as a method for student peer review (see Anson, 2021). However, a very small number of students shared difficulties processing the oral responses (compared with more extensive written marginal and end comments), which provided evidence that not every student is advantaged by the tool. I now show 30 seconds of a fabricated screencast response and offer students the option to request conventional written response.

Although it is beyond the scope of this chapter, it would also be desirable to apply the heuristic to more complex digital tools, such as an entire learning management system (LMS). A team of teachers and/or directors in a department or academic program could work through all the functionalities and affordances of the LMS and consider each in turn. For example, many popular LMSs like Blackboard and Moodle include tools such as group forums for discussion, chats, screencasting or voice recording apps, and wikis, and can have links to (or include) associated tools such as Google Groups, Zoom, Wordpress, and Turnitin. Programs can make informed decisions about which of these should or should not be accessible to or used by instructors. Instructors themselves, either individually or through teacher-development programs, can also decide which ones to use and for what reasons.

The perspectives also drive questions for more formal inquiry, including classroom-based research (Taber, 2013), action research (Mertler, 2020), and full-scale formal studies using a range of methods. What actually happens when students use the tool? How do they feel about it? Is there evidence of learning? How effectively does the tool work in L2 contexts? Anwar et al. (2019), for example, found that students in a functional linguistics course were generally positive about the use of Padlet and felt that it enhanced their learning. But Chuah (2015) found more mixed impressions: students counterbalanced their generally positive feelings about Padlet with concerns about the delay of feedback as others reflected on their comments. Similarly, based on studies of screencasting for teacher commentary (Anson, 2018; Anson et al., 2016), Walker (2017) found "compelling evidence" for screencast-mediated peer review. However, Anson (2021) found that the nature and quality of student peer review using screencast technology varies as a function of instructional ideology and the genre of the writing task.

As further research explores the complexities of digital tool adoption across multiple contexts and populations, the perspectives in the expanded model can become more fully informed, helping teachers to make critical decisions about what to bring into their instruction and how best to utilize it.

References

Anderson, M. & Perrin, A. (2018). Nearly one-in-five teens can't always finish their homework because of the digital divide. PEW Research Center. https://www.pewresearch.org/fact-tank/2018/10/26/nearly-one-in-five-teens-cant-always-finish-their-homework-because-of-the-digital-divide/.

Andrews, K. (2019). *Technologies, pedagogies, and cologies: An analysis of first-year composition faculty's attitudes toward technology and their technological uptake in the writing classroom* [Unpublished doctoral dissertation]. North Carolina State University, Raleigh, North Carolina.

Anson, C. M. (2017). Writing to read, revisited. In A. S. Horning, D. Gollnitz & C. H. Haller (Eds.), *What is college reading?* (pp. 21–39). The WAC Clearinghouse; University Press of Colorado. https://doi.org/10.37514/atd-b.2017.0001.2.01.

Anson, C. M. (2018). "She really took the time": Students' opinions of screen-capture response to their writing in online courses. In C. Weaver & P. Jackson (Eds.), *Writing in online courses: How the online environment shapes writing practices* (pp. 21–45). Myers Education Press.

Anson, C. M. (2021). Correctness revisited: How students (mis)identify and comment on error in peers' drafts. In B. Morrison, J. Chen, L. Lin & A. Urmston (Eds.), *English across the curriculum: Voices from around the world* (pp. 271–291). The WAC Clearinghouse; University Press of Colorado. https://doi.org/10.37514/INT-B.2021.1220.2.15.

Anson, C. M., Dannels, D., Laboy, J. & Carneiro, L. (2016). Students' perceptions of oral screencast responses to their writing: Exploring digitally mediated identities. *Journal of Business and Technical Communication, 30*(3), 1–34. https://doi.org/10.1177/1050651916636424.

Anwar, C., Nugroho, K. Y. & Nurhamidah, I. (2019). Students' perceptions at the use of Padlet in a linguistics class. *Notion: Journal of Linguistics, Literature, and Culture, 1*(1), 35–41. https://doi.org/10.12928/notion.viii.714.

Applebee, A. A. (1984). Writing and reasoning. *Review of Educational Research, 54*(4), 577–596.

Baron, D. E. (1999). From pencils to pixels: The stages of literacy technologies. In G. E. Hawisher & C. L. Selfe (Eds.), *Passions, pedagogies and 21st century technologies* (pp. 15–33). Utah State University Press. https://doi.org/10.2307/j.ctt46nrfk.4.

Bawarshi, A. S. & Reiff, M. J. (2010). *Genre: An introduction to history, theory, research, and pedagogy*. Parlor Press; The WAC Clearinghouse. https://wac.colostate.edu/books/referenceguides/bazerman-wac/.

Bazerman, C. (2004). Intertextuality: How texts rely on other texts. In C. Bazerman & P. Prior (Eds.), *What writing does and how it does it: An introduction to analyzing texts and textual practices* (pp. 83–96). Erlbaum.

Bazerman, C. (2017). The psychology of writing situated within social action: An empirical and theoretical program. In P. Portanova, M. Rifenburg & D. Roen (Eds.), *Contemporary perspectives on cognition* (pp. 21–37). The WAC Clearinghouse; University Press of Colorado. https://doi.org/10.37514/per-b.2017.0032.2.01.

Bean, J. (2011). *Engaging ideas: The professor's guide to integrating writing, critical thinking, and active learning in the classroom* (2nd ed.). Jossey-Bass.

Biggs, J. B. & Tang, C. (2007). *Teaching for quality learning at university*. Open University Press; Mc Graw-Hill Education.

Borrowman, S. (Ed). (2012). *On the blunt edge: Technology in composition's history and pedagogy*. Parlor Press.

Burgstahler, S. (2008). Universal design in higher education. In S. Burgstahler & R. Cory (Eds.), *Universal design in higher education: From principles to practice* (pp. 3–20). Harvard Education Press.

Chen, W. & Wellman, B. (2004). The global digital divide: Within and between countries. *IT & Society, 1*(7), 18–25.

Chuah, K. M. (2015). iTeaching for uLearning: Interactive teaching tools for ubiquitous learning in higher education. In M. A. Embi (Ed.), *e-Learning & interactive lecture: SoTL case studies in Malaysian HEIs* (pp. 89–97). AKEPT.

Clinton, V. (2019). Reading from paper compared to screens: A systematic review and meta-analysis. *Journal of Research in Reading, 42*(2), 288–325. https://doi.org/10.1111/1467-9817.12269.

Condon, W. & Kelly-Riley, D. (2004). Assessing and teaching what we value: The relationship between college-level writing and critical thinking abilities. *Assessing Writing, 9*(1), 56–75.

Croft, M. & Moore, R. (2019). Rural students: Technology, coursework, and extracurricular activities. ACT Center for Equity in Learning. https://equityinlearning.act.org/wp-content/themes/voltron/img/tech-briefs/rural-students.pdf.

Cuban, L., Kirkpatrick, H. & Peck, C. (2001). High access and low use of technologies in high school classrooms: Explaining an apparent paradox. *American Educational Research Journal, 38*(4), 813–834. https://doi.org/10.3102/00028312038004813.

Delagrange, S. H. (2011). *Technologies of wonder: Rhetorical practice in a digital world*. Utah State University Press.

Flower, L. (1979). Writer-based prose: A cognitive basis for problems in writing. *College English, 41*(1), 19–37.

Gee, J. P. (2005). Semiotic social spaces and affinity spaces: From the age of mythology to today's schools. In D. Barton & K. Tusting (Eds.), *Beyond communities of practice: Language, power and social context* (pp. 214–232). Cambridge University Press. https://doi.org/10.1017/cbo9780511610554.012.

Gee, J. P. (2007). *What video games have to teach us about learning and literacy* (2nd ed.). Palgrave/Macmillan.

Gee, J. P. (2018). Affinity spaces: How young people live and learn online and out of school. *Phi Delta Kappan 99*(6), 8–13. https://doi.org/10.1177/0031721718762416.

Goffman, E. (1955). On face-work: An analysis of ritual elements in social interaction. *Psychiatry: Journal of Interpersonal Relations, 18*(3), 213–231.

Harris, J. & Hofer, M. J. (2009). Grounded tech integration. *Learning and Leading with Technology, 37*(2), 22–25.

Hewett, B. L. & DePew, K. E. (Eds.). (2015). *Foundational practices of online writing instruction*. The WAC Clearinghouse; Parlor Press. https://doi.org/10.37514/PER-B.2015.0650.

Hughes, J. (2004). Technology learning principles for preservice and in-service teacher education. *Contemporary Issues in Technology and Teacher Education, 4*(3), 345–362. https://www.learntechlib.org/primary/p/19950/.

Hutchison, A. & Woodward, L. (2014). A planning cycle for integrating digital technology into literacy instruction. *The Reading Teacher, 67*(6), 455–464. https://doi.org/10.1002/trtr.1225.

Kerssen-Griep, J., Trees, A. R. & Hess, J. A. (2008). Attentive facework during instructional feedback: Key to perceiving mentorship and an optimal learning environment. *Communication Education, 57*, 394–414. https://doi.org/10.1080/03634520802027347.

Kluger, A. N. & DeNisi, A. S. (1996). The effects of feedback interventions on performance: A historical review, a meta-analysis, and a preliminary feedback intervention theory. *Psychological Bulletin, 119*(2), 254–284.

Kress, G., Jewitt, C., Ogborn, J. & Charalampos, T. (2001). *Multimodal teaching and learning: The rhetorics of the science classroom*. Bloomsbury. https://doi.org/10.5040/9781472593764.

Kroll, B. M. (1978). Cognitive egocentrism and the problem of audience awareness in written discourse. *Research in the Teaching of English, 12*, 269–281.

Lim, T. & Bowers, J. W. (1991). Facework: Solidarity, approbation, and tact. *Human Communication Research, 17*, 415–450. https://doi.org/10.1111/j.1468-2958.1991.tb00239.x.

McKorkle, B. (2012). *Rhetorical delivery as technological discourse: A cross-historical study*. Southern Illinois University Press.

Melzer, D. (2014). *Assignments across the curriculum: A national study of college writing*. Computers and Composition Digital Press. https://doi.org/10.7330/9780874219401.

Mertler, C. A. (2020). *Action research: Improving schools and empowering educators* (6th ed.). Sage. https://doi.org/10.4135/9781483396484.

Miller, M. D. (2019, Oct. 13). Before adopting classroom technology, figure out your goals. Chronicle of Higher Education. https://www.chronicle.com/article/Before-Adopting-Classroom/247309.

Mishra, P. & Koehler, M. J. (2006). Technological pedagogical content knowledge: A new framework for teacher knowledge. *Teachers College Record, 108*(6), 1017–1054.

Morris, A. M. & Stommel, J. (2017, 15 June). A guide for resisting edtech: The case against Turnitin. Hybrid Pedagogy. https://hybridpedagogy.org/resisting-edtech/.

National Council of Teachers of English. (2018). Beliefs for integrating technology into the English language arts classroom. https://ncte.org/statement/beliefs-technology-preparation-english-teachers/.

Novak, M. (2012, April). *Before the Jetsons, Arthur Radebaugh illustrated the future.* Smithsonian Magazine. https://www.smithsonianmag.com/science-nature/before-the-jetsons-arthur-radebaugh-illustrated-the-future-122729342/.

Pearlman, S. J. & Carillo, D. (2018). *The critical thinking initiative handbook: The Essential guide for critical thinking, reading and writing in any discipline.* Primedia.

Portanova, P., Rifenburg, J. M. & Roen, D. (2017). Introduction. In P. Portanova, J. M. Rifenburg & D. Roen (Eds.), *Contemporary perspectives on cognition* (pp. 3–17). The WAC Clearinghouse; University Press of Colorado. https://doi.org/10.37514/per-b.2017.0032.

Ramo, S. (1957). A new technique of education. *Engineering and Science, 21,* 17–22.

Rice, J. (2012). *Digital Detroit: Rhetoric and space in the age of the network.* Southern Illinois University Press.

Rose, D. H., Harbour, W. S., Johnston, C., Daley, S. G. & Abarbanell, L. (2006). Universal design for learning in postsecondary education: Reflections on principles and their application. *Journal of Postsecondary Education and Disability, 19*(2), 135–151.

Rose, D. H. & Meyer, A. (2002). *Teaching every student in the digital age: Universal design for learning.* Association for Supervision and Curriculum Development.

Russell, D. (1995). Activity theory and its implications for writing instruction. In J. Petraglia (Ed.), *Reconceiving writing, rethinking writing instruction* (pp. 51–78). Erlbaum.

Schön, D. (1983). *The reflective practitioner: How professionals think in action.* Basic Books.

Schorn, S. (2015, March). Replicated text detection: Test of TurnItIn. Unpublished report, University of Texas at Austin. https://www.insidehighered.com/sites/default/server_files/files/2015plagtest.pdf.

Selfe, C. L. & Selfe, R. J. (1994). The politics of the interface: Power and its exercise in electronic contact zones. *College Composition and Communication, 45*(4), 480–504.

Selzer, J. (2004). Rhetorical analysis: Understanding how texts persuade readers. In C. Bazerman & P. Prior (Eds.), *What writing does and how it does it: An introduction to analyzing texts and textual practices* (pp. 279–308). Erlbaum.

Slykhuis, D. A., Wiebe, E. N. & Annetta, L. A. (2005). Eye-tracking students' attention to PowerPoint photographs in a science education setting. *Journal of Science*

Education and Technology, 14(5–6), 509–520. https://doi.org/10.1007/s10956-005-0225-z.

Street, B. (2013). *Social literacies: Critical approaches to literacy in development, ethnography, and education.* Routledge.

Taber, K. S. (2013). *Classroom-based research and evidence-based practice* (2nd ed.). Sage.

Torrance, M. & Galbraith, D. (2006). The processing demands of writing. In C. MacArthur, S. Graham & J. Fitzgerald (Eds.), *Handbook of writing research* (pp. 67–80). Guilford.

Vossoughi, S. & Gutiérrez, K. D. (2016). Critical pedagogy and sociocultural theory. In I. Esmonde & A. N. Booker (Eds.), *Power and privilege in the learning sciences* (pp. 139–161). Routledge.

Walker, A. S. (2017). I hear what you're saying: The power of screencasts in peer-to-peer review. *Journal of Writing Analytics, 1,* 356–391. https://doi.org/10.37514/jwa-j.2017.1.1.13.

Wolfe, J. (2010). *Team writing: A guide to working in groups.* Bedford/St. Martin's.

Wyatt, C. S. (2017). Accessible writing spaces: A framework for inclusive design of virtual composition classrooms. In J. P. Purdy & D. N. DeVoss (Eds.), *Making space: Writing instruction, infrastructure, and multiliteracies.* University of Michigan Press. https://quod.lib.umich.edu/d/drc/mpub7820727/1:7/—making-space-writing-instruction-infrastructure?g=dculture;rgn=div1;view=fulltext;xc=1.

Young, V. A. (2011). Should writers use they own English? In L. Greenfield & K. Rowan (Eds.), *Writing centers and the new racism: A call for sustainable dialogue and change* (pp. 61–72). Utah State University Press. https://doi.org/10.2307/j.ctt4cgk6s.7.

Zylka, J., Gniewosz, G., Kroehne, U., Hartig, J. & Goldhammer, F. (2015). Moving beyond cognitive elements of ICT literacy: First evidence on the structure of ICT engagement. *Computers in Human Behavior, 53,* 149–160. https://doi.org/10.1016/j.chb.2015.07.008.

4. Research Writing, What Do We Know and How to Move Forward

Montserrat Castelló
Universitat Ramon Llull. Barcelona

The chapter starts by framing research writing as a dialogic, collaborative and hybrid activity and discussing the main implications of this conceptualization. Then, based on three representative cases built from evidence from our previous studies, I discuss what we have learned in the last fifteen years regarding the common challenges students—and researchers—confront when dealing with research writing predominantly in social sciences and humanities contexts. Finally, after highlighting what I consider the main remaining research challenges of the field, I explain our recent attempts and related findings to address them, and reflect on pedagogical implications to promote students' and early-career researchers' writing development. Specifically, I discuss two intertwined aspects scarcely addressed by research in the field: a) the need for strategic regulation in authentic and demanding research writing scenarios, which, in turn, requires a new conceptualization of the regulation notion in those situations, and b) the need to understand texts as artifacts-in-activity, not just products resulting from a more or less prescribed writing process. The chapter closes with considerations regarding what I think might constitute a useful and comprehensive agenda to advance our knowledge of the research writing field.

> To steal ideas from a researcher is plagiarism; to steal from many is research.
>
> —*Author unknown?*

I have been using the quip that opens this chapter for so many years that I forgot where I first read or heard it. In some way, it has become part of my discourse, though I learned that the expression has a long history and, with small variations, can be attributed to at least nine authors over the last century. The first was Reverend Charles Caleb Colton in 1820.[1]

---

[1] https://quoteinvestigator.com/2010/09/20/plagiarism/.

The statement is shocking because it emphasizes the thin line between reading and writing. It also points to the type and variety of connections between these two activities, which Bakhtin defined as the dialogue of voices that takes place between the texts that we have read and those that we can produce and thus write (Bakhtin, 1981; Bazerman, 2004). Ultimately, the expression reminds us of the extent to which research writing is a collaborative and dialogic activity[2] (Prior & Thorne, 2014; Russell, 2009).

Despite what the initial quote might suggest, this chapter is not about plagiarism but about dialogue and voices. I conceive research writing as a particular type of conversation in which the writer must acknowledge other voices and stances but must also be able to differentiate his/her voice from others to develop a researcher identity and an authorial self.

In the next sections, I frame research writing as a collaborative, dialogic and hybrid activity and discuss how research-related genres can be characterized accordingly. Then, based on three representative cases built from evidence from our previous studies, I discuss what we have learned in the last fifteen years regarding the common challenges students—and researchers—confront when dealing with research writing. This discussion relies predominantly on social sciences and humanities higher education contexts, not only because these are where my background and the studies I developed come from, but also due to their prevalence in the writing research field. Moreover, most of my research has focused on master and doctoral students as well as on early career researchers, except for some studies conducted with undergraduate students writing their bachelor theses and dissertations.

Finally, after highlighting what I consider the main current research challenges of the field, I explain our recent attempts to address them and related findings and reflect on pedagogical implications to promote students' and early-career researchers' writing development. The chapter closes with considerations regarding what I think might constitute a useful and comprehensive agenda to advance our knowledge of the research writing field.

Characterization of Research Writing: What Are We Talking About?

Borges (1899–1986), who, in addition to being a writer, worked as a librarian in Buenos Aires, defined his work in an interesting way when he affirmed,

---

2   Ideas, comments and arguments in this chapter are grounded in the collaborative research we developed as a team (www.researcher-identity.com); thus, my contribution is also dialogic and includes several voices.

"[O]rdering libraries is exercising, modestly and silently, the art of criticism" (Borges, 1969). I would add that *writing research genres is also exercising, less modestly and silently, the art of criticism*. Criticism required for writers to decide which, how and why previous research should be included in their own work, as well as their alignments, omissions and rhetorical decisions. While it is true that there are different ways to promote "the art of criticism" Borges talked about, the contribution of reading and writing research to this aim cannot be neglected. Understood in this way research writing, involves transversal, interdisciplinary and critical competencies, such as critical thinking or reflective problem-solving, which contribute to transforming information into knowledge, one of highest challenges for societies in the twenty-first century (Paré, 2019; Prior & Bilbro, 2012).

As mentioned, I conceive dialogue as inherent and essential to research writing. This dialogical nature is twofold. First, it involves writing to answer other researchers and studies and expecting to be answered at the same time by other members of the research communities (Bakthin, 1981; Castelló & Iñesta, 2012; Camps & Castelló, 2013). Second, the dialogic nature also involves texts resulting from more or less explicit dialogic situations in which multiple voices intertwine. These situations range from those in which multiple authors explicitly own the text to those in which others' voices participate at different levels and play several roles in single-authored texts and writing processes (e.g., supervisors, research colleagues, reviewers, editors). Understood in that way, dialogue implies conceiving research writing as collaborative even when one single author is credited. Over last century, collaborative research and co-authorship have been progressively growing in all disciplines, though at different pace and available evidence points out that they relate to increased productivity, at the individual, field, and country level, as well as to researchers' satisfaction, learning and commitment (Fanelli & Larivière, 2016; Parish et al., 2018). Moreover, writing (and researching) collaboratively are among those competencies that our students will need in their professional lives. However, our knowledge of what underlies collaborative writing research in different disciplines has not progressed at the same pace. It is urgent for research in the field to discuss what underlies the socially constructed fuzzy notion of authorship in different professional research contexts and to what extent existing practices are ethical and sustainable for students and young researchers (Lokhtina et al., 2020).

The dialogic and collaborative consideration of research writing runs parallel to its hybrid nature. Producing research texts requires a broad range of abilities (e.g., reading, writing, synthesizing, discussing) and discourses (e.g., graphical, numerical, operational). Managing these abilities and discourses is at the core of research writing since all of them are responsible for text quality though they have not always been considered part of the research writing process or research writing interventions. The need to master a broad range of abilities and a variety of discourses and modalities is particularly relevant for students at the bachelor, master, or doctorate stages who are facing complex texts (theses, dissertations and scientific articles), as well as for early career researchers dealing with grant applications, research reports, and other alternative modalities of research dissemination (e.g., blogs, websites or digital presentations). Moreover, the hybrid nature of writing research-related genres refers to the need to produce different types of intermediate or transitional texts, not only drafts. Transitional texts are necessary, for instance, when transforming raw data from analysis into descriptive comments, tables, or graphics. Each genre requires specific transitional texts that range from elaborative and explorative writing (to develop, transform, and elaborate ideas) to communicative writing, and researchers cannot avoid them when writing articles, reports, or grant applications since the final text quality is highly dependent on mastering them. However, transitional texts are rarely taught, and so, they remain occluded and unknown for students, even at the master's or doctoral level.

I also adhere to the consideration of writing as a socially, historically and culturally situated activity (Castelló & Donahue, 2012; Prior, 2006; Prior & Thorne, 2014), which implies that research writing practices and genres evolve as disciplinary communities develop and as purposes and ways to communicate and disseminate research diversify. The growth and dynamism of research-related genres over the last decades, and subsequent difficulty of defining and mapping them, are intrinsically linked to this diversification (Castelló, 2015; Chitez et al., 2015; Hyland & Guinda, 2012; Kruse et al., 2016; Nesi & Gardner, 2018). Despite considerable disciplinary and cultural variability—as well as other genres' relevance for research purposes (e.g., reports or essays)—theses, dissertations or manuscript monograph, research projects and articles are still considered core genres to communicate research plans or results (Hyland & Guinda, 2012; Nesi & Gardner, 2018; Sala-Bubaré & Castelló, 2018; Swales, 2004; Yakhontova, 2002). However, the alignment of these genres with societal challenges and shifts in research is an emerging issue under discussion (e.g., Paré, 2019). Traditional research genres have been claimed no longer to be representative enough of the wide range of scientific and scholarly writing required in contemporary disciplinary, trans- and cross-disciplinary contexts to address different audiences and purposes. Thus, in recent years, an increasing number of multimodal texts, such as blogs, sites, and platforms, have appeared. In a growing number of cases, it is difficult to deny that they serve research purposes though they are not always considered as such even if they are, specifically in academic contexts (e.g., https://thesiswhisperer.com/about/; https://doctoralwriting.wordpress.com/; https://researchers-like-me.com/). Any agenda for future research should include critical reflection on how emergent research genres account for new research and communicative practices researchers inside and outside the academy need to confront.

Diversification of research-related genres adds a layer of difficulty to the complex issue of their acquisition. Available results from different countries (Bekar et al., 2015; Castelló 2015) indicate that students do not confront the most challenging research genres, such as theses and dissertations, until the end of their studies, and show conflicting and unclear ideas regarding their characteristics and functions. In these conditions, it is complicated for students to be able to make sense of these genres.

To help students to unpack the meaning and purposes of these genres, it is necessary to acknowledge their particular constraints when required in formal academic programs. Texts and practices involved in these academic situations are specific and significantly different from those produced by established researchers within scientific and professional communities (Harwood & Petrić, 2016; Russel & Cortes, 2012) and thus, we proposed to consider them as *academic research writing* genres (Castelló & Iñesta, 2012). What characterizes these genres is they are halfway between academic texts, produced exclusively as part of the university curricula and to be read mainly by professors in the teaching and learning community, and disciplinary texts, written to be published and, thus, usually read by the corresponding research and professional community. This halfway situation is complicated for writers, and probably for readers too. As research indicates, students tend to experience contradictions between their previous practices—usually restricted to academic texts—and new and more complex research writing demands, especially in regard to thesis writing and Ph.D. or master's publications (Castelló et al., 2013). Evidence from our studies, like that from different disciplinary and cultural contexts (Lei & Hu, 2019), suggests that contradictions not only relate to the insufficient knowledge of genres characteristics and demands, but also to the need for writers to maintain a dual positioning—as researcher and student—which ultimately call for identity development. We assume this development is crucial for mastering research writing.

Students' and Researchers' Challenges When Writing Research Genres: Lessons from Research

Research on writing research genres has been prolific and extensive in the last ten years, and there is consensus regarding what are the most prevalent challenges writers—mainly students but also experienced researchers—confront (Berkenkotter & Murray, 1983; Gallego et al., 2016; Lei & Hu, 2019). Over the last few years, answers to explain these challenges have consolidated strategies and proposals to help students cope with them effectively. A close look at available research explanations and pedagogical proposals show that most of them are complementary rather than exclusive, with some basic shared premises. In the next sections, I summarize these research agreements, explanations, and answers by analyzing three prototypical cases built on data from our previous studies with Ph.D. students (Castelló & Iñesta, 2012; Castelló et al., 2013). These cases are illustrative of research in the field, which has predominantly concentrated on Ph.D. students, whereas interest in bachelor's, master's and experienced researchers' writing has been much scarcer. The cases refer to Ph.D. students writing their first article, a requirement in almost all doctoral programs in Spain, independently of whether the thesis involves a series of articles or the traditional monograph format. These Ph.D. students share some other characteristics. First, they were enrolled in diverse Catalan doctoral programs within the social sciences (psychology, education, sport sciences). Second, they participated in a workshop we have been developing for the last ten years called "Writing the First Article."

The workshop, which ran fortnightly, extended over a semester and combined online and face-to-face sessions (for more details, see Castelló & Iñesta, 2012; Castelló et al., 2013). Between face-to-face sessions, students developed different tasks that were uploaded to the seminar platform. During the entire seminar, they uploaded at least three drafts of their articles and three writing diaries that prompted them to recall their objectives, their writing processes and activities and their feelings while they were working. Before the final session, they wrote a narrative of their writing process, and at the end of the seminar, they participated in semi-structured interviews. In those weeks of autonomous work and once the drafts were uploaded to the course platform, students read their peers' texts and prepared to provide feedback on them. After the students gave feedback, the teachers did the same. In the next face-to-face session, they discussed written feedback first in peers and then with the whole group.

Maria's Product-Oriented Approach

Maria was a teacher with five years of experience, and she was close to finishing her thesis in a monograph format. At the same time, she was writing her first article, a requirement for her to defend the thesis. Therefore, she was confronted with simultaneously writing in two different genres on the same topic and using shared data.

When she received feedback on her first draft and realized she should revise it, her reaction was to minimize the revision task and to reduce its complexity. It was as if her writing was just a matter of adapting previous texts and making them shorter while using the same content. She considered it a matter of just "telling the knowledge." According to this interpretation, no critical changes would be necessary, so she planned only local revisions and appeared to be quite confident and relaxed when she stated in her reflective writing diary,

> What I liked the most was to see that the literature review . . . which I had to write for my thesis [monograph] didn't need to be changed much to adapt it to this article. (Writing diary entry 2)

This solution was certainly inappropriate and explained the reviewers' feeling that she had not addressed any of their comments in the second draft. Thus, in the next session, reviewers insisted on the requirement to make global changes, emphasizing the need to revise the content and structure of the article. The style was characterized as inappropriate, similar to a textbook style. At that point, she realized something was wrong and felt insecure and uncertain about the results. She admitted that she should change what she was doing to modify the final text. She nicely expressed the consideration of writing products (that is, texts) as strongly dependent on processes in metaphorical terms:

> Writing this article is like making a cake. There's no way of knowing if it is going to come out all right until it is finished, when someone tastes it and can say, "You need more sugar . . . or . . . less . . ." (In-class interaction, session 3)

This comment could indicate a conceptual move, but the real change did not take place until session four when, after realizing her text still had coherence problems, Maria became aware of the importance of managing the writing process without reducing its complexity. She complained,

> This is very difficult. I need to read more. There are too many things to take into account . . . Need to have a clear idea of the structure before writing" (In-class interaction, session 4)

Although painful, this reflection allowed her to write differently by modifying the writing process and planning at the global level, which in turn led to the introduction of more substantial changes that improved the final draft.

These excerpts illustrate Maria's concerns when writing her article and provide a typical example of difficulties in managing the complexity of *processes involved in writing*. Cognitive and sociocognitive approaches to writing have suggested that complexity lies in the writer's capacity to orchestrate the three subprocesses of planning, formulating, and revising, with planning as key to text quality (Baaijen et al., 2014; van den Bergh et al., 2016).

Moreover, and even more interesting for our purposes, research has revealed that the moment and frequency of occurrence of specific strategies have a differential impact on the final text quality. These results suggest that decisions change dynamically during the writing process (Beauvais et al., 2011; van den Bergh & Rijlaarsdam, 2007). Thus, there is no such thing as the ideal writing process but only strategic decisions that make sense in particular communicative situations (Castelló, 2002).

Research has also extensively shown evidence of a lack of appropriate strategies among many students, including Ph.D. students, to manage the complex orchestration of writing processes when dealing with research genres. Responses have focused on helping students adopt a process approach when writing and equipping them with appropriate strategies to manage cognitive processes, such as planning, revising and textualization. Developing courses and seminars has also proven to be a useful approach. There is evidence that some particular proposals aimed at teaching strategies to manage the writing processes in a very structured way are effective to help students engage in research writing (Castelló et al., 2012). However, our data also show that focusing on cognitive strategies and processes is not sufficient to help students cope with ill-defined and challenging sociocultural writing situations, such as writing an article or a thesis (Castelló et al., 2013). Besides learning specific writing strategies to plan, write and revise, it is necessary for students to learn how to regulate these writing processes in complex and real scenarios (Sala-Bubaré et al., 2021), thus, considering the sociocultural nature of writing regulation (Sala-Bubaré & Castelló, 2018).

What is tricky about this approach is that, unfortunately, we still do not have specific knowledge about the writing processes that researchers implement in real and complex scenarios when faced with writing articles or other complex research genres. The majority of studies on writing processes have been located in primary and secondary schools and focused on simple tasks that tend to be very well controlled but poorly contextualized or situated (Sala-Bubaré & Castelló, 2018). Writing a text in one hour without considering sources is entirely different from writing an article or a thesis monograph, which lasts weeks or even months, always requires reading and using many sources in a variety of ways and is socially, disciplinarily, historically and culturally grounded (Bazerman, 1988).

Xavier: Ten Years Writing Experience

Xavier was a psychologist who wrote and published university textbooks on practice-based cases. He loved writing and had been doing it for ten years. He defined himself as a "good writer."

Like Maria, he was writing his first article during his Ph.D., and in the context of the workshop, he received very demanding comments on his first draft that prompted him to revise it extensively. However, Xavier reacted very differently from Maria. Immediately after reading the feedback, he felt lost and realized he was confronting an unknown writing task. He needed to produce a text very different from those he was used to writing in his professional activity. The following reflections illustrate his thinking:

> I don't know how to decide what is important and how to structure the text. I'm not clear about the focus of the article. It's difficult for me to prioritize information and restructure the previous draft. (Writing diary entry 2)

He made some minor changes, and in the second draft, the reviewer again mentioned the need to reduce information and revise the structure in addition to noticing that the link with the previous literature was not clear. At this point, Xavier explicitly mentioned that he was facing a new modality of writing with particular characteristics. For the first time, he reflected on the aims and audience guiding his decision-making regarding content selection and structure:

> I am used to writing 70 pages, but now this is not the case. I've had to put much effort into reducing and synthesizing to make objectives clearer to readers. There are some concepts that you don't have to explain in an article because readers already know them. (In-class interaction, session 3)

Finally, a significant change was evident in the third draft in which reviewers detected only minor problems. At that point, Xavier showed increased awareness of the discursive mechanisms that characterize research articles when he said,

> Now I can see what I want to say and how to say it more clearly. It's also been very helpful to learn "ways of saying" and typical statements of articles. I think this is a fundamental issue in research. Another topic is citations. Above all, I was surprised at all the "playing" one can do with the references to others' articles. (In-class interaction, session 4)

The kind of difficulties Xavier's case illustrates is strongly related to the knowledge and mastery of genre-related issues. Genre studies have demonstrated that although research genres are highly typified texts, they are also dynamic (Bazerman, 1988; Swales, 2004). Thus, their content and structure evolve depending on communities' history, characteristics and aims. Research practices and the writer's position in those communities also influence genre evolution (Hyland, 2005).

Moreover, we know that research genres accomplish different functions and purposes. First, they have an epistemic function since they contribute to the construction and growth of scientific knowledge. Second, they have a dialogic function since they aim to respond to previous studies and to be responded to by others, thus participating in discussions and debates within the scientific community. Finally, they have a relational function through citation and other discursive mechanisms that permit authors to create and maintain influential networks and indicate their position in the community (Iñesta & Castelló, 2012). Managing all these functions in a single piece of text is not easy, and research has extensively reported that students' lack of knowledge of genre characteristics and constraints accounts for various difficulties in research writing (Castelló et al., 2013). Accordingly, several successful proposals have been developed to facilitate students' learning of the discursive mechanisms related to writing research genres, such as theses, dissertations or articles, including students' reflection on and awareness of their learning and writing processes (Negretti & McGrath, 2018; Tardy 2016).

However, learning about genre characteristics might not be sufficient to guarantee that Ph.D. students will develop as research writers. There is evidence that students tend to interpret genres as formal and rigid structures and apply examples and resources in a nonreflective way (Castelló et al., 2013; Kamler & Thompson, 2008). Recent studies note that this reductionist interpretation is associated with the meaning students attribute to research, which, in turn, accounts for their authorial position when writing, either as students or researchers (Castelló et al., 2017; Lei & Hu, 2019). Moreover, some of our data indicate that both doctoral students and researchers are unable to strategically use their knowledge to decide when and why specific discursive mechanisms or resources are appropriate in meaningful writing situations (Castelló & Iñesta, 2012; Castelló et al., 2009).

Berta's Isolation

The last case is Berta, a young Ph.D. student who, after finishing her MSc, obtained a doctoral grant. She was a less experienced writer than the other two students; the most extensive and recent research texts she had written were her bachelor's dissertation and master's thesis. When we started to discuss students' feelings as research writers within the workshop, she expressed that she had many problems because she felt unable to write an article despite trying. She considered herself *only* a student and not part of the researcher community and therefore not legitimate as an author. In her own words, "Perhaps I will be able to feel that I am someone [in the disciplinary community] in the future when I get my paper published" (Final interview).

After receiving the reviewers' comments on her second draft, she began to modify this perception and considered that authorship could be established through writing, not just publishing. She explained,

> Through an article, you communicate an orientation, a certain way of conducting a study. That is, not only is it a study with its results and conclusions presented but also the researcher's motivation and orientation. (In-class interaction, session 4)

This quote also reveals a different way of understanding participation, not just through outputs but also through intentions and positioning. At the end of the workshop, she added to her comments a critical issue involving recognition and writer identity development when she stated,

> I feel I am part of the research community because I feel a very close identification with the community I am addressing, although I know I'm not an important part of this community. They are not going to cite me. (In-class interaction, session 5)

Evidence from research relates Berta's concerns to doctoral students' and, more generally, early-career researchers' socialization and acculturation issues in disciplinary research communities. Writing an article is difficult for students and early-career researchers because it requires not only knowing the rules and conventions of the community they are addressing, but also understanding when, how and why some particular conventions, ways of speaking, or discursive mechanisms are appropriate and using them intentionally to play the desired role and positioning in this disciplinary research community (Castelló et al., 2013). Studies on researcher identity development have explained such complex accomplishments—strategic decisions, regulation and positioning—particularly in the writing transition from academic to researcher communities (Castelló, McAlpine et al., 2021), when students must write in situated and authentic situations.

In these transitions, according to Ivanič's developmental framework, writers are expected to progress from learning to write like others to being read by others until they reach a final stage in which they are recognized as authors by others talking and writing about their work (Ivanič, 1998). This dynamic and interactive process requires time to learn the strategic management of different selves: the autobiographic "self" that a person brings to the act of writing, the authorial and discoursal "self" constructed through the act of writing, and how the writer is perceived by the reader(s) (Burguess & Ivanic, 2010; Castelló et al., 2011). Knowledge of these selves allows writers to be aware of their *identity kit* (Gee, 1996) and its fit to specific disciplinary research communities when translated into texts.

Acculturation processes have been studied extensively, especially regarding doctoral students' transitions from peripheral practices to increasingly legitimate and central ways of participation in research and disciplinary communities (Canagarajah, 2003; Lave & Wenger, 2001). Complementarily, the notion of identity trajectories (McAlpine & Amundsen, 2018) emphasizes how past, present, and anticipated future experiences explain researchers' identity development. Moreover, recent theoretical and empirical contributions have stressed the role of networks, interactions and processes to account for the dynamics of individuals' positioning and communities' participation (Castelló et al., 2021; Castelló, Sala-Bubaré & Pardo, 2021; Suñé-Soler, 2019; Lemke, 2000).

Based on these identity development approaches, in the last ten years, we have developed a series of studies and related pedagogical proposals addressed to undergraduate and graduate students as well as experienced researchers writing research-related genres (e.g., theses, dissertations, articles). These initiatives underline writer positioning and authorship development through strategic uses and regulation of discursive mechanisms that are useful to participate in—or confront—the specific discourses of disciplinary and research communities in which they are inserted in addition to promote a process approach and genre knowledge. These discursive mechanisms refer to the process, rhetorical and genre but also to the knowledge regarding values, premises, methods and restrictions that characterize research thinking in each discipline, subject, approach and community. Strategic uses involve reflective and intentional decisions regarding when, how and why specific mechanisms might help in adjusting texts to the writer's aims and authorial purposes whereas regulation refers to adjustments of these intentional decisions when facing a challenge or difficulty (Castelló, 2016; Castelló & Iñesta, 2012; Sala-Bubaré & Castelló, 2018).

Students' and Researchers' Writing Development: Recent Findings and Pedagogical Implications

Despite remarkable advances, evidence from research still shows that difficulties, struggles and contradictions remain even after students learn about the writing process, genres, and disciplinary research communities. Thus, focusing on knowledge acquisition and writing practices might not be sufficient to equip researchers to develop as writers. Based on our recent findings, developing a researcher identity is necessary to grow as a research writer and, in turn, to be aware of the authorial voice in social writing scenarios (Burgess & Ivanič, 2010; Castelló et al., 2013; Castelló & Iñesta, 2012). This process of identity development requires writers' agency to regulate cognitive, social and affective processes in particular communicative situations where individual or collaborative writing is required. Conceptions also play a major role in this development. When talking about conceptions, I refer not only to how writers understand the processes of writing but also how they consider texts and the interrelations of texts with processes and with general research activity. This involves developing a sophisticated understanding of texts as semiotic artifacts that evolve with the writing activity, or *artifact-in-activity* (Prior, 2006; Castelló et al., 2013).

In what follows, I address these aspects and draw a more complex picture to explain how research writing relates to acting, feeling and thinking like a researcher, that is, someone able to advance credible knowledge to solve disciplinary and societal challenges through responsible and innovative approaches (European Union, n.d.). To do so, I rely on our recent studies to discuss evidence regarding the persistence of a variety of difficulties relating to the two mentioned intertwined aspects, still scarcely addressed by research in the field: a) the need for strategic regulation of different types of knowledge in authentic and demanding research writing scenarios, which, in turn, requires a new conceptualization of the regulation notion in those situations, and b) the need to understand texts as artifacts-in-activity, not just products resulting from a more or less prescribed writing process.

The Social Nature of Research Writing Regulation. Relationship with Positioning, Voice and Authorial Self.

Writing regulation in higher education is a growing field with a broad distribution of studies framed into different theoretical and methodological perspectives, not all of them equally committed with the search for comprehensive methods that account for regulation in situated writing contexts. The results from a recent review of writing regulation research in Higher

Education indicate that, surprisingly, most studies adopt cognitive and sociocognitive approaches and focus on the writing processes of tasks that are more manageable and shorter than the complex tasks writers find in their professional careers or others that are not aligned with their disciplinary genres (Sala-Bubaré & Castelló, 2018). Moreover, there is a lack of studies exploring research writing regulation from a micro perspective, that is, observing master, bachelor or doctoral students' writing processes synchronously when dealing with complex research genres, such as theses or research articles.

To address the methodological challenge of the complexity of research writing in ecological conditions, we designed a first study (Iñesta & Castelló, 2012) in which we followed two participants, expert writers, who were writing a research article. They had the freedom to work anytime they wanted, with no time or space restrictions. Both of them worked on the research article for approximately one and a half months. We collected several types of data: writing diaries the participants completed after every writing session, the text-draft evolution, video recording of their writing activity in every session (through the Camtasia screen-capture software) and short interviews conducted weekly during the writing process to reflect upon their writing process. Finally, once they finished the article, they participated in a retrospective recall interview in which they discussed the recorded processes.

We combined macroanalysis of the discursive data and changes in drafts with microanalysis of the writing activity in which we compared the writers' discourse and interpretation of their processes with what they did—the registered writing activity (screen recorded) and draft evolution during the entire process of writing the research article. We integrated all this information in a double-scope representation. On the one hand, we considered the *writing sessions*: what they wrote and did during each session. On the other hand, we included what we called *the regulation episodes*, a new unit of analysis that accounted for intra- or intersession regulation activity.

A *regulation episode* was defined as the sequences of actions writers strategically implement to solve a difficulty or a challenge identified during the writing process. According to this definition, we initially expected regulation to be intentional and conscious (Castelló & Iñesta, 2012; Castelló et al., 2013; Iñesta & Castelló, 2012). Surprisingly, the results revealed the existence of some episodes that, although intentional, appeared to be implicit. Table 4.1 shows a condensed excerpt of one of these implicit episodes. In this case, to address the discussion of the results, the writer introduced a new sentence: "It is necessary to have more data but" and started to reformulate it (bursts 1 to 5).

Later in the same session, she started correcting the sentence by changing expressions, words, and verbs. That initial stage of reformulation lasted three minutes (bursts 6 to 11). Then, a second phase started, and for at least ten more minutes, she continued to edit the same sentence, making small changes in words and expressions (bursts 12 to 15). The final version of the sentence occurs after a couple of bursts in which she included content and structure changes (bursts 16 & 17).

Table 4.1. Implicit Regulation Episode (I). Experienced Writer Sentence Generation (Changes Highlighted)

Burst	Time code	Transcript
1	0:35:45	New sentence: "It is necessary to have more data but
5	0:37:40	Continuing: "It would be necessary to have more research but the mechanisms through which [one's] own action is decided could move along different paths to those which explain the acquisition of conceptual knowledge (authors cited)."
		Pause
11	0:43:40	Correcting: "It would be necessary to have more research in order to try to explore the hypothesis regarding the possibility that the mechanisms through which [one's] own action is decided could move along different paths to those which explain the acquisition of conceptual knowledge (authors cited)."
		Pause
15	0:54:41	Highlighting in yellow a fragment of the sentence here marked in bold: "It would be necessary to have more research but the working hypothesis appears to be clear; it could be possible that the mechanisms through which one's own action is decided could move along different paths to those which explain the acquisition of conceptual knowledge (authors cited)."
		Pause
16	1:16:21	Correcting: "It would be necessary to have more research information to validate some but the working hypothesis appears to be clear that results point towards; it could be possible that the mechanisms through which one's own action is decided could move along different paths to those which explain the acquisition of conceptual knowledge (authors cited)."
17	1:16:56	Correcting: "It would be necessary to have more information to validate some working hypothesis that results point towards; firstly, it could be possible that the mechanisms through which one's own action is decided could move along different paths to those which explain the acquisition of conceptual knowledge (authors cited)."

Adapted from Iñesta & Castelló (2012)

In total, the writer invested almost thirty minutes on this single sentence aimed at interpreting her results, which conflicted with previous results. In the writer's words, she was trying to *sound* polite. Thus, she was hedging some of the statements, whereas at the same time, she was interested in making her stance quite clear. To achieve this twofold goal, writers need to know quite well how the genre works and what the discursive mechanisms are that fit a specific community. In particular, they must have a clear sense of their voice and position in this community, which, in turn, is linked to their projected or desired authorial identity.

What surprised us the most was that the writer did not report any trouble or difficulty in this session. She was not aware of the amount of time and effort she invested in this single sentence until we confronted her with the Camtasia recordings and the sentence bursts transcription during the final interview. At that point, she mentioned being aware that the author with whom she was interacting—and criticizing—could be one of the reviewers; even if this was not the case, she expected him to be one of the readers when the article was eventually published. She considered him a colleague, but she felt distant from him epistemologically and empirically. From her perspective, this distance made writing this sentence more difficult. She explained that she did not report these considerations as concerns because she was not aware of the high number of linguistic decisions linked to discussing findings in scientific articles. The example reveals writing regulation can happen at the implicit level, at least for experienced researchers when writing scientific articles. We do not have enough real time data from different writers—not only experts—to explain why. It might be that our writer was aware of her positioning but did not link it to the rhetorical sphere, which was implicitly triggered by the situation, as a routine, due to her condition of expert writer; or it might be an issue of whether and how these mechanisms were taught and learned.

Moreover, the revised episode and its writer's interpretation offer a clear example of the extent to which research writing regulation is social as well as linguistic and cognitive. The discursive mechanisms put into play in this regulation episode were linked not only to the writer's intention of adjusting the sentence to the community standards, genre characteristics and audience but also to her aims and particular stance in the text.

These refined forms of regulation are extremely difficult for our students, only partially due to their lack of knowledge about the genre characteristics or writing processes necessary to understand how to discuss their results in an article. The results from studies in which writers participate in communities of practice where research writing is part of a meaningful and functional activity showed students' struggles to go beyond genre and strategy knowledge and practices (Castelló & Iñesta, 2012; Castelló et al., 2013). The strategic management of this knowledge within the research and writing activity that allows writers to position themselves, make their stance visible, and bring their voices into the conversation constitutes a significant challenge for students and early-career researchers.

Studies of students writing their bachelor's (Cano et al., 2012; Corcelles et al., 2017) and master's theses (Iñesta & Castelló, 2012) offer illustrative examples of this challenge. A first excerpt comes from psychology students participating in writing seminars with their peers and supervisors when writing their bachelor's theses. As in the doctoral workshop described in the previous section, peer-review was a key component of these seminars. Carol was one of these students. When reviewing Felipe's text, she mentioned the need for him to hedge some expressions, which seems a quite compelling recommendation. What are shocking are the arguments used to justify the need for hedging (see Figure 4.1). She first asked for a citation as a way to reduce Felipe's agency in the statement; then, she considered it necessary to hedge the statement because it compromised the writer's neutrality, which seems far from considering hedges as mechanisms to help writers' stance (Castelló et al., 2011; Castelló et al., 2012; Hyland, 2005).

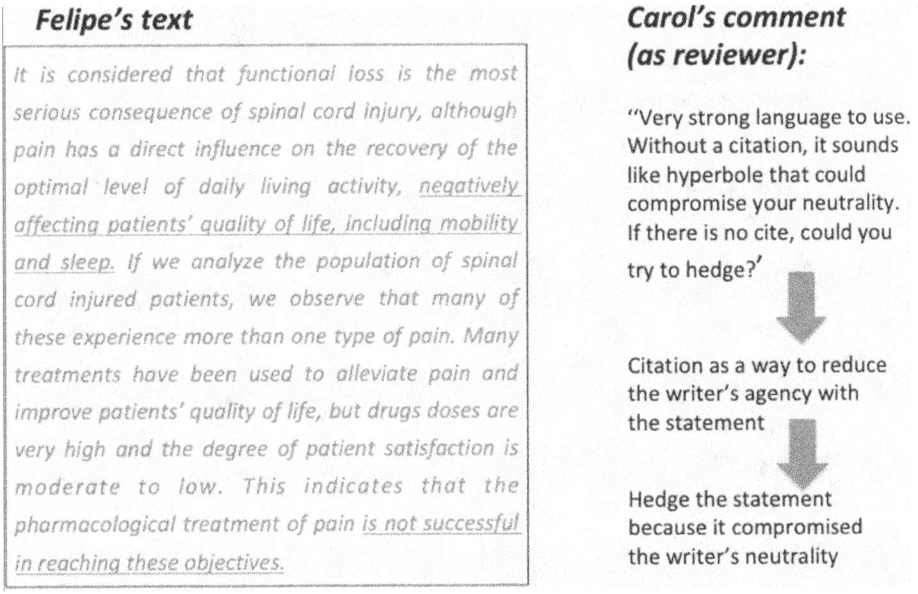

Felipe's text

It is considered that functional loss is the most serious consequence of spinal cord injury, although pain has a direct influence on the recovery of the optimal level of daily living activity, negatively affecting patients' quality of life, including mobility and sleep. If we analyze the population of spinal cord injured patients, we observe that many of these experience more than one type of pain. Many treatments have been used to alleviate pain and improve patients' quality of life, but drugs doses are very high and the degree of patient satisfaction is moderate to low. This indicates that the pharmacological treatment of pain is not successful in reaching these objectives.

Carol's comment (as reviewer):

"Very strong language to use. Without a citation, it sounds like hyperbole that could compromise your neutrality. If there is no cite, could you try to hedge?'

Citation as a way to reduce the writer's agency with the statement

Hedge the statement because it compromised the writer's neutrality

Figure 4.1. Felipe's text and Carol's comments (excerpt from Castelló et al., 2011).

A plausible explanation has to do with her struggles in combining *normative* knowledge in a challenging part of the text when Felipe is attempting to explain the gap and justifying the relevance of his study. Combining hedging and citation is always a result of strategic decisions by which authors manifest their stance—the authorial voice (Ivanič, 1998)—in specific parts of a text. Understanding such strategic decisions requires students—and their teachers—to participate in learning scenarios embedded in meaningful research activity systems in which decisions about tools (semiotic, physical, multimodal and others), goals, and the relationship and contextual constraints of actions in their research communities (Castelló et al., 2013; Prior & Thorne, 2014; Russell, 1995) are not optional but constitutive.

A second and much more frequent challenge relates to the variability of the discursive mechanisms' purposes, which remain obscure or occluded, to many students. In the following example, Laia was attempting to integrate different sources into a coherent synthesis when writing the introduction to her bachelor's thesis on the topic of *dissociation* (see Figure 4.2). In her text she summarized the different sources separately without the level of argumentation and integration that a synthesis requires (Mateos et al., 2020), which, in turn, prevented the identification of her stance in relation to the cited authors.

Laia's text	Reviewer's comment:
Richard (2007) argues for dissociation as a process in which experiences and psychological interpretations are not related and meanings are altered. He explains how experiences are distorted and interpretations for personal and interpersonal experiences are subtly but deeply altered.	"Ok but, do you agree or disagree with those authors' assumptions?"
In addition, Steinberg & Schnall (2002) suggest [y] dissociation is an adaptive behavior to face up with tensions or traumas.	 **Laia's answer:**
On the other hand, Bernstein and Putnam (1996) argue for different levels of dissociation, which imply memory loss and disconnection from the context. (M1)	"I agree, obviously!"

Figure 4.2. Laia's text and reviewer's comment (excerpt from Castelló et al., 2011).

Noticing this issue, the student who was acting as a reviewer asked her whether she was agreeing or disagreeing with the cited authors' assumptions. Laia answered that she agreed with all of them; what is relevant in this example is that she was stunned when she realized this was not self-evident to the reader. Later in the same session, when the reviewer claimed it was difficult to understand her stance because "she"—the author—was not visible in the text, Laia mentioned the contradiction she experienced between having an authorial stance and at the same time crediting the authors she read. From her perspective, the mere act of citing those authors and explaining and paraphrasing their assumptions was a sufficient sign of her own (agreeing) stance.

This contradiction referred to frequent recommendations from her supervisor regarding the requirement to cite every statement *versus* the significance of making the author's stance clear. From Laia's perspective, these were opposite moves. She felt unable to integrate both when writing the introduction; thus, she resolved the contradiction using a sequential structure consisting of writing short summaries of the readings first and then presenting her stance separately.

These examples illustrate the type of contradictions students experience when starting to make decisions about writing and need to regulate their knowledge and strategies in real research scenarios. However, these data come from retrospective designs and relationships between students' decisions to deal with these contradictions and changes in their writing processes are still fairly unknown. To advance our knowledge, we need to confront students' perceptions and discourse about their decisions (what they say) to their actions (what they do) along the writing process in authentic and complex research writing conditions.

To this end we recently designed an exploratory study in which we followed one Ph.D. student *when starting to write* a research article (RA) during the first three sessions of a writing workshop. In the first session, the writer started to draft the initial draft (extended abstract) of her research article which was peer reviewed and comments discussed in the second session. The third session was devoted to revising the text according to the received feedback.

As in the previous study with expert writers, we looked for regulation episodes in real time combining data about both the writing process and its products, and about participant's actions and perceptions about these actions (Sala-Bubaré et al., 2021). Considering what we discussed regarding implicit regulation processes (Castelló & Iñesta, 2012), we added a synchronous instrument such as keystroke logging, which, combined with screen capture software, helped us to obtain information about the moment-by-moment creation of the text and the resources used to that end. Other asynchronous instruments were an initial questionnaire and writing logs, which rendered crucial insight about the context of writing. The feedback session was also recorded to get access to the social context through the feedback comments, the problems writers encountered and the rationale for some of the decisions taken.

Although exploratory, some aspects of this study design and preliminary results can contribute to the ongoing discussions in the field of writing research and thus, the purpose of this chapter. First, besides identifying changes in writing processes at different levels (micro and macro) among sessions, the multimethod approach allowed us to relate writing regulation processes to the writer's aims and stance. Evidence showed writer reflection and positioning, integrating rhetorical, genre, community, and disciplinary (subject-related) issues, triggered by feedback, resulting in more complex writing regulation processes. Second, results offer new empirical evidence of the social nature of the regulation writing processes. Unlike expert writers, it seems this student (from social sciences) struggled, through the whole writing process, to reconcile what she considered her "personal" and natural way of writing with the constraints of the writing situation imposed by the genre characteristics (article), her position (as Ph.D. student) and the perceived authorial self (provided by feedback) (Burgess & Ivanič, 2010). At the same time, looking at discussions regarding the feedback and changes required in texts from her perspective, I also consider these struggles might indicate potential dissociations of herself as writer and researcher. Although the student accepted almost all the reviewers' critical comments and recommendations, she justified her previous decisions and difficulties by claiming her in-between position as an advanced Ph.D. student but not yet a researcher, and as a good writer but not as good at writing an article or thesis.

These results, though their reduced scope and preliminary nature, not only offer evidence of these dissociations but also show that appropriately introducing other voices (in our case, reviewers' voices) in writers' inner dialogues and interpretations can modify the writing processes involved in cognitive and emotional regulation when they write the second version of their abstract. To what extent these results might transfer to other disciplinary and alternative contexts remains unknown, a pending issue for the research writing agenda.

Conceiving Texts as Artifacts-in-Activity

Another series of studies we developed relates to conceptions and how to help students consider texts as mediating *artifacts* (Prior, 2006). Considering texts as *artifacts-in-activity* implies that successive drafts can be considered as tools for writers to think about the text content, its structure and linguistic formulation as well as tools to evolve as authors—that is, as identity development tools.

This conceptualization contradicts the idea of texts as just final outputs resulting from a more or less prescribed writing process, that we found in previous studies (Castelló et al., 2012). As mentioned, students, probably due to previous experiences, consider research genres to be highly typified and normative; thus, they believe as research writers they are expected to use a specialized lexicon and a fixed structure and have no freedom to write (Castelló et al., 2012; Castelló & Iñesta, 2012). In these cases, students struggle to attain the correct or the good final version of the text as soon as possible, which in turn prevents them from taking a stance, from defining and developing a plan to achieve their objectives and, ultimately, from developing their authorial voice and researcher identity. Therefore, their conceptions regarding research genres might contradict the possibility of reflecting upon linguistic resources and using these resources strategically.

The following example, from one of our first studies on writing conceptions, illustrates the students' struggling to find what they consider the "correct version" of a text. In this example, Sofia acted as a reviewer of the manuscript written by Maria, both of whom were psychology students writing their bachelor's theses (Cano et al., 2012; Castelló et al., 2013; Corcelles et al., 2017). Sofia's comments (see Figure 4.3) suggested changing Maria's words and sentences she defined as *incorrect*, and, as displayed in Figure 4.3, they were quite direct. Interestingly, Sofia was not an exception. More than half of the bachelor's students participating in the study did something similar when reviewing their peers' texts. This result was unexpected because these students were trained as reviewers and learned to offer indirect and critical comments instead of direct suggestions for change, like those displayed by Sofia. Students knew that when acting as reviewers, they should first clarify and explain their concerns with specific issues in the texts; second, they should justify the reasons underlying the concerns; and finally, they should make recommendations or ask questions to promote the writer's reflection. Possibly because of this, Sofia realized that she was being too directive and tried to excuse herself at the end of her comments by saying she was only offering suggestions but not "the absolute truth." Still, evidence showed she looked for the "truth," the ideal text she considered to be the only correct one.

In this study, students tended to offer simple comments, asking for changes only at the word level rather than considering texts as mediating artifacts. However, these results also offer evidence regarding how conflicting writers' conceptions and their interpretation of genre characteristics unfold in social writing contexts. Consequently, we assumed that the nature and diversity of writing experiences might mediate writing conceptions and developed series of studies to explore whether and how researchers' experiences and writing conceptions are intertwined (Castelló et al., 2017; Castelló, Sala-Bubaré & Pardo, 2021; Sala-Bubaré et al., 2018;). Within experiences, we included the students' trajectories and their social relationships and research-related networks in addition to other aspects, such as the thesis language, discipline or country.

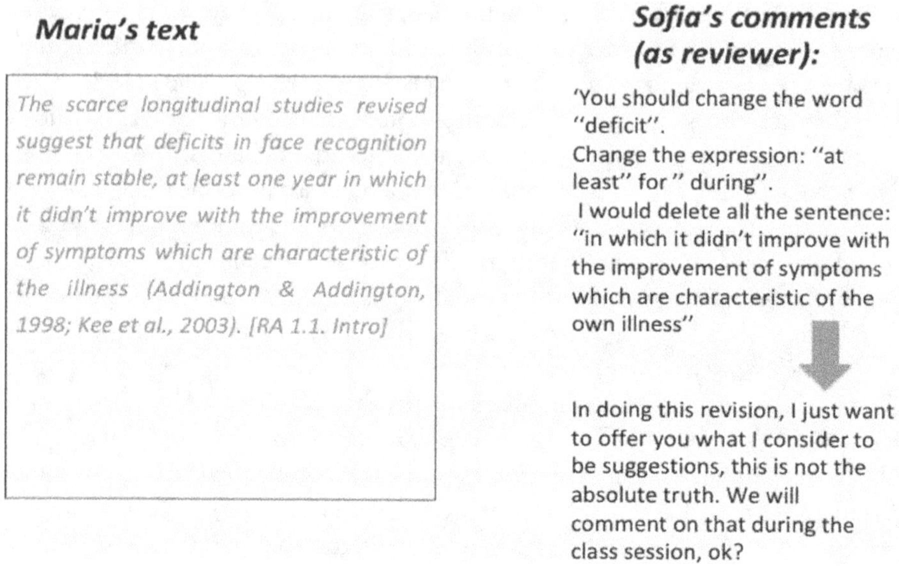

Maria's text	Sofia's comments (as reviewer):
The scarce longitudinal studies revised suggest that deficits in face recognition remain stable, at least one year in which it didn't improve with the improvement of symptoms which are characteristic of the illness (Addington & Addington, 1998; Kee et al., 2003). [RA 1.1. Intro]	'You should change the word "deficit". Change the expression: "at least" for " during". I would delete all the sentence: "in which it didn't improve with the improvement of symptoms which are characteristic of the own illness"
	In doing this revision, I just want to offer you what I consider to be suggestions, this is not the absolute truth. We will comment on that during the class session, ok?

Figure 4.3. Sofia's comments related to conceiving research texts as highly typified and normative.

We combined cross-sectional with longitudinal mixed-method studies using the Cross-Country Doctoral and Post-Ph.D. Researcher Experience surveys (C-DES & C-PDR) and so-called *multimodal interviews* to collect different types of data regarding both perceptions and experiences development through time. A *multimodal interview* is a semi-structured interview in which we combine discursive data with visual methods to elicit different types of information (McAlpine et al., 2017). In our case, we used two visual methods, the *Journey Plot* and the *Network Plot* (Castelló et al., 2018; Sala-Bubaré & Castelló, 2017).

The *Journey Plot* is a two-axes graphic in which students think about and mark significant events or experiences they faced over time; thus, the resulting line represents their trajectories. Figure 4.4 shows an example of a Ph.D. student's Journey Plot over a year. Time is situated in the horizontal X-axis, whereas the vertical Y-axis reflects the intensity and the value (positive or negative) of the experiences.

The *Network Plot* consists of circles that represent the individuals, groups or institutions with which students interact when writing research genres (see Figure 4.5). Students are asked to organize these circles freely to display their research writing-related network while explaining the type of relationship and activity they share (writing together, publishing, discussing drafts, writing grants or other) as well as how these relationships were created and maintained.

Research Writing

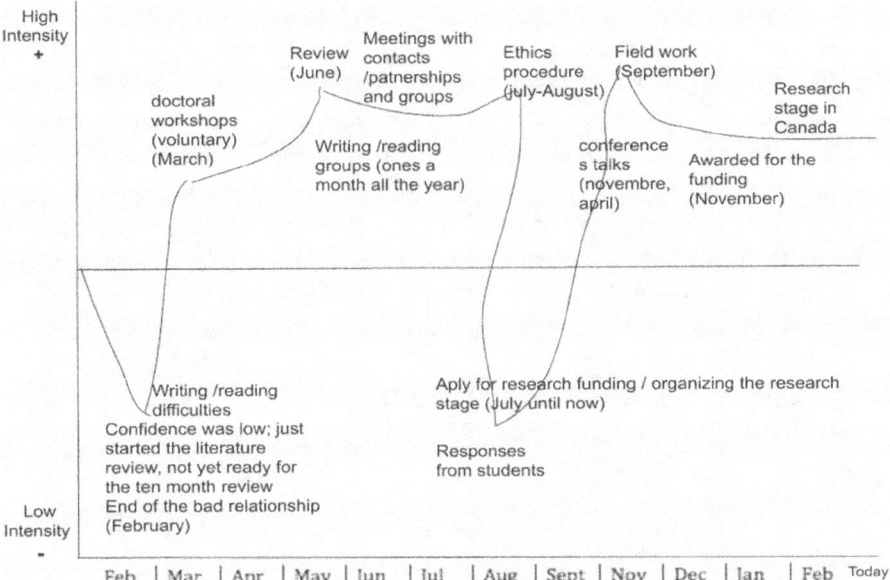

Figure 4.4, Journey Plot example.

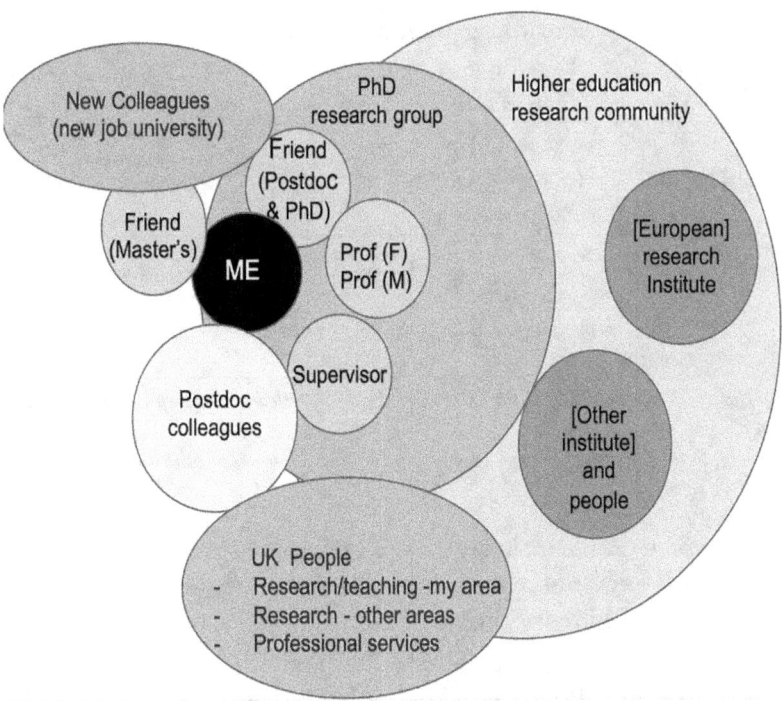

Figure 4.5. Network Plot example.

In what follows I transversally discuss results of the mentioned series of studies we developed so far to offer an integrated and comprehensive picture of their accounts. Cross-sectional results, based on person-centered analysis, allowed us to differentiate writing conception profiles of both doctoral students (Sala-Bubaré et al., 2018) and post-Ph.D. researchers (Castelló et al., 2017; Castelló, Sala-Bubaré & Pardo, 2021) with similar characteristics across countries, disciplines and researcher expertise. As summarized in table 4.2, Ph.D. students and post-Ph.D. researchers share the productive and struggler profiles, the two ends of a continuum while the two other profiles—the productive struggler and the reduced productivity—were found within each group respectively.

Table 4.2. Ph.D. Students' and Post-Ph.D. Researchers' Writing Perceptions Profiles

Profiles	Characteristics	Ph.D. (n=1.463)*	Post-Ph.D. (n=134)**
Productive	Transformative writing perceptions Few problems when writing High publication experience as first and co-authors	x	x
Productive struggler	Transformative writing perceptions Struggles when writing High publication experience	–	x
Reduced productivity	Transformative writing perceptions Some problems when writing Low publication experience	x	–
Struggler	Less transformative writing perceptions Struggles when writing Low (Ph.D.) to medium (post-Ph.D.) publication experience	x	x

*See Sala-Bubaré et al. (2018) for a Ph.D. profiles results detailed account and their statistical significance.
** See Castelló, Sala-Bubaré & Pardo (2021) for a Post-Ph.D. profiles results detailed account and their statistical significance

The *productive* profile includes those who consider writing as a tool to think and create new knowledge, thus held the most transformative writing perceptions, and experienced fewer problems than the rest of the profiles when writing. Moreover, they had more publication experience as both first and second authors and perceived themselves as productive. This profile was the most frequent among the post-Ph.D. researchers and the second most frequent among the doctoral students (see Figure 4.6). The Ph.D. students and post-Ph.D. researchers included in the *struggler* writer profile reported suffering several problems when writing, such as high levels of procrastination, blocks and anxiety when writing, which prevented them from writing; thus, they were less productive than writers in the rest of the profiles. They also held less transformative writing conceptions, and Ph.D. students considered writing to be an innate ability more frequently than writers in the other profiles.

The two other profiles were specific to each group of participants. The *productive struggler* was the second most predominant writer profile among post-Ph.D. researchers. It included those who experienced blocks and had difficulties when dealing with research writing even though they were almost as productive as the first profile participants and also held transformative writing perceptions.

In the case of doctoral students, we found a *reduced productivity* writer profile. In this case, participants held transformative writing perceptions and experienced fewer problems in writing than *struggler* writers but more than *productive* writers. Nevertheless, they were the least productive among the doctoral students' profiles with regard to both their perceptions and the reported number of publications. These doctoral candidates were also more likely not to have determined the format of their dissertation. These last two profiles were unexpected according to previous findings (Castelló et al., 2018; Lonka et al., 2019) in that they both had transformative writing perceptions but differed in productivity.

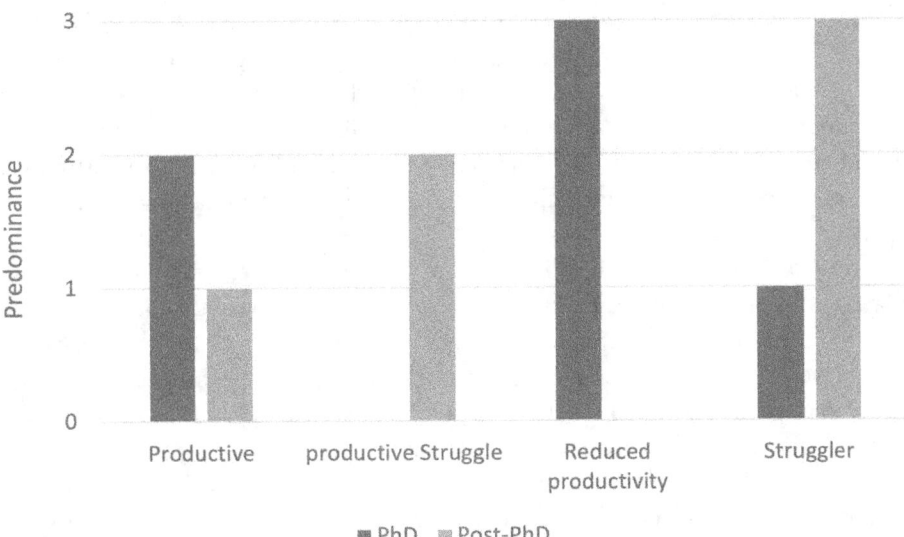

Figure 4.6. Profiles distribution and significant predominance among Ph.D. and Post-Ph.D.

In the case of doctoral candidates, low productivity was related to not knowing the format of the thesis and to a higher focus on research-related tasks other than writing, such as data collection and analysis. In both cases, there were no differences among profiles regarding the writing language, countries (data discussed here come from Switzerland, UK, Spain, and Finland) and, even more surprisingly, in the case of postdocs regarding the perceived social support from their research team, their supervisor or their disciplinary research community.

These results offer a complex picture of how writing conceptions evolve through early-career researchers' development but, at the same time, appear to contradict previous findings and assumptions about the mediating role of social experiences and writing trajectories on writing conceptions, one of our primary concerns when trying to understand research-writing development. Nevertheless, when looking at the qualitative multimodal data, we found inspiring patterns complementing the quantitative analysis that shed new light on the relationships between the profiles and their trajectories and networks (Castelló, Sala-Bubaré & Pardo, 2021).

Participants included in the *productive* writer profile reported mainly positive and rather stable research writing trajectories. Consistently, their Journey Plots displayed either horizontal or ascendant trajectories. Moreover, they mentioned writing a diverse variety of genres: articles as well as conference presentations, workshops and project proposals, among others.

In contrast, *productive struggler* writers' trajectories went from very negative to more positive points; therefore, their Journey Plots were also ascendant but looked less stable since they displayed very negative experiences. Writers in this profile detailed many specific difficulties they experienced when writing particular genres, mainly articles, such as inability to finish them or dealing with bad reviews. Most of their discourse focused on how much they suffered and struggled, though they ultimately managed to solve challenges and thus finished very satisfied.

The post-Ph.D. researchers included in the third profile, *struggler writer*, displayed a roller-coaster, upside-down trajectory in their Journal Plots. Although these writers reported positive writing experiences, the transitions between events were often abrupt, changing from very positive to very negative in a short time. In most cases, the explanation for such radical changes was unclear and did not offer evidence of the participants being agentive in solving the issues they experienced. An excerpt from one representative student of this profile, Víctor, is illustrative of this lack of agency when talking about the rejection of a paper:

> Well, this was a bit difficult because we had very good chances. In theory, it is well done, with the same methodology [as the

previous paper] and everything, but they did not like it. At the end, we will not publish it, and we will add the physiological variables to the second article.

Instead of taking an active role in solving the problems they encountered, postdocs included in this profile frequently expected that the passing of time or other people would solve them (i.e., Victor explained that his supervisor rewrote the paper because, after rejection, he was unable to work on it again). The majority mentioned almost exclusively writing articles and rarely reported other genres.

Differences among profiles also appear in the postdocs' relational research networks. Participants from the *productive writer* profile demonstrated that they built mainly international networks and offered clear evidence of what we have called a relational agency, meaning that their networks were created primarily by themselves. They explained how they actively contacted people they were interested in, whether through email, conferences or stays, and how they started to write together. In contrast, postdocs' networks representative of the *struggler writer* profile mainly focused on their local context, either the university or the department. Thus, their writing and publishing experiences were restricted to researchers from the local context with no evidence that they actively looked for opportunities to write with other remote partners. Accordingly, their co-authors were mainly supervisors or their research team members.

Altogether, these results indicate the extent to which social relationships and researchers' positioning in any particular community mediate writing perceptions, practices and outputs. Therefore, participating in a variety of communities and experiencing different roles as researcher, but also as a writer—either single or in collaboration—reviewer or discussant in such communities might impact on developing more complex conceptualizations and ideas regarding research writing and on using texts as artifacts-in-activity.

Final Remarks

In this chapter, I discussed consolidated and emergent research that relies on several related premises, the dialogical, social, hybrid, and epistemic nature of research writing. Producing research texts is a particular form of conversation that requires a broad range of abilities and a variety of discourse modalities, all of them related to particular communicative contexts that not only might transform and create knowledge through critical reflection but also develop research writers through positioning and authorial development.

I have also argued that research-writing development involves transversal, interdisciplinary and critical competencies, such as critical thinking or socially-shared regulation. Considering that these competencies have been progressively included during the last 20 years in many of the world's bachelor's curricula and study programs and they appear as critical in the knowledge society (Castells, 2000), it seems reasonable to include research writing in higher education from the first years of bachelor's programs through a variety of formats and in connection with particular disciplinary requirements. Moreover, if research writing is a complex and hybrid activity, it cannot be taught via short and straightforward tasks or an isolated subject.

My point here is that preparing students as professionals currently requires equipping them with research competencies and attitudes. This consideration relates to the need to rethink the role and purpose of research training and education in higher education curricula. Identifying challenges, designing ways to address them, and interpreting and communicating results are crucial not only for professionals' lifelong learning but also to innovate in their professional contexts. Consequently, it is urgent to analyze the role of research training, understood in a broad sense, which also incorporates different research genres in higher education curricula. It is not only a matter of knowing, writing, and doing research but also of being able to decide *when*, *how*, and *why* a particular way of thinking, acting, and feeling is appropriate and necessary to deal with social and disciplinary challenges.

When envisaging the role of research in twenty-first century societies and how professions will evolve, it is plausible to assume the professionals capable of generating cycles of reflection-inquiry-innovation are probably those who will have better and more exciting workplaces in any sector. From my perspective, this assumption has significant consequences for writing research and intervention and alludes to the need for what we may consider, following Yore's (2012) idea, a new *scientific literacy*. To move forward in this direction and confront the most urgent challenges research writing is already facing, future research in the field would require, at least, considering the following challenges.

First, clarifying and mapping the situation of research-related genres in higher education as well as how students but also faculty interpret the so-called scientific literacy in different disciplines and at the graduate and undergraduate levels. Understanding when, how and why students learn research-related writing genres and to what extent they are familiar with their purposes and tools is necessary to enhance both students' research competencies and writing development. Moreover, any agenda for future research should include critical reflection on how emergent research genres account for new research and communicative practices researchers inside and outside the academia need to confront.

Second, knowing how writing processes unfold when writing research-related genres in a variety of ecological research contexts and disciplines is a pending task necessary to build comprehensive and non-reductionist explanations of such processes. Advancing on such knowledge not only would ground theory and models adjusted to specific research writing conditions but would also open spaces for those with teaching responsibilities to reflect, think and sometimes rethink research writing interventions.

From my perspective, focusing on research writing processes has to do with accounting not only for the social dimension of writing but also for writing-in-the-activity. As mentioned, this implies looking both at processes and writers' knowledge, as well as taking into account time and space signifying historical and cultural rules and practices. Understanding how these systemic components intertwine in particular research communities remains a priority for those committed to improving research writing in the twenty-first century. It might also be a promising way to develop a comprehensive framework to facilitate the competent and harmonious development of research writers in diverse, global and complex research scenarios.

Dialogue, discussions, and cross-fertilization among different streams, approaches, and disciplinary traditions that converge on the study of research-related genres and research writing is imperative for future research in the field. A vast body of knowledge has been built based on these traditions, which in many cases has remained confined within their own boundaries. The development of cross-, trans- and multidisciplinary projects and teams that are just emerging can be the first step to bridge those boundaries and move forward to the integration of existing evidence and the promotion of meaningful and relevant, though complex and challenging, research. This volume assembles a promising step forward towards this direction.

References

Baaijen, V. M., Galbraith, D. & de Glopper, K. (2014). Effects of writing beliefs and planning on writing performance. *Learning and Instruction, 33*, 81–91. https://doi.org/10.1016/j.learninstruc.2014.04.001.

Bakhtin, M. (1981). *The dialogic imagination*. University of Texas Press.

Bazerman, C. (1988). *Shaping written knowledge: The genre and activity of the experimental article in science* (Vol. 356). University of Wisconsin Press.

Bazerman, C. (2004). Intertextualities: Volosinov, Bakhtin, literary theory, and literacy studies. In A. F. Ball, S. Warshauer Freedman & R. Pea (Eds.), *Bakhtinian perspectives on language, literacy, and learning* (pp. 53–65). Cambridge University Press.

Beauvais, C., Olive, T. & Passerault, J. M. (2011). Why are some texts good and others not? Relationship between text quality and management of the writing processes. *Journal of Educational Psychology, 103*(2), 415–428. https://doi.org/10.1037/a0022545.

Bekar, M., Doroholschi, C. I., Kruse, O. & Yakhontova, T. (2015). Educational genres in eastern Europe: A comparison of the genres in the humanities departments of three countries of three different universities in three different countries. *Journal of Academic Writing, 5*(1), 119–132. https://doi.org/10.18552/joaw.v5i1.164.

Berkenkotter, C. & Murray, D. M. (1983). Decisions and revisions: The planning strategies of a publishing writer, and response of a laboratory rat: Or, being protocoled. *College Composition and Communication, 34*(2), 156–172. https://doi.org/10.2307/357403.

Borges, J. L. (1969). *Elogio de la sombra*. Emece.

Burgess, A. & Ivanič, R. (2010). Writing and being written: Issues of identity across timescales. *Written Communication, 27*(2), 228–255. https://doi.org/10.1177/0741088310363447.

Camps, A. & Castelló, M. (2013). La escritura académica en la universidad [Academic writing at university]. *Revista de Docencia Universitaria, 11*(1), 17–36. https://doi.org/10.4995/redu.2013.5590.

Canagarajah, A. S. (2003). A somewhat legitimate and very peripheral participation. In C. P. Casanave & S. Vandrick. (Eds.), *Writing for scholarly publication: Behind the scenes in language education* (pp. 197–210). Routledge.

Cano, M., Corcelles, M., Castelló, M. & Fuentealba, M.O. (2012). Características y funciones de las ayudas en la revisión colaborativa de textos científico-académicos. *Proceedings CIDUI*. UPF.

Castelló, M. (2002). De la investigación sobre el proceso de composición a la enseñanza de la escritura. *Revista signos, 35*(51–52), 149–162. http://dx.doi.org/10.4067/S0718-09342002005100011.

Castelló, M., Iñesta, A. & Monereo, C. (2009). Towards self-regulated academic writing: an exploratory study with graduate students in a situated learning environment. *Electronic Journal of Research in Educational Psychology, 9*(3), 1107–1130. http://www.investigacion-psicopedagogica.org/revista/new/english/ContadorArticulo.php?367.

Castelló, M., Corcelles, M., Iñesta, A., Bañales, G. & Vega, N. (2011). La voz del autor en la escritura académica: una propuesta para su análisis. *Signos, 44*(76), 105–117. http://dx.doi.org/10.4067/S0718-09342011000200001.

Castelló, M. & Donahue, C. (2012). Introduction. In M. Castelló & C. Donahue (Eds.), *University writing: Selves and texts in academic societies* (pp. i-xxvii). Brill. https://doi.org/10.1163/9781780523873.

Castelló, M. & Iñesta, A. (2012). Texts as artifacts-in-activity: Developing authorial identity and academic voice in writing academic research papers in M. Castelló & C. Donahue (Eds.), *University writing: Selves and texts in academic societies* (pp. 179–200). Brill. https://doi.org/10.1163/9781780523873.

Castelló, M., Iñesta, A., Pardo, M., Liesa, E. & Martinez-Fernández, R. (2012). Tutoring the end-of-studies dissertation: Helping psychology students find their academic voice. *Higher Education, 63*(1), 97–115. https://doi.org/10.1007/s10734-011-9428-9.

Castelló, M., Iñesta, A. & Corcelles, M. (2013). Ph.D. students' transitions between academic and scientific writing identity: Learning to write a research article. *Research in the Teaching of English, 47*(4), 442–478. http://www.jstor.org/stable/24397847.

Castelló, M. (2015). La investigación sobre escritura académica en los procesos de enseñanza-aprendizaje en la universidad Española. *Culture and Education, 27*(3), 465–476. https://doi.org/10.1080/11356405.2015.1072362.

Castelló, M. (2016). Escribir artículos de investigación. Aprender a desarrollar la voz y la identidad del investigador novel. In G. Bañales-Faz, M. Castelló & N. A. Vega-López. *Enseñar a leer y escribir en la educación superior. Propuestas educativas basadas en la investigación* (pp. 209–232). Fundación SM. http://web.metro.inter.edu/facultad/esthumanisticos/crem_docs/Ensenar%20a%20leer%20y%20escribir.pdf.

Castelló, M., McAlpine, L. & Pyhältö, K. (2017). Spanish and UK post-Ph.D. researchers: Writing perceptions, well-being and productivity. *Journal of Higher Education Research & Development, 36*(6), 1108–1122. https://doi.org/10.1080/07294360.2017.1296412.

Castelló, M., Pyhältö, K. & McAlpine, L. (2018). European cross-national mixed-method study on early career researcher experience. In A. J. Jaeger & A. J. Dinin (Eds.), *The postdoc landscape. The invisible scholars* (pp. 143–174). Academic Press.

Castelló, M., McAlpine, L., Sala-Bubaré, A., Inouye, K. & Skakni, I. (2021). What perspectives underlie "researcher identity"? A review of two decades of empirical studies. *Higher Education, 81*, 567–590. https://doi.org/10.1007/s10734-020-00557-8.

Castelló, M., Sala-Bubaré, A. & Pardo, M. (2021). Post-Ph.D. researchers' writing conceptions as mediators of trajectories and networking. *Written communication, 38*(4). https://doi.org/10.1177/07410883211027949.

Castells, M. (2000). Materials for an exploratory theory of the network society. *The British Journal of Sociology, 51*(1), 5–24. https://doi.org/10.1111/j.1468-4446.2000.00005.x.

Chitez, M., Kruse, O. & Castelló, M. (2015). *The European writing survey (EUWRIT): Background, structure, implementation, and some results.* Zürcher Hochschule für Angewandte Wissenschaften (ZAHW).

Colton, C. C. (1820). *Lacon: Or, many things in few words; Addressed to those who think* (5th ed.) [Quote Page 229]. Longman, Hurst, Rees, Orme, and Brown. http://books.google.com/books?id=fcQsAAAAYAAJ&q=%22steal+thoughts%22#v=snippet&.

Corcelles, M., Cano, M., Mayoral, P. & Castelló, M. (2017.) Enseñar a escribir en la Universidad: el Trabajo final de grado. *Signos, 50*(95), 337–360. http://dx.doi.org/10.4067/S0718-09342017000300337.

European Union (n.d.) *Science with and for Society (SwafS), Horizon 2020*. Retrieved December 2, 2021, from *https://rb.gy/44uq6x*.

Fanelli, D. & Larivière, V. (2016). Researchers' individual publication rate has not increased in a century. *PloS one, 11*(3), e0149504. https://doi.org/10.1371/journal.pone.0149504.

Gallego, L., Castelló, M. & Badia, A. (2016). Faculty feelings as writers: Relationship with writing genres, perceived competences, and values associated to writing. *Higher Education, 71*(5), 719–734. https://doi.org/10.1007/s10734-015-9933-3.

Gee, J. P. (1996). *Social linguistics and literacies: Ideology in discourses* (2nd ed.). Taylor Francis.

Harwood, N. & Petrić, B. (2016). *Experiencing master's supervision: Perspectives of international students and their supervisors*. Taylor & Francis.

Hyland, K. (2005). Stance and engagement: A model of interaction in academic discourse. *Discourse studies, 7*(2), 173–192. https://doi.org/10.1177/1461445605050365.

Hyland, K. & Guinda, C. S. (Eds.). (2012). *Stance and voice in written academic genres*. Palgrave Macmillan.

Iñesta, A. & Castelló, M. (2012). Towards an integrative unit of analysis: Regulation episodes in expert research article writing. In C. Bazerman, C. Dean, J. Early, K. Lunsford, S. Null, P. Rogers & A. Stansell (Eds.), *International advances in writing research: Cultures, places, measures* (pp. 441–448). The WAC Clearinghouse; Parlor Press. https://doi.org/10.37514/PER-B.2012.0452.2.24.

Ivanič, R. (1998). *Writing and identity: The discoursal construction of identity in academic writing*. John Benjamins.

Kamler, B. & Thomson, P. (2008). The failure of dissertation advice books: Toward alternative pedagogies for doctoral writing. *Educational Researcher, 37*(8), 507–514. https://doi.org/10.3102/0013189X08327390.

Kruse, O., Chitez, M., Rodriguez, B. & Castelló, M. (2016). *Exploring European writing cultures. Country reports on genres, writing practices and languages used in European higher education*. Winterthur: ZHAW Zurcher Hochschule fur Angewandte Wissenschaften. https://doi.org/10.21256/zhaw-1056.

Lave, J. & Wenger, E. (2001). Legitimate peripheral participation in communities of practice. In J. Clarke, A. Hansson, R. Harrison & F. Reeve. *Supporting lifelong learning* (pp. 121–136). Routledge.

Lei, J. & Hu, G. (2019). Doctoral candidates' dual role as student and expert scholarly writer: An activity theory perspective. *English for Specific Purposes, 54*, 62–74. https://doi.org/10.1016/j.esp.2018.12.003.

Lemke, J. (2000). Across the scales of time: Artifacts, activities, and meanings in ecosocial systems. *Mind, Culture, and Activity, 7*(4), 273–290. https://doi.org/10.1207/S15327884MCA0704_03.

Lokhtina, I., Löfström, E., Cornér, S. & Castelló, M. (2020). In pursuit of sustainable co-authorship practices in doctoral supervision: Addressing the challenges of writing, authorial identity and integrity. *Innovations in Education and Teaching International*, 1–11. https://doi.org/10.1080/14703297.2020.1799839.

Lonka, K., Ketonen, E., Vekkaila, J., Cerrato, M. & Pyhältö, K. (2019). Doctoral students' writing profiles and their relations to well-being and perceptions of the academic environment. *Higher Education, 77*(4), 587–602. https://doi.org/10.1007/s10734-018-0290-x.

Mateos, M., Rijlaarsdam, G., Martín, E., Cuevas, I., Van den Bergh, H. & Solari, M. (2020). Learning paths in synthesis writing: Which learning path contributes most to which learning outcome? *Instructional Science, 48*, 137–157. https://doi.org/10.1007/s11251-020-09508-3.

McAlpine, L. & Amundsen, C. (2018). *Identity-trajectories of early career researchers*. Palgrave Macmillan.

McAlpine, L., Pyhältö, K. & Castelló, M. (2017) Building a more robust conception of early career researcher experience: What might we be overlooking? *Studies in Continuing Education, 40*(2), 149–165. https://doi.org/10.1080/0158037X.2017.1408582.

Negretti, R. & McGrath, L. (2018). Scaffolding genre knowledge and metacognition: Insights from an L2 doctoral research writing course. *Journal of Second Language Writing, 40*, 12–31. https://doi.org/10.1016/j.jslw.2017.12.002.

Nesi, H. & Gardner, S. (2018). The BAWE corpus and genre families classification of assessed student writing. *Assessing Writing, 38*, 51–55. https://doi.org/10.1016/j.asw.2018.06.005.

Paré, A. (2019). Re-writing the doctorate: New contexts, identities, and genres. *Journal of Second Language Writing, 43*, 80–84. https://doi.org/10.1016/j.jslw.2018.08.004.

Parish, A. J., Boyack, K. W. & Ioannidis, J. P. (2018). Dynamics of co-authorship and productivity across different fields of scientific research. *PloS One, 13*(1), e0189742. https://doi.org/10.1371/journal.pone.0189742.

Prior, P. (2006). A sociocultural theory of writing. In C. A. MacArthur, S. Graham & J. Fitzgerald (Eds.), *Handbook of Writing Research* (pp. 54–66). The Guilford Press.

Prior, P. & Bilbro, R. (2012). Academic enculturation: Developing literate practices and isciplinary identities. In M. Castelló & C. Donahue (Eds.), *University writing selves and texts in academic societies* (pp. 19–31). Brill. https://doi.org/10.1163/9781780523873.

Prior, P. & Thorne, S. L. (2014). Research paradigms: Product, process, and social activity. In E.-M. Jakobs & D. Perrin (Eds.), *Handbook of writing and text production* (pp. 31–54). Mouton de Gruyter.

Russell, D. (1995). Activity theory and its implications for writing instruction. In J. Petraglia (Ed.), *Reconceiving writing, rethinking writing instruction* (pp. 51–77). Lawrence Erlbaum.

Russell, D. R. (2009). Writing in multiple contexts: Vygotskian CHAT meets the phenomenology of genre. In C. Bazerman, R. Krut, K. Lunsford, S. McLeod, S. Null, P. Rogers & A. Stansell (Eds.), *Traditions of writing research* (pp. 365–376). Routledge.

Russell, D. R. & Cortes, V. (2012). Academic and scientific texts: The same or different communities? In M. Castelló & C. Donahue (Eds.), *University writing: Selves and texts in academic societies* (pp. 3–17). Brill.

Sala-Bubaré, A. & Castelló, M. (2017). Exploring the relationship between doctoral students' experiences and research community positioning. *Studies in Continuing Education, 39*(1), 16–34. https://doi.org/10.1080/0158037X.2016.1216832.

Sala-Bubaré, A. & Castelló, M. (2018). Writing regulation processes in higher education: A review of two decades of empirical research. *Reading and Writing, 31*(4), 757–777. https://doi.org/10.1007/s11145-017-9808-3.

Sala-Bubaré, A., Castelló, M. & Rijlaarsdam, G. (2021). Doctoral students' writing regulation processes. *Journal of Writing Research, 13*(1), 1–30. https://doi.org/10.17239/jowr-2021.13.01.01.

Sala-Bubaré, A., Peltonen, J. A., Pyhältö, K. & Castelló, M. (2018). Doctoral candidates' research writing perceptions: A cross-national study. *International Journal of Doctoral Studies, 13*, 327–345. https://doi.org/10.28945/4103.

Suñé-Soler, N. (2019). *The dialogical self of doctoral candidates* [Unpublished doctoral dissertation]. Universitat Autònoma de Barcelona. Bellaterra.

Swales, J. M. (2004). *Research genres: Explorations and applications*. Cambridge University Press.

Tardy, C. M. (2016). *Beyond convention: Genre innovation in academic writing*. University of Michigan Press.

van den Bergh, H. & Rijlaarsdam, G. (2007). The dynamics of idea generation during writing: An online study. In G. Rijlaarsdam (Series Ed.), M. Torrance, L. van Waes & D. Galbraith (Eds.), *Writing and cognition: Research and applications* (pp. 125–150). Elsevier.

van den Bergh, H., Rijlaarsdam, G. & van Steendam, E. (2016). Writing process theory: A functional dynamic approach. In C. A. MacArthur, S. Graham & J. Fitzgerald (Eds.), *Handbook of writing research* (pp. 57–71). The Guilford Press.

Yakhontova, T. (2002). "Selling" or "telling"? The issue of cultural variation in research genres. In J. Flowerdew (Ed.), *Academic discourse* (pp. 216–232). Routledge.

Yore, L. D. (2012). Science literacy for all: More than a slogan, logo, or rally flag! *Issues and Challenges in Science Education Research*, 5–23. https://doi.org/10.1007/978-94-007-3980-2_2.

5 Fostering Multilingual Academic Writing Knowledge in Interdisciplinary EMI Degree Programs

Ina Alexandra Machura
JUSTUS LIEBIG UNIVERSITY, GERMANY

This contribution presents a course curriculum as well as conclusions drawn from a quasi-interventional study on the development of advanced English writing skills in an interdisciplinary English-medium instruction (EMI) management degree program at the master's level, offered at a Midwestern German university. Two English for specific purposes (ESP) writing instructors and seven discipline-specific lecturers in the life and social sciences contributed to a writing-intensive course design in team-teaching partnerships (Lasagabaster, 2018) formed during the implementation of a 14-week core module in the interdisciplinary degree program. The student group in the present project (n=20) provides an illustrative example of today's superdiverse student populations in higher education (Donahue, 2018). In order to document developments in the students' EFL writing skills, EFL source-based academic writing assignments were collected from the students prior to and after the module. Also prior to and after the module, students completed extensive writing-focused surveys, documenting the students' declarative writing skills and the students' attitudes towards different types of advanced EFL writing.

Based on the writing curriculum implemented in the module, on the texts produced by the students, on the student surveys, and on the responses gathered in a lecturer workshop discussion, the present contribution discusses how writing-intensive course designs informed in team-teaching partnerships between writing instructors and discipline-specific faculty can help EFL writers in interdisciplinary EMI programs develop their EFL professional writing knowledge.[1]

---

[1] I would like to dedicate this publication to the memory of Prof. Dr. Susanne

In today's increasingly globalized and interdisciplinary landscape in higher education, discipline-specific lecturers as well as language teachers and writing instructors more often than not have to cater to the highly heterogeneous needs of *superdiverse* student groups. Today's student bodies' *superdiversity*, according to Blommaert and Rampton (2012), is characterized by a "tremendous increase in the categories of migrants, not only in terms of nationality, ethnicity, language, and religion, but also in terms of motives, patterns and itineraries of migration, processes of insertion into . . . the host societies" (p. 1). In order to remain academically, educationally, and economically attractive, universities in Europe currently advance their institutions' internationalization in a variety of ways (Göpferich et al., 2019).[2] The institutions' measures of internationalization contribute substantially to the superdiversity of students and faculty, as was precisely the case for the interdisciplinary management degree program at the master's level in which the course detailed in the present contribution was taught with a *superdiverse* group of students and a *superdiverse* group of lecturers. Importantly, Madiba (2018, p. 508) points out that the appropriateness of the term *superdiversity* may be contextually dependent, particularly when languages in higher education are concerned. Educational settings in the global South, for instance, have historically been characterized by a different kind and extent of linguistic diversity than educational contexts in the global North, so that learning environments striking people as *superdiverse* in the latter would represent familiar diversity in the former. The argument why the term *superdiversity* is indeed applicable in the present context is twofold: First, the sheer number and combination of languages in the present context (plus the fact that the language of instruction was a foreign language for most persons involved) is still relatively uncommon in the context of higher education in Germany (Göpferich et al., 2019, p. 114). Second, the diversity of the people involved in the project transcended linguistic diversity and also comprised disciplinary, cultural, and national diversity. Courses in the interdisciplinary management degree program are usually held with *superdiverse* student groups since the program accepts both domestic and international students with undergraduate degrees in business and economics, agriculture, legal studies, nutrition, environmental sciences, and the social sciences. Accordingly, this interdisciplinary master's program offers an institutional opportunity to

---

Göpferich who single-handedly created a fertile institutional background for our projects in the form of a versatile writing center. It was thanks to her dedication and expertise that we were able to form interdisciplinary partnerships for writing instruction across the university. She is deeply missed.

    2   Please note that Professor Göpferich's 2019 publications followed her death in 2017.

foster students' academic literacies by transcending the disciplinary boundaries students have experienced during their undergraduate studies (Barrie, 2006). The student group in the present project (n=20) can be regarded as an illustrative example of today's *superdiverse* student populations in higher education (Donahue, 2018) with 14 different native languages, seven different undergraduate disciplinary backgrounds, and English proficiency levels between 4 and 7 on the IELTS scale (British Council, 2018) present in the course. Additionally, there were also a number of English native speakers taking the class.[3]

Based on the wide accessibility for German students as well as for students from abroad, the program can be classified as a hybrid between two modes in which universities introduce English Medium Instruction (EMI) and internationalization into their institutional portfolio: (a) The "internationalization at home modality," as described by Dafouz (2014), is characterized by the introduction of international foci and lecturers into the curriculum; (b) The "student mobility modality" defined for EMI programs by Baker and Hüttner (2017) enables a considerable internationalization of universities' student body. Both of these modalities usually necessitate the switch from local languages of instruction to English as *lingua franca*, as was the case for the program in question here.

The present study was completed collaboratively by two English for specific purposes (ESP) writing instructors and seven discipline-specific lecturers in the life and social sciences in team-teaching partnerships (Lasagabaster, 2018) formed by a top-down mandate during the implementation of a 14-week core course in the program. Importantly, adding to the *superdiversity* of the teaching context was the fact that the discipline-specific lecturers involved in the course also represented a range of different disciplinary, linguistic, and national backgrounds, with each lecturer contributing distinct disciplinary input to the course.

In the interdisciplinary collaboration between the writing instructors and the discipline-specific lecturers, the latter providing input to varying degrees, attitudes towards EMI differed markedly from, e.g., the attitudes among faculty documented by Galloway et al. (2017). Surveying students and lecturers in several universities across China and Japan, the authors reported a substantial mismatch between students' and lecturers' expectations and attitudes towards

---

3   Please see also Dengscherz and Zenger/Pill, this volume, who offer insights into the multilingual, multicultural professional writing that students need to be prepared for in increasingly superdiverse educational environments. In the present contribution, participants were first introduced to multilingual writing strategies in an international context. Allowing students to draw on their full idiosyncratic linguistic repertoire may serve as a steppingstone towards the more advanced, layered multilingual writing processes illustrated in Dengscherz and Zenger/Pill, where personal multilingual writing strategies intersect with multilingual learning environments.

EMI classes. Students conceptualized the instruction delivered to them in English as sites for engaging in English-language-learning (ELL) activities, while lecturers positioned themselves as oblivious or even sceptical towards including ELL opportunities in the content courses they were teaching in English. Findings similar to Galloway et al. (2017) were reported by Airey (2012) for a European science, technology, engineering, and mathematics (STEM) context. Airey (2012) identified commonly held beliefs among the physics lecturers surveyed for the study who taught their courses in English as a foreign language. For instance, the lecturers in Airey (2012) appeared to hold the implicit belief that no particular introduction to *English for physics purposes* was necessary for students even if these students were taking the physics EMI courses as part of non-physics degree programs and might not be familiar with the conventional English discourse in physics courses. Also, the lecturers surveyed in Airey (2012) were mostly skeptical towards introducing students' dominant languages (mostly Swedish) as a valid linguistic resource in an EMI physics classroom. Finally, the lecturers contributing to the data set in Airey (2012) refrained from specifying language learning outcomes for their courses and, accordingly, did not engage in any dialogue with students about the English language requirements of the courses. Similar attitudes among STEM lecturers in other European EMI contexts were reported by Block and Moncada-Colmas (2019) in an interview study. Importantly, the lecturers shared that they themselves would need formal specialized training to position themselves as competent enough to address English language issues in their STEM classrooms, a training that none of the lecturers had received or planned on seeking out (Block & Moncada-Colmas, 2019, p. 13).

Thus, in contrast to findings and positions reported in studies like Galloway et al. (2017), Airey (2012), and Block and Moncada-Colmas (2019), the following shared beliefs and positions for the team-teaching collaboration were established in the present project: First, the course developed in collaboration was clearly designed as a course with an integrating content and language in higher education (ICLHE) framework in mind. As Pecorari has noted (2020), course formats that combine content teaching with some form of language instruction come in many forms and under many designations, among them ICLHE or also content and language integrated learning (CLIL). In comparison to CLIL, ICLHE designs cater to the specific exigencies in post-secondary academic education (Dafouz, 2020). The co-operative teaching approach in the course stands in noticeable contrast to merely "CLIL-ized EMI," criticized adamantly by Block and Moncada-Colmas as

> what happens when [Higher Education] stakeholders—program administrators and lecturers—draw on a naïve theory

of language learning, seemingly based on an under-theorised version of Krashen's (1985) input hypothesis. In effect, they assume that the mere fact of sitting in classrooms in which content is taught in English will lead to the learning of English. (Block & Moncada-Colmas, 2019, p. 3)

In contrast, the ICLHE approach in the present project was clearly aligned with the conception of CLIL put forward by Gustafsson and colleagues (2011) who contend that "CLIL appears to require collaboration not only in materials or curriculum development but also in course design, learning activities, teaching and assessment" (p. 8). The authors stress that CLIL approaches should "be sensitive to where the students are coming from, building on home languages/literacies to transition into content area language/ literacy" (2011, p. 5), specifically the approach taken in the present project.

The team-teaching approach in the present project could be termed *transdisciplinary*, as suggested by Hendricks (2018), since it allowed for "interdisciplinary faculty [to] be granted proactive input into curricular design" (p. 58). However, since each lecturer retained specific evaluative tasks that would not be shared with the writing instructors, a more apt classification for the present project would be *interdisciplinary*. Since lecturers and instructors collaborated mainly in topic choice, material selection, material design, and evaluation, instead of teaching lessons together, the team-teaching partnerships established in the present project can be described a hybrid between two modes of team-teaching suggested by Creese (2005), namely (a) the *temporary withdrawal mode*, in which subject teachers and language teachers inform each other about the material covered and support each other in selecting material and activities, and (b) *observational and advisory support mode*, in which language teachers provide feedback and support to content lecturers on how they can establish more clear-cut language requirements and intended language learning outcomes for their EMI courses, and also on how they can communicate these requirements and intended outcomes more clearly to their students. Accordingly, the present course design was implemented with two-fold intended learning outcomes in place, including subject-matter knowledge and writing knowledge development outcomes.

As a second general position in the collaborative course design, it was decided to introduce students' multiple linguistic backgrounds as potentially valuable resources into the superdiverse EMI course sessions. Adopting this approach was deemed relevant especially for the superdiverse context of the group as a range of empirical investigations have provided support for the idea that students' dominant language, especially for students with lower and intermediate foreign-language proficiency, can serve important self-regulatory functions in students' private and inner speech (cf. De Guerrero, 2018). Private speech is defined as speech that students employ subvocally to guide themselves through cognitively taxing tasks (Ewert, 2010; Jiménez Jiménez, 2015), and that in all probability mirrors their inner speech, which is not actually pronounced. Superior results for bilingual cognitive strategies used by bilingual speakers in comparison to monolingual cognitive strategies have been documented in comparison to monolingual cognitive strategies for non-linguistic tasks (Centeno-Cortés & Jiménez Jiménez, 2004; Van Rinsveld et al., 2016). In a similar vein, using their dominant language for private and probably also inner speech appears to support students' writing performance in a foreign language and can help students perform better on the basis of multilingual writing strategies than on the basis of monolingual writing strategies (Kobayashi & Rinnert, 1992; Uzawa, 1996; Woodall, 2002). Thus, a collaborative multilingual teaching approach was chosen in the present project in accordance with the recommendations by Palmer et al. (2014), where specifically one writing instructor and occasionally the discipline-specific lecturers would (a) model dynamic bilingualism in front of the students in the course by responding to students and to fellow lecturers in English, German, French, Spanish, or Russian, as far as possible, for addressing language, content, as well as administrative issues; (b) instruct and encourage students to draw on their full linguistic repertoires for completing the content- and writing-related assignments in the course; and (c) celebrate in-class interactions in which students spontaneously contributed meta-linguistic comments whenever they realized how their prior knowledge about other languages or writing in general could benefit them when completing the course-specific writing tasks in English as a foreign language.

What students were thus encouraged to accomplish in the interdisciplinary writing context of the course can be termed *adaptive transfer*, which DePalma and Ringer (2011) define as "*the conscious or intuitive process of applying or reshaping learned writing knowledge in order to help students negotiate new and potentially unfamiliar writing situations*" (p. 135; emphasis in the original). This approach was judged by the interdisciplinary collaborators to be particularly relevant for the course in question since a range of students indicated that, after completing their master's degree, they might not necessarily stay in Germany, but instead, e.g., return to the countries where they had completed their primary, secondary, and undergraduate education in a language other than English.

The purpose of the present chapter is twofold. First, the course design including the writing assignments and strategies discussed with the students in the superdiverse course group are presented. The assignments and strategies were designed specifically to help the students (a) differentiate between intradisciplinary and interdisciplinary writing in terms of target audiences in and beyond the university (Gustafsson et al., 2011); (b) draw on their full linguistic repertoire in two or more languages at different times and for different purposes during their English writing processes (Baker, 2003; Canagarajah, 2011); and (c) draw on their individual writing knowledge to establish shared communicative goals and strategies in interdisciplinary collaborative writing projects. The second purpose of the present contribution is to shed light on the developments in the students' individual English-language writing knowledge and in the students' beliefs and attitudes towards writing: English-language source-based academic writing assignments were collected from the students prior to and after the course. Also prior to and after the course, students completed extensive writing-focused surveys, documenting the students' declarative writing knowledge and the students' attitudes towards different concepts in connection with advanced English writing. Based on the writing curriculum implemented in the course, on the texts produced by the students, and on the student surveys, the present contribution discusses how teaching materials and strategies developed in team-teaching partnerships between writing instructors and discipline-specific faculty can (a) cater to student and lecturer groups that are highly diverse in terms of linguistic, cultural, and disciplinary backgrounds, and English-language proficiency levels; and (b) lay the groundwork for the development of professional English writing knowledge in highly diverse student populations.

Project Framework: Course Design of the ICLHE Course

For implementing English writing training in the course, seven discipline-specific lecturers cooperated with two writing instructors from the university's writing center. The course was taught during a regular semester with four hours of instruction per week. The mandatory structure of the course was that of a lecture series, with each lecturer providing different disciplinary input. Different discipline-specific lecturers held 90-minute lectures in English, introducing their specific area of expertise and their current research projects. A range of these lectures were followed by English writing training sessions tailored to the content of each previous lecture. The disciplinary foci of the seven lecturers involved ranged from food security, eco-efficiency, groundwater management, and field spectroscopy to ecosystems services. Five of the seven lecturers had already completed their Ph.D.s and were working on post-doctoral research projects while two lecturers were in the process of completing their Ph.D. degrees. One of the seven lecturers held a position as course coordinator for the present project. All of the lecturers had learned English as a foreign language and described themselves as advanced users and writers. While employed at the university, they had not participated in faculty development courses providing support to faculty teaching in English as a foreign language.

As the first step in the course development, one of the writing instructors provided a substantial online survey[4] to the collaborators serving as a basis for a "transaction space" (cf. Winberg et al., 2013, p. 96). In this "transaction space," discipline-specific lecturers and the writing instructors could articulate and negotiate their understandings of the intended learning outcomes for students in the course. In the online survey, the discipline-specific lecturers indicated in which genres the students enrolled in the interdisciplinary master's degree program should be able to write well in English, and also which genres the lecturers felt students struggled with the most. The survey also asked lecturers to indicate which of five core areas they thought students needed to progress in most substantially in order to meet the communicative standards of the degree program. The five core areas targeted in the survey were *source-based writing, audience awareness, rhetorical writing competence, genre knowledge,* and *linguistic correctness.* The lecturers ordered these concerns in accordance with the priority they thought the core area should have in the interdisciplinary degree curriculum. The writing tasks and approaches implemented in the collaborative course design directly reflect the priorities identified by the discipline-specific lecturers. The discipline-specific lecturers also collaborated with the two writing instructors in a course debriefing meeting (cf. Winberg et al., 2013) to evaluate the course design in a focus group discussion. Thus, the project offers both individual and group "transaction spaces": Session designs in individual collaborations were complemented with a joint debriefing, as a communal "transaction space."

The ICLHE course framework designed by the interdisciplinary faculty team was first implemented in the fall semester of 2018/2019. Table 5.1 illustrates the task types (pre-writing, in-class writing, out-of-class writing, assessment, feedback, revision, meta-cognitive reflection, or collaborative writing) that were used in the six training sessions in the course design. In the remaining weeks of the 14-week semester, lectures and input were provided by faculty who were not involved in the implementation of the writing training. In three of the remaining 14 sessions, students gave oral presentations. Table 5.1 also specifies which tasks were completed monolingually and in which other tasks students were encouraged to draw on their personal multilingual repertoires. Additionally, the table specifies the intended learning outcomes for each training session.

---

4   Thank you to Dr. Janine Murphy for designing this elaborate and versatile instrument.

Table 5.1. Course Design

Writing training: Session 01		
Task type	**Intended learning outcome**	**Task**
Pre-writing monolingual	Ability to gage time needed for • reading • note-taking in source-based English writing tasks	Timed *reading and note-taking tasks* with academic journal articles, discipline-specific and interdisciplinary
Pre-writing monolingual	Ability to identify • readers' genre expectations for **summaries** of specialized articles • the level of detail and the range of specialized vocabulary appropriate to use in **summaries** for different clients depending on the clients' professional background and the clients' inquiry • relevant types of information for **summaries** and where to find these types in specialized articles	Composing and discussing *written client profiles* based on fictitious client scenarios
In-class writing monolingual	Ability to choose between 12 paraphrasing strategies for article **summaries**, e.g., • listing • condensing, etc.	*Discussion and revision* of sections from the students' pre-semester **summaries** of English academic articles
Writing training: Session 02		
Task type	**Intended learning outcome**	**Task**
Pre-writing multilingual + In-class writing monolingual	Ability to switch between L1 and FL for different sub-processes of English source-based writing, e.g., • note-taking • planning • formulating, etc.	*Summary* of main findings in an English research article *Description* of main observations illustrated in figures and charts
Revision multilingual	Ability to draw on the L1 in English revision processes, e.g., for • grammar assessment • content assessment, etc.	*Discussion and revision* of **summaries** of research findings provided by the lecturers
Meta-cognitive mono/multi	Ability to determine individually which language/s serve/s best for which sub-process of source-based writing	*Critical reflection* writing task, documenting perceived advantages & disadvantages of multilingual writing strategies

Writing training: Session 03		
Task type	**Intended learning outcome**	**Task**
Pre-writing multilingual	Ability to draw on full multilingual idiolect irrespective of sub-process of writing, e.g., by • switching • mixing • meshing For a differentiation between language switching, mixing, and meshing, please see Michael-Luna and Canagarajah (2007).	*Annotation* of English academic articles, identification of CARS components
Collaborative mono/multi	Ability to draw on full multilingual idiolect irrespective of sub-process of writing, but respectful of interlocutor	*Discussion and revision* of article annotations

Writing training: Session 04		
Task type	**Intended learning outcome**	**Task**
Assessment mono/multi	Ability to identify and remedy ambiguous formulations in research reports	*Discussion* of **summaries** of research findings provided by the lectures
Pre-writing multilingual + In-class writing monolingual	Ability to • identify readers' genre expectations for **summaries** of specialized articles • establish text structures & use connectors in **summaries** for different clients depending on the clients' professional background and the clients' inquiry	Composing and discussing *written client profiles* based on client simulations Composing text *outlines*
Out-of-class writing monolingual + Collaborative mono/multi	Ability to • adapt **summary** writing strategies to the composition of funding applications • organize & monitor collaborative writing processes • compose & revise texts in groups	Composing *annotated outlines* of funding proposals for interdisciplinary boards

Writing training: Session 05		
Task type	**Intended learning outcome**	**Task**
Pre-writing multilingual	Ability to understand and apply findings from applied linguistics research to • assess & optimize English writing processes and products • assess & optimize multilingual writing strategies in English writing processes	*Annotation* of English academic articles from other disciplines *Documentation* of applicable multilingual writing strategies
In-class writing monolingual + Peer feedback multilingual	Ability to • differentiate between higher-order and lower-order concerns in peer feedback processes • deploy one's own multilingual resources in peer-to-peer discussions of English texts	Composing *memos* Giving and receiving *feedback* in bilingual pairs
Assessment mono/multi	Ability to • identify appropriate sources and publications in accordance with specific writing purposes • avoid different forms of plagiarism	*Classifying* source types *Classifying* types of plagiarism
Pre-writing monolingual	Ability to identify • readers' genre expectations for **summaries** of specialized articles • the level of detail and the range of specialized vocabulary appropriate to use in **summaries** for different clients depending on the clients' professional background and the clients' inquiry • relevant types of information for **summaries** and where to find these types in specialized articles	Composing and discussing *written client profiles* based on client simulations
Out-of-class writing monolingual + Collaborative mono/multi	Ability to • adapt **summary** writing strategies to the composition of funding applications • organize & monitor collaborative writing processes • compose & revise texts in groups	Composing & revising *funding proposal drafts* for interdisciplinary boards Using written & oral feedback for proposal revisions

Writing training: Session 06		
Task type	Intended learning outcome	Task
Pre-writing mono/multi	Ability to • make use of oral feedback for the revision of extensive texts produced in collaboration. • organize & monitor collaborative revision processes • revise texts in groups	Composing & revising *complete funding proposals* for interdisciplinary boards Using written & oral feedback for proposal revisions

Five of the total of six writing training sessions followed immediately after the lectures given by the discipline-specific lecturers and lasted between 90 and 180 minutes. In the last of the six writing training sessions, students received oral feedback on their writing. Each of the writing training sessions comprised different combinations of *pre-writing tasks, in-class writing tasks*, and *collaborative out-of-class writing tasks*. The tasks were based either on journal articles that the discipline-specific lecturers had provided to the writing instructor to design writing tasks with or on journal articles that the writing instructor had suggested to the discipline-specific lecturers in connection with their research foci.

Session 01 of the writing training sessions was dedicated to discussing the strengths and weaknesses of the students' pre-semester summaries, and to clarifying appropriate summarizing strategies for interdisciplinary writing. In this session, the writing approach was still a monolingual one.

Session 02 marked the first introduction of the *translanguaging* approach as championed by Baker (2003), among others. In this approach, specific functions are assigned to specific languages in the classroom, i.e., by distinguishing clearly between input and output language for source-based writing tasks. For example, as their first introduction to multilingual writing strategies, students were given two types of English source material, i.e., a short excerpt from an academic article as well as a figure illustrating findings from an empirical study. Students were asked to formulate summaries of the main observations detailed in the article excerpt as well as of the findings illustrated in the figure. For their summaries, students were asked to use their dominant language, i.e., the language in which students felt most flexible, comfortable, and confident. Importantly, students were told not to switch between, mix, or mesh languages, but to remain in their dominant language for writing. Students who had indicated that English was one of their dominant languages were asked to compose their formulations in a noticeably less formal register than they would usually be expected to use in academic settings. The students who shared dominant languages with other students in the class were encouraged to compare formulations and discuss the excerpt and the figure in their dominant language together. The subsequent joint discussion of the observations and findings was held with all students in the course in English.

A complementary form of *translanguaging* was introduced in Session 03. Students were asked, as a pre-writing assignment, to use their dominant language for annotating an English journal article. As a basis for the annotation, students were introduced to the CARS model that would help students recognize a range of different textual moves that are used in academic writing and that can be used in funding proposal writing to articulate (a) the research or the funded projects already available in a certain field of expertise, (b) the gaps or shortcomings of the research and funded projects that are already available, and, importantly, (c) the findings and projects the writers wish to produce or accomplish with their own contributions to the field (Swales, 1990). Students read an introduction from a research report that one of the discipline-specific lecturers had published as a co-author in a joint project; subsequently, students identified the CARS moves in the text. As a *translanguaging* strategy, students were introduced to the translanguaging approach suggested by Canagarajah (2011) and by García (2009), namely "intermingl[ing] linguistic features that have hereto been administratively or linguistically assigned to a particular language or language variety" (p. 51). Instead of formulating their text annotations exclusively in their dominant language, students were told to use whatever type of language use felt most comfortable and cognitively economical to them; students were allowed to switch between languages and to mix or mesh languages as they saw fit. Whenever students wanted to discuss passages from the text with other students sharing the same linguistic repertoire, students were encouraged to also switch, mix, and mesh in their conversations where they saw fit. The subsequent joint discussion of the English article was held with all students in the course in English.

In session 04, the writing instructor illustrated how the summarizing strategies students had been using with full articles, with excerpts, and with figures, were to be applied in the out-of-class collaborative writing tasks. The writing instructor explained the task in English and in German and the explanations were repeated by one of the discipline-specific lecturers in Russian. Whenever possible, the writing instructor also used French or Spanish with individual course participants.

Session 05 started with introducing students to two texts chosen not from their fields of study, but from applied linguistics. First, students were given the opportunity to familiarize themselves with a theoretical text on the expected benefits of multilingual writing strategies for FL text comprehension and

FL text production (cf. Göpferich, 2017). Subsequently, students read the findings from a study conducted among EFL writers where the EFL texts that the study participants had produced in their dominant language first and subsequently translated into English received significantly better ratings than texts that the students had produced directly in the foreign language (cf. Uzawa, 1996). Thus, students in the present course discussed how using their dominant language during EFL reading and writing processes could help them allot their cognitive capacities more effectively, e.g., by completing pre-writing activities in their dominant instead of a foreign language.

A central pre-writing task used repeatedly in the writing training was the written *client profile task*. This task was integrated into sessions 01, 04, and 05, as well as referenced repeatedly in the task descriptions and guides for the summaries and the collaborative writing project. The client profile task was also referenced in the written and oral feedback that students received on their writing. In this task, students were given different scenario descriptions in which different fictitious clients reached out to them and asked for summaries of the source material that students were working with. The fictitious clients represented a range of different disciplinary backgrounds and specified different foci and purposes for the summaries that they requested. Students had to discuss which kind of background knowledge they could expect the different clients to have, which level of specialized or general vocabulary would be appropriate for the clients, and where to find the specific information that the clients were asking for in the sources that the students worked with.

In the present project, the *summary genre* was chosen as the central genre for the writing training. The summary task was agreed upon since it represents a written version of what Cheng and Feyten (2015) term "legitimate peripheral participation" (p. 8). The task comprises *legitimate* reading and writing activities, such as extrapolating relevant information from legitimate specialized journal articles and presenting the information to a particular target audience; the summarization task is *peripheral* in that it does not conform to the standards set for actual scientific papers and publications, but instead is tailored to the students' current semester and academic abilities. Lastly, the summarization task is *participatory* as it constitutes direct written engagement with the research basis of the interdisciplinary degree program. Also, the summary task was chosen because Graham and Perin (2007) report the highest effect-size in terms of fostering writing knowledge development for writing interventions that specifically train summary writing knowledge. The overall rationale for selecting the summary genre was to help students learn how to present specialized literature to interdisciplinary readerships in a comprehensible and concise manner. Thus, students composed individual summaries as well as summaries that constituted the building blocks for their collaborative interdisciplinary writing projects. The *collaborative writing projects* built directly on the summary tasks discussed with the students in the writing training, as students had to summarize both theoretical as well as empirical publications in order to articulate the interdisciplinary backbone of extensive funding proposals in groups of students with different disciplinary backgrounds.

The course coordinator collaborated with the writing instructor in designing guiding documents that would help students revise and expand their texts in an iterative process. The guiding documents (a) identified the main points that the students had to summarize in the different text drafts, (b) provided specific tasks that students needed to complete in writing to argue their point, and (c) contained examples of well-formulated as well as ill-formulated text sections. Table 5.2 provides a section of the instructions that students were given in the guiding document for revising their initial drafts to create further drafts.

Table 5.2. Section from the Documents Designed by the Writing Instructor in Collaboration with the Course Coordinator

Focus	Specific Objectives
Overall task	**Summarize** the specific objectives of the project = What is necessary to achieve the main objective? Specific objectives should be achieved within the project duration.
Specific tasks	*Consult* the feedback that you have received on the initial draft.
	Revise your descriptions of your specific objectives in your initial draft.
	Make sure that your descriptions of the specific objectives EXACTLY fit your main objective stated earlier in your initial draft.
	Indicate your sources with precision.
Examples	NOT: "Each nutritional base value will be addressed." 💀💀💀
	INSTEAD: "There are in total xx nutritional base values not met by the population in the region (SOURCE). For the base value of yy, this means that people lack bb (SOURCE). Accordingly, the supply of bb needs to be stabilized. The next problematic base value is cc (SOURCE). Here, people lack hh (SOURCE). Accordingly, the supply of hh needs to be increased in the target region." 👍👍👍

For the individual as well as the collaborative writing tasks, the students received written feedback from the writing instructor focused on the appropriate use of source material, the comprehensibility of the texts for the intended interdisciplinary readership, the lexical precision and structural coherence of the texts, the adherence to genre conventions, as well as the linguistic correctness of the texts. The discipline-specific lecturers provided oral and written feedback on the students' drafts by assessing the proposed projects' feasibility and persuasiveness. The lecturers and the writing instructor involved in the course design coordinated their feedback to the students and agreed that a clear division of responsibilities would be communicated to the students: Students received feedback on the comprehensibility, lexical precision, register, style, and linguistic correctness only from the writing instructor. The content lecturers assessed and provided feedback mainly on the scope, practicality, and feasibility of the students' projects.

Data Collection

Data were collected prior to and after the semester, in the form of individual English summaries, and responses to a self-assessment survey as well as to two beliefs-and-attitudes surveys. The collaborative team assumed that students would develop a more nuanced view of the purpose of their writing, upon participating in writing training that was (a) closely linked to the discipline-specific lectures; (b) specifically focused on text comprehensibility for interdisciplinary readerships; (c) inclusive of writing-to-learn recommendations; and (d) sensitive to the individual students' multilingual profiles. Their learning might also translate into improved text quality (cf. Crosthwaite, 2017). Table 5.3 offers a chronological overview of the phases of data collection in the present project.

Participants

In the present project, twenty students in their first year in the interdisciplinary management master's degree program enrolled in the mandatory course, seven of them female, and thirteen male, with a mean age of 25.6 years (SD=3.7 years). Eighteen of them had learned English as a foreign language, while two indicated that they had been raised as bilinguals from birth and that they regarded English as one of their native languages. On average, the EFL students in the course had been learning English as a foreign language for 12 years (SD= 4.2 years), with two of the students having started learning English as recently as three and six years ago. As an English language proficiency test, the online assessment offered by the university's language center was administered prior to the start of the course; this test is a c-test, a timed online cloze-test in which students are presented with a number of texts in order of increasing difficulty in which the second half of every second word is deleted and students have to fill in the blanks (see Eckes & Grotjahn, 2006, for a detailed analysis of the c-test assessment logic). In the course, there was no significant correlation between the English language proficiency score achieved in the online c-test and the number of years for which the students had been learning English as a foreign language (r_s=-.052, p >.05, n = 18). Table 5.4 illustrates the range of languages and educational backgrounds represented in the group of course participants, with the number of participants represented in parentheses. English proficiency levels are indicated in terms of IELTS score equivalents.

Table 5.3. Chronological Order of Data Collection

Data Collection: One Week Prior to the First Session (PRE)	
Data collection instrument	Resulting data type
Individual *summary* task	English summaries of ca. 600 words each
Self-assessment *survey*: English writing knowledge	(a) Source-based writing (6 closed items) (b) Audience awareness (6 closed items) (c) Coherent writing (8 closed items) (d) Genre knowledge (3 closed items) (e) Linguistic correctness & stylistic appropriateness (6 closed items)
Self-report *survey*: beliefs and attitudes towards writing	(a) Usefulness of Academic Writing for Writing in the Professions (max. no. of points: 24) (b) Using writing as a learning tool (max. no. of points: 32)
Self-report *survey*: beliefs and attitudes towards multilingual writing strategies	Usefulness & appropriateness of multilingual writing strategies in academic writing processes (max. no. of points: 44)
English *proficiency* test	c-test results expressed in IELTS scores
Data Collection: Final Week of the Semester (POST)	
Data collection instrument	Resulting data type
Individual **summary** task	English **summaries** of ca. 600 words each
Self-assessment *survey*: English academic writing knowledge	(a) Source-based writing (6 closed items) (b) Audience awareness (6 closed items) (c) Coherent writing (8 closed items) (d) Genre knowledge (3 closed items) (e) Linguistic correctness & stylistic appropriateness (6 closed items)
Self-report *survey*: beliefs and attitudes towards writing	(a) Usefulness of Academic Writing for Writing in the Professions (max. no. of points: 24) (b) Using writing as a learning tool (max. no. of points: 32)
Self-report *survey*: beliefs and attitudes towards multilingual writing strategies	Usefulness & appropriateness of multilingual writing strategies in academic writing processes (max. no. of points: 44)

Table 5.4. Participant Characteristics

Native languages	Russian (4), English (2), Mandarin Chinese (2), Persian (2), Spanish (2), Amharic (1), Azerbaijani (1), German (1), Indonesian (1), Tamazight (1), Tatar (1), Turkish (1), Urdu (1), Vietnamese (1)
Bachelor's degrees	Business and economics (10), environmental studies and agriculture (4), social sciences (4), legal studies (1), history (1)
Languages of instruction: undergraduate degree	Russian (5), English (4), Mandarin Chinese (2), Persian (2), Arabic (1), French (1), German (1), Spanish (1), Tatar (1), Urdu (1), Vietnamese (1)
Country of instruction: undergraduate degree	Russia (4), Afghanistan (1), Azerbaijan (1), Belarus (1), Brazil (1), Cameroon (1), China (1), Colombia (1), Germany (1), India (1), Indonesia (1), Iran (1), Morocco (1), Pakistan (1), Poland (1), Turkey (1), Vietnam (1)
Results in English proficiency test	IELTS 7/proficient English users (4)
	IELTS 6/upper-intermediate English users (6)
	IELTS 5/lower-intermediate English users (5)
	IELTS 4/basic English users (3)
	Additionally, two of the 20 students taking the course self-identified as native speakers of English.

None of the students had ever been diagnosed with any language-related disorder or learning disability. Out of the twenty students in the class, three indicated in the survey that they had taken bilingual classes during secondary education, combining either English with Urdu or Persian with German. Six students had completed their bachelor's degree in a language other than the language they grew up speaking at home. Twelve of the students indicated that they had had no formal training in either translation or interpreting, while eight students indicated that they had received at least some training in either translation or interpreting.

Data Collection Instrument: Individual English Summary Task

Students were asked to summarize English journal articles for interdisciplinary readerships. The summary was well-suited as the genre of the pre- and post-tests as one can perform a more or less clear comparison of what the writers might have wanted to express and what they eventually formulated in their text: summary writing, as stated by Byrnes (2011),

> bypasses the dilemma for L2 writing research of determining what an author intended to mean in the first place.

Though that dilemma can never be entirely removed, the task of summary writing proves a sufficiently knowable environment of objectively stable criteria—derived from the source text—to investigate the writer's meaning-wording choices not just in terms of occurrence or non-occurrence but in terms of the nature and significance of either of these options. (p. 144)

For the writing task prior to the first session and after the last session of the course, the writing instructor and the discipline-specific course coordinator selected two academic articles topically suited to the content of the course, one article each for the pre- and post-test on the basis of which students' individual writing knowledge were assessed in the summary writing task. The following measures were taken to ensure that the original articles were equal in terms of a range of key parameters. Both the discipline-specific course coordinator and the writing instructor had to agree that the articles would be equal in terms of three critical parameters:

1. *Content fit*: the articles had to discuss one of the topics covered in the lectures offered in the mandatory in-class sessions of the course.
2. *Representativeness*: the articles had to be representative of the type of source material that students were expected to use for the summaries in the written group proposal.
3. *Familiarity*: the articles had to be chosen from specialized journals in which one or more of the discipline-specific lectures involved in the collaborative design of the course had already published.

Both articles were roughly equal in terms of number of words, average number of words per sentence, average number of syllables per word, and additional parameters such as the Flesch Reading Ease Score, as listed in Table 5.5.

Table 5.5. Measures of Equality for the Journal Articles Used in the Pre- and Post-Tests

Parameter	Pre-test article	Post-test article
Number of tables	4	4
Number of images	4	4
Number of words	6,700	6,000
Average number of words per sentence	25.53	26.92
Average number of syllables per word	1.77	1.79

Parameter	Pre-test article	Post-test article
Gunning Fog Index The Gunning Fog Index is calculated based on the number of words comprising one or two syllables and the number of words comprising more than two syllables in a text (Kincaid et al., 1975).	17.42	18.00
Coleman Liau Index The Coleman Liau Index is computed on the basis of the average number of words per sentence and the average number of syllables per word (Kincaid et al., 1975).	13.90	14.22
Automated Readability Index The Automated Readability Index is computed on the basis of the average number of words per sentence and the average number of strokes per word in a text (Kincaid et al., 1975).	16.03	16.92
SMOG The SMOG Grading is calculated based on the number of words of three or more syllables in a text (McLaughlin, 1969).	16.09	16.89
Flesch Reading Ease Score The Flesch Reading Ease Score is computed on the basis of the average word length in syllables and the average number of words per sentence in a text (Flesch, 1948). Texts with a Flesch Reading Ease Score equal or lower to 30 are classified as "Very difficult," i.e., "scientific" (1948, p. 230).	30.31	27.92

From both articles, the abstracts were removed so that students would not use them as examples for their own summaries. Additionally, the students themselves were asked immediately after submitting the post-test summary to compare the article used for the post-semester writing task with the article that was the basis for the pre-semester writing task concerning the following six parameters:

1. *Perceived text length*: students were not asked to actually count the words in the different documents, but to indicate whether they had perceived the two texts to be of equal length;
2. *Reading effort*: students were asked whether they felt that they had to put an equal amount of effort intro reading the text prior to the semester as they had into reading the text after the semester;
3. *Summarizing effort*: students were asked to indicate whether they felt they had to put an equal amount of effort into summarizing the

article they worked with prior to the semester as they had to put into summarizing the article they worked with after the semester;
4. *Difficulty of vocabulary*: students were asked to indicate whether they felt that both texts contained an equal amount and range of difficult vocabulary;
5. *Relevance*: students indicated whether they perceived both texts to be equally relevant for the course topic; and finally,
6. *Personal interest*: students were asked to indicate whether they had found both texts equally interesting.

In designing the writing task itself and specifically the written task instructions that students had to observe, the following five criteria were applied in accordance with Bachmann and Becker-Mrotzek (2010) to make the writing task instructions maximally comprehensible and accessible to the students:

1. *The final text's function was specified in the task description*: it was made clear that the students had to produce a summary serving a purely informative function without interpretative, persuasive, or evaluative elements;
2. *The readership for the final text was specified in the task description*: students were asked to compose their summary for fellow students in the same interdisciplinary degree program who had not yet enrolled in the core course and had not read the academic article that students were asked to summarize;
3. *The intended impact or outcome was specified in the task description*: it was explicitly stated that the prospective interdisciplinary readers, after reading the students' summaries, should be well-informed about (a) the hypothesis undergirding the study detailed in the academic article, (b) the empirical testing procedure and the data collected to verify the authors' hypothesis, (c) the observations that the authors reported, and (d) the specific conclusions that the authors drew based on their observations in light of their initial hypothesis;
4. *The task description was tailored to the students' assumed general knowledge, i.e., genre conventions*: a list of the specific features of academic summaries was provided to the participants so that they would be aware of, e.g., citation conventions.
5. *The task description comprised linguistic specifications*: the expected text length, the level of formality, and the required textual structure were indicated in the task description. Students were also explicitly informed that they were not allowed to use direct quotations, but that they had to explain the study entirely in their own words.

Students also completed (a) an online self-assessment survey concerning their English writing knowledge; (b) an online self-report survey on their beliefs and attitudes towards improving their professional English writing knowledge; (c) an online self-report survey on their beliefs and attitudes towards using multilingual writing strategies; and (d) an online English proficiency test. With the exception of the English proficiency test, all data collection instruments were used again immediately after students had completed the course, in the second round of data collection.

Text Quality Assessment

The text quality assessment for the study was focused on the summaries that students produced prior to and after the course. In the present team-teaching design, it was decided to forgo assessing the final funding proposal together mainly for workload reasons (for a discussion of common pitfalls in team-teaching partnerships, including the negotiation of workload, see Lasagabaster, 2018). Each of the summaries produced prior to and after the semester was assessed by two independent raters using a five-point scale (1 = "excellent"; 2 = "good"; 3 = "average"; 4 = "sufficient"; 5 = "insufficient"), first focusing on the overall quality of the complete text and assigning a holistic rating, and subsequently with an analytical text quality scheme comprising eight different parameters of text quality, provided in Table 5.6. For both, the holistic assessment and the assessment for eight sub-parameters, raters were instructed to base their evaluation on the task description that the students received for the summary task. In the task description, the purpose and the intended audience were explicitly specified. See Table 5.6 for the eight parameters the raters used.

All raters involved had substantial experience in text feedback, editing, and proof-reading. In two separate training rounds, raters received the task description students had been working with, a model summary of each of the academic articles that the students had summarized, as well as a number of summaries with the rating schemes already completed. The two independent raters were given the opportunity to ask individual questions and the responses were collected in a written training summary. Each rater was given several training summaries to rate and received feedback on each of the training rounds by the researcher. After the final training round, the two raters had reached the following levels of interrater agreement as indicated by Cohen's kappa: *holistic*: $\kappa = .874$, $p < .0005$; *completeness & accuracy* $\kappa = .676$, $p < .0005$; *focus*: $\kappa = .504$, $p < .0005$; *macrostructural coherence* $\kappa = .637$, $p < .0005$; *microstructural coherence* $\kappa = .776$, $p < .000$; *lexical precision* $\kappa = .729$, $p < .0005$;

stylistic appropriateness κ = .814, p < .0005; *source use* κ = .50, p < .000; and *linguistic correctness* κ = .586, p < .000. Cohen's kappa was chosen as an indicator of interrater agreement as it "indicates the proportion of agreements between two raters after adjusting for chance agreements" (Tinsley & Weiss, 2000, p. 112). The values for Cohen's kappa that are commonly deemed acceptable in studies where two raters provide ratings independently from one another usually are κ ≥ 0.65 (cf. Lesterhuis et al., 2018). Accordingly, the kappa values for interrater agreement achieved in the present study for the *holistic* rating, for *completeness & accuracy*, for *microstructural coherence*, for *lexical precision*, and for *stylistic appropriateness* are within the realm of the values accepted in the literature. In contrast, acceptable values for the agreement concerning *focus*, *macrostructural coherence*, *source use*, and *linguistic correctness* were not achieved. Accordingly, different training rounds will be implemented in subsequent installments of the project.

Table 5.6. Parameters for Text Quality Assessment

Parameter	Guiding questions
Completeness & accuracy	Does the summary include all the information needed by the interdisciplinary target audience as detailed in the task description? Is the information in the summary correct?
Focus	Does the summary focus on the relevant information specifically asked for in the task description? Does the summary contain irrelevant details that might be misleading for an interdisciplinary readership?
Macrostructural coherence	Does the argument in the summary progress clearly from a hypothesis to a design description, to a description of the observations and, finally, to the conclusions drawn based on the observations? Does the summary establish a clear connection between the closing sentences and the study rationale established in the beginning of the summary?
Microstructural coherence	Are the sentences in the summary ordered in a comprehensible manner? Does the summary contain appropriate connectors to link the sentences with one another?
Lexical precision	Does the student use precise and unambiguous formulations? Has specialized terminology been appropriately explained for an interdisciplinary readership?
Stylistic appropriateness	Is the register of the summary sufficiently formal for the interdisciplinary professional setting specified in the task description?
Source use	Is the source article indicated in accordance with the style sheets commonly used in the interdisciplinary degree program? Are prepositions like *according to source* used correctly?
Linguistic accuracy	Is the summary correct in terms of grammar, spelling, and punctuation?

The ratings were completed anonymously, and raters were not aware of the pre/post-design of the study. For the values in the actual rating in which the raters did not agree, the mean value was calculated for those ratings where the raters disagreed by merely one level. For the remaining disagreements, a third rater, in this case the researcher, adjudicated between the two disagreeing raters.

Data Collection Instrument: The Self-assessment Survey

The self-assessment survey for the students enrolled in the course was based on the survey that the lecturers had completed as the first step in the course design and comprised three components. The survey asked students to (a) pick genres from an open list that the students felt they could already write well in English; (b) rate their overall English academic writing ability on a five-point scale ("Unable to assess"; "Basic"; "Intermediate"; "Advanced"; "Mastery"); and (c) use a six-point scale ("Unable to assess"; "Unsure"; "Basic"; "Intermediate"; "Advanced"; "Mastery") to self-assess their *source-based writing* ability, their *audience awareness*, their ability to *write coherently*, their *genre knowledge*, and their ability to produce *linguistically correct and stylistically appropriate* texts in English. For assessing their abilities, students were given between six to eight parameters per component to self-assess. The exact number of items per core area is indicated in Table 5.3. For instance, the core area of *source-based writing* was represented through items like "I can use sources to generate my own ideas," while *audience awareness* was captured in items like "I can identify my readers' expectations." Items like "I can establish an outline for my texts" represented the core area of *coherent writing*, and *genre knowledge* was represented with items like "I can select appropriate genres for specific purposes." Finally, the core area of *linguistic correctness & stylistic appropriateness* was represented in the self-assessment survey through items like "I can use a broad range of appropriate vocabulary."

Data Collection Instrument: The Beliefs-and-attitudes Surveys

The beliefs-and-attitudes survey comprised three components designed to measure (a) students' beliefs about the relevance of advanced writing knowledge for their future professional lives (*writing in the professions*); (b) students' attitudes towards using writing as a learning tool (*writing-to-learn*); and (c) students' attitudes towards using multilingual writing strategies (*multilingual writing strategies*). Students were given between nine and eleven closed items per component and had to indicate their opinion on a four-point, bipolar Likert-scale ("I strongly disagree"; "I disagree"; "I agree"; "I strongly agree"). For each of the survey components, a maximum number of points could be achieved by completely agreeing to each of the items in the section, indicating a high degree of interest and a positive attitude towards *writing in the professions*, *writing-to-learn*, or *multilingual writing strategies*. The component *writing in the professions* (maximum number of points: 24) was represented with items like "Formulations from my academic texts will also be useful for my texts in my future profession." Items like "Writing helps me organize my ideas about the topics from my field of studies" constituted the component *writing-to-learn* (maximum number of points: 32). Finally, items like "During my English writing processes, I use all of my languages for my reflections" represented the *multilingual writing strategies* component (maximum number of points: 44) in the beliefs-and-attitudes survey.

Findings

Of the 20 students enrolled in the course, 19 completed the c-test prior to the semester (one student of the two self-identifying as English native speakers did not complete the test) as well as the self-assessment survey prior to and after the semester. Among these 19 students, one did not hand in the post-semester summary and did not complete the post-semester beliefs-and-attitudes survey.

Student perceptions of the original article

A total of 15 students submitted their comparisons for the articles used in the pre- and post-writing task. Although the articles can be said to have been more or less equal based on the parameters listed in Table 5, a more substantial variety of impressions can be documented in the students' responses, as documented in Table 5.7.

Table 5.7. Number of Students Per Response Option: Comparing the Pre/Post Articles

Parameter	Equal	PRE	POST	Total
Which article was perceived to be longer?	6	8	1	15
Which article necessitated a higher reading effort?	6	8	1	15
Which article necessitated a higher summarizing effort?	6	8	1	15
Which article contained more difficult terminology?	7	8	/	15
Which article was more relevant for the course?	13	1	1	15
Which article was of higher personal interest?	5	5	5	15

The most obvious agreement among the students can be seen for students' view on the texts' relevance for the overall course theme: most students agreed that the studies reported in the articles the students were working with corresponded well to the overall course design and the topics discussed in the course. The most substantial variation can be seen in students' personal interest: the same number of students found both articles equally interesting as the number of students who found the first the most interesting or the number of students who found the second more interesting than the first.

Text quality

The text quality of the summaries composed prior to and after the semester was assessed first *holistically*, and subsequently separately for *completeness, focus, macrostructural coherence, microstructural coherence, lexical precision, stylistic appropriateness, source use,* and *linguistic correctness*. Table 5.8 shows the percentage of students who improved the quality of their EFL texts, ordered by parameters of text quality.

Table 5.8. Percentage of Students Who Improved, Ordered by Parameters*

Macrostructural Coherence	Source use	Lexical Precision	Microstructural Coherence	Stylistic Appropriateness
61.0%	50.0%*	33.0%	33.0%	33.0%
Linguistic Correctness	Completeness	Focus	Holistic	
28.0%	11.0%	6.0%	6.0%	

*Planned comparisons showed that only the difference between pre- and post-scores for source use reached statistical significance (pre mean = 4.4; post mean = 3.7; exact Wilcoxon-test $z = -2.234$, $p = .01$, $n = 18$; $r = .5$).

The two parameters for which most students improved were *macrostructural coherence* and *source use*. This means that 61 percent of the students were able to convey the argumentative structure of the original article in their summaries better after the course than before. Likewise, 50 percent of the students improved their ability to cite and paraphrase purposefully and to indicate their source where needed. On average, students progressed from a sufficient level to a lower-intermediate level in their ability to use and indicate sources appropriately.

The Self-assessment Survey

In the self-assessment survey, most students indicated that they felt their abilities in the core areas had improved, while a lower percentage of students had become somewhat more critical of their own writing knowledge. For instance, as Figure 5.1 illustrates, most students felt that their abilities had improved particularly where *audience awareness* was concerned. Among the students who felt they had improved their ability to understand and adhere to audience expectations, and to tailor their texts to the characteristics of specific readerships, two were basic English speakers, three were lower-intermediate, and four were upper-intermediate English speakers. All of the proficient speakers (n=5) and one of the native speakers felt they had progressed from their initial competence level. In contrast, 16%, i.e., three of the students indicated in the post-semester survey that they had realized their abilities in understanding and adhering to audience expectations and tailoring their texts to the characteristics of specific readerships were not as well developed as they had supposed at the beginning of the semester.

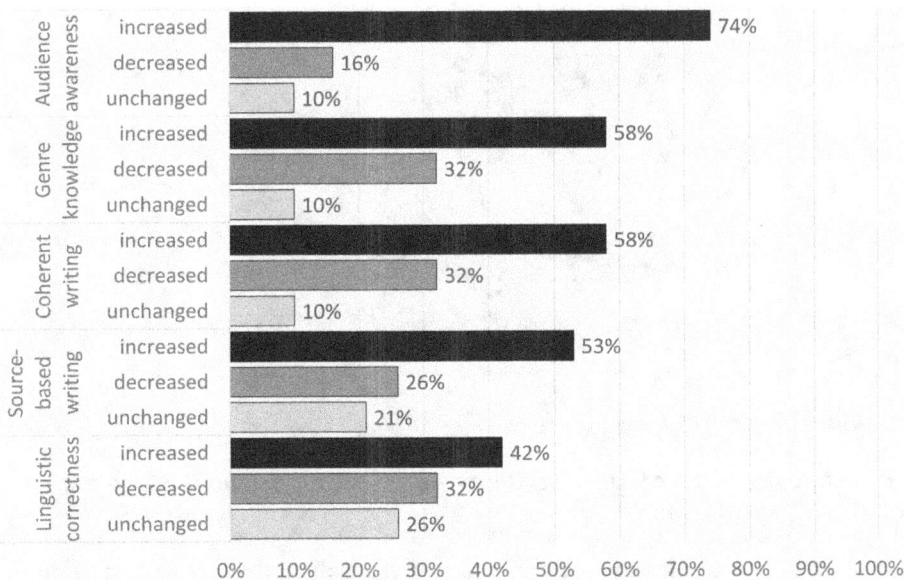

Figure 5.1. Percentage of students who indicated that their confidence in their own writing knowledge had either increased, decreased, or remained unchanged; ordered by the five themes in the self-assessment survey.

The difference between the average score prior to the semester and the average score after the semester for *audience awareness* proved to be statistically significant in a planned comparison (pre mean =1.8; post mean = 2.2; exact Wilcoxon-test z = -2.835, p = .001, n= 19; r = .65). On average, students felt that their ability to understand their audience and cater to their audience's needs had progressed from a basic to an intermediate level during the semester. Additionally, more than half of the students indicated that their ability to identify and adhere to *genre* conventions had improved, as well as their ability to establish and signal argumentative coherence in their English writing.

The Beliefs-and-Attitudes Surveys

As can be seen in Figure 5.2, the majority of students in the course indicated a shift in opinion in what concerns the *Relevance of Writing for their Profession*, *Writing-to-learn*, and *Multilingual Writing Strategies*.

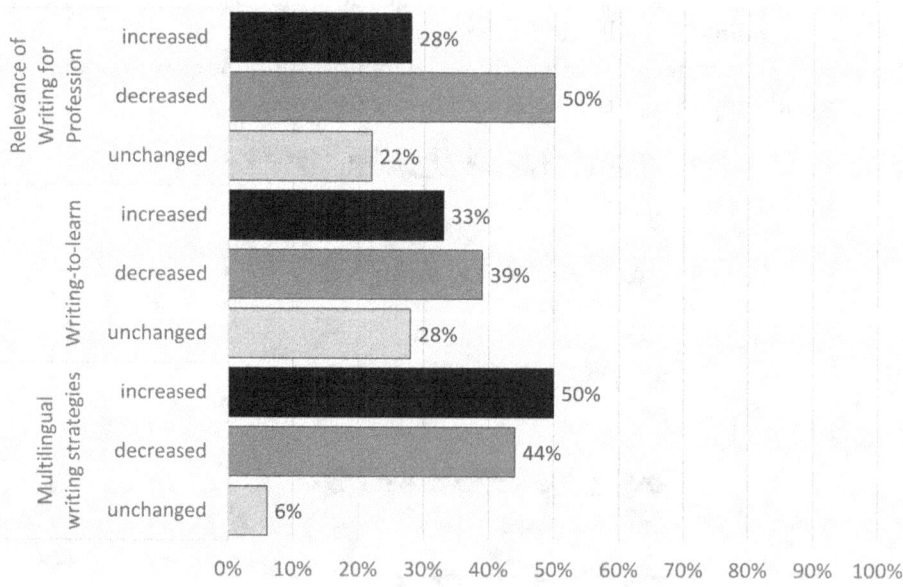

Figure 5.2. Percentage of students whose attitude did/did not change.

Interestingly, most of the writers who had come to regard writing at the university as *less* relevant for their future workplace than they had thought it to be at the beginning of the semester were at a lower-intermediate level of English proficiency. Conversely, the students indicating at the end of the course that they thought writing in academic contexts to be *more* relevant for their prospective workplaces than they had thought it to be prior to taking the writing-intensive course were at the upper-intermediate, proficient, or even native level. A differentiation between the closed items contributing to the relevance score reveals that, while most students came to think that text production would constitute a substantial part of their professional lives and that formulations from their university writing would be helpful for them in their professional text production, most students agreed that the specific texts produced and read at university (summaries and scientific articles) were not what they expected to resurface in their professional text production later on.

Concerning the use of writing for *writing-to-learn* purposes, shifts in attitude were observed among the majority of students taking the course in that over 70 percent of students expressed a different attitude towards writing as a learning tool after than prior to the semester. Thirty-nine percent of the students were less inclined, while 33 percent were more inclined to use writing as a learning strategy after having taken the course.

With regard to the use of *multilingual writing strategies*, most students, i.e., 94 percent, changed their attitude and became either *more* or *less* inclined to make use of their full linguistic repertoire in their English writing processes. Importantly, 50 percent indicated that their interest in multilingual writing strategies had actually increased at the end of the semester.

Discussion

Overall, the results documented in the present study in terms of text quality development and shifts in self-assessments as well as in beliefs and attitudes need to be qualified as *mixed* for each instrument of data collection.

Developments in EFL text quality

It is interesting to note that a substantial percentage of students wrote higher-quality texts in terms of, e.g., *source use* at the end of the semester than at the beginning while the percentage of students who improved for the other parameters of text quality was less noteworthy. The students in the present project, eager to avoid plagiarism, started indicating and presenting their sources more carefully; at the same time, students' taking more risks when trying to make their own formulations as unlike the original texts as the students could possibly make them explains why improvements in other areas of text quality were less encouraging. Mixed results for university students' development of their ability to summarize foreign-language texts are documented in the literature, e.g., by Ko (2009), who also argues that students take more risks in their formulations once they understand how carefully they need to avoid accusations of plagiarism. In a similar vein, fewer students in the present project progressed in terms of *lexical precision, linguistic correctness,* or *holistic* quality: the students might have taken too many and/or too substantial linguistic risks when trying to avoid plagiarism, thus not paying sufficient attention to other parameters of text quality. Also, while the course in the reported form may have laid some ground-work for students' writing knowledge concerning *macrostructure* and *source use*, it may not have been long or intensive enough for students to show significant gains in, e.g., *lexical precision* or *linguistic accuracy*. These findings align with findings reported by Crosthwaite (2017) who found that 14 weeks of instruction for international student EFL writers did not lead to gains in these particular areas, but that longer periods of instruction (two semesters and more) were necessary.

It is also interesting to note that a substantial percentage of students improved their understanding of the macrostructural requirements of the source-based *summary* genre, but that most students still struggled with determining which information from the original articles the interdisciplinary readership would need in the summary to make sense of the content from the original article. The written *client analyses* that students completed repeatedly during the course in preparation for their summaries might thus need to offer more balanced instructions, foregrounding the genre expectations of their readers less and focusing more on the clients' background knowledge and informational needs.

A further element that might have been added to the range of pre-writing assignments in the course could have been a section on reading strategies and comprehension checking. Du (2014) reports in a qualitative interview study that students struggled with their ESL summary writing task already during the reading stage and did not necessarily arrive at a good enough understanding of the source texts to produce satisfactory ESL summaries. Students in the present course might have shown more substantial improvements in summary text quality if reading strategies had been included in the course curriculum. This addition will be discussed in further installments of the course.

Self-assessment survey

As already indicated, *audience awareness* emerged as the focus of writing knowledge for which the most substantial percentage of students, i.e., 74 percent, reported an increase in confidence concerning their own abilities. It appears that the *client analyses* used in the course design helped students to analyze prospective readerships in more systematic ways, identifying their audiences' specific interests, prior content knowledge, and prior linguistic knowledge. Given that students completed the client profile activity multiple times during the course, the strategies used to identify their readership's probable characteristics possibly were more present in students' minds than other pre-writing and writing activities they had completed in the course. Similarly positive results were reported in a study completed by Robles and Baker (2019) with 51 student writers in technical and professional communication courses: in their written reflections on the course, the students indicated that creating case profiles for prospective readers had helped them understand the demographic characteristics as well as the ensuing needs and values of their readerships, and to communicate their intentions with more credibility, persuasiveness, and appropriateness to their prospective readers. Positive developments in students' self-awareness associated with guided self-assessment have also been documented, e.g., by Wang (2017), where 80 student writers in higher education indicated in their reflective journals and during a range of interview sessions that they had developed their ability to set goals for writing, to self-monitor more effectively while writing, and to assess their own texts more carefully. Similar writing process advantages of guided self-assessment were also reported by sixty student writers in higher education by Covill (2012) where students felt the guided self-assessment had led them to a more reliable understanding of what constitutes a good paper. Additionally, it can be argued that, for more advanced students in the present project, their self-assessment may not have been be too far off from their actual development, as specifically guided self-assessment has been observed to mirror actual assessment in writing performance in higher education to a substantial degree (Hawthorne et al., 2017).

However, in the present project, students' self-perceived heightened awareness of their audiences' characteristics did not necessarily translate into students' ability to, e.g., select information appropriately from the source texts that students were working with, or to select vocabulary sufficiently comprehensible for interdisciplinary readerships. Thus, students might need more time and training to put their audience awareness into practice in their texts, even given the fact that the students in the present project had already completed their bachelor's degree and were thus not inexperienced or novice readers and writers of academic texts.

While the substantial variations in students' confidence in their own abilities concerning different parameters illustrated Figure 5.1 are certainly not an ideal outcome, they may be regarded as a positive outcome even given the substantial percentage of students whose confidence actually decreased: The less confident students may either have learned to scrutinize their own writing with a more critical eye or may have developed higher standards to hold their own writing to. Students in the present project may thus feel that while their ability to produce adequate texts for their prospective readers might not be as substantial as they had believed, they have become more acute in monitoring their own writing processes.

Beliefs-and-attitudes survey

Interestingly, half of the students in the present study indicated that they perceived university writing to be less relevant for their prospective workplaces than they had thought it to be at the beginning of the course, while other students found academic writing to be more professionally relevant than they had thought it to be before. The different shifts observed in students' perception of the relevance of writing at university for writing in the professions may be associated with the different workplace profiles that students envision for their professional future. The perceived mismatch between the writing trained at university and the writing probably done at the prospective workplaces could thus be addressed by introducing students early on to workplace writing demands, such as documented by Knoch and colleagues (Knoch et al., 2016). For their report, Knoch et al. (2016) surveyed employers/supervisors for graduates with, e.g., economics degrees. The employers/supervisors in Knoch et al. (2016) stressed that workplace writing involved tailoring the lexical specificity of their writing to non-specialist clients (p. 14). Knoch et al. (2016) also documented that the qualities most valued in workplace writing were clarity, prioritization of key points, conciseness, brevity, relevance, and logical sequencing. Possibly, the approach to writing trained in the present project invited transfer to the workplace to a more substantial extent than some students in the course apparently perceived: The priorities identified in Knoch et al. (2016) are precisely the points that were targeted in the present project course with, e.g., the summary writing assignments, the readership profiles, and the joint writing projects. In a similar vein, Blythe et al. (2014), documented in a survey study with over 200 professionals in ten different fields (among them also management professionals) that presentations and grant proposals were among the ten most frequent workplace writing tasks they had to complete. Thus, the text types chosen for the course in the present project resemble prospective workplace writing for management degree graduates closely. Interestingly, while the discipline-specific course coordinator in the present project clearly indicated the proposal genre and its building blocks as relevant genres for the students' prospective careers, it was not clear to which extent students had already formed a clear idea of writing in the workplace for their specific careers. Thus, a more substantial access to work-integrated learning (WIL) (Dean et al., 2020) should be added to the course design to help students identify how academic writing can be transferred into actual workplace writing.

While the possibility of using writing as a learning tool was discussed with students in the course, this aspect was not foregrounded in the writing training; in the training, more emphasis was put onto readership analysis and interdisciplinary comprehensibility. Students were made aware of how they could use writing to consolidate their personal course learning, but the communicative goals of summary writing and proposal writing were trained with more emphasis and repetition. Thus, students were more autonomous in their choice of how much they wanted to experiment with writing-to-learn, and the percentage of students who came to appreciate writing as a tool for learning was similar to the percentage of students who were less interested in writing-to-learn at the end of the course. Interestingly, a range of studies and meta-analyses (e.g., Bangert-Drowns et al., 2004) report mixed and moderate effects for writing as an instrument for learning. Similarly, Klein et al. (2007, p. 595) concede that "a growing body of literature shows that writing can contribute to the recall, comprehension, and transfer of content area knowledge. . . . However, the effects of writing are inconsistent, and on average, small." Nückles et al. (2012) echo Klein et al. (2007) in acknowledging that "the available empirical evidence suggests that the effect of writing-to-learn interventions are typically rather small, though positive" (p. 180). Thus, even though writing activities have been demonstrated to support knowledge acquisition, this support has not been substantial in the studies reviewed by, e.g., Bangert-Drowns et al. (2004) and Nückles et al. (2012). Given the inconclusiveness of the findings reported in the literature as well as the fact that *writing-to-learn* was not prioritized over *writing-to-communicate* in the present project, it is not surprising that some students deepened their appreciation towards writing-to-learn, while other students became more skeptical.

Hardly any students in the course did not shift their view towards multilingual writing strategies: while half of the students increased their appreciation of multilingual writing, 44 percent actually became less interested in multilingual strategies for writing. These findings are in line with previously reported outcomes for students' attitudes towards multilingual writing strategies, since it still remains unclear which type of multilingual writing strategy is most useful for which language combination, for which learner, at which proficiency level, and for which purpose during their EFL writing processes (cf. Göpferich, 2017; Plata-Ramírez, 2016). The students in the present project who had developed a more positive attitude towards multilingual writing strategies may have experienced the translanguaging component of the course in a similar way as participants observed by Plata-Ramírez (2016), who reported in stimulated-recall interviews conducted after the students had completed recorded writing sessions involving think-aloud, that the students benefited from having "another language to verify the language you are writing in" (p. 62). The perceived benefits concerned, e.g., assessing the macrostructural coherence of their texts as students would "go back to [their] native language and . . . see how the organization makes sense to me in my own language" (p. 62). In a similar vein, the students in Plata-Ramírez (2016) reported using their dominant language for cognitive relief, indicating that "if [they] feel stuck thinking in English [the FL] then [they] switch and think in Spanish [their] native language" (p. 65). In the present context, five of the students who had become more positive towards using multilingual writing strategies had scored above average in the English proficiency test, while the remaining four had scored below average. In the literature reporting process-oriented findings, resorting to the dominant language had been reported to be particularly attractive for lower-proficiency FL learners (cf. Göpferich, 2017). However, among the five writers who had scored above average in the English proficiency test in the course, three had achieved advanced scores for English language proficiency. They appear to have experienced advantages of translanguaging strategies even though their EFL proficiency was advanced.

The decline in motivation to use multilingual writing strategies among some students may have resulted from students' experiencing momentary cognitive fixedness when switching between languages during the translanguaging tasks. Göpferich (2019) argues that FL writers, upon using other languages during their FL writing processes, might experience not cognitive relief, but indeed increased cognitive load if the writers lack the translation skills necessary to prevent L1 fixedness and interference phenomena. Viewed from this angle, translanguaging strategies, supposedly the most authentic and cognitively economical strategies for multilingual writers, would have to be introduced to multilingual students in combination with at least rudimentary translation training. On the basis of such training, students could make the most of their multilingual writing knowledge without experiencing interference between their languages. The students in the present project who became more reluctant to make use of translanguaging during their EFL writing processes may have encountered difficulties in their writing processes due to interference between their languages.

Focus-group Discussion in the Post-semester Debriefing Workshop

In the focus group discussion with the content lecturers and two writing instructors at the end of the semester, the seven discipline-specific lecturers agreed that they experienced a lack of confidence in their own metalinguistic awareness and in their metalinguistic vocabulary. While all of them felt confident and flexible when using English as a medium of instruction and also as a language of publishing and presenting, they felt they would not necessarily be able to identify the exact nature and extent of students' English language struggles, specifically in written texts. This apprehension is in line with findings reported by Lasagabaster and Doiz (2018), i.e., that language teachers, unsurprisingly, outperform content teachers in identifying and specifying language problems in their students FL written work. The discipline-specific lecturers' position is also frequently reported in other studies detailing content lecturers' resistance to acting as English language support for their students in EMI contexts (cf. Airey, 2012; Block & Moncada-Colmas, 2019).

The discipline-specific lecturers in the present context also came to realize that, while learning outcomes and communicative standards had been agreed upon for the project course and specifically for students written work based on the writing training, there was no coherent framework across the master's degree program for assessing writing. The lecturers also discussed the possibility that the difference of feedback foci between content lecturers and writing instructors might have suggested to the students that the content lecturers valued professional communication less than the writing instructor did. Students might have perceived inconsistencies in the content lecturers' responses to their writing, similar to the inconsistencies reported in Block and Moncada-Colmas (2019), where a substantial paradox emerged in the interview data collected among STEM lecturers: When the interviews were no longer focused on English as a foreign language, but also encompassed language issues in connection with most students' shared dominant language, the lecturers' view on the importance of language instruction shifted. This is illustrated by the following excerpt from one of the interviews: "Yes I'm training them in engineering . . . but in the end I'm teaching people who will end up having to write reports . . . and here language is very important for EVERYTHING" (Block & Moncada-Colmas, 2019, p. 12, emphasis in the original). In both contexts, i.e., the present project and the STEM context in Block and Moncada-Colmas (2019), content lecturers did recognize the importance of writing in their discipline but did not necessarily feel confident enough in their metalinguistic knowledge to insist on this importance to a sufficient degree in front of students.

In subsequent installments of the present project, students might progress in their writing knowledge development more substantially if the content lecturers involved stress the importance of professional writing knowledge more adamantly; the content lecturers could take a more resolute stance even while refraining from offering language training and assessment themselves and delegating these tasks to the writing instructors. Recommendations could thus be formulated on the basis of Gustafsson et al. (2011) who argue that between content specialists on the one hand and language specialists on the other "awareness of congruence helps form and design the collaboration" (p. 5), not only in individual course contexts for assessment and communication with students, but for entire curricular program frameworks.

Conclusion

The mixed observations demonstrated, e.g., that students on the whole improved their writing knowledge in terms of *source use*, and that a substantial percentage of students improved their writing knowledge in terms of *macrostructural coherence*. These positive results were obtained in spite of the fact that a substantial number of students in the superdiverse writing environment struggled with lower-level EFL concerns and in spite of the fact that EFL writers in higher education may need two semesters of instruction or more to show significant progress in EFL academic writing knowledge (Crosthwaite, 2017). However, no sizable gains were observed in other areas of text quality. The mixed results also show how most students changed their beliefs and attitudes about writing in terms of its *professional relevance*, its *relevance for learning*, and the potential benefits of *multilingual writing strategies*. However, these changes in beliefs and attitudes did not progress in similar directions but varied substantially.

On the basis of these heterogeneous observations, the study serves to highlight the complexity of the intersecting exigencies that need to be navigated in *superdiverse* student and faculty groups. Thus, as concluding remarks, three recommendations can be offered:

> *Establish a climate of language professionalization in superdiverse learning environments.* A range of students in the present project experienced substantial writing struggles due to their comparatively low levels of English language proficiency. However, to our knowledge, these students did not seek additional English language support. What might have encouraged these students to seek more language learning opportunities? The discipline-specific faculty as well as the writing instructors might have been more adamant in presenting additional language courses not as remedial courses for students with "language deficits," but

as professionalization opportunities where students could enhance their perfectly valuable multilingual repertoires with more professional English language knowledge.

Systematize language professionalization across course contexts in superdiverse learning environments. In the evaluation workshop, the content lecturers related how the coordinated language standards in the course did not have coordinated equivalents on the program level. With a coordinated communication curriculum throughout the program, students might have had a more coherent basis of writing knowledge to build upon for the lecture-series course.

Systematize peer support in superdiverse learning environments. For many students enrolled in the course, it was a new and challenging experience to have to produce texts in collaboration. However, collaborative text production in highly diverse teams is likely to become a stable feature of these students' professional careers (cf. Schrijver & Leijten, 2019). Experiences with collaborative writing in superdiverse environments might prove to be an asset then, especially when appropriately fostered in higher education. Specifically, in superdiverse learning environments, students who themselves represent highly diverse backgrounds in terms of linguistic, cultural, and disciplinary knowledge may be more likely to take diversity among their readers into account than writers from less diverse backgrounds, as related by, e.g., Poe and Zhang-Wu (2020). Surveying over 2,000 domestic and international students, Poe and Zhang-Wu (2020) report that "on the learning goal related to awareness of diversity, international students out-performed . . . domestic students" (p. 13).

Thus, in designing writing training for superdiverse HE contexts in collaboration with content faculty and program administrators, the focus might have to be on *adaptive transfer* as called for by DePalma and Ringer (2012): Writing instructors and discipline-specific faculty need to constantly apply *and reshape* their writing knowledge to negotiate new and potentially unfamiliar situations of writing training. Efficient approaches to fostering professional writing knowledge within linguistically, disciplinarily, and culturally multifaceted environments in higher education might have to be as superdiverse as the student and faculty groups these approaches cater to.

References

Airey, J. (2012). I Don't teach language. The linguistic attitudes of physics lecturers in Sweden. *AILA Review, 25*, 64–79. https://doi.org/10.1075/aila.25.05air.

Bachmann, T. & Becker-Mrotzek, M. (2010), Schreibaufgaben situieren und profilieren. In T. Pohl & T. Steinhoff (Eds.), *Textformen als Lernformen* (pp. 191–210). Gilles & Francke Verlag.

Baker, C. (2003). Biliteracy and transliteracy in Wales: Language planning and the Welsh National Curriculum. In N. H. Hornberger (Ed.), *Continua of Biliteracy: An Ecological Framework for Educational Policy, Research and Practice in Multilingual Settings* (pp. 71–90). Multilingual Matters. https://doi.org/10.21832/9781853596568.

Baker, W. & Hüttner, J. (2017). English and more: A multisite study of roles and conceptualisations of language in English medium multilingual universities from Europe to Asia. *Journal of Multilingual and Multicultural Development, 38*(6), 501–516. https://doi.org/10.1080/01434632.2016.1207183.

Bangert-Drowns, R. L., Hurley, M. M. & Wilkinson, B. (2004). The effects of school-based writing-to-learn interventions on academic achievement: A meta-analysis. *Review of Educational Research, 74*(1), 29–58. https://doi.org/10.3102/00346543074001029.

Barrie, S. C. (2006). Understanding what we mean by the generic attributes of graduates. *Higher Education, 51*, 215–241. https://doi.org/10.1007/s10734-004-6384-7.

Block, D. & Moncada-Comas, B. (2019). English-medium instruction in higher education and the ELT gaze: STEM lecturers' self-positioning as NOT English language teachers. *International Journal of Bilingual Education and Bilingualism*, 1–17. https://doi.org/10.1080/13670050.2019.1689917.

Blommaert, J. & Rampton, B. (2012). Language and superdiversity. *MMG Working papers, 12*(9), 1–36.

Blythe, S., Lauer, C. & Curran, P. G. (2014). Professional and technical communication in a web 2.0 world. *Technical Communication Quarterly, 23*(4), 265–287. https://doi.org/10.1080/10572252.2014.941766.

British Council (2018). *Understand and explain the IELTS score.* https://takeielts.britishcouncil.org/teach-ielts/test-information/ielts-scores-explained.

Byrnes, H. (2011). Beyond writing as language learning or content learning. In R. Manchón (Ed.), *Learning-to-write and writing-to-learn in an additional language* (pp. 133–157). John Benjamins. https://doi.org/10.1075/lllt.31.

Canagarajah, S. (2011). Translanguaging in the classroom: Emerging issues for research and pedagogy. *Applied linguistics review, 2*, 1–28. https://doi.org/10.1515/9783110239331.1.

Centeno-Cortés, B. & Jiménez Jiménez, A. F. (2004). Problem-solving tasks in a foreign language: The importance of the L1 in private verbal thinking. *International Journal of Applied Linguistics, 14*(1), 7–35. https://doi.org/10.1111/j.1473-4192.2004.00052.x.

Cheng, R. & Feyten, C. M. (2015). L2 students' academic literacy development guided by teacher written feedback: A writing-to-learn perspective. *Studies in Applied Linguistics, 6*(2), 7–25.

Covill, A. E. (2012). College students' use of a writing rubric: Effect on quality of writing, self-efficacy, and writing practices. *Journal of Writing Assessment, 5*(1), 11–29.

Creese, A. (2005). *Teacher collaboration and talk in multilingual classrooms* (Vol. 51). Multilingual Matters.

Crosthwaite, P. (2017). Does EAP writing instruction reduce L2 errors? Evidence from a longitudinal corpus of L2 EAP essays and reports. *International Review of Applied Linguistics in Language Teaching, 56*(3), 315–343. https://doi.org/10.1515/iral-2016-0129.

Dafouz, E. (2014). Integrating content and language in European higher education: An overview of recurrent research concerns and pending issues. In P. Joycey, E. Agathopoulou & M. Mattheoudakis (Eds.), *Cross-curricular approaches to language education* (pp. 289–304). Cambridge Scholars Publishing.

Dafouz, E. (2020). Postscript: Moving forward in integrating content and language in multilingual higher education. In S. Dimova & J. Kling (Eds.), *Integrating Content and Language in Multilingual Universities* (pp. 179–183) (Educational Linguistics, vol. 44). Springer. https://doi.org/10.1007/978-3-030-46947-4_11.

Dean, B. A., Yanamandram, V., Eady, M. J., Moroney, T. & O'Donnell, N. (2020). An institutional framework for scaffolding work-integrated learning across a degree. *Journal of University Teaching & Learning Practice, 17*(4), 6. https://ro.uow.edu.au/jutlp/vol17/iss4/6/.

De Guerrero, M. C. (2018). Going covert: Inner and private speech in language learning. *Language Teaching, 51*(1), 1–35. https://doi.org/10.1017/S0261444817000295.

DePalma, M. J. & Ringer, J. M. (2011). Toward a theory of adaptive transfer: Expanding disciplinary discussions of "transfer" in second-language writing and composition studies. *Journal of Second Language Writing, 20*(2), 134–147. https://doi.org/10.1016/j.jslw.2011.02.003.

Donahue, C. (2018). We are the "other": The future of exchanges between writing and language studies. *Across the Disciplines, 15*(3), 130–143. https://doi.org/10.37514/ATD-J.2018.15.3.17.

Du, Q. (2014). Bridging the gap between ESL composition programs and disciplinary writing: The teaching and learning of summarization skill. In T. Myers Zawacki & M. Cox (Eds.), *WAC and second language writers: Research towards linguistically and culturally inclusive programs and practices* (pp. 113–128). The WAC Clearinghouse; Parlor Press. https://wac.colostate.edu/books/perspectives/l2/.

Eckes, T. & Grotjahn, R. (2006). A closer look at the construct validity of C-tests. *Language Testing, 23*(3), 290–325. https://doi.org/10.1191/0265532206lt330oa.

Ewert, A. (2010). An educational language community: External and internal language use by multilingual students. In J. Arabski & A. Wojtaszek (Eds.), *Neurolinguistic and psycholinguistic perspectives on SLA* (pp. 159–174). Multilingual Matters. https://doi.org/10.21832/9781847692429.

Flesch, R. (1948). A new readability yardstick. *Journal of Applied Psychology, 32*(3), 221–233. https://doi.org/10.1037/h0057532.

Galloway, N., Kriukow, J. & Numajiri, T. (2017). Internationalisation, higher education and the growing demand for English: an investigation into the English medium of instruction (EMI) movement in China and Japan. *ELT Research papers, 17*(2), 1–39. https://www.research.ed.ac.uk/en/publications/internationalisation-higher-education-and-the-growing-demand-for-.

García, O. (2009). *Bilingual education in the 21st century: A global perspective*. Wiley/Blackwell. https://doi.org/10.1017/S0047404513000304.

Graham, S. & Perin, D. (2007). A meta-analysis of writing instruction for adolescent students. *Journal of educational psychology, 99*(3), 445–476. https://doi.org/10.1037/0022-0663.99.3.445.

Gustafsson, M., Eriksson, A., Räisänen, C., Stenberg, A. C., Jacobs, C., Wright, J., Wyrley-Birch, B. & Winberg, C. (2011). Collaborating for content and language integrated learning: The situated character of faculty collaboration and student learning. *Across the Disciplines, 8*(3), 1–11. https://doi.org/10.37514/ATD-J.2011.8.3.09.

Göpferich, S. (2017). Cognitive functions of translation in L2 writing. In J. W. Schwieter & A. Ferreira (Eds.), *The handbook of translation and cognition* (pp. 402–422). Wiley. https://doi.org/10.1002/9781119241485.ch22.

Göpferich, S. (2019). Translation competence as a cognitive catalyst for multiliteracy—Research findings and their Implications for L2 writing and translation instruction. In D. Li, V. Lei & Y. He (Eds.), *Researching cognitive processes of translation* (pp. 169–197). Springer. https://doi.org/10.1007/978-981-13-1984-6_8.

Göpferich, S., Machura, I. A. & Murphy, J. T. (2019). Supporting english medium instruction at German institutions of higher education. In R. Hickey (Ed.), *English in the German-speaking world* (pp. 114–140). Cambridge University Press. https://doi.org/10.1017/9781108768924.007.

Hawthorne, K., Bol, L. & Pribesh, S. (2017). Can providing rubrics for writing tasks improve developing writers' calibration accuracy? *The Journal of Experimental Education, 85*(4), 689–708. https://doi.org/10.1080/00220973.2017.1299081.

Hendricks, C. C. (2018). WAC/WID and transfer: Towards a transdisciplinary view of academic writing. *Across the Disciplines, 15*(3), 48–62. https://doi.org/10.37514/ATD-J.2018.15.3.11.

Jiménez Jiménez, A. F. (2015). Private speech during problem-solving activities in bilingual speakers. *International Journal of Bilingualism, 19*(3), 259–281. https://doi.org/10.1177/1367006913509902.

Kincaid, J. P., Fishburne, R. P., Jr., Rogers, R. L. & Chissom, B. S. (1975). *Derivation of new readability formulas (automated readability index, fog count and Flesch reading Ease Formula) for Navy enlisted personnel*. Institute for Simulation and Training.

Klein, D., Piacente-Cimini, S., Williams, L. A. (2007). The role of writing in learning form analogies. *Learning and Instruction, 17*(6), 596–611. https://doi.org/10.1016/j.learninstruc.2007.09.006.

Knoch, U., May, L., Macqueen, S., Pill, J. & Storch, N. (2016). Transitioning from university to the workplace: Stakeholder perceptions of academic and professional writing demands. *IELTS Research Report Series, 1*, 1–37.

Ko, M. H. (2009). Summary writing instruction to university students and their learning outcomes. *English Teaching, 64*(2), 125–149.

Kobayashi, H. & Rinnert, C. (1992). Effects of first language on second language writing: Translation versus direct composition. *Language learning, 42*(2), 183–209. https://doi.org/10.1111/j.1467-1770.1992.tb00707.x.

Lasagabaster, D. (2018). Fostering team teaching: Mapping out a research agenda for English-medium instruction at university level. *Language Teaching, 51*(3), 400–416. https://doi.org/10.1017/S0261444818000113.

Lasagabaster, D. & Doiz, A. (2018). Language errors in an English-medium instruction university setting: How do language versus content teachers tackle them? *Porta Linguarum: Revista internacional de didáctica de las lenguas extranjeras, 30*, 131–148.

Lesterhuis, M., Daal, T. van, Van Gasse, R., Coertjens, L., Donche, V. & De Maeyer, S. (2018). When teachers compare argumentative texts: Decisions informed by multiple complex aspects of text quality. *L1-Educational Studies in Language and Literature, 18*, 1–22. https://doi.org/10.17239/L1ESLL-2018.18.01.02.

Madiba, M. (2018). The multilingual university. In A. Creese & A. Blackledge (Eds.), *The Routledge handbook of language and superdiversity* (pp. 504–517). Routledge.

McLaughlin, G. H. (1969). SMOG grading-a new readability formula. *Journal of reading, 12*(8), 639–646.

Michael-Luna, S. & Canagarajah, A. S. (2007). Multilingual academic literacies: Pedagogical foundations for code meshing in primary and higher education. *Journal of Applied Linguistics, 4*(1), 55–77. https://doi.org/10.1558/japl.v4i1.55.

Nückles, M., Hübner, S., Renkl, A. (2012). How should instructional support be designed to promote high-quality learning? In J. Kirby & M. Lawson (Eds.), *Enhancing the quality of learning. Disposition, instruction, and learning Processes* (pp. 178–200). Cambridge University Press.

Palmer, D. K., Martínez, R. A., Mateus, S. G. & Henderson, K. (2014). Reframing the debate on language separation: Toward a vision for translanguaging pedagogies in the dual language classroom. *The Modern Language Journal, 98*(3), 757–772. https://doi.org/10.1111/modl.12121.

Pecorari D. (2020) English medium instruction: Disintegrating language and content? In S. Dimova & J. Kling (Eds.), *Integrating content and language in multilingual universities* (p. 15–36). Educational Linguistics, vol. 44. Springer. https://doi.org/10.1007/978-3-030-46947-4_2.

Plata-Ramírez, J. M. (2016). Language switching: Exploring writers' perceptions on the use of their L1s in the L2 writing process. *Revista Internacional de Lenguas Extranjeras/International Journal of Foreign Languages, 5*, 47–77. https://revistes.urv.cat/index.php/rile/article/view/1003.

Poe, M. & Zhang-Wu, Q. (2020). Super-diversity as a framework to promote justice: Designing program assessment for multilingual writing outcomes. *Composition Forum, 44*. http://compositionforum.com/issue/44/northeastern.php.

Robles, V. D. & Baker, M. J. (2019). Using case-method pedagogy to facilitate audience awareness. *IEEE Transactions on Professional Communication, 62*(2), 192–207.

Schrijver, I. & Leijten, M. (2019). The diverse field of professional writing: Current perspectives on writing in the workplace. *Hermes—Journal of Language and Communication in Business, 59*, 7–14. https://doi.org/10.7146/hjlcb.v59i1.117315.

Swales, J. M. (1990). *Genre analysis: English in academic and research settings*. Cambridge University Press. https://doi.org/10.1017/S0272263100011773.

Tinsley, H. E. & Weiss, D. J. (2000). Interrater reliability and agreement. In H. E. Tinsley & D. J. Weiss (Eds.), *Handbook of applied multivariate statistics and mathematical modeling* (pp. 95–124). Academic Press. https://doi.org/10.1016/B978-012691360-6/50005-7.

Uzawa, K. (1996). Second language learners' processes of L1 writing, L2 writing, and translation from L1 into L2. *Journal of Second Language Writing, 5*(3), 271–294. https://doi.org/10.1016/S1060-3743(96)90005-3.

Van Rinsveld, A., Schiltz, C., Brunner, M., Landerl, K. & Ugen, S. (2016). Solving arithmetic problems in first and second language: Does the language context matter? *Learning and instruction 42*, 72–82. https://doi.org/10.1016/j.learninstruc.2016.01.003.

Wang, W. (2017). Using rubrics in student self-assessment: Student perceptions in the English as a foreign language writing context. *Assessment & Evaluation in Higher Education, 42*(8), 1280–1292. https://doi.org/10.1080/02602938.2016.1261993.

Winberg, C., Wyrley-Birch, B. & Jacobs, C. (2013). Conceptualising linguistic access to knowledge as interdisciplinary collaboration. *Journal for Language Teaching, 47*(2), 89–108. https://doi.org/10.4314/jlt.v47i2.5.

Woodall, B. R. (2002). Language-switching: Using the first language while writing in a second language. *Journal of Second Language Writing, 11*(1), 7–28. https://doi.org/10.1016/S1060-3743(01)00051-0.

6 Considering Individual and Situational Variation in Modeling Writing Processes

Sabine Dengscherz
UNIVERSITY OF VIENNA

> Writing processes vary individually and situationally. Writing process models that focus on *writing activities* cannot capture these variations. In this chapter, I present and discuss a new model which shifts the focus from activities during writing towards *factorial conditions* that influence *writing situations*. This way, the PROSIMS writing process model explicitly considers individual and situational variation in writing processes. It was developed within the scope of a research project of the same title (PROSIMS: Strategien und Routinen für **pro**fessionelles **S**chreiben **i**n **m**ehreren **S**prachen; Strategies and Routines for Professional Multilingual Writing). Based on 17 case studies with 13 multilingual students and four researchers, mainly at the University of Vienna, and tested in a survey, the model conceptualizes the writing process as a dynamic system with a certain range of influence factors on several levels. The chapter focuses on the theoretical background of the model while illustrating it with some examples from the case studies and providing additional insights from the survey, especially concerning the handling of language resources in writing.

Academic writing is a social and cognitive activity. It takes place in multiple contexts and implements a variety of genres and writing situations (Dengscherz, 2019). Scholars and students write to generate knowledge (Estrem, 2016) and/or to demonstrate knowledge, and to make research results, theories, and reflections accessible to their readers (Ehlich, 2018). Writers act against the background of their language and writing biographies, as well as of the traditions of institutions and discourse communities (Russell, 2010; Zenger and Pill, this volume) or instruction and reflection practices (see Anson in this volume, especially for digital contexts). They have to meet a broad variety of requirements and overcome several challenges (see also Castelló in this volume).

The complex act of writing has been described from various perspectives. Knorr (2019) suggests three categories of traditions in writing research: First, approaches from the angle of cognitive psychology, understanding writing mainly as a problem-solving activity (for example Beaugrande, 1984; Hayes, 2012; or Hayes & Flower, 1980). Second, approaches that focus on social contexts and discourse and describe writing as a situated activity in professional workplace contexts (like Beaufort, 2005; Beaufort & Iñesta, 2014; Jakobs 1997; or Pogner, 1997), and third, approaches that focus on writing development, competence and skills (e.g., Becker-Mrotzek and Schindler, 2007; Bereiter, 1980; Knappik, 2013; or Pohl, 2007; Steinhoff, 2007).

Each of these research traditions has provided valuable insights for the field. For covering the complexity of writing in a deeper, multi-faceted view on writing processes, intersections of these perspectives need to be integrated. Several studies may serve as successful examples for such integrations: Knappik (2018) combines a social perspective with a focus on writing development, Knorr (2019) has developed a "language-sensitive" model of writing competence in bundling together approaches from cognitive psychology, social discourse and writing development with a focus on the role of language in writing, and Adler-Kassner and Wardle (2015) give a multifaceted overview of insights into writing activities in their programmatic book on "threshold concepts" of writing, addressing writing from a variety of perspectives.

The PROSIMS writing process model described in this chapter is inspired by such intersecting viewpoints of writing. It is empirically based on 17 case studies on writing processes in multilingual academic contexts and, furthermore, has been tested in a quantitative survey at the Centre for Translation Studies (CTS) of the University of Vienna.

The model consists of three parts, each covering a specific perspective on writing situations occurring in the process. It seeks to apply multi-perspectivism and complexity by integrating cognitive and competence-oriented approaches as well as perspectives on writing as a situated activity. Additionally, it explicitly focuses on variation according to individual prerequisites, attitudes towards writing and personal preferences. The model focuses on academic text production in multilingual contexts and aims to conceptualize writing processes, with a special focus on individual and situational variation.

The PROSIMS writing process model is to some extent inspired by Dynamic Systems Theory (DST). Initially derived from natural science, DST addresses complex systems with a high number of interfering and interrelating factors (De Angelis & Jessner, 2012). In complex systems, changes are not predictable. Since the factors shaping the system interrelate, a change of one factor very likely leads to changes in other factors and so on. Since writing

Modeling Writing Processes

processes can be regarded as complex systems in this sense (Jacobs & Perrin, 2014), individual behavior in text production cannot be forecasted (Risku & Windhager, 2015). The model addresses writing processes as dynamic systems by articulating and describing adjustments in specific situations.

Another important aspect in the PROSIMS project is multilingualism and the handling of language resources in the writing process. Language is central to all writing. However, the crucial role of language resources becomes especially obvious when it comes to writing in multilingual contexts: Writers might use their multilingual repertoires strategically as resources in the writing process. But how do they do that? How do they apply their language resources strategically to address heuristic and rhetorical requirements and challenges in writing situations? These are important research questions in the PROSIMS project. The PROSIMS writing process model aims at supporting the analysis of factors that contribute to individual multilingual writing behavior and the functional use of language resources in the writing process.

In this chapter, I first set out the theoretical and empirical background and provide information about the case studies and the survey conducted in the project. Then, the three parts of the PROSIMS writing process model are described in more detail. The first part of the model describes the general holistic view of the writing process, the second part zooms into a writing situation and focuses on factors shaping that specific situation, while the third part focuses on interrelations between the conditions of the situation and the strategies and routines applied by the writers, as well as their handling of language resources. Further, I present and discuss the quantitative results of the project, first in their relevance for testing the model, and, second, in eliciting additional information about the quantitative distribution of writing behavior that could be observed in the case studies, especially concerning the handling of language resources in multilingual writing settings. Limitations and desiderata for further research will be addressed in the closing section, along with scopes of application of the model.

The PROSIMS Project: Aims, Methodology, and Database

The PROSIMS project was conducted from May 2014 to October 2019 at the Centre for Translation Studies (CTS) of the University of Vienna and was third-party funded by the Austrian Science Fund FWF. PROSIMS is an acronym of the German project title "Strategien und Routinen für **Pro**fessionelles **S**chreiben **i**n **m**ehreren **S**prachen" (Strategies and Routines for Professional Multilingual Writing). The project refers to "professional writing" in multiple senses: First, it aims at writing tasks that simulate writing at the workplace in focusing on audience awareness and various communication situations that might occur in workplace-settings. At the CTS, the students fulfil a broad range of short writing tasks during their studies that simulate order-specific writing, and, they engage with various genres (for example journalistic reports or commentaries, blog-texts, business letters, etc.). Second, "professional" in a broad sense includes academic writing in the job, not only in a narrow sense referring to research articles, monographs, and related genres but also to "supporting genres" (Swales & Feak, 2011) such as project reports. Third, "professional writing" refers to kinds of writing that afford extended writing expertise (for a detailed discussion see Dengscherz, 2019, pp. 37-86).

The PROSIMS project carried out an exploratory research study on authentic writing in multilingual academic contexts, and pursued several goals: Mainly, it aimed at a "thick description" (Geertz, 1973) of the writing behavior and the application of language resources by multilingual academic writers. It focused on individual challenges in writing and writer's strategic ways in which they respond to these challenges. The empirical data were mainly elicited in case studies, applying screen-capturing and retrospective interviews. The data from the case studies were supplemented by an antecedent analysis of CTS students' statements about their approaches to writing (Dengscherz & Steindl, 2016) and a final quantitative questionnaire screening with teachers, researchers and students at the CTS.

Theory Building, Modeling, and Methodological Background

The process of theory building in the PROSIMS project is inspired by Grounded Theory Methodology (GTM). The empirical base for the "grounded theory" in the PROSIMS project consists of 17 case studies. A "thick description" (Geertz, 1973) of the observations in the case studies was deeply interlinked with theory building. Since case studies are focused on the exploratory analysis of highly diverse authentic material, a declared inductive data processing of GTM is supposed to ensure a certain openness for even unexpected findings. Nevertheless, instead of applying the pure strain of GTM described by Glaser and Strauss (1967), it seemed more appropriate for the aims of the project to follow the more recent suggestions of Charmaz (2006) and Breuer (2009). While Glaser and Strauss (1967) recommend to largely exclude academic discourse and former findings from the current analysis, Charmaz (2006) and Breuer (2009) interpret the objective of openness in a more moderate way. Glaser and Strauss argue for a fundamental openness without being distracted by existing theories, models and claims of other researchers, whereas Charmaz and Breuer point out that it is not realistic and would not even be desirable for a current analysis to ignore pre-existing knowledge of the field.

To avoid the risk of re-inventing the wheel in the case study analysis, it seems quite fortunate and necessary to draw on previous research and discussions in writing research discourse. Nevertheless, the claim for inductive openness is not to be neglected either. As a method for combining both aims, openness and theoretical awareness, Kruse (2015) suggests a stereoscopic "squinting hermeneutics" ("schielende Hermeneutik," p. 363): The data can be viewed by one eye remaining as unprejudiced as possible, while the other eye scans it against the background of former research in the field (or categories developed in former phases of the analysis). Kruse focuses on interview analysis, but his suggestion of a "squinting" analysis proved to be useful for the entire case study analysis: Theory building evolved together with the analysis of the empirical data *and* in-depth investigation of the discourse of the field. For example, research on individual differences in writing behavior (Chandler, 1995; Keseling, 2004; Ortner, 2000; Wyllie, 2000) influenced the analysis of the case studies in that *differences* in writing processes were at the core of the analysis. Nevertheless, openness for similarities in writing processes was required as well.

The Empirical Data: Case Studies and a Survey

The empirical data relevant for the PROSIMS writing process model consist of case studies and a survey. While the case studies provided the base for the *development* of the model, the survey was used for *testing* the model. Seventeen multilingual writers (13 students and four researchers) participated in the case studies. The participants were chosen by theoretical sampling (Glaser & Strauss, 1967). The aim of the case studies was to gain insights into a broad range of writing situations in German, English, French, and Hungarian (see also the remarks on professional writing above). The participants were chosen subsequently according to their current writing projects and working languages. Another important aspect was their willingness to participate in the study. Since the participants allowed us to watch over their shoulders during writing and provided deep insights into their writing behavior, the participation in the study was also a question of trust. Most of the student participants (all from the University of Vienna, studying at the CTS, the German Department or the Institute for Culture and Social Anthropology) knew me from institutional contacts and lectures at the CTS and the German Department, the researchers (three from the CTS, another from a German academic institution) knew me as a colleague (for an overview over all participants in the case studies and their institutional background as well as language biographies see Dengscherz, 2019, pp. 259-278).

The participants recorded their writing processes, or parts thereof, with the screen capturing software Snagit (Techsmith). The number and length of the screen capturing videos differ between the case studies: The shortest covers just a single half-hour video, while the most extensive one contains 25 videos adding up to 24 hours of writing process. All in all, 111 hours of screen capturing videos were analyzed in the project. The case studies focus on authentic writing assignments. In other words, the participants were working on texts that were independent from their participation in the project.

Therefore, the case studies cover a broad range of writing tasks and genres which can be clustered into four categories: first, *voluminous academic texts* such as term papers, research articles or a master's thesis; second, *short academic texts* like abstracts or components for a project report; third, *short texts with professional requirements*, for example commentaries or glosses; and fourth, *other texts* that draw on specific competences needed for academic writing, for example summaries or reflections. The case studies focused on individual writing. However, forms of collaboration could be observed in some of the cases (for detailed information on the writing tasks see Dengscherz, 2019, pp. 299-350). The case studies focus on text production in various genres that are demanding in a rhetorical and/or heuristic dimension. The writing tasks have in common, that they are all based on "focused writing" in the sense of Hicks and Perrin (2014) and not just on "writing by the way" (p. 237). The case studies explore writing with requirements that might lead to challenges for the writers.

The perception of specific demands and challenges varies between both writers and writing situations over the writing process (Dengscherz, 2019). An important focus of the PROSIMS project is the exploratory analysis of circumstances and influence factors on the perception of requirements that might lead to challenges—and of routines and strategies[1] (including the application of—multilingual—language resources) that address those requirements and challenges. The case study methodology was used to explore the interrelations of writing behavior, writing tasks, language and writing biographies, situational factors, etc. in specific writing situations. Therefore, a broad variety

---

[1] I understand routines and strategies as partial activities or procedures in the writing process. While strategies explicitly and consciously focus on a specific problem/challenge that has to be solved/overcome or a goal that is to be achieved, routines are mainly habituative, often unconscious and less focused: they are rather forms of writing behavior that (seem to) have proven useful in the past and thus became individual habit. The distinction between routines and strategies is not a rigid one, though. To which extent an activity/a procedure in the writing process can be interpreted as a routine or a strategy, depends on the interrelation between the writer, the activity/procedure and its function in the writing process (Dengscherz, 2019).

of writing tasks and genres is a crucial factor for the analysis—and not an obstacle. Though, such variety makes it necessary to forgo direct comparability between the individual writing behavior in the processes observed, it allows the analysis of individual *and* situational variation in the writing process.

Diversity in genres entails diversity in requirements in rhetorical and heuristic dimensions. Additionally, writers differ in their perception of requirements, their writing habits and their individual needs and abilities. The exploratory design of the case studies makes it possible to observe a broad range of writing situations with a broad variety of influence factors and interrelations.

The screen capturing videos are a rich data source. However, additional background information is needed for triangulation and for the interpretation of these data. A deeper understanding of writers' (choices of) acting in specific writing situations requires insights into their personal language and writing biographies, their attitudes towards writing in general and the specific writing tasks in particular, etc. To gain information about these aspects, we conducted interviews with a multiple focus: We addressed the writing processes observed in the screen capturing videos as well as the contexts of these writing processes, including language and writing biographies, individual attitudes towards writing and writing habits, institutional background, the specifics of the particular writing tasks and possible challenges perceived. By these means, writing behavior in situ ("Aktualverhalten") could be interpreted against the background of the participants' writing habits ("Habitualverhalten," Ortner, 2000).

In the analysis of the case studies, the interviews proved important for the interpretation of the screen capturing videos (Dengscherz, 2017). One example can be illustrative: Daniel (CS2) centered his writing very close to the source texts. This could have misled a researcher to the conclusion that he found it difficult to develop his own ideas in a text. But the opposite was the case: Actually, Daniel loves to write poems and other genres in literature (in his L1 Spanish as well as in his L2 German).[2] He is quite a successful young writer—albeit outside university. However, for his homework texts in

---

[2] Categorizing language repertoires into L1 and L2 is quite problematic since the categories mainly mirror views on multilingualism that are based on a monolingual paradigm (Canagarajah, 2012). Such categories cannot cover the diversity and complexity of individual language biographies (Blommaert, 2010; García & Kleyn, 2016; García & Wei, 2014). Nevertheless, those categories provide at least first proximations to the role that language resources play in the repertoire of a writer. For these reasons, I chose to use the terms L1 and L2 in this chapter—while, however, pointing to problems arising along those ways of categorizing (for an extensive analysis and discussion of "named languages" for language biographies and repertoires of the participants in the PROSIMS project see Dengscherz, 2019, pp. 523-568)

a course, he often gets the feedback that he exceeds the topic, misinterprets the task, or maybe does not even understand the source text. Daniel's efforts to rely closely on the source texts can be interpreted as a strategy to hold back his overwhelming fantasy and creativity. This, additionally, affects the revision of his texts: In the interview, Daniel talked a lot about revising his literary texts, whereas a "university text," once drafted, is pretty much a finished product for Daniel, and his attention shifts straight away to writing tasks more motivating for him: literature. Without this background information from the interview, the analysis of the screen capturing videos might have elicited inappropriate interpretations (Dengscherz, 2017).

During the analysis of the screen capturing videos together with the interviews, a second means for reconciliation and quality control was implemented. The data was analyzed in single case studies first, and these written case studies (32-150 pages long) were sent to the participants with a request for their opinion on the analysis of their writing behavior and their approaches to writing. Additionally, the participants were asked to answer questions that had arisen during the case study analysis. Sixteen of the 17 case studies were read and commented on by the participants. This step exceeds usual forms of quality control: The participants were integrated as partners in the research process, and the data could be refined recursively in repeated comparison of the single case studies integrating additional information from the participants, if needed, also during the data analysis. In a next and final step of the case study research, the single case studies were integrated in a cross-case analysis focused on systematic theory building.

At the end of the project, in October 2019, a quantitative survey with additional participants was carried out. On one hand, the questionnaire was used for testing the PROSIMS writing process model. On the other hand, it elicits information about the quantitative distribution of writing strategies that could be observed in the qualitative case studies. The questionnaire especially focuses on the handling of language(s) during the writing process and on the strategic use of multilingual resources.

The HRRC Concept: Insights into the Process of Integrated Analysis and Theory Building

While the survey was a separate step in the project, theory building and case study analysis were strongly interlinked. The development of the HRRC concept, which is a central theory component of the PROSIMS writing process model, may serve as an example for this interwoven process of theory building and analysis. The concept points to a double distinction: first, between (task-oriented) requirements and (writer- and process-oriented) challenges, and, second, between a heuristic and rhetorical level.

The HRRC concept was developed quite early in the project, mainly during the analysis of some single case studies (Dengscherz, 2018), especially the ones of the researchers Kerstin (CS12) and Lajos (CS5) and the student Andrea (CS1). The cases of Kerstin, Lajos, and Andrea illustrate that is useful to distinguish between requirements and challenges, and between a heuristic and a rhetorical level.

Kerstin had to write a 700-character abstract for a project proposal. When she started to draft her texts, she knew already exactly what she wanted to say. The heuristic challenges were quite low, because she had met them before, in a former writing process: while writing the proposal. The only challenge for her was to put her thoughts elegantly and eloquently into 700 characters which required a high-density text. Thus, the challenge Kerstin had to meet was merely a rhetorical one.

A similar pattern occurred in the case study with Lajos (CS5): He writes abstracts for planned conference contributions, in re-using material from his doctoral thesis. In the interview, he explicitly addresses the low heuristic demands of those texts for him and calls this writing "Verwurstelung" (stuffing, re-using like bits of meat in a sausage).

Andrea (CS1), in turn, met high challenges with a text that might be a routine genre for many experienced writers: a book review for an academic journal. She engaged with this genre for the first time in her life and perceived it as extremely challenging (to some extent because the text was to be published).

These examples show more than just differences between experienced and novice writers. In a closer look, they illustrate the importance of *task-related* preliminary work for the perception of challenges. The HRRC concept (and the entire PROSIMS writing process model) takes such task-related preliminary work into account. For later[3] case studies, the HRRC concept provided already useful categories for analysis. Nevertheless, following the "squinting hermeneutics" described above, we tried to remain unprejudiced and open for new categories and refinements during the entire analysis. This way, step by step, the whole picture of the model was completed during the cross-case analysis.

---

3   The chronological numbering of the case studies refers to their first delivery of a screen capturing video, not to the time when a case study was completed. In fact, CS12 was already the second case study that could be completed (after CS2). Some of the participants delivered screen capturing videos over a long time (for example Andrea, CS1, over a year), others over a few days (for example Kerstin, CS12, or Terèz, CS17).

The PROSIMS Writing Process Model

To produce functional texts, writers address several requirements during the writing process. They develop ideas, reflect on connections between them, and (virtually) communicate with their readers about those ideas and connections. They find out what they want to say and put it in a linear macrostructure. They refine ideas in language(s) and juggle with interrelations between all those aims and aspects thereof. Writers carry out various activities during the writing process to meet the aims described.

Several models have focused on these mental and physical activities. Overviews of writing process models have been provided by Molitor-Lübbert (1996), Alamargot and Chanquoy (2001), Göpferich (2002), Heine (2010), Girgensohn and Sennewald (2012) or Heine (2021), each following different selection criteria and thus come to different selection of models. Some models have become quite influential for further research. Among these are the models of Hayes and Flower (1980), Bereiter and Scardamalia (1987), Baer et al. (1995), Hayes (1996 and 2012) or Göpferich (2002). While the respective focus of writing process models differs, they have (at least) one aspect in common: They aim to cover *supra-individual commonalities* of writing and the sequencing of activities.[4]

Other approaches (like Bridwell-Bowles et al., 1987; Chandler, 1995; Keseling 2004; Lange 2012; Ortner 2000; or Wyllie 2000) shift the focus to *individual differences* in writing processes concerning activities, strategies applied, and the role and succession of these strategies during the writing process. These approaches, again, have in common that they point out individual variation—and refrain from designing writing process *models*.

The PROSIMS writing process model, in turn, tries to cover both aims: It takes individual differences and situational variation into consideration *and* it aims to process them in a model. To make this possible, the model shifts the focus from labeling writing *activities* to exploring specific *contextual and situational conditions*. Writing activities, then, can be analyzed in interrelation with those situational conditions and other (biographical, institutional, etc.) contexts. In the following subsections, the three parts of the PROSIMS writing process model are described in detail.

---

4   Writing process models sometimes have been misunderstood concerning the sequencing of the activities concerned. For example, in German speaking countries, the Hayes & Flower (1980) model was whispered down from academic discourse to curricula until the activities of planning, translating and reviewing were interpreted as "phases" of the writing process (see Baurmann, 1995, p. 52).

The Situations-Sequence Model

The situation-sequence model (Figure 6.1) conceptualizes the writing process as a sequence of *writing situations*, each shaped by specific heuristic and rhetorical requirements and challenges (HRRC)—instead of addressing a sequence of specific writing activities. Writing *activities* come into play where the writing situations are linked together: Through applying strategies and routines, writers change the current writing situation and shape those that follow. Whatever a writer does in a specific writing situation alters the conditions of the situation and creates a new one. Therefore, writing processes can be considered as a succession of altering writing situations, which are linked by writers' acting. The dynamics of writing vary from writer to writer and from writing process to writing process. The PROSIMS writing process model focuses on task-driven and *successful* writing with the objective to lead to an effective text at the end of the writing process. (This does not mean that every writing process reaches this end, and that every text at the end is a high-quality text that meets all requirements it should. However, the writing process *aims* at this goal, and writing situations are geared for it.)

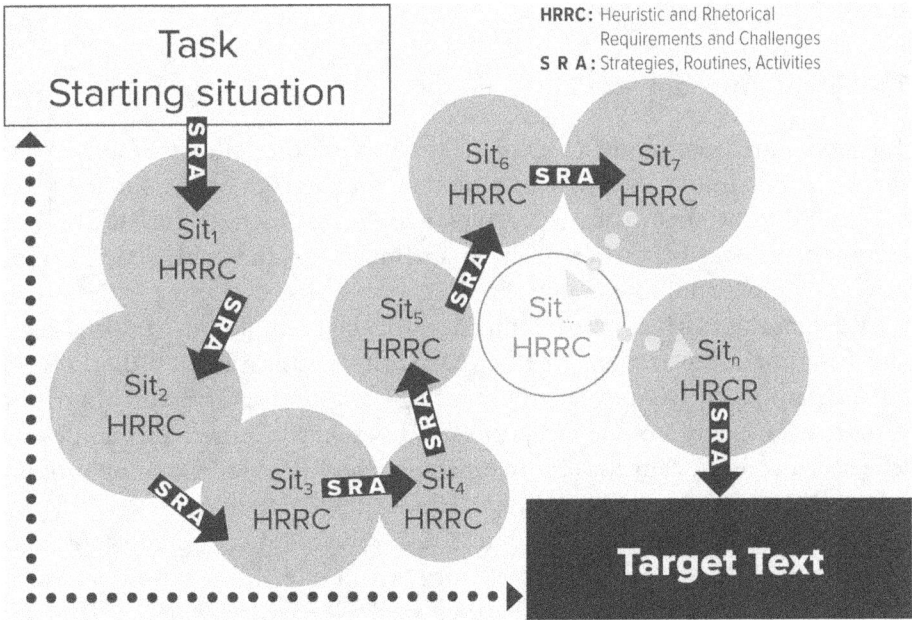

Figure 6.1. PROSIMS writing process model part 1— the situations-sequence model.[5]

---

5   A German version of the model was initially published in Dengscherz

From the perspective of writing success and efficacy, functional writing routines and strategies can be considered as activities that alter a specific writing situation in a direction the writer is comfortable with. In other words, successful, efficient writing means creating writing situations the writer *likes* to enter and to deal with. From this perspective, processual success means that the writer shapes situations in a way (s)he is fine with, and this way navigates through the writing process. The criteria that distinguish a *welcome* situation from a situation from an *unwelcome* one differ individually, and, the activities that lead to the respective next situation differ situationally. The model deliberately does not answer the question *which* situations are convenient to enter or *which* activities are carried out during writing. Situational preferences vary individually, and activities vary according to the conditions of the writing situations and the aims, experience and needs of individual writers.

The situations-sequence model determines neither specific writing activities nor the number of writing situations in a writing process. It addresses the writing process in a very general manner. To learn more about the conditions of writing situations and their respective interrelating influence factors, we need to zoom into the situation. And this is what the situation-zoom model does.

The Situation-zoom Model

The situation-zoom model (Figure 6.2) focuses on the influence factors that shape the conditions of a writing situation. At the core of the situation are heuristic and/or rhetorical requirements and/or challenges (HRRC). Task requirements and other factors have an impact on these HRRC. Further environmental conditions frame the situation and its conditions.

We met the HRRC concept already with the examples of Kerstin, Lajos, and Andrea (in the section "The HRRC Concept: Insights into the Process of Integrated Analysis and Theory Building"). Its double distinction between a heuristic and a rhetorical dimension and between requirements and challenges is a core concept for all three parts of the PROSIMS writing process model. Therefore, the concept will be discussed in detail now.

The heuristic dimension refers to the development of thoughts through writing, the rhetoric dimension is focused on the presentation of those thoughts for a specific audience. In other words: The writers work *on their own understanding* of a topic in the heuristic dimension, whereas in the rhetorical

---

(2019). In this chapter, the PROSIMS writing process model is published for the first time in English.

dimension they try to make their insights *understandable for others*. The heuristic and the rhetorical dimensions must not be equated with content and language. In fact, writers work with language in both dimensions. But they can do it in different ways. The heuristic dimension aims at knowledge transforming in the sense of Bereiter and Scardamalia (1987) while the rhetoric dimension is focused on *knowledge crafting* in the sense of Kellogg (2008).

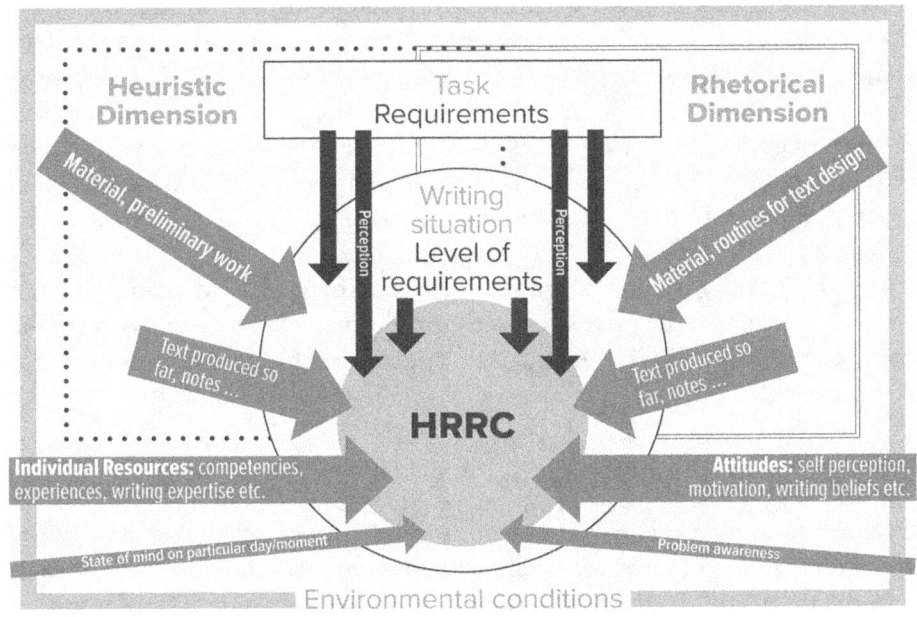

Figure 6.2. PROSIMS writing process model part 2—the situation-zoom model.

The HRRC concept explicitly addresses the writing process in situ (instead of focusing on writing development or writing competence, as in Kellogg, 2008). However, writing development and writers' competences implicitly become important when it comes to the second distinction: the distinction between requirements and challenges. *Requirements* refer to the level of the writing task, to the needs of the *product*, the *text* to be written, whereas *challenges* depend on *the writers' perception* of these requirements. Their perception partly depends on the level of requirements in a specific writing situation. And the level of requirements, in turn, depends on the writing task as well as on preliminary work (in the heuristic and the rhetorical dimension) and on several other factors like individual resources (competencies, experiences, writing expertise, etc.), attitudes (self-perception, motivation, writing beliefs, etc.), problem awareness and the writer's state of mind on the day or in the moment.

The distinctions in the HRRC concept help to understand writing behavior in its functional dimensions and to explain individual and situational variation. Furthermore, the HRRC concept helps to distinguish between strategies and routines: Requirements can often be addressed through routines, whereas strategies are usually needed for overcoming challenges. While requirements refer to the product level, challenges refer to the writing situation and the writers' perceptions. Therefore, challenges do not only depend on the demands of the target text but also on the material, experience and competence that writers bring into a writing situation. In some cases, even high text requirements on the product level do not lead to the perception of difficulties, while in other cases even seemingly low text requirements can be perceived as quite challenging. To paraphrase Wrobel (1995, p. 23), in extreme cases, a holiday postcard can become a writing problem, and a novel routine.

In the writing situation, the factors that shape this situation and the writer's background as well as activities interact with each other. The third part of the model, the situation-interaction model, focuses on these interactions.

The Situation-interaction Model

The distinction between requirements and challenges helps to analyze writers' actions in the process, especially when it comes to strategies and routines and the (strategic) handling of language resources in (multilingual) writing processes.[6] In the third part of the model, the situations-interaction model, we take a closer look at the factors that determine the interrelations between writing activities and other factors in a specific writing situation. The situation-interaction model (Figure 6.3) takes up the HRRC concept, again, from another perspective and locates it in its interactions in the writing situation.

The situation-interaction model conceptualizes the interrelation of writing activities and other factors shaping a writing situation. Writing behavior is contextualized in the writers' verbal and strategy repertoire as well as in

---

6   The handling of language resources—and maybe of more than one language during writing—is especially important for writing in an L2. However, in academic writing as well as other forms of professional/demanding writing, the rhetorical text design often affords kinds of language use that differs from vernacular L1. Against this background, Knorr and Pogner (2015) point out that academic language can be interpreted as a kind of foreign language for everybody. The HRRC concept points to the possibility of separating rhetorical text design and heuristic aspects when this perceived as necessary or helpful by the writers.

writing habits on the one side, and the writing tasks and its requirements on the other side. While repertoires and habits are embedded into individual approaches and individual needs in general, the writing task is embedded into an institutional environment. The tasks' general requirements lead to specific levels of requirements in specific writing situations. The interaction between HRRC and writing behavior (such as routines, strategies or handling of language/s) is further influenced by motivation and individual goals within the writing situation as well as by writing experience[7] and suggestions of guidebooks and writing didactics. (This does not mean that the writers *follow* these suggestions. Actually, they might oppose them as well). Thus, the model covers interrelations at several levels: some referring to the specific writing situation, others to more general influence factors on the writing process.

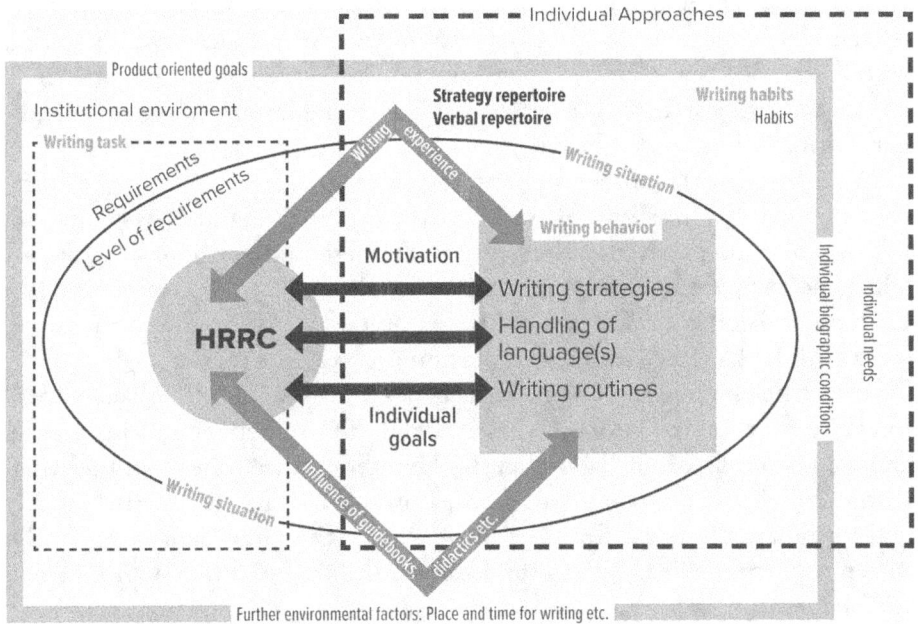

Figure 6.3. PROSIMS writing process model part 3— the situation-interaction model.

---

7   Writing experience refers to previous writing processes, to the perceptions and the memories that come along with them. It refers to transferable knowledge as well as to emotional factors. Reflecting writing experience is an important source for the development of strategy repertoires: writers have learned about their strengths and weaknesses as well as their preferences for specific kinds of writing situations. On this base, they can apply their strategies and routines in the writing process.

The case studies provide rich material with examples for individual preferences, for instance concerning the field of tension between spontaneous writing in the flow, the (feeling of) security that is provided by planning and the need for revision of draft versions. Some writers rely on writing in the flow and the feeling of discovering their own thoughts through writing. Carmen (CS11), for example, hates revising when it affects higher order concerns. However, this does not mean that she would apply low quality standards for her texts. On the contrary, if she considers a text part or entire text as not satisfying, she re-writes it. Her re-writing can be interpreted as an especially radical form of revision that effects even "highest order concerns" (Dengscherz, 2019, p. 498).

With her writing habits, Carmen shapes writing situations that offer starting points for following ones she can rely on and meet her preferences. A first version, even if not yet satisfying, allows her to work on some aspects on the text while writing spontaneously in the flow. If she writes a second version, the first one serves as a starting point for a mental text plan that will be revised during writing. Since Carmen likes formulating and writes quickly, her writing habits work efficiently for her.

Manuel (CS10), another student and very experienced writer (he came back to university after approximately 20 years of working life), has quite different habits and preferences. He starts with rough draft versions of thoughts, which he revises and refines in adding details step by step. In contrast to Carmen, revision is a main part of his text production. It often takes up to 20 steps until he has reached the final version of a single sentence.

Nevertheless, he shares some similarities with Carmen: He likes to formulate sentences and text passages in detail, the sentences and texts parts early look complete and elaborated (in the interview, he states that the visual aesthetic is important for him). Both, Carmen and Manuel, write quickly and formulate their text from the beginning in the target language (on the screen capturing videos, this is the L2 English for Carmen and L2 German for Manuel).

While Carmen and Manuel enjoy writing, Andrea (CS1) perceives it as very difficult, not only in her L2 German but also in her L1 Hungarian. She *is* able to produce functional texts but it takes a lot of time and energy, and she applies multiple strategies to reach her goals. One of those strategies is to split heuristic and rhetorical demands of the text. Unlike Carmen and Manuel, she considers formulating as very difficult and energy-consuming and tries to minimize the formulating expense. Therefore, she works a lot with plans and notes, and leaves formulating for the final version of a text or paragraph. For her notes, she often draws on multilingual language resources, especially when she is working on a complex heuristic problem and tries to find out what exactly she wants to say.

As we see, writers apply their repertoires of strategies and routines according to their competences and preferences and the needs of the actual situation (for example drafting and fixing meaning, working on a complex heuristic problem or elaborating thoughts, in a next version or by adding details). For example, it makes a difference if a writer likes or dislikes phrasing in the target languages: Some strategies focus on reducing this phrasing in early phases or to make it easier through preliminary work. The PROSIMS writing process model aims at covering the complex interrelations between the requirements and challenges of writing situations in their specific context—and in the context of individual needs, habits and preferences (for reflections on the complexity of professional learning see also Melonashi et al. in this volume).

The Quantitative Dimension: A Survey on Writing Behavior at the CTS

The quantitative survey, which was conducted at the end of the project, fulfilled mainly two goals: First, it was used for testing the model, especially concerning the relevance of influence factors on writing behavior. Second, it aimed at eliciting quantitative information about writing strategies and routines that could be observed in the case studies, especially concerning the handling of languages in the writing process.

Via the German platform "Umfrage online," the questionnaire was sent to students, teachers and researchers at the CTS in October 2019. Since multilingual writing was at the core of the project, the context of translation studies and transcultural communication was considered as appropriate for the survey because students as well as most teachers and researchers write in multiple working languages. Additionally, they share a disciplinary context which makes the results more comparable. While in the case studies, comparability was side-lined in favor of a preferably broad range of writing situations as well as diverse individual backgrounds, comparability is more important in the survey

However, the survey does not aim at comparing patterns of writing behavior between groups of writers (like students or researchers), since the case study analysis illustrated that writing experience cannot be reduced to the categories of students or teacher/researcher. More experienced and less experienced writers can be found in both groups (Dengscherz, 2019). Instead, the survey is interested in the overall quantitative distribution of writing behavior that could be observed in the case studies.

Three hundred ninety-six persons participated in the survey. Three hundred ten of them completed the entire questionnaire. The largest groups of the participants are students in the BA program (49.4%) and in the MA program (36.1%). Additionally, teachers (10.3%), researchers (6.9%), and tutors (1.3%) at the CTS participated in the survey. Some of the participants (7%) belong to more than one of those groups (they are, for example, MA students and tutors, or teachers and researchers). Two hundred thirty-one participants affirmed that in the past year they had been engaged in forms of professional writing that the PROSIMS project was interested in (such as academic writing or text production in other demanding genres, see "The HRRC Concept: Insights into the Process of Integrated Analysis and Theory Building"). The tables hereafter focus on the answers of those 231 participants.

The following sections summarize important results from this survey. First, I focus on testing the model, thus on results concerning influence factors on writing behavior. Second, I analyze the participants' answers concerning the handling of language resources in multilingual writing contexts and compare them with observations from the case studies. Based on this triangulation of data, I reflect on multilingual repertoires as strategic resources in writing processes.

Testing the Model: Influence Factors on Writing Behavior

For testing the PROSIMS writing process model, the survey participants were asked to rate the impact of several factors influencing their writing. The provided response options are related to factors occurring in the PROSIMS writing process model. Though the perception of these factors varies individually, the results show clearly that the factors mentioned in the model are influential for most writers (see Table 6.1).

The main results of this part of the survey can be summarized as follows. First, most participants seem to be aware of influence factors on their writing behavior: The option "I can't tell" was hardly taken. Second, the influence factors mentioned in the model and listed in the questionnaire seem to be accurate for most writers. Only few of them noted that a factor had no (or little) influence on their writing. The factors were mostly rated to be of strong (or at least moderate) influence (between 1.29 and 1.97 with a maximum standard deviation of 0.85). Further, the questionnaire offered the possibility of including additional influence factors, but the participants hardly made any use of this option.

Table 6.1. Survey Participants Rate the Influence of Different Factors on their Writing Behavior*

Provided response options	Strong influence (1)	Moderate influence (2)	Little influence (3)	No influence (4)	I can't tell	Average score	SD
	numbers in %					∅	±
Requirements of the target text	74.89	22.08	1.30	1.30	0.43	1.29	0.56
Frame-work conditions (for example time)	63.64	26.84	7.79	1.73	—	1.48	0.72
Previous experience (with the genre)	58.08	34.93	5.24	0.87	0.88	1.48	0.64
Anticipated difficulties concerning the target text	46.29	36.68	13.10	0.87	3.06	1.58	0.74
Own attitudes towards writing	54.82	32.02	7.02	3.95	2.19	1.59	0.79
Notes and text produced so far	47.19	39.39	11.69	1.30	0.43	1.67	0.73
State of mind at a day/moment	48.48	32.02	16.02	1.74	1.74	1.70	0.80
Importance of the target text	45.89	35.50	13.85	4.33	0.43	1.77	0.85
Already existing/previous elaborated material	33.04	51.30	12.17	1.30	2.19	1.81	0.69
Routines: I do what has proven successful in previous writing situations	30.43	42.17	17.83	4.78	4.79	1.97	0.84

*1=strong influence; 4=no influence; n=231

It can be concluded that the qualitative and the quantitative research led to matching results. According to the participants in the survey, the PROSIMS writing model seems to cover the most important influence factors on writing situations. Nevertheless, it would be interesting to test the validity of the model by implementing it in further contexts and to carry out additional research.

Patterns in the Handling of Language Resources

Writing in multilingual contexts allows for various ways of handling language(s) in the writing process (see also Lange, 2012, and Machura, this volume). In the case studies, some patterns of strategic application of language resources could be observed. Based on these findings, the participants in the survey were asked about the ways they apply their language resources in second language writing settings. The language command expected from students at the CTS is quite high (minimum B2 for their working languages, for German and English it is C1). Most of them prefer to write immediately in the target language. A quarter of the participants stated to use only the target language in writing, an even larger group (40.2%) rely on the target language whenever possible. However, nearly half of the group (44.6%) confirmed to take notes in different languages, and a third of the participants shifts to another language when they cannot express in the target language what they want to say. Nearly a quarter of the writers (23.7%) indicated to use their entire language repertoire (see Table 6.2).

Table 6.2. Individual Variation in the Handling of Language Resources: "Which language(s) do you use when writing in a foreign/second language?" (Multiple Answers Allowed)

	%
Only the target language.	25.0
The target language whenever possible.	40.2
I like to take notes in different languages.	44.6
I shift to another language when I can't express in the target language what I want to say.	31.3
I use my entire language repertoire for writing.	23.7
It varies.	8.9
I can't tell. I did not observe myself consciously.	2.2

The participants seem to be quite aware of their handling of languages in the writing process, and their language use varies. Some of them (8.9%) explicitly state this variation, and most writers chose more than one of the answering options. As observed in the case studies: Individual variation is only one side of the coin—situational variation is just as important. Therefore, another question of the survey focused more specifically on writing situations. The participants were asked, in which situations they apply language resources from other languages than the target language. Table 6.3 summarizes their answers.

Table 6.3. Situational Variation in the Handling of Language Resources: "In which situations do you apply other languages than the target language?" (Multiple Answers Allowed)

	%
For investigation.	80.4
For gaining ideas.	71.4
When developing the structure of the text.	29.2
When I use writing to ponder a difficult issue.	31.3
When I have difficulties to express my thoughts in the target language.	63.1
Other.	6.0

Investigation is the most common option (80.4%) for the use of another language than the target language. Similarly, in the case studies, even writers who tried to write entirely in the target language, *did* take advantage of their multilingual repertoire for investigation. Further, writers make use of multilingual resources for gaining ideas (71.4%), for developing the macrostructure of the text (29.2%) or for thinking over a complex problem (39.9%). Further, a large majority of the participants (63.1%) stated that they shift to another language when they cannot express in the target language what they want to say.

The writers' choice of language resources depends to some extent on individual attitudes. Individual attitudes towards multilingual writing and their own multilingual repertoires are an important aspect: In the case studies, it became obvious that some writers try to "switch" to the target language entirely and get confused when alternating between languages, while others experience a creative potential in working multilingually.

Further, situational foci are important. For a deeper understanding of the strategic, functional handling of language resources the HRRC concept is helpful. In the case studies, it could be observed that heuristic and rhetorical aspects were sometimes addressed separately. For overcoming heuristic or rhetorical challenges, it proved a reasonable strategy for some writers to single out either heuristic or rhetorical aspects and address them specifically while ignoring other problems of the text in the meantime. When working on complex heuristic problems, some writers largely leave aside the rhetorical requirements of the target text (as recommended by Elbow as early as 1973). When those writers focus explicitly on the epistemic-heuristic function of writing (Molitor, 1985), on knowledge transforming and knowledge making during writing, they do not address an external audience in the first place. Draft versions need not be accessible and understandable for an external audience, the drafting rather enables the writers to take further steps with their texts. This opens spaces for translanguaging (García & Kleyn, 2016; García & Wei, 2014) and other forms of multilingual and translingual writing.

This does not necessarily mean that all writers occupy translingual spaces or separate heuristic and rhetorical requirements at all. In the case studies, some writers disassemble challenges in another way: They break down complex heuristic challenges into smaller parts (instead of separating them from rhetorical requirements). Manuel, for example, adds details step by step, and Carmen elaborates thoughts in writing a new version of a paragraph (or even an entire text), if necessary. Some writers, like Lajos or Manuel, explicitly write everything in the target language, even when focused on heuristic aspects and/or taking notes.

In most cases, however, multilingual and translingual strategies could be observed. Some writers used to write multilingual text passages, others took notes in their L1, and one of the participants (Andrea, CS1) "invented" a special orthography for notes in Hungarian which was compatible with German keyboard settings (she wrote her MA thesis in German but often took notes in Hungarian). Andrea reduces formulating (in the target language) to a minimum.[8] In her multilingual notes, Andrea applies specialist terminology in the target language (German), embedded in multilingual or Hungarian sentences (the syntax mainly in Hungarian). Andrea types economically, sparing characters (often using abbreviations or switching to another language for a shorter word; for example, writing "done" instead of the German "erledigt" or the Hungarian "elvégzett").

Multilingual strategies are valued differently by the writers, depending on their focus on heuristic or rhetorical aspects. Those writers who applied multilingual or translingual strategies in the writing process, appreciated them when working on heuristic or macrostructural aspects of their texts. When

---

8   When it comes to the final version, even Andrea tries to phrase everything immediately in the target language, using online dictionaries and drawing on her notes. If she cannot find the right words, she leaves a gap, uses a related word in the target language or some (Hungarian or multilingual) hints on what should be said at this point.

focused on the heuristic dimension, multilingual and translingual writing tends to be perceived as a free decision, for example a strategy for openness and creativity. When it comes to rhetorical questions of the text design, in turn, the case study participants mostly prefer to formulate in the target language—if their language command allows it (Dengscherz, 2019). The writers shift to another language when they have no other choice, thus, when they are not able to express their ideas in the target language. While multilingual notes and drafts that focus on the heuristic dimension of the text production are an individual strategy of those writers who deliberately opt to employ them, code shifting while addressing the rhetorical aspects of the target text is rather perceived as a "provisional prosthesis," a temporary aid for dealing with the unfortunate lack of language proficiency: a problem-solving strategy for a problem the writers would prefer not to have in the first place (Dengscherz, 2019; 2020).

Based on these observations in the cased studies, the participants of the survey were asked explicitly about the functions of applying language resources beyond the target language. Most of the writers point to reasons of "security" (51.2%), or creativity, in pointing out that they gain different ideas in different languages (54.8%), or feelings of "freedom" when they can use all language resources that come to their mind (51.2%). The need for compensation is stated by a third of the participants (33.9). Additionally, a smaller group of participants (7.1%) sometimes deliberately writes multilingual texts (see Table 6.4). In an open answer box, the participants were encouraged to elaborate the category "other": They referred to spontaneity and to the precision of expressions on the one hand, and to maintaining the writing flow or silencing their inner critic on the other hand. Additionally, they stated variation according to audience or genre.

Table 6.4. Functions of Using Other Language/s than the Target Language in Writing (Multiple Answers Allowed)

	%
I choose a language in which I feel secure.	51.2
I have different ideas in different languages.	54.8
I feel free when I can use all languages that come to my mind.	51.2
I would prefer to use the target language only but this does not always work (at once).	33.9
I write deliberately multilingual texts.	7.1
Other.	6

All in all, the survey complemented observations from the case studies with information about their quantitative distribution. The survey results can be interpreted best when compared to the "thick description" of the case studies and the theoretical insights in the PROSIMS writing process model (and HRRC concept). Together, the theory development, the quantitative case studies and the quantitative data make the whole of the project results concerning individual and situational variation in the handling of multilingual language resources in writing.

Conclusion and Outlook

The PROSIMS writing process model supports the analysis of writing activities in the context of the writing situation and its specific conditions. The model addresses writers' actions systematically on context levels: First, it locates writing situations in the context of the writing process, and, second, it conceptualizes heuristic and rhetorical requirements and challenges in the context of writing situations, writing tasks, institutional and biographical factors, etc.

In its focus on factorial interrelations in writing situations, the model supports a deeper understanding of writing processes in their individual and situational variation. Activities, such as strategies or routines, meet specific heuristic/rhetorical requirements/challenges (HRRC) in writing situations. The PROSIMS writing process model aims at the comprehensibility of variations in writing behavior, since it provides a theoretical base for the analysis of individual strategies, routines, and applications of language resources in their functionality.

Based on empirical data from 17 case studies with students and researchers, the three parts of the model draw on "thick descriptions" (in the sense of Geertz, 1973; for the entire description of the case studies see Dengscherz, 2019) of situational factors in their context and delve step by step into the factorial interrelations in writing situations. While the first part of the model provides a rough sketch of the writing process as a sequence of writing situations that are interlinked by writers' actions, the second part zooms into the writing situation and points out influence factors shaping that specific situation. The writing process is conceptualized as a dynamic system in which the altering of one factor affects several other factors as well. Against this background, the third part of the model focuses on the interrelations between writing activities and the context factors of the writing situation.

The PROSIMS writing process model addresses (epistemic-heuristic) writing processes in quite a general way and is meant to be applicable to various contexts. The empirical base of the model covers a broad range of writing situations and writing tasks. However, they still present just a fraction of all possible writing situations. Therefore, the following limitations should be taken into account: First, the case studies are focused on writing in academic contexts. Second, they are focused on writing in specific disciplines of the humanities (mainly translation studies). Third, the case studies are focused on quite successful multilingual writers. "Successful" is interpreted as writing that leads to functional texts in the end. While, of course, also successful writers may perceive difficulties and challenges, they can rely on their strategy repertoire for overcoming those difficulties and challenges. Fourth, while the model was tested in a survey at the CTS, the questionnaire data does not claim to be representative for other contexts and domains. The survey carried out can be regarded as an example of how the model can be used for further research.

In view of these limitations, it would be desirable to test the model for further contexts, for example in supervision situations (as described by Ankersborg and Pogner, this volume), or for writing in other disciplines or beyond academia, or for different groups of writers (for example writers that struggle with writing block and thus do not come to a target text at all). Further research will be needed to find out to what extent the model can be transferred to those contexts, and how it could or should be adapted for them. Thus, the model provides several starting points for further research. If the model is to be applied to collaborative writing, researchers have to consider that the conditions of the writing situation are even more complex when it comes to simultaneous collaborative writing. The other writers in the group shape the writing situations with their competences, attitudes, and preferences as well as their repertoire of strategies and routines. Their approaches are interconnected in the joint writing process. When applied to collaborative writing, the model can build a base for reflecting the different perspectives of individual writers in the group that collaborates. Modes of collaboration can be interpreted as factors that shape the specific writing situation, and a writing situation might be or feel different for every single writer that is part of the group. The model can serve as base for reflecting and discussing these different perceptions and help negotiating modes of collaboration that work best for the specific group.

Overall, the PROSIMS writing process model is designed to support a closer look into strategies and routines applied in writing situations. It aims at perceiving them in their functionality for specific aims that are important for individual writers at particular moments in the writing process. Though writing behavior is not predictable, it is not random either. Addressing individual writing activities in their situational functionality against the background of additional context factors leads to a deeper understanding of the individual and situational variation in writing processes. Such a deeper understanding, again, is helpful for writing support and didactics, especially for the reflection of individual writing habits in interrelation with their specific functions in writing situations. In defining factors that influence individual writing activities, and conditions that lead to challenges, the model helps to analyze the specific nature of situational challenges against the background of individual needs and attitudes. This way, the PROSIMS writing process model supports the reflection of strategies that might be useful for overcoming these challenges in the writing process.

Acknowledgments

The PROSIMS project was third-party funded by the Austrian Science Fund FWF in the Elise Richter program (Project No. V-342). I would like to thank the FWF for this funding, my project assistant Melanie Steindl for her reliability and her contributions to the research: She wrote many of the extensive video sequence protocols, guided the interviews with me, and was a great partner for discussing the results. Additionally, I would like to thank Judith Platter who did the transcriptions of the interviews. Last but not least, I am grateful to all participants for their time, efforts, and trust in my research, and to the editors and reviewers of this book for their helpful suggestions and their support.

References

Adler-Kassner, L. & Wardle, E., (Eds.). (2015). *Naming what we know. Threshold concepts of writing studies*. Utah State University Press.
Alamargot, D. & Chanquoy, L. (2001). *Through the models of writing*. Kluwer Academic Publishers.
Baer, M., Fuchs, M., Reber-Wyss, M., Ueli, J. & Nussbaum, T. (1995). Das "Orchester-Modell" der Textproduktion. In J. Baurmann & R. Weingarten (Eds.), *Schreiben. Prozesse, Prozeduren und Produkte* (pp. 173–200). Springer. https://doi.org/10.1007/978-3-322-97050-3_9.
Baurmann, J. (1995). Schreiben in der Schule: Orientierung an Schreibprozessen. In J. Baurmann & R. Weingarten (Eds.), *Schreiben. Prozesse, Prozeduren und Produkte* (pp. 51–69). Springer. https://doi.org/10.1007/978-3-322-97050-3_3.
Beaufort, A. (2005). Adapting to new writing situations. How writers gain new skills. In E.-M. Jakobs, K. Lehnen & K. Schindler (Eds*.)*, *Schreiben am Arbeitsplatz* (pp. 201–216). VS Verlag für Sozialwissenschaften. https://doi.org/10.1007/978-3-322-80777-9_11.
Beaufort, A. & Iñesta, A. (2014). Author profiles: Awareness, competence, and skills. In E.-M. Jakobs & D. Perrin (Eds.), *Handbook of writing and text production* (pp. 141–158). De Gruyter. https://doi.org/10.1515/9783110220674.

Beaugrande, de R. (1984). *Textproduction. Toward a science of composition.* Ablex.
Becker-Mrotzek, M. & Schindler, K. (2007). Schreibkompetenzen modellieren. In M. Becker-Mrotzek & K. Schindler (Eds.), *Texte schreiben* (pp. 7–26). Gilles & Francke.
Bereiter, C. (1980). Development in writing. In L. W. Gregg & E. R. Steinberg (Eds.), *Cognitive processes in writing* (pp. 73–93). Erlbaum. https://doi.org/10.4324/9781315630274.
Bereiter, C. & Scardamalia, M. (1987). *The psychology of written composition.* Routledge. https://doi.org/10.4324/9780203812310.
Blommaert, J. (2010). *The sociolinguistics of globalization.* Cambridge University Press. https://doi.org/10.1017/CBO9780511845307.
Breuer, F. (2009). *Reflexive Grounded Theory. Eine Einführung für die Forschungspraxis.* VS Verlag für Sozialwissenschaften. https://doi.org/10.1007/978-3-531-92580-6.
Bridwell-Bowles, L., Johnson, P. & Brehe, S. (1987). Composing and computers: Case studies of experienced writers. In A. Matsuhashi (Ed.), *Writing in real time. Modeling production processes* (pp. 81–107). Ablex Publishing Corporation.
Canagarajah, S. (2012). *Translingual practice. Global Englishes and cosmopolitan relations.* Routledge. https://doi.org/10.4324/9780203073889.
Chandler, D. (1995). *The act of writing: A media theory approach.* UWA.
Charmaz, K. (2006). *Constructing grounded theory. A practical guide through qualitative analysis.* SAGE.
De Angelis, G. & Jessner, U. (2012). Writing across languages in a bilingual context: A dynamic systems theory approach. In R. Manchón (Ed.), *L2 writing development: Multiple perspectives* (pp. 47–68). de Gruyter. https://doi.org/10.1515/9781934078303.47.
Dengscherz, S. (2017). Potentiale und Grenzen retrospektiver Interviews in der Schreib(prozess)forschung. In M. Brinkschule & D. Kreitz (Eds.), *Qualitative Methoden in der angewandten Schreibforschung* (pp. 139–158) (Theorie und Praxis der Schreibwissenschaft, Bd. 1). wbv. https://doi.org/10.3278/6004549w.
Dengscherz, S. (2018). Heuristische und rhetorische Herausforderungen meistern—Strategien für wissenschaftliches Formulieren in der L2 Deutsch. In M. Nied Curcio & D. Cortés Velásquez (Eds.), *Strategien im Kontext des mehrsprachigen und lebenslangen Lernens* (pp. 211–232). Frank & Timme.
Dengscherz, S. (2019). *Professionelles Schreiben in mehreren Sprachen. Strategien, Routinen und Sprachen im Schreibprozess.* Peter Lang. https://doi.org/10.3726/b16495.
Dengscherz, S. (2020). Professionelles schreiben in mehreren sprachen—das PROSIMS-schreibprozessmodell. *ZIF Zeitschrift für Interkulturellen Fremdsprachenunterricht, 25*(1), 397–422. https://tujournals.ulb.tu-darmstadt.de/index.php/zif/article/view/1023/1020.
Dengscherz, S. & Steindl, M. (2016). "Prepare an outline first and then just write spontaneously"—An analysis of students' writing strategies and their attitudes towards professional writing. In S. Göpferich & I. Neumann (Eds.), *Developing and assessing academic and professional writing skills* (pp. 173–202). Peter Lang. https://doi.org/10.3726/978-3-653-06614-2.

Ehlich, K. (2018). Wissenschaftlich schreiben lernen—von diskursiver Mündlichkeit zu textueller Schriftlichkeit. In S. Schmölzer-Eibinger, B. Bushati, C. Ebner & L. Niederdorfer (Eds), *Wissenschaftliches schreiben lehren und lernen. Diagnose und Förderung wissenschaftlicher Textkompetenz in Schule und Universität* (pp. 15–32). Waxmann.

Elbow, P. (1973). *Writing without teachers*. Oxford University Press.

Estrem, H. (2016). Writing is a knowledge-making activity. In L. Adler-Kassner & E. Wardle (Eds.), *Naming what we know. Threshold concepts of writing studies* (pp. 19–20). University Press of Colorado.

García, O. & Kleyn, T. (2016). Translanguaging theory in education. In O. García & T. Kleyn (Eds.), *Translanguaging with multilingual students. Learning from classroom moments* (pp. 9–33). Routledge. https://doi.org/10.4324/9781315695242.

García, O. & Wei, L. (2014). *Translanguaging. Language, bilingualism and education*. Palgrave. https://doi.org/10.1057/9781137385765.

Geertz, C. (1973). Thick description. Toward an interpretive theory of culture. In C. Geertz (Ed.), *The interpretation of cultures: Selected essays* (pp. 3–30). Basic Books.

Girgensohn, K. & Sennewald, N. (2012*). Schreiben lehren, Schreiben lernen*. Wissenschaftliche Buchgesellschaft.

Glaser, A. & Strauss, B. G. (1967). *The discovery of grounded theory: Strategies for qualitative research*. Aldine Publishing Company. https://doi.org/10.1007/978-3-658-13213-2_59.

Göpferich, S. (2002). *Textproduktion im Zeitalter der Globalisierung. Entwicklung einer Didaktik des Wissenstransfers*. Stauffenburg.

Hayes, J. R. (1996). A new framework for understanding cognition and affect in writing. In M. Levy & S. Ransdell (Eds.), *The science of writing: Theories, methods, individual differences, and applications* (pp. 1–27). Erlbaum.

Hayes, J. R. (2012). Modeling and remodeling writing. *Written Communication, 29*(3), 369–388. https://doi.org/10.1177/0741088312451260.

Hayes, J. R. & Flower, L. S. (1980). Identifying the organization of writing processes. In L. W. Gregg & E. R. Steinberg (Eds.), *Cognitive processes in writing* (pp. 3–30). Erlbaum. https://doi.org/10.4324/9781315630274.

Heine, C. (2010). *Modell zur Produktion von Online-Hilfen*. Frank & Timme.

Heine, C. (2021). Einflussfaktor Kontext: Modelle und Methoden in Schreib- und Übersetzungswissenschaft. In S. Reitbrecht (Ed.), *Schreiben in Kontexten* (pp. 15–33). ESV.

Hicks, T. & Perrin, D. (2014). Beyond single modes and media: Writing as an ongoing multimodal text production. In E.-M. Jakobs & D. Perrin (Eds.), *Handbook of writing and text production* (pp. 231–253) De Gruyter. https://doi.org/10.1515/9783110220674.

Jacobs, G. & Perrin, D. (2014). Production modes: Writing as materializing and stimulating thoughts. In E.-M. Jakobs & D. Perrin (Eds.), *Handbook of writing and text production* (pp. 181–208). De Gruyter (Handbook of Applied Linguistics, Vol. 10). https://doi.org/10.1515/9783110220674.

Jakobs, E.-M. (1997). Textproduktion als domänen- und kulturspezifisches Handeln. Diskutiert am Beispiel wissenschaftlichen Schreibens. In K. Adamzik, E.-M. Jakobs & G. Antos (Eds.), *Domänen- und kulturspezifisches Schreiben* (pp. 9–30). Peter Lang.

Kellogg, R. T. (2008). Training writing skills: A cognitive developmental perspective. *Journal of Writing Research, 1*, 1–26. https://doi.org/10.17239/jowr-2008.01.01.1.

Keseling, G. (2004). *Die Einsamkeit des Schreibers. Wie Schreibblockaden entstehen und erfolgreich bearbeitet werden können.* VS Verlag für Sozialwissenschaften. https://doi.org/10.1007/978-3-322-80533-1.

Knappik, M. (2013). *Wege zur wissenschaftlichen Textkompetenz. Schreiben für reflexive Professionalisierung.* Bundesministerium für Unterricht, Kunst und Kultur. https://dafdaz.univie.ac.at/fileadmin/user_upload/lehrstuhl_daf/schreibenfuer reflexiveprofessionalisierung_web-1.pdf.

Knappik, M. (2018). *Schreibend werden. Subjektivierungsprozesse in der Migrationsgesellschaft* (Theorie und Praxis der Schreibwissenschaft, Bd. 6). wbv. https://doi.org/10.3278/6004651w.

Knorr, D. (2019). Sprachsensibles Kompetenzmodell wissenschaftlichen Schreibens. *Zeitschrift für Interkulturellen Fremdsprachenunterricht 24*(1), 165–179. https://tujournals.ulb.tu-darmstadt.de/index.php/zif/article/view/956/955.

Knorr, D. & Pogner, K.-H. (2015). Vom Schreiben zum "Texten" - Akademische Textproduktion unter den Bedingungen von Mehrsprachigkeit. *Fremdsprachen Lehren und Lernen, 44*(1), 110–122.

Kruse, J. (2015). *Qualitative Interviewforschung. Ein integrativer Ansatz. 2., überarbeitete und ergänzte Auflage.* Beltz Juventa.

Lange, U. (2012). Strategien für das wissenschaftliche Schreiben in mehrsprachigen Umgebungen. Eine didaktische Analyse. In D. Knorr & A. Verhein-Jarren (Eds.), *Schreiben unter Bedingungen von Mehrsprachigkeit* (pp. 139–154). Peter Lang. https://doi.org/10.3726/978-3-653-01784-7.

Molitor, S. (1985). Personen- und aufgabenspezifische schreibstrategien. Fünf Fallstudien. *Unterrichtswissenschaft, 1985*(4), 334–345.

Molitor-Lübbert, S. (1996). Schreiben als mentaler und kognitiver Prozeß. In H. Günther & O. Ludwig (Eds.), *Schrift und Schriftlichkeit* (pp. 1005–1027). De Gruyter. https://doi.org/10.1515/9783110147445.2.7.1005.

Ortner, H. (2000). *Schreiben und Denken.* Niemeyer. https://doi.org/10.1515/9783110943313.

Pogner, K.-H. (1997). Diskursgemeinschaft und interaktion. Zum Schreiben von beratenden IngenieurInnen. In K. Adamzik, G. Antos & E.-M. Jakobs (Eds.), *Domänen- und kulturspezifisches schreiben* (pp. 127–150). Peter Lang.

Pohl, T. (2007). *Studien zur Ontogenese wissenschaftlichen Schreibens.* Niemeyer. https://doi.org/10.1515/9783110946116.

Risku, H. & Windhager, F. (2015). Extended translation. A socio-cognitive research agenda. In M. Ehrensberger-Dow, S. Göpferich & S. O'Brien (Eds.), *Interdisciplinarity in translation and interpreting process research* (pp. 35–47). Benjamins. https://doi.org/10.1075/bct.72.04ris.

Russell, D. R. (2010). Writing in multiple contexts: Vygotskian CHAT meets the phenomenology of genre. In C. Bazerman, R. Krut, K. Lunsford, S. McLeod, S. Null, P. Rogers & A. Stansell (Eds.), *Traditions of writing research* (pp. 353–364). Routledge. https://lib.dr.iastate.edu/engl_pubs/278.

Steinhoff, T. (2007). *Wissenschaftliche Textkompetenz. Sprachgebrauch und schreibentwicklung in wissenschaftlichen Texten von Studenten und Experten.* Niemeyer. https://10.1515/9783110973389.

Swales, J. M. & Feak, C. B. (2011). *Navigating academia. Writing supporting genres.* University of Michigan Press.

Wrobel, A. (1995). *Schreiben als handlung. Überlegungen und Untersuchungen zur Theorie der textproduktion.* Niemeyer.

Wyllie, A. (2000). On the road to discovery: A study of the composing strategies of native and non-native academic writers using the word processor. In E. Broady (Ed.), *Second language writing in a computer environment* (pp. 95–116). CILT.

7

Conform, Transform, Resist: The Scandinavian Way of Master's Thesis Supervision and Its Contribution to Acquiring Research Literacy and Practice

Vibeke Ankersborg and Karl-Heinz Pogner
COPENHAGEN BUSINESS SCHOOL

Our contribution explores the concept of supervision in the context of Scandinavian (Danish) Higher Education by investigating how student-centered supervision ("vejledning") can foster and advance students' research literacies when managing their master's thesis project and writing their master's thesis. The theoretical and analytical framework links three different pedagogical models of supervision with three types of supervisor roles. The models describe different kinds of relationships between supervisors and students; the nature of this relationship enables and/or constrains the students' chances to develop research literacy. Our findings show that the partnership model allows for the enactment of all three types of supervisor roles, gives a high degree of flexibility for the supervisor and assigns a high degree of responsibility, autonomy, and independence to the students. The qualitative analyses investigate how the combination of the perceived supervision model and supervisor role affects the students' opportunities to acquire and develop research literacies. In the partnership model, supervision can enhance students' research literacies by empowering the students to make well-informed choices concerning their knowledge production and text production. This shift in responsibility from supervisor to students shapes the meaning and content of student-centered supervision. The combination of the partnership model with student responsibility and autonomy, which is deeply rooted in the problem-oriented project learning approach, can be a fruitful and productive approach in higher education aiming at fostering students' ability to identify, define, and research a relevant "problem." It further contributes to students' competencies to transform and produce knowledge as a contribution to the academic discourse community and community of practice. As legitimate peripheral members of the academic community, students can develop academic and research literacies, in order to become able to INTERPRET the discourse and to decide if they want to conform, transform or resist.

We offer an insight into the characteristics of Danish (and Scandinavian) student-centered supervision, which does not take charge of the students' projects, nor of their research and writing processes, but empowers students to learn to find their own way (in Danish: "vej") to develop academic literacy. We are aiming at unfolding the relationship between supervisor and student in order to show how and why this relationship enables and constrains students in acquiring research literacies that enables them "to 'read' the discourse and then to decide if they want to conform to, transform, or to resist" (Badenhorst & Guerin, 2016, p. 15) existing discourses, cultures and established perceptions. This leads to the following research question: *How can the Danish perception of the act of supervision foster master's students' research literacies including their chance to conform to, transform, or resist established expectations and norms of the academic community?*

We investigate this question by looking at the role of different pedagogical models of supervision (supervision models) and different approaches to supervision (supervisor roles) in student-centered master's thesis supervision in the tradition of problem-oriented project work. The students are enrolled at the Copenhagen Business School, a Danish (business) university offering a wide range of mono- and interdisciplinary study programs mostly with a focus on social science disciplines. We study the influence of the models and roles on the students' chances to acquire knowledge, capabilities, and skills in academic writing (AW) and research literacies (RL).

Lea and Street (1998) have identified three models of student writing in higher education: (1) study skill model: student writing as technical and instrumental skill; (2) academic socialization model: student writing as transparent medium of representation; and (3) academic literacies model: student writing as "meaning-making" and taking into account the "conflicting and contested nature of writing practices" (Lea & Street, 1998, p. 158). In the academic literacies model (3) the focus is on students' "negotiation(s) of literacy practices," literacies are seen as social practices including epistemology and identities; "institutions as sites of/constituted in discourses and power," and the curriculum has to deal with a "variety of communicative repertoire, e.g., genres, fields, disciplines" (Lea & Street, 1998, p 172). In accordance, we conceptualize academic writing as a situated social practice of master's thesis students. This practice is both a process of text production and knowledge production embedded in academic discourse communities and academic communities of practice where the main practice is producing research and discourse (Pogner, 1999, 2003, 2007 & 2012).

When it comes to academic literacies (AL) (Lillis & Scott, 2007a, 2007b), especially to research literacies (Badenhorst & Guerin, 2016) as an essential part of AL, the literacies model goes beyond the study skill approach and includes features of the academic socialization model:

> Literacy is seen as acquiring the epistemologies necessary for participating in a particular discourse. For example, students need to learn what knowledge is valued, what questions can be asked and who is allowed to ask, while at the same time recognizing what they know and how they write what they know (Lea & Street, 2014). (Badenhorst & Guerin, 2016, p. 15)

Socialization is much more than conforming to the expectations and norms of the disciplinary domains and academic discourse communities and communities of practice (Pogner, 2007) in academic "Action and Discourse Spaces" (Knorr & Pogner, 2015, pp. 113-115):

> An academic literacies approach suggests that students should not merely be socialized into academic contexts and taught how to conform to existing cultures; it conversely advocates that students should be able to "read" the discourse and then decide if they want to conform, transform or resist. (Badenhorst & Guerin, 2016, p. 15)

Our analyses focus on the question under which conditions supervision can enable or constrain this conforming, transforming, and resisting of master's thesis students and how supervision models and supervisor roles contribute to shaping learning spaces, which can support the awareness about and ultimately contribute to the acquisition of research literacies.

Lee (2010) interviewed successful (doctoral) supervisors in the UK and from the US. In her analysis a framework emerged which she tested with groups of supervisors at universities in the UK, Sweden, Denmark, South Africa, and Estonia (Lee, 2010). This framework consists of the interrelation of a wide range of different approaches to supervision on the continuum of professional to personal approaches. She conceptualized the approaches as the functional approach (accumulation of knowledge), the enculturation approach (professional and disciplinary practices), the critical thinking approach (cognitive skills), the emancipation approach (discovery) and relationship development approach (shared development) (Lee, 2010). She also reflects on the consequences for the supervisors' knowledge and skills as directing, project management and negotiating; diagnosing and coaching; reasoning and analyzing; facilitating and reflecting; emotional intelligence (Lee 2010).

We want to investigate how different *supervisor roles* and *supervision models* enacted in student-centered supervision embedded in problem-oriented project work can create and constrain a space for balancing or bridging the mentioned, different but interrelated, approaches in practice—according to context, situation, institutional frame, and learning culture. Our analyses complement the different expectations that students might have (certainty, belonging, ability to think in new ways, self-awareness, and friendship), which Lee derives from applying her framework to identifying (doctoral) students' needs (Lee, 2010), with an analysis of master's students' own perspectives and expectations. Within our theoretical and analytical framework of a matrix of supervising models and roles, we analyze 11 qualitative research interviews (Kvale & Brinkmann, 2014) which we have conducted with Danish master's thesis students at the Copenhagen Business School (CBS). In the interviews, the students open a door to their "supervision space" (see Nexø Jensen, 2010).

The remainder of our contribution introduces our methodological reflections about the qualitative data collection and hermeneutical analysis and our theoretical frame, which we operationalize as an analytical framework for our analysis. The framework introduces the educational-cultural background in which the supervision we investigate is embedded. It further introduces supervision models and supervisor roles. Models and roles serve as our preliminary analytical framework for the empirical analysis of qualitative research interviews with master's students in order to analyze supervision practice from the student's perspective. We discuss the results of our analysis by answering the question how the Danish or Scandinavian way of student-centered supervision can foster students' research literacies including the students' ability and capability to conform to, transform, or resist expectations and established norms of the academic research community, they are becoming temporary and peripheral members of. Finally, we conclude by reflecting on the implications of our findings for supervision in general, i.e., beyond master's thesis supervision, and suggest the adaptive extension of student-centered supervision (vejledning) to non-Scandinavian educational cultures.

Hermeneutics and Semi-Structured Qualitative Research Interviews

Our study is based on philosophical hermeneutics according to Hans-Georg Gadamer (2004) and thus uses abductive reasoning. In terms of research design, this means that the point of departure is the *horizon of understanding* of the social scientist. Our "horizon of understanding" is shaped by years of experience as supervisors at universities in Denmark. Therefore, we are thoroughly embedded in the Scandinavian tradition of supervision endorsed by the educational-cultural basis discussed in the section "Educational-cultural basis." We had, however, an assumption that educational reforms in Denmark in recent years had created a gap between the ideals inherent in the tradition and possible ways of conducting supervision in present day Denmark. Based on the hermeneutical concept "prejudice," which should be read and understood as a priori "pre-judice" (Gadamer, 2004, p. 289), we follow Gadamer (2004) and put our assumptions ("horizon of understanding," Gadamer, 2004, p. 143) at stake by selecting two theoretical frameworks embedded in the Scandinavian tradition (supervision models and supervisor roles) and by interviewing 13 students exposed to supervision. The interviews are then interpreted in accordance with the hermeneutical circle, which means that a circular movement is formed between the interpreter (us) and the texts to be interpreted. In this study, we first extended our horizon of understanding with the theoretical frameworks containing the supervision models and the supervisor roles. Then, based on the extended horizon of understanding we have created a first draft of understanding of the interviews. This first draft of understanding modifies our understanding of the supervision models and the supervisor roles, which in turn leads to a second draft of interpretation of the interviews and so on. The (iterative) hermeneutical circle of interpretation is in principle endless, but a valid interpretation, and thus a study's conclusion, is reached when it is no longer possible to find statements in the texts that contradict the interpretation. According to philosophical hermeneutics, each text should be interpreted in its own right. The number of texts supporting a given interpretation does therefore not in itself strengthen or weaken an interpretation. In the present study, the interpretation results in the supervision matrix (vejledning matrix) explained below in "The 'Vejledning' Matrix."

The students also have a horizon of understanding through which they perceive the supervision they receive, their own role as part of the relationship with the supervisor as well as their own learning process and learning outcome. The students are first-hand witnesses to the link between supervision and learning outcome. According to philosophical hermeneutics, the purpose of interpretation is to understand a text, in this case the interviews, on its own terms. Thus, we use the students' expectations toward and first-hand experience of supervision as a lens to investigate how different supervision models and supervisor roles enable and constrain the potential of supervision for students' acquisition of research literacies. To investigate this relation, we conducted interviews with master's thesis writers during or shortly after their master's thesis project and production process. We used the method of purposeful sampling by inviting all master's thesis students with primarily Danish educational backgrounds enrolled in one of the master's programs at the Copenhagen Business School in 2018. This approach allowed us to reach out to students not familiar to us before the interviews. The students were selected in the order they volunteered to participate in order to avoid any biases in the selection, and, thus, we have used a convenience random data collection technique.

The students represent a wide range of CBS' full-time programs most of which are cross- or interdisciplinary study programs in accordance with one of the principles in Illeris' pedagogy (see "Educational-Cultural Basis"). Together, the study programs involved in this study represent a wide range of academic disciplines within social science, the humanities, business administration, and mathematics. This eliminates a possible bias due to any perceived or real differences in supervision styles across study programs. The interviews were conducted in Danish to allow interviewers and interviewees to use the concepts inherent in the problem-oriented project work tradition laid out in the section "Educational-Cultural Basis," which in turn allows us to detect any changes in the perception of these concepts. These selection criteria lead to a group of interviewees who share the same cultural-educational background and at the same time represent variations across disciplines within that background. Given our hermeneutical approach, the aim is to understand each student's perception, reception, and perspective on supervision as well as on the learning and writing process. We use the students' individual experiences and sensemaking of thesis processes to get insights into the potentials of different combinations of supervision models and supervisor roles for students to acquire research literacies.

Through "analytical generalizability" (Kvale, 2007, pp. 121-122; Kvale & Brinkmann, 2014, pp. 260-266; see also Kvale, 1994, pp. 164-166, and Kvale, 1983, pp. 164-169) we expand the insights from the interviews to more general insights into the relationship between supervision models, supervisor roles, and students' possibility to acquire and develop research literacies. With the problem-oriented project work tradition as a point of departure, analytical generalization allows us to suggest what might happen in (partially) similar situations and contexts. By combining the hermeneutical interpretation of the interviews with theories and models about supervision that originate from the same tradition, we are in principle able to falsify, verify, and/or modify these theories and models. This, in turn, results in a new conceptual model, the vejledning matrix, which provides the answer to our research question. The range of our analytical generalization is limited, however, by the focus on the students' perspective and study programs deeply embedded in social science, as well as our choices on epistemology, research design, and method of investigation. We follow Kvale and Brinkmann's seven stages for an interview investigation (2014) when designing, conducting, analyzing and reporting semi-structured qualitative research interviews. According to Kvale, the purpose of qualitative research interviews is to understand each interviewee's views on the topic of the interview from the perspective of the interviewee. Thus, interviewees should not be regarded as respondents representative of a given population, but as a unique source supplying insights into their "horizon of understanding." Thus, epistemologically the semi-structured qualitative research interview method is in accordance with hermeneutics (Kvale, p. 1997; see Kvale 1983). The students in the present study were interviewed in accordance with Kvale and Brinkmann's guidelines (2014, p. 123-142) (for our interview guide see Appendix A).

Our empirical qualitative data consist of 11 semi-structured research interviews with 13 master's thesis students about 11 master's theses projects (see Appendix B). Seven students wrote their master's thesis as a one person's project and were interviewed on their own. Of the remaining six students, two pairs of students wrote their master's thesis as a pair project. All four students participated in the interviews and were interviewed in pairs. The remaining two interviews were conducted with one student each. Both students wrote their master's thesis as a group/pair project, but their respective master's thesis partners did not participate in the interview. The interviews lasted between 45 and 90 minutes. The students were informed about the purpose and topic of the interview in the call for volunteer interviewees and again immediately before each interview began. All students agreed to have the interviews recorded and all students were promised anonymity, therefore the names of the students have been changed. The interviews' first part deals with the students' views on and experience with supervision and the second part deals with the students' writing habits and processes partially using the students' texts as boundary objects and basis for the interview questions. The interviews were transcribed, and the content was analyzed based on the hermeneutic paradigm as discussed above.

Theoretical and Analytical Framework

In this section, we explain the theoretical components of the hermeneutical circle. The two theoretical frameworks (typologies of supervisor models and supervisor roles) are presented in the section "Supervision Models and Supervisor Roles." However, in order to allow the reader to understand the teaching and learning tradition we come from, and in which the master's thesis supervision practice we investigate is embedded in, we start this section by presenting the educational-cultural basis of the Danish education system including the historical background.

Educational-Cultural Basis

A key feature of the Danish educational-cultural basis is problem orientation. Problem orientation is a way of thinking that runs through all levels of the Danish education system. In 1974, Knud Illeris published his seminal book *Problem orientation and participant control: Outline for an alternative didactics* (Illeris, 1974, authors' translation). In the following, we present the principles, which problem orientation is built on, including a number of related key concepts.

Some of the key principles of this pedagogical approach are that pupils and students should work with real societal and social problems, that the students' work has to be research based, and that the problem, not the syllabus, should determine how the problem should be researched. These principles together lead to a cross-disciplinary approach. Other important principles are participant control, which means that the students themselves identify the problem they wish to investigate within the frame of their educational institution, program and discipline/s, as well as the students' ultimate responsibility for designing, planning and conducting the research project. The supervisor neither sets nor states the problem to investigate, nor provides or determines research approach, design, or methodology, because supervisors act primarily as consultants. Participant control implies that students work autonomously, i.e., as independent from their supervisor as possible. Wirenfeldt Jensen (2018) has confirmed the rootedness of autonomy in the problem-orientation tradition in a recent study of the master's thesis genre in Denmark. Across 20 interviews conducted with master's thesis supervisors, the category *autonomy/independency* was mentioned 89 times—even though the category was not part of the interview questions (Wirenfeldt Jensen 2018). Similarly, in our own interviews with thesis supervisors (Ankersborg & Pogner, in press) interviewees referred to autonomy repeatedly regardless of the questions asked.

The emphasis on student autonomy is closely linked to the Danish word for supervision: vejledning. In Danish, the concept vejledning means to enable someone to make their own decisions on an informed basis, and thus the concept vejledning emphasizes the person who receives vejledning, i.e., the student. In comparison, the English concept "supervision" connotes the action or function of overseeing, directing, or taking charge of a person, organization, activity, etc., and thus "supervision" emphasizes the person who supervises, i.e., the supervisor. In accordance, the Danish word for "supervisor" is "vejleder," which corresponds to supervisors acting as consultants. Thus, vejledning follows the logic of problem-oriented project work with its emphasis on participant (= student) control and opens up for empowerment, transformation, and the ability to acquire (academic) literacies (Lillies et al., 2015). Taken together, the essence of vejledning contributes to learners transforming, creating and producing their knowledge themselves.

The term vejledning translates poorly into English. However, in order to avoid confusion, we use the term supervision as the generic term in the remaining part of our contribution, as supervision is the most commonly used term in the English language literature. We reserve vejledning for instances where this term is needed in order to clarify points in the argument. The Danish concept of master's thesis also corresponds with the problem-oriented project work tradition. The Danish word for master's thesis is "speciale," which is an abbreviation for specialization. According to Danish legislation, this means that the student should specialize within a tightly delimited part of their study program's academic discipline/s, and that students must show that they are able to apply theory and methodology within that discipline (Danish Ministry for Education and Science, 2020, § 18). Thus, a speciale (master's thesis) is a problem-oriented comprehensive, but delimited research project, including literature reviewing and (primary) data collecting, conducted independently by (a group of) students. Mainhard et al. (2009) have shown that the term "master's thesis" itself is understood in very different ways across European countries (see also Nissen, 2019, and Wirenfeldt Jensen, 2018, pp. 66-71 for an international perspective). In this chapter, we use the term master's thesis in accordance with the Danish definition.

Problem-orientation is closely linked to time as students work on the same research project for at least several weeks and often up to a whole semester. Another originally crucial aspect of problem orientation is group work, where groups of students work (together) for a longer period and manage the process themselves. Problem-oriented group projects foster the students' collaborative skills and creates an environment for mutual inspiration and even provocation (Illeris, 1974). It also promotes creativity and flexibility, which in turn enables the students to transform and produce knowledge of and on their own, thereby acquiring skills and competencies that can be used across contexts (Illeris, 1974). These skills and competencies allow students to liberate themselves from established norms (Illeris, 1974), which, in the case of our investigation, can facilitate the students' ability to acquire research literacies, including being able to "decide if they want to conform to, transform or resist" (Badenhorst & Guerin, 2016, p. 15) established norms. Learning in the problem-oriented way, therefore, does not focus on small "cases" defined by the teacher, concrete problem-solving on the basis of predefined problem definitions, or students working for a short period of time on cases based on the syllabus as part of classroom teaching. Such learning context characteristics, in contrast, can be present in approaches under the Anglo-Saxon term "problem-based learning" (Krogh & Wiberg, 2015, p. 215).

Illeris' originally alternative didactics quickly became mainstream at all levels of the Danish educational system and has been in force ever since, although with adjustments. In the 1990s, emphasis was no longer on societal problems or challenges; a problem could instead deal with a gap in a discipline's knowledge (Keiding & Laursen, 2008, Olsen & Pedersen, 1997). Thus, the term "problem" should nowadays not be understood as something that went wrong and needs to be fixed, but rather as a question about a matter of a certain complexity, which the academic community in question has not yet answered and therefore needs to be researched—also by students as young members of the academic community. Furthermore, the cross-disciplinary aspect has not been adopted everywhere. However, at the business university Copenhagen Business School (CBS), where we conducted our interviews, cross-disciplinary programs and interdisciplinary specializations are a distinct part of the university's portfolio. The group aspect has also been disputed, which has left traces in Danish legislation. In 2005–2012, oral group exams, but not group projects themselves, were abolished by the Ministry of Education and Science based on a vote by the majority of the members of the Danish parliament. The students at all Danish colleges and universities were in 2018 granted the right to write their bachelor's thesis and master's thesis as a one-student project. At CBS, approximately 40% of the master's students who graduated in 2019 conducted the research project and wrote their master's thesis in groups (mostly of two students); 60% of the students conducted and wrote it individually.

To sum up, problem-oriented master's theses are the standard at Danish universities, and problem-oriented research projects and master's theses still imply student participant control, autonomy/independency, ownership, and responsibility. This means that the students themselves identify and select a problem relevant to their academic discipline. Furthermore, it means that the students plan their research process and conduct their own research over a period of approximately six months as independently as possible from their supervisor, and that the students are responsible for the quality of their research and the submission of the final master's thesis. This has consequences for the role of the supervisor, which will be discussed in the subsequent sections.

Supervision Models and Supervisor Roles

Our analytical framework is designed as a matrix composed of three supervision models and three supervisor types. It is inspired by models of supervisory management and supervisory styles (Boehe, 2016; Gatfield, 2005), different approaches to supervision (Lee, 2010) and the supervisor-student relationship (Mainhard et al., 2009), and on research about supervisors as learners and teachers (Maher & Say, 2016), primarily in doctoral supervision. Although, it is primarily informed by Scandinavian research on supervisor roles (Nexø Jensen, 2010), models of the relationship between supervisor and student/s (Dysthe, 2006; Wichmann-Hansen & Wirenfeldt Jensen, 2015) in master's thesis supervision and supervision in higher education in general. In accordance with the hermeneutical circle, the final matrix and research design has been developed and assessed in the course of our analysis of the interviews.

The central part of the framework for our analysis consists of three supervision models and three supervisor roles mainly originating from research at the University in Bergen, Norway (Dysthe, 2006, Dysthe, Brinkstein et al., 2006, Dysthe, Samara et al., 2006; Dysthe et al., 2007) and the University of Copenhagen, Denmark (Nexø Jensen, 2010). Models and roles will be combined in a supervision matrix (vejledning matrix), where we present the findings of our analysis of interviews with master's thesis students. The matrix and our analysis show how the different supervision models allow different supervisor roles and which influence the flexibility to shift supervisor roles has on the students' chance to acquire research literacies.

Supervision Models

Based on her empirical research in Norway, Olga Dysthe (Dysthe, 2006; Dysthe, Samara et al., 2006; Dysthe et al., 2007) has developed the following three models of supervision: (1) The partnership model, (2) the apprenticeship model, and (3) the teaching model. The models express distinct approaches to supervision, to the nature of the relationship between supervisor and student, and to the consequences of this relationship for the role, the students' texts play in supervision. Wichmann-Hansen and Wirenfeldt Jensen (2015) argue that all of Dysthe's three supervision models have their strengths and weaknesses; therefore, we include those as well in our interpretation of the supervision models.

The partnership model is characterized by a symmetrical relationship based on dialogue, from which students (and supervisors) acquire and produce knowledge, and especially the students develop their skills and competencies. Student and supervisor share complementary responsibilities for the master's thesis. Thus, the purpose of supervision is not to supply the student with ready answers, but to foster the student's identity as academic in their own right. From a text production perspective, explorative texts form the basis for a dialogue, where feedback on the text is meant as suggestions open for discussion and not as correction of errors and where the revision of text is seen as learning something new (Dysthe, 2006). The focus on dialogue calls for a certain view on supervision meetings, which frames the dialogue. In the words of the Norwegian scholars Lauvås & Handal (2015):

> A conversation is a human activity that contributes to the development of our understanding of the world and strengthens our capability to reflect, or in other words, talk with ourselves. The conversation has the potential of knowledge development, which hardly can be replaced by anything else. (p. 231; authors' translation)

The strength of this model lies in allowing students to play an active part and have an impact on the supervision received and obtaining genuine responsibility for the master's thesis. The weakness in this supervision model lies in demanding much from students themselves and especially from university students without prior experience with the partnership model in their primary and secondary school career finding it difficult to meet the demands inherent to the model (Wichmann-Hansen & Wirenfeldt Jensen, 2015).

The apprenticeship model is characterized by a close work relationship between student and supervisor. The knowledge acquired by the student is in part tacit knowledge because it is acquired as the student observes and solves research tasks together with the supervisor as master. The apprenticeship model is thus mostly in play when student and supervisor are part of the same research team. The student-supervisor relationship is more hierarchical than in the partnership model, but less hierarchical than in the teaching model (see below), and the student learns to work both autonomously on their own and as part of a team. From a text-production perspective, the student shares work-in-progress with other members of the research group as part of an ongoing dialogue. The student thus receives feedback from many people, not only from the supervisor. The apprenticeship model is mainly used in natural sciences and technical programs, and to a lesser degree within social sciences and the humanities (Dysthe, 2006).

The strength of this model lies in students being socialized or enculturated into the community of practice within their discipline, which makes supervision highly efficient. The weakness is that this supervision model makes learning context-dependent and focuses on problem solving (Wichmann-Hansen & Wirenfeldt Jensen, 2015), which makes it difficult for students to transfer knowledge to other (types of) contexts.

The teaching model is characterized by the teacher-pupil relationship, where the teacher (= supervisor) knows best and the pupil mainly listens. Thus, the model emphasizes the hierarchical distance between supervisor and student, and asymmetric communication situations, where the student does not dare to question the supervisor's comments, making the student strongly dependent on the supervisor. From a text production perspective, the student treats the supervisor's feedback as errors to be corrected, and the student only shares almost finished text with the supervisor, neither preliminary drafts, nor work-in-progress reflections (Dysthe, 2006).

The strength of this model is that it ensures an efficient and systematic transfer of knowledge from the supervisor to the student—if the student adapts the assigned role. The weakness of the supervision model is that it assigns the student a submissive position without any right to take an initiative of their own and in which the supervisor speaks in a kind of monologue and thereby controls the communication encounter (Wichmann-Hansen & Wirenfeldt Jensen, 2015), which prevents the supervisor from (active) listening to the student.

Supervisor roles

Hanne Nexø Jensen (2010) has researched the triangle of supervision, supervisor, and master's thesis student at the University of Copenhagen. Based on her empirical research, she has identified three supervisor roles: (1) The role of an expert within the discipline/s, (2) a supervisor on methodology, and (3) a supervisor on the learning process. According to Nexø Jensen, a supervisor takes on all three roles at different stages of the students' thesis research and writing process, but how much each of the roles is enacted depends on the type of research project the student is conducting and how far the student has come in the research and learning process.

1. The expert on the discipline is the predominant supervisor role in any supervision as the thesis topic is at the core of the dialogue between

supervisor and student. According to Nexø Jensen, successful supervision supports the student's clarification and orientation process if the supervisor's comments foster the students' reflections on their own research. The supervisor approach as an expert on discipline should therefore mainly be understood as an expert on sound academic thinking, and to a lesser degree as an expert who knows best and supplies the student with the correct answer.

2. The supervisor on methodology deals with crucial considerations about methodology, such as data collection techniques, choice of case location or organization, and qualitative or quantitative data analysis methods. Like in the case of the supervisor as an expert on the discipline/s, dialogue fosters the students' reflection. However, students tend to be more insecure about methodology than about their thesis topic; therefore, the supervisor on methodology is more directing and guiding.

3. The supervisor on the learning process deals with the intersection of writing and research, and text and project, e.g., inadequate thesis structure or writer's block. In contrast to the other two roles, according to Nexø Jensen's (2010) findings, student-supervisor sessions about the learning process are not marked by dialogue; rather the student listens and the supervisor is expected to offer concrete advice.

Supervision Seen from the Student's Perspective: Models and Roles in Practice

In this section, we discuss the analysis of the interviews. In accordance with hermeneutics, we view each interview as one unit in its own right, but each interview is also a part of the entire collection of interviews. This collection is in turn part of a broader collection of texts (the research literature) included in this study. Thus, the iterative hermeneutic circle of understanding the individual parts and the whole is in play on three levels: the single interview, the sample of interviews, and research literature (especially on supervision models and supervisor roles) merged with the interview/s. The analysis is structured in accordance with the supervision models discussed in the section "Supervision Models." The statements from the students are fused with the characteristics of the supervision models as well as the characteristics of the supervisor roles ((from the section "Supervisor Roles"). This reveals how the different supervision models do or do not facilitate the enactment of the supervisor roles and how that influences the students' ability to learn and acquire research literacies when exposed to the logic of supervision inherent in each supervision model. Based on these analyses we are able to assign the interviews to the different supervision models (see also Appendix C). Statements from eight of the interviews are analyzed across interviews and included in the following section, since the students' accounts in these interviews all paint a picture of supervision in accordance with the partnership model. The three remaining interviews match each one of the other supervision models discussed below with a new model, the laissez-faire model, extending Dysthe's typology of supervision models. The findings of the analysis developed below lead us to the supervision matrix (vejledningmatrix) shown in Figure 7.1.

Partnership Model

When the supervisor acts as an expert on the discipline within the partnership model, the purpose is to foster the student's reflections. There is clear evidence of this in all of the eight interviews, which we have categorized within the partnership model: To Natalie the supervisor made the biggest difference for her research when the supervisor challenged Natalie's own perceptions by asking questions without supplying the answers. Johan tells a similar story about his supervisor who asked critical questions but offered no answers; this led to new insights, which in turn led to momentum in his research project. None of the supervisors, who supervise within the partnership model, offer any concrete expert answer but initiate a dialogue about possible and adequate answers, which in the eyes of the students is the way it is supposed to be.

In the partnership model, students have responsibility for their own research, which is in accordance with participant control in the problem-oriented project work tradition. At CBS, students formally hold sole responsibility for the production, quality and submission of their own master's thesis; the interviewed students take this responsibility for granted. This contradicts Dysthe's (2006) definition of the partnership model where supervisor and student have a shared responsibility for the research process and product. Supervisors, on the other hand, hold responsibility for supervision itself, which is not covered by the interviews with the students. In comparison, our research on supervision seen from the supervisors' perspective (Ankersborg & Pogner, in press) shows that supervisors loyal to the partnership model do manage to combine their individual approaches to supervision with student autonomy. Student autonomy does not imply that supervisors do not offer any opinion about research methods. As Nexø Jensen (2010) notes, the dialogue between supervisor and student tends to be more concrete and thus more guiding, when they discuss methodology, rather than when they discuss the overall thesis topic. Thor, for example, was introduced by his supervisor to a method hitherto unknown to him. Thor decided to apply that method as it seemed more promising than his own suggestion, but he did not feel any hidden pressure from his supervisor to do so. The supervisors' suggestions aid the students to make qualified choices on methodology, but since students themselves are expected to identify relevant problems to research within their discipline, it follows that they have to have the final say about how they should conduct that research. All the students participating in the eight interviews, which we assign to the partnership model, report that they have declined suggestions from their supervisor and that the supervisor was fine with that. As Katherina puts it: "the supervisor is of course not familiar with the evidence in my data." Rasmus adds another dimension: "'You can do this, or you can do that' [said the supervisor], but it is the student's call." In hermeneutical terms, a fusion of horizons is established on the function of the supervisors' suggestions in the light of student autonomy. Thus, in the eyes of the students, their supervisors meet the goals and objectives of vejledning: they enable the students to make their own decisions on an informed basis.

In agreement with Nexø Jensen's definition of the supervisor on the learning process, the supervisors in our study are perceived as being even more specific, when the dialogue between supervisor and student is concerned with the student's learning process. Rasmus for instance lost sight of his own research as he drowned himself in research literature and reading whereupon the supervisor helped him select a relevant model. Natalie's supervisor did a reality check, when Natalie's research design seemed to be too ambitious, and Johan was advised to write an introduction, which helped him shape the research question. Students exposed to the partnership model thus seem to feel confident in sharing their work-in-progress and uncertainty about the process with their supervisor.

In contrast to the role of texts in the teaching model, where the supervisor is expected to approve final parts of the thesis before submission, both students and supervisors perceive the draft texts, which the students share with their supervisors, as work-in-progress. Given the students' horizon of understanding, they do not expect the supervisor to approve or proofread their text, as this would contradict the notion of student autonomy. Instead, the students display confidence in sharing work-in-progress, which underline that approval is not involved. The students regard supervisor comments as the right kind of input for their learning process, although this approach is a little frustrating at times. Katherina's supervisor shared knowledge about the academic genre by suggesting a structure for the analysis chapter before this part of the thesis even was written. To Katherina that advice proved to be a breakthrough. Katherina is split between knowing that she learns better without supervisor's interference and her wish for more direction. Katherina does not particularly like the text writing part of thesis work, and she expresses the frustration that sometimes comes with the partnership model. The supervisor offers concrete advice on work-in-progress, but Katherina does not expect the supervisor to read the final text before submission. Thor also felt a touch of frustration and insecurity when the supervisor chose not to comment in detail on the structure of the analysis thereby refraining from supplying the answers. However, in hindsight, Thor is pleased with the unobtrusiveness of the supervisor at the time, and in general, Thor's supervisor does not offer detailed comments on the text. This is reflected by Per's account that his supervisor only read the introduction, which was sufficient according to Per. Similarly, Simon managed to improve the quality of the chapter on theory by integrating the project's empirical case in the chapter. He did so on the advice of the supervisor after the supervisor had read a draft version of the chapter. Apart from this, Simon and his thesis partner wrote most of the thesis without text feedback from the supervisor. Finally, Laura and Line's supervisor made it clear from the beginning that he would only read draft versions of the introduction and the chapter on methodology. He did however glance through the theoretical part and added comments in the text, which Laura and Line still at the time of the interview had to decide if they would follow or not. To sum up, our data confirm Dysthe's (2006) typology in which the text is perceived to be a step on the way in the learning process and is therefore subject to revision. The supervisor does not read the final version of the whole master's thesis before the thesis is submitted for assessment as that would compromise participant control inherent in the problem-oriented project work tradition.

Wichmann-Hansen and Wirenfeldt Jensen (2015) stress that the partnership model is the most suitable model to facilitate students' critical thinking and reflection, active participation, responsibility and sense of ownership for their own research project. Adding to this, our study shows that the supervisor, based on dialogue with the student/s, acts both as an expert on sound academic thinking, as a supervisor on methodology, and as a supervisor on the (learning) process. In return, the supervisors do not oversee the student, nor do they take charge of the student's research project. Hence, supervision is actually enacted not as supervisor-centered "supervision," but as student-centered vejledning. The supervisor's task of making suggestions demands on the student's side that they possess or develop the skills and capabilities of assessing the suggestions before making a choice about what suggestions, if any, to include in the thesis. One student felt that he had to test every single suggestion before he could turn them down, which in hindsight led to a waste of time. The partnership model thus also demands that students know how to handle confusion and frustration as inherent parts of doing research, that they have sufficient self-confidence to make their own decisions without knowing the subsequent consequences for their research, and that they trust in the symmetrical relationship and communication with the supervisor. This symmetrical relationship allows them to decline suggestions from the supervisor. To be supervised according to the partnership model can thus both be rewarding, demanding, and frustrating for students, but it ultimately results in the students acquiring the skills to decide whether and when it makes sense to conform to, transform or resist existing norms.

Apprenticeship Model

As noted in section 3.2.1, the apprenticeship model is mainly used within natural sciences. This is supported by Fimreite and Hjertaker (2005, 2006) who, based on Dysthe's three supervision models, have compared supervision at a natural science department and at a social science department at the University in Bergen, Norway. They concluded that the science department mainly used the apprenticeship model, whereas the social science department mainly used the partnership model. One of our interviewees, Jonas, studies business administration and mathematics, which is a cross-disciplinary program that combines elements from both natural science and social science. In principle, this student could therefore be supervised within either the partnership model or the apprenticeship model. In practice, Jonas reports a supervision style that points towards the apprenticeship model.

Jonas has chosen to work with a mathematical model beyond master's level, which is more complex than he is supposed to master. Following Jonas' horizon of understanding, this decision was not to be discussed, and Jonas thus enacts student autonomy. The supervisor respects Jonas' choice, but he also requests that the student and the supervisor meet once a week. The supervisor thereby facilitates a close work relationship inherent in the apprenticeship model. This is also seen in a situation where the supervisor vetoed Jonas' attempt to change model assumptions too much. In this situation, the supervisor acts as an expert who knows best, but at the same time he agreed to help modify the model because the student insists on applying this particular model. Thus, the student assumes responsibility for the chosen methods, but applies the methods in a much closer work relationship than the students within the partnership model would have with their supervisors. Because supervisor and student work so closely together, the role of supervisor on the learning process is interwoven with the other two supervisor roles (expert within discipline/s and supervisor on methodology), but as in the partnership model the student feels free to decline suggestions from the supervisor.

Jonas' draft texts are perceived as work-in-progress, which corresponds with Dysthe's definition of the role of the text in the apprenticeship model, but in this case, the student does not discuss the text with other people than the supervisor. It is also in accordance with the apprenticeship model that the supervisor helps explain particularly challenging parts of the text. However, the student sets the agenda for the supervision meetings and adds questions intended to guide the dialogue between supervisor and student. In addition, the supervisor does not read the entire thesis manuscript before submission. Furthermore, the role of Jonas' draft texts illustrates that the horizons of understanding of both student and supervisor are marked by the problem-oriented project work tradition in the way the student takes in participant control of the research design and the agenda for supervision meetings. As in Dysthe's definition of the apprenticeship model, the supervisor in this case acts as master, but in contrast to the teacher-pupil relation, the supervisor creates space for the student's independent and autonomous contribution.

Teaching Model

The logic of the teaching model completely contradicts the Danish problem-oriented project work tradition, and we should therefore not expect to find accounts of this approach to supervision in our interviews. Nevertheless, one interview clearly falls within this supervision model. According to the student, the supervisor argues with reference to his position as professor, thereby establishing a strong hierarchical distance between supervisor and student. The supervisor directs the student's work and process in detail, making the student highly dependent on the supervisor; the student eventually gave up any attempt to start a dialogue. Concerning the text production and the interaction around it, the directing of the supervisor became visible in the supervisor's detailed remarks ordering the student to correct specific phrases in the text. According to Dysthe (2006), students exposed to the teaching model treat such remarks as errors to be corrected. In this case, the student attempted to discuss the supervisor's remarks at first, but eventually gave up and executed the corrections in order to avoid more trouble. The student finally submitted a master's thesis, which he describes as "supervisor's baby" (Peter), knowing that he had not learned what he had hoped to learn from this thesis project. The student expresses a horizon of understanding that is clearly marked by the problem-oriented project work tradition, as he expressed that this is not how supervision is supposed to be, "It is just so wrong, has no place at a university" (Peter). In his opinion, supervision should follow the partnership model. Peter thus establishes a fusion of horizons with the tradition but not with his supervisor.

In the interview with Peter, we could only identify one supervisor role, the role as expert on the discipline. We are not referring here to the kind of expert that initiates student reflection, but rather an expert who knows best and pushes in an asymmetrical communication situation his version as the correct answer, e.g., when it comes to philosophy of science. This supervisor approach corresponds with the understanding of the concept of supervisor-centered supervision as the supervisor oversees, directs and takes charge of another person. It does not correspond with the student-centered concept vejledning, as the supervisor does not allow the student to make his own decisions. Although we only found one instance of the teaching model in our data, we assume that supervision in accordance with the logic of this model happens from time to time. Nexø Jensen (2010), who also found traces of this kind of supervision in her data, supports this assumption.

Laissez-faire Model

Our interview with Nadia and Michala falls outside Dysthe's description of the three supervision models. The supervision the students report points towards the existence of a fourth supervision model. In defining this model, we are inspired by Gatfield's (2005) "laissez-faire" style of supervision. Gatfield (2005) has identified different management styles of (doctoral) supervision at a metropolitan Australian university. He has shown that the "contractual" (high level of support and high level of structure) is the predominant style, whereas the "laissez-faire" (low support, low structure), pastoral (high support, high structure) and "directional styles" (low support, high structure) are hardly to be found in statements of experienced and successful supervisors, but exist (Gatfield, 2005, p. 319). Gatfield bases his typology partially on a conceptual model that results from his literature review, partially on interviews with 12 Ph.D. supervisors from social science disciplines at an Australian university. Nevertheless, our findings in one of the interviews about master's thesis supervision at Copenhagen Business School resemble Gatfield's definition of the laissez-faire management style to a high degree.

As mentioned above, the Danish problem-oriented project-work tradition emphasizes students' autonomy and independence from their supervisor. Taken to its extreme, this notion could lead to supervisors becoming afraid of influencing the student/s, and therefore they do not offer any kind of suggestion or opinion except from stressing the students' right to make their own choices. In terms of text production, they simply insist that the students should just write. Nadia and Michala, who are writing their master's thesis together, describe the resulting confusion with a touch of desperation in their voices:

> Nevertheless, what we hear is that, no matter what you choose, it may be good, but it can also get really bad . . . After all . . . that we have been too insecure and felt that no matter what we chose . . . in the beginning; that no matter what we chose, so, we were potentially doomed because we had, we were not good in coming to grips of the direction. (Nadia & Michala)

Following the doctrine of non-interference with students' work, neither of the three supervisor roles come into play with this type of supervision. The supervisor approach is thus neither student-centered vejledning nor supervisor-centered "supervision." In fact, there is not supervision at all. The result of this non-supervising is the opposite of vejledning, as the supervisor style constrains students by forcing them to make their own decisions on an *un*informed basis. Following Nadia and Michala's horizons of understanding, they do not expect the supervisor to supply the answers, but at the same time, they struggle more than anticipated with their thesis project. As they are unable to pinpoint the intended role of the supervisor in this situation, a fusion of horizons between students and supervisor does not occur. Although only one of our interviews reports this approach to supervision, we choose to label it as a supervision model of its own. Outside the scope of our study, we have been reported this approach to supervision many times by students over the years, and thus we have an evidence-based assumption that Nadia and Michala are not the only students to have been exposed to this approach to supervision. We label this supervision model the laissez-faire model. It is characterized by a low degree of structure of the supervision and a low degree of support by the supervisor. The supervisor is non-directive and perceived by the student as not committed to high levels of personal interaction, which may make the supervisor appear as uncaring and uninvolved. This, in turn, risks demotivating the students.

The Vejledning Matrix

At the third level of the hermeneutical circle, we tie the three elements—the educational-cultural basis, the two theoretical frameworks, and the 11 interviews—together and create a vejledning matrix for our empirical material. In the interviews, we have identified the enacted supervisor roles and linked them to the corresponding supervisor models, as the chosen supervision model influences the roles of a supervisor. This in turn affects the students' research process and learning intake and outcome. As the interviews largely confirm the characteristics of Dysthe's typology of supervision models, we conclude based on analytical generalizability that the partnership model allows for enactment of all three supervisor roles as illustrated in the matrix (see Figure 7.1) in similar cases in the context of problem-oriented work and student-centered supervision.

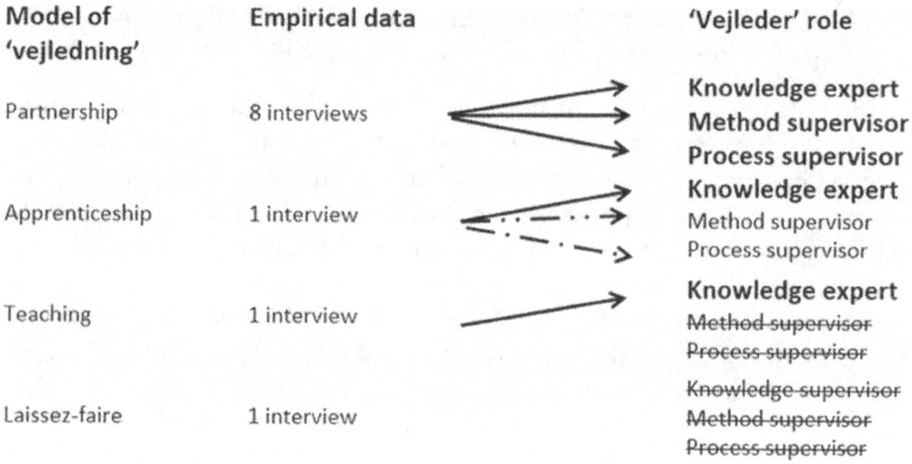

Model of 'vejledning'	Empirical data		'Vejleder' role
Partnership	8 interviews	→	Knowledge expert Method supervisor Process supervisor
Apprenticeship	1 interview	→	Knowledge expert Method supervisor Process supervisor
Teaching	1 interview	→	Knowledge expert ~~Method supervisor~~ ~~Process supervisor~~
Laissez-faire	1 interview		~~Knowledge supervisor~~ ~~Method supervisor~~ ~~Process supervisor~~

Figure 7.1. The vejledning matrix: Enacted models and roles in the interviews.

The four models of vejledning in the vejledning matrix allow for different kinds of vejledning/supervision. Supervision according to the partnership model enables vejledning with its emphasis on student autonomy and responsibility. The logic of the partnership model draws heavily on the problem-oriented project work tradition. Our data show that also the students' perception of supervision and supervisor is aligned with this logic. Thus, a fusion of horizons of understanding is established between students and supervisors within the context of problem orientation. Supervision according to the apprenticeship model enables a student-centered form of vejledning in a moderated form with its closer contact and (co-)working relation between supervisor and student. In addition, in this case, a fusion of horizons is established between student and supervisor that pays respect to problem orientation, but in a slightly different form. Supervision according to the teaching model enables "supervision" in the sense of supervisor-centered directional "supervision" with its emphasis on hierarchy between supervisor and student. It does not enable student-driven vejledning and it is not connected to problem-orientation. Supervision according to the laissez-faire model is a kind of misunderstood student-driven vejledning. It is characterized by low levels of structure and support and high level of student frustration and limited level of management skills (Gatfield, 2005). It results in not suggesting any direction, and a lack of commitment to high levels of personal interaction. The supervisor may be perceived by the students as uncaring and uninvolved. Thus, the fusion of horizons between student/s and supervisor is not established, although its logic might be traced back to the problem-oriented project work tradition.

We call the matrix we have developed in our analysis vejledning matrix, not "supervision" matrix, in order to emphasize the student-centered perspective fostering autonomy/independence and responsibility of master's thesis writers and hereby the skills and competencies of research literacies that the students gain. As shown in figure 7.1, the partnership model allows supervisors to conduct student-driven supervision and simultaneously enact the roles of an expert on sound academic thinking, as an advisor on methodology, and as a guide on the learning and research process. These findings are confirmed in our previously mentioned study on thesis supervisors where nine out of 15 interviewed supervisors supervise according to the partnership model and report the flexibility of enacting different roles. They also emphasize that the ultimate goal of students should be becoming able to deliver independent work (see Ankersborg & Pogner, in press). Since both the mono-disciplinary and interdisciplinary master's study programs, which Copenhagen Business Schools offers, are all primarily embedded in social sciences/the humanities and business administration/economics (Appendix B), only one interview from an interdisciplinary program with a mathematical focus (business administration and mathematics) is included in the research. In this case, the apprenticeship model, often found in the natural sciences and engineering (as indicated by the work of Eriksson & Nordrum (2018) for Chemical Engineering) may also include all three types of vejleder roles but gives predominance to the role of the knowledge expert. In our matrix, the teaching model, which is most prominent in study programs of science, technology, engineering, and mathematics (see Filippou et al., 2021), is solely connected to the expert role (for STEM and subject knowledge, see Pelger & Sigrell, 2016). The laissez-faire model does not enact any vejleder roles in our matrix; actually, supervision in the laissez-faire model does not enact any form of supervision at all.

When we asked the student interviewees to describe their understanding of an ideal supervisor and they all described a vejleder that matches the partnership model when the expert role is enacted, regardless of the kind of supervision, they actually receive (see table 7.1).

Table 7.1. The Ideal Vejleder/Supervisor from the Students' Perspective

Concerning expertise on knowledge and supervisor on method	Concerning supervisor on process
Discussion partner	Dedicated
Supportive, not controlling	Good chemistry
Respects that it is the student's thesis	Flexible
An expert in his/her field and research process	Available
Using that expertise • to initiate student's reflections • to challenge student's perceptions • to point in new directions • to help the student to explore	Does not control the process
Does not supply the answers him/herself	

The words they use to describe the master's thesis itself (see table 7.2) contain many traces back to the problem-oriented project work tradition:

Table 7.2. Perception of a Master's Thesis from the Students' Perspective

A Master's thesis (speciale) is:	A Master's thesis (speciale) is about:
• Genuine academic • Complex • The jewel in the crown • Long term • A test of the skills to create a product that reflects the student's learning process. • The student's own specialization somewhere between previous studies and future career • Research into a specific area, specialization on Social Science terms within a specific area relevant to the student's academic profile	• Absorption/ immersion • Analytical skills • Focus • Intellectual, academic and personal competences

The master's thesis is a long-term research project where the skills and insights the students acquire from writing the thesis play an important part. Illeris' pedagogy and didactics became mainstream in Denmark many years ago, and it is still thoroughly embedded in the horizons of understanding of present Danish students. So much so that unless proven otherwise by a supervisor it does not even occur to the students that vejledning could be something else, that vejledning could be supervisor-centered supervision.

Discussion

The predominant approach in our analysis is the partnership model. The partnership model grants a high degree of flexibility for *supervisor* (teacher and researcher) and *student* (write, learner and becoming or as-if-"researcher") because of its capacity of enacting and negotiating different supervisor roles and student roles, voices and identities. This flexibility to enact different roles enables the choice and negotiation of different roles, relations, and styles according to different phases in the supervision process (see Gatfield, 2005. pp. 322f. for the phases). It also fosters the ability to react to process-treated contingency factors (uncertainty, organizational complexity) and product-related contingency factors (power and expertise; goals and expectations) (Boehe, 2016).

The model allows *supervisors* to choose deliberately and shift between supervisor roles and enables the supervisor to cope with the duality of their role as expert of the academic (cross-, inter-) disciplinary knowledge at stake (Andersen & Wirenfeldt Jensen, 2007) and expert of the learning and research process. Furthermore, it permits them to shift between personal supervision and disciplinary-processual supervision (Andersen & Wirenfeldt Jensen, 2007). The partnership model's dynamics and flexibility also allow different goals to be set in different phases and beliefs and values to be enacted and negotiated such as practical applicability (functionalist), belonging (enculturation, socialization), rigor (critical thinking), autonomy (emancipation and empowerment), and sympathy (relational) (see Lee, 2010, p. 22). The model facilitates the choice and interactive negotiation of the situation-adequate roles with the students in the course of the supervision process: "A supervisor should be able to be coaching, motivating, insistent, criticizing, appreciatively controlling, appreciative, personal, authoritarian, friendly and determined" (Andersen & Wirenfeldt Jensen, 2007, p. 157). The partnership model allows supervisors to balance their interpersonal behavior related to the dominance and submission continuum (influence) and to the opposition and cooperation continuum (proximity) (Mainhard et al., 2009).

The partnership model gives main, if not full, responsibility for the research project and master's thesis to the *student*. We have analyzed supervision from the student's perception, their perspectives on and expectations towards the interactive enactment of supervision and of the ideal enactment as points of departure. In the analysis of the student's perspective, we found a lot of alignment of the students with the delegation of responsibility for the project and the thesis' academic rigor and relevance for business and society to the student.

A number of aspects come into play to form the complexity that enables students to conform to, transform or resist established discourses and norms. When exposed to supervision based on the partnership model, students feel both challenged and supported. The requirement of autonomy is central for both supervisors' and students' perceptions and enactments of student-centered vejledning. Supervisors' options of supervising both as an expert on sound academic thinking, on methodology and on the learning process at an abstract and a concrete level widens the scope of supporting students without taking charge of neither the person nor the project and without taking responsibility for the learning process at all. Supervisors' critical questions can provoke students to think in new ways. Supervisors' reluctance, restraint or caution to provide direct answers can force students via Socratic dialogue methods to make their own decisions and to argue for those. In the partnership model, students in turn feel comfortable with discussing and rejecting supervisor's suggestions and finding their own way. This is due to the symmetrical relationship, which creates an atmosphere of trust where the students' work-in-progress is seen as a step on the way in a learning process. Since the master's thesis is a long-term research project, it fosters the students' skills in managing complex and comprehensive projects with their inherent obstacles. Since master's thesis students conduct their research as independently and autonomously as possible, they carry the main or sole responsibility for the consequences of those decisions. Hereby, they learn to master blocks, barriers, insecurities, and frustrations. Taken together, students gain capabilities in critical, independent, and autonomous thinking in order to become able to decide whether or when to conform to, transform or resist existing discourses and norms of disciplinary and professional cultures. Problem-oriented master's theses can be seen as students' research projects contributing to an academic research conversation. It is a contribution of legitimate peripheral (still learning) members of academic communities conceptualized as discourse community (Swales, 1990) and community of practice (Lave & Wenger, 1991) in a space of action (here: research) and discourse (here: the master's thesis) (see Pogner, 2007, Knorr & Pogner, 2015). It gives the opportunity to create spaces for the development of the students' academic literacies in the students' zone of proximal development (Vygotsky, 1978).

The partnership model enables students to develop their research literacies and thereby their ability to understand the academic discourse and practice of the respective disciplinary domain and community. This does not only count for master's students but to a certain degree for bachelor's students and for sure for doctoral students. And this counts not only for the context of vejledning embedded in the Scandinavian tradition of problem-oriented project-based pedagogy, where it stems from and in which it has been transformed over time, but also for any form of student-centered supervision. It fosters both critical thinking, independence from the supervisor and students' responsibility for the project and thesis. It enables students to acquire technical and instrumental (writing) skills or being passively socialized/acculturated into academic discourse, but also to develop academic literacies, which give their text production a meaning-making and meaning negotiating perspective. Furthermore, it can offer students' independence and autonomy by fostering their ability to understand expectations and norms of the disciplinary domains and spaces of action and discourse (Knorr & Pogner, 2015). Based on this understanding, the partnership model can empower the students to decide independently whether and when to conform, transform or resist. These competencies open up for academic writing both as "knowledge telling," "knowledge transforming" and "knowledge building" (Bereiter & Scardamalia, 1989 and 2014).

Conclusions and Reflections

We have analyzed the Danish perception of the interaction of vejledning as student-centered supervision and shown its strong embeddedness in the pedagogical approach and ideology of problem-oriented project work. The Danish perception and problem-oriented project work stresses in theory and practice the independency of the students' problem-oriented research project, their main responsibility for the process and the quality of project and thesis demonstrated in the written report and in the oral discussion ("defense") of the report. The predominant partnership model can offer students' independence and autonomy by fostering their ability to understand expectations and norms of the disciplinary domains and spaces of action and discourse. Based on this understanding, the partnership model can empower the students to decide independently whether and when to conform, transform or resist. These competencies open up for academic writing as knowledge production. We propose to consider expanding the central role of the partnership model for the development of academic literacies from supervision of master's thesis students to supervision of students in general. We further propose to expand it from the Danish/Scandinavian context to the context of higher education in general. In the following, we reflect on the implications of this proposal.

In the context of creating space for students' development of academic literacy/ies the partnership model and its flexibility can contribute to

> empowering students to find ways of becoming more visible (to themselves, their lecturers and institutions) and thus less peripheral to the processes of knowledge telling, transformation and creation, getting their voices as writers heard, and their writer authority respected. (Gimenez & Thomas, 2015, p. 32)

At the same time, the partnership model allows both supervisors and students to become aware of and reflect on their own expectations, assumptions, and perceptions. This is "integral to the practice of teaching as informed by an Academic Literacies approach—and it is itself transformative, and empowering, for both teachers and students" (Lillis et al., 2015, p. 12).

Our findings have implications for the supervision practice aiming at supporting the development of academic literacies in order to strengthen students'/writers' independence, voice and identity (Wirenfeldt Jensen, 2019). Thereby, the model could contribute to the students' reflections on and awareness of their identity as learners. At the same time, it could support the students' temporal and peripheral—but legitimate—membership of the academic discourse community (Swales, 1990) and the academic community of practice (Lave & Wenger, 1991). Furthermore, it could and foster the students' ability to navigate and participate actively in the academic "space of action and discourse" (Knorr & Pogner 2015), which combines the concepts of discourse community and community of practice.

The partnership model in student-centered supervision could stimulate a nuanced understanding of the pedagogical techniques of instructional scaffolding and of the pedagogical concept of the learner's zone of proximal development. Scaffolding "refers to the steps taken to reduce the degrees of freedom in carrying out some task so that the child can concentrate on the difficult skill she is in the process of acquiring" (Bruner, 1978, p. 19). When it comes to (master's) students, these techniques can help students to develop greater independence and autonomy in and more responsibility for their learning processes. Vygotsky defines the zone of proximal development as "the distance between the actual developmental level as determined by independent problem solving and the level of potential development as determined through problem solving under adult guidance, or in collaboration with more capable peers" (Vygotsky, 1978, p. 86). In the case of student-centered supervision following the partnership model, the scaffold is constructed and torn down in a joint effort of adult supervisor and adult student/s, and the students' learning processes are shaped by his joint effort. The zone of proximal development is determined in collaboration and dialogue of adult supervisor and adult student/s. Furthermore, in the case of group research projects, the students' zones of proximate development are enabled and constrained by collaborative knowledge and text production with not necessarily more capable peers. Student-centered supervision enables the students both to acquire academic literacies (learning) and at the same time to display the acquired literacies (competencies).

Academic writing as text and knowledge production takes place under specific conditions in academic discourse communities and academic communities of practice in the discourse and action space of academia. This counts also for master's thesis students, who simultaneously do research in a broad sense and learn how to create and communicate with and about research knowledge. Novices and peripheral members of these communities do neither know these conditions nor the norms, expectations, discourses and genres (Knorr & Pogner, 2015). Therefore, it is also vital to establish transparency about those and make tacit knowledge explicit both for students socialized in the local learning culture and those from other learning cultures.

This counts also for project supervision where international students sometimes are unsure about "what is, in the Danish system, a *learning moment*, with an *assessment moment* that would affect their grade" (Blasco, 2015, p. 96). However, even if a high degree of transparency and awareness about differing supervisor/student role expectations can be reached (Harwood & Petrić, 2019); there will still be doubt and uncertainty: "Mystery persists alongside notions of communication, objectivity and equality; hence, its presence needs to be recognized and accepted" (Knowles, 2016, p. 311). Research (knowledge production, subject knowledge) and writing processes (text production, writing skills) also have unique and idiosyncratic elements. Supervising process may also include doubt and uncertainty. Moreover, this calls for a feedback process in the supervision conversations that "needs to be flexible and open-ended and tolerant of ambiguity" (Knowles, 2016, p. 311).

Our conclusions and reflections are based on analytical generalizing of our findings in order to expand the insights from our qualitative studies of master's thesis supervision, which is deeply rooted in the problem-oriented project work tradition, to more general insight into the interrelation of supervision models, supervisor roles, and acquiring and developing academic literacies. The sampling, the quantity and quality of our empirical data (mainly social-science-based study programs and predominance of the partnership model), the scope of our study, and the focus on the students' perceptions and understanding limit the range of the analytical generalizability. Therefore, further research should look at how internal and external contingent factors (Boehe, 2016) and non-contingent factors have an influence on our vejledning matrix, such as the composition of the groups of students/writers, students doing the master's thesis alone versus doing it in a pair or small group, and face-to-face supervision vs. digital and remote supervision. Further research should also investigate different practices as aspects of solo and collaborative writing (Ede & Lunsford, 1990), new forms of supervision, e.g., collective academic supervision (Nordentoft et al., 2019). It should also consider multi-voiced (and multi-lingual) supervision in a mix of discussion groups, group or cluster supervision and individual supervision (Dysthe et al., 2007), and the influence of different educational-cultural experiences of students and supervisors on supervising in a student-centered way.

In order to counterbalance the focus on the students' perspective and to open the door to the "closed room" (Nexø Jensen, 2010) of supervising and learning further, and to investigate the supervisors' contribution to shape problem-oriented project work, we have already started interviewing supervisors. We are looking at how supervisors understand and adapt to student-centered supervision in the Scandinavian way—both in cases where the supervisor has a Scandinavian educational socialization or another education-cultural background—and which supervision models supervisors and students enact.

In their case studies, Harwood and Petrić (2017) have investigated master's thesis supervision in international study programs at a UK university from the supervisor/advisor and student perspective in order to demystify supervision (Harwood & Petrić, 2017) and to help international students to navigate master's thesis supervision in this intercultural context (Harwood & Petrić, 2019). For the same reasons, we have started interviewing international students with non-Danish or non-Scandinavian educational backgrounds studying at the Copenhagen Business School, i.e., in the context and encounter of the local Scandinavian educational culture and ideology. In order to investigate the impact of these encounters on the acquisition and development of research literacy/ies are we exploring how novices (students and supervisors) in the Danish educational culture handle student-centered supervision (vejledning) when enacting or being exposed to different supervision models.

References

Andersen, H. L. & Wirenfeldt Jensen, T. (2007). *Specialevejledning: Rammer og roller. En universitetspædagogisk undersøgelse*. Samfundslitteratur.

Ankersborg, V. & Pogner, K.-H. (in press). Specialevejledning fra studenter-selvstændighed til vejlederdiktat: En vejledningsmatrix. *Dansk Universitetspædagogisk Tidsskrift*, Special Issue: Vejledning på højere læreanstalter.

Badenhorst, C. & Guerin C. (Eds.) (2016). *Research literacies and writing pedagogies for masters and doctoral writers*. Brill.

Bereiter, C. & Scardamalia, M. (1989). Intentional learning as a goal of instruction. In L. B. Resnick (Ed), *Knowing, learning, and instruction: Essays in honor of Robert Glaser* (pp. 361–392). Lawrence Erlbaum.

Bereiter, C. & Scardamalia, M. (2014). Knowledge building and knowledge creation: One concept, two hills to climb. In S. C. Tan, H. J. So & J. Yeo (Eds.), *Knowledge creation in education* (pp. 35–52). Springer.

Blasco, M. (2015). Making the tacit explicit: Rethinking culturally inclusive pedagogy in international student academic adaption. *Pedagogy, Culture & Society*, *23*(1), 85–106. https://doi.org/10.1080/14681366.2014.922120.

Boehe, D. M. (2016). Supervisory styles: A contingency framework. *Studies in Higher Education*, *41*(3), 399–414. https://doi.org/10.1080/03075079.2014.927853.

Bruner, J. S. (1978). The role of dialogue in language acquisition. In A. Sinclair, R. J. Jarvella & W. J. M. Levelt (Eds.). *The child's concept of language* (pp. 242–256). Springer.

Danish Ministry for Education and Science (2020). *Executive orders of Education BEK nr. 20* (09/01/2020). Copenhagen: The Danish Ministry for Education and Science. https://www.retsinformation.dk/Forms/R0710.aspx?id=212490#idc3caa998-351c-4176-82a6-5e2a38e442eb.

Dysthe, O. (2006). Rettleiaren som lærar, partner eller meister? In O. Dysthe & A. Samara (Eds.), *Forskningsveiledning på master- og doktorgradsnivå* (pp. 228–248). Abstrakt.

Dysthe, O., Breistein, S., Kjeldsen, J. & Lied, L. I. (2006). Studentperspektiv på rettleiing. In O. Dysthe & A. Samara (Eds). *Forskningsveiledning på master- og doktorgradsnivå* (pp. 207–227). Abstrakt.

Dysthe, O., Samara, A. & Westrheim, K. (2006): En treleddet veiledningsmodell i masterstudiet. In O. Dysthe & A. Samara (Eds.). *Forskningsveiledning på master- og doktorgradsnivå* (pp. 37–55). Abstrakt.

Dysthe, O., Samara, A. & Westrheim, K. (2007). Multivoiced supervision of master's students: A case study of alternative supervision in higher education. *Studies in Higher Education*, *31*(03), 299–318. https://doi.org/10.1080/03075070600680562.

Ede, L. & Lunsford, A. (1990). *Singular texts/plural authors: Perspectives on collaborative writing*. Southern Illinois University Press.

Eriksson, A. & Nordrum, L. (2018). Unpacking challenges of data commentary writing in master's thesis projects: An insider perspective from chemical engineering. *Research in Science and Technological Education*, *36*(4), 499–520. https://doi.org/10.1080/02635143.2018.1460339.

Filippou, K., Kallo, J. & Mikkilä-Erdmann, M. (2021). Supervising master's theses in international master's degree programmes: Roles, responsibilities and models.

Teaching in Higher Education, 26(1), 299–318. https://doi.org/10.1080/13562517.2019.1636220.

Fimreite, A. L. & Hjertaker, B. J. (2005). Sammenligning av eksisterende mastergrads veiledning ved institutt for administrasjons- og organisasjonsvitenskap og Institutt for fysikk og teknologi (UPED-skrift nr. 1/2005).

Fimreite, A. L. & Hjertaker B. J. (2006). Sammenligning av eksisterende mastergrads veiledningen ved to institutt. In O. Dysthe & A. Samara (Eds.). *Forskningsveiledning på master- og doktorgradsnivå* (pp. 249–268). Abstrakt.

Gadamer, H.-G. (2004). *Truth and method* (2nd ed.). (J. Weinsheimer & D. G. Marshall, Trans). Bloomsbury. (Original work published 1990)

Gatfield, T. (2005). An investigation into Ph.D. supervisory management styles: Development of a dynamic conceptual model and its managerial implications. *Journal of Higher Education Policy and Management, 27*(3), 314–325. https://doi.org/10.1080/13600800500283585.

Gimenez, J. & Thomas P. (2015). A framework for usable pedagogy: Case studies towards accessibility, criticality and visibility. In T. Lillis, K. Harrington, M. R. Lea & S. Mitchell (Eds.), *Working with academic literacies: Case studies towards transformative practice* (pp. 29–44). WAC Clearinghouse; Parlor Press. https://doi.org/10.37514/PER-B.2015.0674.2.01.

Harwood, N. & Petrić, B. (2017). *Experiencing master's supervision: Perspectives of international students and their supervisors.* Routledge.

Harwood, N. & Petrić, B. (2019). Helping international master's students navigate dissertation supervision: Research-informed discussion and research awareness-raising activities. *Journal of International Students, 9*(1), 150–171. https://doi.org/10.32674/jis.v9i1.276.

Illeris, K. (1974). *Problemorientering og deltagerstyring. Oplæg til en alternativ didaktik.* Munksgaard.

Keiding, T. B. & Laursen, E. (2008). *Projektmetoden iagttaget. Metodens didaktik og anvendelse i universitetsuddannelse* (Forskningsrapport 19). Institut for Uddannelse, Læring og Filosofi, Aalborg Universitet.

Knorr, D. & Pogner, K.-H. (2015). Vom schreiben zum "texten": Akademische textproduktion unter den bedingungen von mehrsprachigkeit. *Fremdsprachen Lehren und Lernen, 44*(1), 2015, 110–122.

Knowles, S. S. (2016). Underground murmurs: Disturbing supervisory practices of feedback. In C. Badenhorst & C. Guerin (Eds.). *Research literacies and writing pedagogies for masters and doctoral writers* (pp. 295–313). Brill.

Krogh, L. & Wiberg, M. (2015). Problem-based and project-organised teaching. In L. Rienecker, P. Stray Jørgensen, J. Dolin & G. Holten Ingerslev (Eds.), *University teaching and learning* (pp. 215–228). Samfundslitteratur.

Kvale, S. (1983). The qualitative research interview: A phenomenological and a hermeneutical mode of understanding. *Journal of Phenomenological Psychology, 14*(2), 171–196.

Kvale, S. (1994). Ten standard objections to qualitative research interviews. *Journal of Phenomenological Psychology, 25*(2), 147–173.

Kvale, S. (1997). Interview. *En introduktion til det kvalitative interview*. Hans Reitzel.
Kvale, S. (2007). *Doing interviews*. Sage.
Kvale, S. & Brinkmann, S. (2014). *InterViews: Learning the craft of qualitative research interviewing* (3rd ed.). Sage.
Lave, J. & Wenger, E. (1991). *Situated learning: Legitimate peripheral participation*. Cambridge University Press.
Lauvås, P. & Handal, G. (2015). *Vejledning og praksisteori: Vejledning og profession* (2nd ed.) Klim.
Lea, M. R. & Street, B. V. (1998). Student writing in higher education: An academic literacies approach. *Studies in Higher Education*, *23*(2), 157–172. https://doi.org/10.1080/03075079812331380364.
Lea, M. R. & Street, B. V. (2014). Writing as academic literacies: Understanding textual practices in higher education. In C. N. Candlin & K. Hyland (Eds.), *Writing: Texts, processes and practices* (pp. 62–81). Routledge.
Lee, A. (2010). New approaches to doctoral supervision: Implications for educational development. *Educational Developments*, *11*(2), 18–23.
Lillis, T., Harrington, K., Lea, M. R. & Mitchell, S. (Eds.). (2015). *Working with academic literacies: Case studies towards transformative practice*. WAC Clearinghouse; Parlor Press. https://doi.org/10.37514/PER-B.2015.0674.
Lillis, T. & Scott, M. (2007a). Introduction to special issue. *Journal of Applied Linguistics*, *4*(1), 1–4. https://doi.org/10.1558/japl.v4i1.1.
Lillis, T. & Scott M. (2007b). Defining academic literacies research: Issues of epistemology, ideology and strategy. *Journal of Applied Linguistics*, *4*(1), 5–32. https://doi.org/10.1558/japl.v4i1.5.
Maher, M. A. & Say, B. H. (2016). Doctoral supervisors as learners and teachers of disciplinary writing. In C. Badenhorst & C. Guerin (Eds.), *Research literacies and writing pedagogies for masters and doctoral writers* (pp. 277–313). Brill.
Mainhard, T., van der Rijst, R., van Tartwijk, J. & Wubbels, T. (2009). A model for the supervisor-doctoral student relationship. *Higher Education*, *58*, 359–373. https://doi.org/10.1007/s10734-009-9199-8.
Nexø Jensen, H. (2010). "Det lukkede rum"—en dør på klem til specialevejledning. *Dansk Universitetspædagogisk Tidsskrift*, *8*, 17–22. https://tidsskrift.dk/dut/article/view/5580.
Nissen, C. F. R. (2019). *Blind spots of internationalization of higher education* [Doctoral dissertation, University of Copenhagen, Faculty of Humanities]. Zbook. Org. https://static-curis.ku.dk/portal/files/222323139/Ph.d._afhandling_2019_Nissen.pdf.
Nordentoft, H. M., Hvass, H., Mariager-Anderson, K., Bengtsen, S. S., Smedegaard, A. & Warrer, S. D. (2019). *Kollektiv akademisk vejledning. Fra forskning til praksis*. Århus Universitetsforlag.
Olsen, P. B. & Pedersen K. (1997). *Problemorienteret projektarbejde - en værktøjsbog* (2nd ed.) Roskilde Universitetsforlag.
Pelger, S. & Sigrell, A. (2016). Rhetorical meta-language to promote the development of students' writing skills and subject matter understanding. *Research in*

Science & Technological Education, 34(1), 15–42. https://doi.org/10.1080/02635143.2015.1060410.

Pogner, K.-H. (1999). *Schreiben im beruf als handeln im fach*. Forum für Fachsprachen-Forschung 46. Narr.

Pogner, K.-H. (2003). Writing and interacting in the discourse community of engineering. *Journal of Pragmatics, 35*, 855–867. https://doi.org/10.1016/S0378-2166(02)00122-4.

Pogner, K.-H. (2007). Text- und wissensproduktion am arbeitsplatz: Die rolle der diskursgemeinschaften und praxisgemeinschaften. *Zeitschrift Schreiben. Schreiben in Schule, Hochschule und Beruf*, 1–12.

Pogner, K.-H. (2012). A social perspective on writing in the workplace: Communities of discourse (DC) and communities of practice (CoP). In A. Rothkegel & S. Ruda (Eds.), *Communication on and via technology* (pp. 220–235). De Gruyter Mouton.

Swales, J. M. (1990). *Genre analysis: English in academic and research settings*. University Press.

Vygotsky, L. S. (1978). *Mind in society: The development of higher psychological processes*. Harvard University Press.

Wichmann-Hansen, G. & Wirenfeldt Jensen, T. (2015). Supervision: Process management and communication. In L. Rienecker, P. Stray Jørgensen, J. Dolin & G. Holten Ingerslev (Eds.), *University teaching and learning* (pp. 220–235). Samfundslitteratur.

Wirenfeldt Jensen, T. (2018). *Det danske universitetsspeciale: Topografi, tekster og tendenser*. Århus Universitetsforlag.

Wirenfeldt Jensen, T. (2019, July 3). *Becoming a master's thesis writer: Authorial identity, autonomy, and impossible choices* [Conference session]. EATAW 2019 conference, Chalmers University of Technology, Gothenburg, Sweden.

Appendix A: Interview Guide (translated from Danish by the authors)

General questions

- What do you study? In which study program are you enrolled?
- What is the topic of your thesis?
- When did you submit your thesis/when do you expect to submit?
- What is a master's thesis?
- Do you see it as a process or a product (NB ownership, who is coming up with solutions, role of critical thinking)?
- Where in the process are you now?
- What has been the biggest challenge/difficulty until now?
- What has been the easiest part until now?

About supervision

Questions about vejledning (supervision)

- Conditions/media for vejledning (supervision), e.g., f2f, skype, email, etc., how often did you have meetings, is vejleder reading drafts, which types of drafts, feedback on drafts/texts?
- Who initiated the vejledning (supervision) meetings?
- How much did you make use of your vejleder (supervisor)?
- Who did most of the talking during meetings?

About the vejleder (supervisor)

- Vejleders (supervisor's) background (position) and nationality/language (L1) [NB external supervisors: without research; internal supervisors: with research]
- Did you know your vejleder (supervisor) in advance?
- Is there any relation between your topic and the vejleder's (supervisor's) research/profession?

Content of vejledningen (supervision)

- Did the vejleder (supervisor) recommend/suggest literature? To what extent?
- Did you discuss theories? On what level and how often?
- What did you talk about with your vejleder (supervisor) concerning methodology/methods? On which level and to which extent?
- Did you employ your vejleder (supervisor) when it comes to the process? (Process: any halt, doubt about academic issues, the structure of the thesis, writing "hurdles" and "barriers," organization of project work?)
- Were there any moments of "Now I really have learned something"?

The nature of vejledning (supervision)

- What kind of comments did you get from the vejleder (supervisor)?
- How did you react? What did you do with the comments?
- Which specific advice did the vejleder (supervisor) give? Did s/he give any at all?
- Did the vejleder (supervisor) suggest things that you have not followed?
- If yes, what was the reaction of the vejleder (supervisor)?
- If no, did you have the impression that you were forced to reach a compromise/agreement by giving up your initial position?
- Was there anything the vejleder (supervisor) insisted on you should do?

- Did the vejleder (supervisor) frustrate you?
- Any doubts like "Should I do that?" Any reactions like "Well, the vejleder (supervisor) was right."
- Where did your vejleder (supervisor) make the biggest difference?
- In a positive way? In a negative way?
- Did the vejleder (supervisor) suggest things that did not make sense for you?
- How much autonomy/independence did you have in respect to your thesis?

The ideal vejleder (supervisor)

- What do you think should be the supervisor's contribution, your contribution?
- Could you please describe the perfect vejleder (supervisor)?

The vejledningsplan (supervision plan)

- In how much detail did you talk about and help you fill out the plan?
- About the writing process?
- What have you written so far?
- Which other actions have you done, e.g., literature search, method chapter, data collection, reading?
- What status has the text you have brought with you (loose notes, first draft, almost finished) text?
- What do you use writing for, in addition to manuscript writing?
- How many times did you add text/delete in the same part of the manuscript?
- Do you use writing in the idea phase?
- Do you write when you are reading?
- Take me into your "writing cell (writing space)." What is going on in there?
- How do you write? One sentence at a time, structured writing based on disposition/structure, loose writing in all directions, across manuscript, one chapter at a time?
- Can you put into words something you have learned until now?
- What courses and activities about master's thesis (writing) have you participated?
- What else do you use for help or as a source of inspiration?
- How do you feel about method and methodology? How do you cope with it?

Appendix B: Details on Data Collection

The empirical data distributed on students' study programs and supervisors' terms of employment and nationality.

The students' study programs	Supervisor (position and educational-cultural background)
Business Administration and Psychology	Researcher*, Danish
Business Administration and Philosophy	Researcher*, Danish
Business Administration and Mathematics	Researcher*, Danish
Business Administration and Political Science	Researcher*, Danish
Applied Economy and Finance	Researcher*, Danish
Economic Marketing (1 student from a pair)***	Researcher*, Danish
Intercultural Marketing	Researcher*, Danish
Intercultural Marketing (2 students)****	Researcher*, Danish
Human Resource Management (2 students)***	Researcher*, Danish
Business and Development studies	Researcher*, Austrian **
Multicultural Communication in Organizations (1 student from a pair)***	Non researcher*, Danish

*Researcher: internal (teachers/ supervisors) with research obligations, Non-researcher: external (teachers/ supervisors) without research obligations
** Austrian, but has adopted Danish educational culture/ideology
*** Student has conducted the project and written the thesis together with another student, but only one student was interviewed.
**** The two students have conducted the project and written the thesis together.

Appendix C: Distribution of Interviews across the Supervision Models

Supervision models	Empirical data
Partnership	Eight interviews with: Johan, Katherina. Laura and Line, Nathalie. Per, Rasmus, Simon, and Thor
Apprenticeship	One interview with Jonas
Teaching	One interview with Peter
Laissez-faire	One interview with Nadia and Michala

8 The Challenges of Professional Development in the European Higher Education Area: Targeting Success in Writing, Research, Learning and Teaching

Erika Melonashi
UNIVERSITY COLLEGE WISDOM, ALBANIA

Paul Donovan
MAYNOOTH UNIVERSITY, IRELAND

Basak Ercan
AKDENIZ UNIVERSITY, TURKEY

Alison Farrell
MAYNOOTH UNIVERSITY, IRELAND

Sonia Oliver
AUTONOMOUS UNIVERSITY OF BARCELONA, SPAIN

In this chapter we report on an element of a European COST Action which set out to explore centralised models of professional learning for higher education staff across writing, research, learning and teaching. Specifically, we report on our examination of three things: the provision of professional support across writing, research, learning and teaching; the factors which influence the research participants' engagement in writing, research, learning and teaching; the sort of professional support that the research participants found either effective or desirable in terms of writing, research, learning and teaching. Based on analysis of the data, in the context of the COST Action, we suggest three themes to be considered with regard to the provision of professional learning for higher education colleagues across these four areas, namely, character, community and context. In our discussion and concluding remarks we emphasize the importance of the human component of higher education and the need for collaborative approaches which are meaningful and context sensitive.

The work underpinning this chapter began with a conversation between colleagues from teaching and learning/academic/educational/faculty development backgrounds, and colleagues from composition and rhetoric/writing traditions. When we met, we discovered that we were often talking about the same or related matters but that we were coming at them from different directions. We found that we could identify strong links in the nature of the work we were doing and similar challenges. The common thread of enquiry which ran through our work, and our being situated in higher education, meant that we all had experience of four key areas within that sector, namely, writing, research, learning, and teaching. We realised that our professional trajectories had necessitated that we develop across these four areas. In some instances, this development was mapped carefully and strategically to a career plan, more often, however, it was haphazard and responsive in nature. Similarly, we observed that the professional development support we were offered by our institutions, and the support we offered within our institutions in our professional roles or as colleagues had both distinctive threads and woven patterns.

With the benefit of our combined years of experience, we reflected on whether we could make more of the common ground between writing and research, learning, and teaching, and, in turn on whether our institutions could provide support for their staff which would capitalise on this common ground. We decided to try to explore this idea by writing a bid for European Union (EU) funding through a mechanism called COST—European Cooperation in Science and Technology. COST is a "funding organisation for research and innovation networks" (COST, n.d.). COST supports networking by providing funding which facilitates co-enquiry and collaboration between colleagues from across Europe and beyond. The work these colleagues do is called an Action; according to the COST Association, "Actions help connect research initiatives across Europe and beyond and enable researchers and innovators to grow their ideas in any science and technology field by sharing them with their peers. COST Actions are bottom-up networks with a duration of four years that boost research, innovation and careers" (COST, n.d.). Our COST Action was called *We ReLaTe* or COST Action 15221. In our Action we examined the challenge of creating synergy among centralised institutional supports for staff across the four key areas of writing, research, learning, and teaching (COST Action 15221, n.d., a). Practically, we knew that our institutions provided, to varying degrees and with different institutional emphases, professional development support for staff in their roles as writers and researchers, as learners and teachers but we were unsure about the extent of support in each of these spaces and we wondered if these supports did, or could, complement each other. Our Action allowed us to find out more about this challenge and in this chapter, we present a portion of the findings of our Action work.

As part of the Action, we conducted research with colleagues across Europe about the personal (internal) and contextual (external) factors that contribute to success in teaching, learning, research and writing. Specifically, we wanted to do two things:

1. To capture the knowledge, skills, values, motivations and processes that have led to success, effectiveness and/or productivity in each of the four areas of writing, research, learning and teaching.
2. To explore what institutions can and/or should do to support effectiveness and/or productivity in each of the four areas of writing, research, learning and teaching.

Prior to presenting our findings we situate this chapter in the COST Action. We then locate our work in literature which has helped us to understand the contemporary higher education context and the place of professional development therein. Next, we present our methodology and our findings. Finally, we present a discussion of our findings and some concluding remarks.

Situating This Chapter in the COST Action

A full description of the COST Action from which the findings discussed in this chapter are drawn is available in the Memorandum of Understanding (COST, 2016)[1] between the Action and COST. That document states the Action's rationale which is summarised here:

- There is a need for a global conversation about professional development across writing, research, learning and teaching which will take place "alongside, and building on, the 'disciplining' approach that has predominated [and] . . . will offer an alternative for consideration in a transdisciplinary and interdisciplinary space" (COST, 2016, p. 1).
- This conversation is needed because of three key factors in the higher education landscape:
    1. the massification of higher education in terms of growth in student numbers and diversity of the student population (Altbach et al.,

---

1 http://www.werelate.eu/wp-content/uploads/2017/10/MoU-.pdf

2009; Arum & Roksa, 2011; Barber et al., 2013; European Commission, 2013; Guri-Rosenblit et al., 2007; OECD, 2012, 2014; Shavit et al., 2007)

2. neoliberal, managerial approaches in higher education including an ever-growing range of stakeholder demands, a transactional approach to the higher education experience and the need for alternative models (Barnett, 2012; Lynch et al., 2012)

3. the growing use of technology in higher education (Conole, 2013; Laurillard, 2012; Wheeler & Gerver, 2015) (COST, 2016, pp. 1-2).

- These, and other factors mean that higher education is changing in a range of ways.
- These factors combined, or even taken separately, mean that scaffolding and enhancing the staff and student experience of teaching, learning, research and writing has become ever more complex in terms of institutional organisation and professional and student support (COST, 2016, p. 2).
- New models and frameworks that identify synergies across the four areas of writing, research, learning, and teaching could help us to reimage central supports for these four areas which would focus on effectiveness, success and productivity, and would serve to capitalise on commonalities and synergies.

COST Actions facilitate co-enquiry and collaboration. In terms of partnership, our Action began with a small group of proposers from 16 countries. Over its lifetime from October 2016 to April 2021, the Action grew to include colleagues from 41 countries (COST Action 15221, n.d., b; Appendix 1).

Contemporary Higher Education and the Need for Professional Learning

More and more is being required of higher education and the environment in which it is operating is becoming more complex; Barnett suggests it is a modern world of supercomplexity (2000). In addition, higher education is increasingly required to demonstrate where the return on the investment in it might be observed particularly in publicly funded higher education which is subject to greater demands for accountability and improved efficiency, more competition, and a requirement for ever more sophisticated reporting mechanisms (Torres, 2011). This tendency is identified as part of the "neoliberal" move in higher education about which much has been written (readers are directed to Malcolm Tight's article entitled "The neoliberal turn in Higher

Education" which traces the use and evolution of the term in this space). Whether we see neoliberalism in higher education as a "fright term" (Tight, 2019, p. 273) or as what Giroux has suggested is the cause of "bare pedagogy" (Giroux, 2010, p. 185) there is no questioning its prevalence in the discourse around higher education. Neither can one deny the inclination towards greater accountability and transparency and their associated tools in this sector. Van Vught and Ziegele define transparency tools as "instruments that aim to provide information to stakeholders about the efforts and performance of higher education and research institutions" (2011, p. 25). Gunn, with reference to Neave, makes a useful distinction in his work in this area between quality assurance and transparency tools; he notes

> In origin, quality assurance comes from within the higher education community whereas transparency tools tend to be imposed from outside. Quality assurance is rooted in an ethos of institutional autonomy and the principles of peer review undertaken by self-regulating professionals. It is focused on assurance, and increasingly concerned with enhancement, rather than performance measurement and comparison (Neave 2014). Transparency tools, alternatively, may serve agendas and stakeholders outside the academic community, and they typically have characteristics more akin to external audit and public scrutiny. (2018, pp. 505-506)

Both of these elements are broadly associated with demonstrating some impact of the combined efforts associated with higher education.

Higher education is a human endeavour. As such demonstrating its impact will depend in no small part on higher education staff. The growing complexity of, the relentless demands on, and the increasing changes in, higher education mean that the staff working within it need support including professional development as higher education continues to evolve. Reflecting the growth and increased complexity of the field, research into higher education itself has grown exponentially especially in the past 50 years (Tight, 2017). Our chapter is concerned with writing, research, learning and teaching (WRLT) and so it connects with research into higher education which considers all four of these areas, against the bigger higher education landscape. As we note in the COST MoU, there is an abundance of work which explores these four individual areas specifically—we refer to but a few in that document including: Åkerlind, 2005; Bain, 2004; Geller & Eodice, 2013; Kuh et al., 2010; Pascarella & Terenzini, 2005; Sorcinelli et al., 2006; Stefani, 2011; Thaiss et al., 2012; Trowler et al., 2012 (COST, 2016). Strands of the higher education research into writing, research, learning and teaching (WRLT) are concerned with professional development or professional learning for higher education staff. The professional learning for higher education staff in their role as teachers has been categorised variously and under broad headings such as simply "teaching and learning in higher education," as educational development, as academic development, as faculty development, as the scholarship of teaching and learning, etc. The absence of an agreed nomenclature points to the fluid and expansive nature of this work. At the outset, work in this space sought to establish a research and evidence basis, and practical guidance for academics in terms of their teaching practice in higher education. Sutherland notes that the "field of 'academic development' (or educational, faculty, or instructional development as it is variously known internationally) has had a clear focus on supporting academics in their teaching endeavours" (2018, p. 262). In her editorial for a special issue of the *International Journal for Academic Development,* Sutherland sketches the development of this field and concludes that "the focus of most academic development literature . . . is still clearly on the development of teaching" (2018, p. 263). However, she also remarks that "Around the same time as academic development as a field of research was emerging, organisational development was becoming more prominent in universities worldwide" (2018, p. 263). And that subsequently "researcher development" emerged as "a more recent phenomenon" but one which shares an ambiguity with academic development in that "its definition is as slippery as academic development's appears to be" (Sutherland, 2018, p. 264). In turn, educational development and researcher development might both overlap with research into supporting colleagues as writers. Part of the work of our Action was to find out more about, and from, colleagues who have been clearly successful across the four areas writing, research, learning and teaching (WRLT) and to decipher their professional purposes (goals-motivations), their processes, their knowledge and skills, and their values. We believed that if we could learn more about these experts, or as we titled them "stellar" colleagues, we could extrapolate from that data the sort of support that might be beneficial for other colleagues who were seeking to succeed in a similar way. We also asked these key informants about the sorts of supports that they considered most beneficial.

Methodology

The primary partners in a COST Action are the Management Committee (MC). There can be two MC members from each partner country. In our Action the MC identified stellar colleagues in their countries using agreed criteria (COST Action 15221, 2018). MC members identified stellar colleagues either within their home institutions or from other institutions in their home country. All of these colleagues were working in COST member countries (there are 38 European COST member countries and one cooperating member country, namely Israel). These stellar colleagues became the key informants for the Action's data gathering. Working with our key informants, we tried to learn about professional learning, including institutional models of professional learning, through an individual lens.

Our data gathering included a two-stage process starting with the creation of focus groups composed of multilingual and multicultural colleagues selected by the Management Committee. Six online focus groups were held with a total of 16 participants involved. The data from the focus groups was analysed using thematic analysis and reported in Carmody (2019). The findings from the focus groups informed the design of a questionnaire, which was the second stage of data gathering. The questionnaire was designed by colleagues who had participated in one of the Action's training schools and by MC members. It was piloted with a small group of colleagues known to MC members. Following feedback from the pilot group the questionnaire was refined. Once the questionnaire was finalised, MC members invited colleagues, by email, to complete it. In total, 252 colleagues, from across 31 countries answered the questionnaire which considered the four areas of writing, research, learning and teaching (WRLT). Across the sections that considered support and development there were 16 Likert scale questions and four open text questions. The quantitative results of the questionnaire (minus the open text questions) were analysed by co-author of this chapter Erika Melonashi (2020), and it is that data that we concentrate on in this chapter.

Findings

As noted at the outset of this chapter, in our Action we were examining professional learning across the research participant settings. We asked about the factors which influence engagement with writing, research, learning and teaching, the provision or lack thereof of centralised professional support across writing, research, learning and teaching, and the sort of professional support participants found either effective or desirable across the four areas. We report our findings here under the headings of internal (personal) and external (contextual) factors.

Internal Factors—Personal: Character, Personal Traits and Motivation

As a result of our focus groups, we discovered that a key determinant of success across WRLT was the academic disposition. Because we began to see a pattern from the focus group data about the importance of individual, personal characteristics in our key informants, we decided to explore this to a greater extent in the questionnaire.

In order to assess personal traits, participants were asked "To what extent have the following personal traits/dispositions influenced your success across the four areas of writing, research, teaching and learning where five is most influential, and one is least influential." Table 8.1 shows means and standard deviations for 13 personal traits. They are ranked in descending order of mean values from most influential to least influential. As can be seen in the table, the top six traits rated as most influential by participants included: Curiosity, Openness to New Experiences, Optimism, Freedom, Determination/Persistence, and Ability to Problem Solve.

Table 8.1. Mean Values and Standard Deviations for Personal Traits

Personal Traits	Mean*	SD
1. Curiosity	4.59	.65
2. Openness to new experiences	4.47	.74
3. Optimism, positive attitude	4.45	.76
4. Freedom	4.43	.79
5. Determination/persistence	4.42	.73
6. Ability to problem solve	4.42	.70
7. Openness to collaboration	4.33	.85
8. Sound values—respect, equality, fairness, integrity	4.20	.93
9. Imagination	4.09	.92
10. Strategic thinking and planning	3.97	1.05
11. Willingness to travel for work	3.89	1.18
12. Kindness and compassion	3.83	1.05
13. Willingness to take risks	3.73	1.05
14. Willingness to live and work overseas	3.33	1.41

Range of values 1-5.

Motivation was investigated across two dimensions: "Motivation for Writing" and "Motivation for research." Table 8.2 shows means and standard deviations for nine items assessing "Motivation for writing," ranking them from strongest (higher means) to weakest (lower means) motivating factors. It is clearly noticed that "Passion for your discipline" was rated as the strongest motive, followed by "The wish to advance my career," "Desire to share your work," "Wish to be recognized in the field," and "Desire to learn more about my work" (See Table 8.2).

Table 8.2. Mean Values and Standard Deviations for "Motivation for Writing"

Motivation for Writing	Mean*	SD
1. Passion for your discipline	4.02	1.16
2. The wish to advance my career	3.78	1.27
3. Desire to share your work	3.76	1.25
4. The wish to be recognized in the field	3.72	1.22
5. Desire to learn more about my work	3.66	1.14
6. Belief that your writing can make a difference	3.62	1.16
7. The obligation to publish as a requirement around funding secured	3.39	1.26
8. The opportunity to co-author	3.32	1.33
9. The support of colleagues	3.05	1.32

Range of values 1-5.

Table 8.3 shows means and standard deviations for the twelve items regarding motivation for research, in descending order. It can be noted that "Intrinsic motivation" is at the top of the list, followed by "Desire to learn more," "Desire to progress the field," "Connectedness," "Desire to improve the quality of my teaching." The weakest motive was "Industry needs."

Table 8.3. Mean Values and Standard Deviations for "Motivation for Research"

Motivation for Research	Mean*	SD
1. Intrinsic motivation	4.70	.62
2. Desire to learn more	4.37	.81
3. Desire to progress the field	4.31	.86
4. Connectedness	4.05	1.08
5. Desire to improve the quality of my teaching	3.98	1.08
6. The opportunity to collaborate with colleagues	3.95	1.04
7. Mobility—the opportunity to travel	3.84	1.21
8. Recognition by my institution	3.55	1.11
9. Institutional demands	3.47	1.06
10. Job security	3.44	1.17
11. Sense of competition within my field	3.22	1.26
12. Industry needs	2.69	1.30

Range of values 1-5.

5.2 External Factors—Context

In addition to the asking key informants about personal traits, colleagues were asked about centralised support that was offered to them by their institutions, and about what enables or creates barriers to success and development. By centralised support we meant an office or centre, which is managed by dedicated staff, whose primary role is to provide institution-wide support for writing, research, learning and teaching. We present the findings in answer to these questions as

1. Presence/existence of support for teaching, learning, research and writing
2. The most useful types of support and or enablers across all four dimensions

Figure 8.1 show participants' answers on the existence of support for staff at their institutions. As can be noticed, the presence of support is poorest for writing; only 23% of participants reported having support for writing at their institutions. The most extensive support was reported for research, as 38% of the sample reported this type of support at their institutions. Additionally, teaching and learning support was reported by 31.6% of the sample, while professional development by 35% of the sample. To be noted is the percentage of individuals who answer "Difficult to say," which varies from 1/5 to 1/3 of the sample reporting so across the different areas, suggesting perhaps a lack of information or confusion regarding the specific types of support.

It should be highlighted that this question did ask specifically about centralised support for these areas. We know from our work across the Action, and from our own experience, that professional learning can take many guises outside of that which is offered by institutions centrally. Hence, while support for centralized support for writing was reported as low that is not to say that there were no other forms of support that participants may have been availing of, or indeed extending to, colleagues.

One interesting finding is that cross-tabulation between supports across different areas indicated that institutions providing one type of support, e.g., writing support, were also more likely to provide other types of support too, e.g., research support, teaching and learning, etc. (Chi Square value was significant at p<.001.) Tables 8.4-8.9 provide more detailed information for the cross-tabulations; for instance, Table 8.4 suggests that participants who answered "yes" to "teaching and learning support" were also more likely to answer "yes" on "writing support" and vice versa.

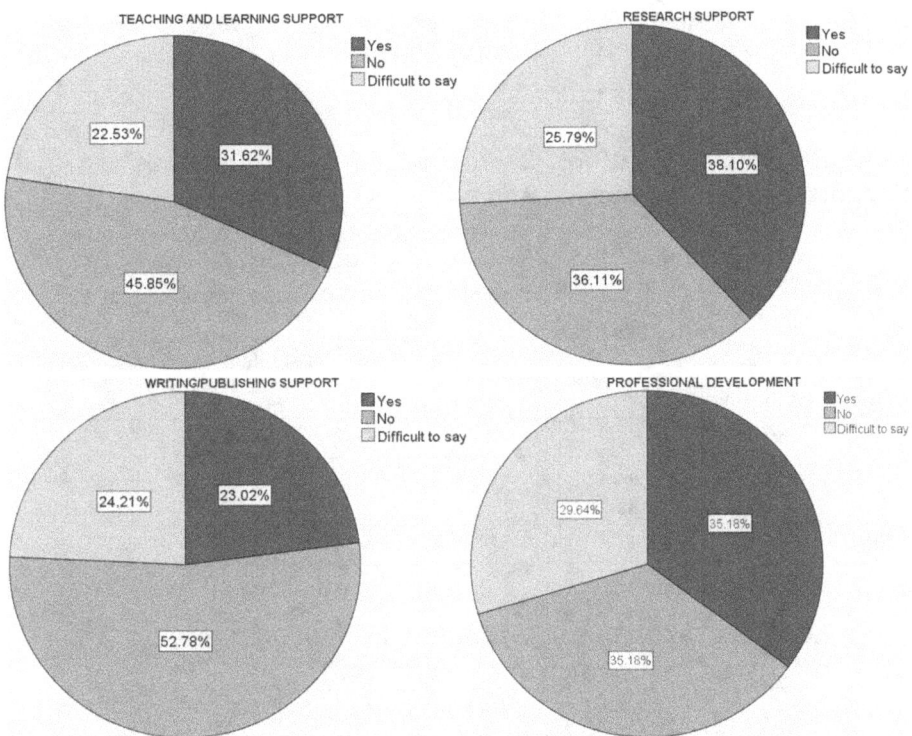

Figure 8.1. Percentages of respondents who answered "yes," "no," or "difficult to say" in answer to the question of the provision by their institution of centralised support for teaching and learning (support for staff in their role as teachers), research, professional development (or staff training/development) and writing/publishing for staff.

Similar patterns are discernible across the cross-tabulations reported in Tables 8.5-8.9. In the cases of cross tabulation between "writing/publishing support for staff" and "research support for staff" (Table 8.5) and between "writing/publishing support for staff" and "professional development and/or staff training" (Table 8.6), we can see that in both instances the numbers reported for "no" support in either area are higher than reported support for each area. The gap between the provision of two supports closes as we move through the cross-tabulation tables. In Tables 8.7 and 8.8, respectively, there is slightly greater provision of support across "research support" and "teaching and learning support," and nearly identical provision and no provision numbers in the cross-tabulation between "research support for staff" and "professional development and/or staff training." In Table 8.9 again those answering "yes" to "professional development and/or staff training" are more likely to answer "yes" to "teaching and learning support"; those answering "no" to one are more likely to answer "no" to the other. The cross-tabulated "difficult to say" numbers remain relatively stable throughout the tables all of them within a range of 24 and 35.

Table 8.4. Cross-tabulations: Overlap between Writing/Publishing Support for Staff? x Teaching and Learning Support

		Teaching and learning support (for example through a teaching and learning centre which aims primarily to support staff as teachers)?			
		Yes	No	Difficult to say	Total
Writing/publishing support for staff?	Yes	42	6	10	58
	No	19	91	23	133
	Difficult to say	18	19	24	61
Total		79	116	57	252

Table 8.5. Cross-tabulations: Writing/Publishing Support for Staff? x Research Support for Staff?

		Research support for staff?			
		Yes	No	Difficult to say	Total
Writing/publishing support for staff?	Yes	44	5	9	58
	No	29	78	26	133
	Difficult to say	22	8	30	60
Total		95	91	65	251

Table 8.6. Cross-tabulation: Writing/Publishing Support for Staff? x Professional Development and/or Staff Training

		Professional development and/or staff training and development?			
		Yes	No	Difficult to say	Total
Writing/publishing support for staff?	Yes	39	5	14	58
	No	26	71	36	133
	Difficult to say	23	13	25	61
Total		88	89	75	252

Table 8.7. Cross-tabulation: Research Support for Staff? x Teaching and Learning Support

		Teaching and learning support			
		Yes	No	Difficult to say	Total
Research support for staff?	Yes	50	28	18	96
	No	10	67	14	91
	Difficult to say	20	21	24	65
Total		80	116	56	252

Table 8.8. Cross-tabulation: Research Support x Professional Development

Yes		Professional development and/or staff training and development?			
		Yes	No	Difficult to say	Total
Research support for staff?	Yes	57	19	20	96
	No	13	58	20	91
	Difficult to say	18	12	35	65
Total		88	89	75	252

Table 8.9. Cross-tabulation: Teaching and Learning Support x Professional Development and/or Staff Training and Development?

Yes		Professional development and/or staff training and development?			
		Yes	No	Difficult to say	Total
Teaching and learning support?*	Yes	52	9	19	80
	No	21	68	27	116
	Difficult to say	16	12	29	57
Total		89	89	75	253

For example through a teaching and learning centre which aims primarily to support staff as teachers.

With regard types of support which colleagues find mostly useful, Table 8.10 indicates opinions on writing supports. As can be observed from the table: "Access to relevant literature" ranks first (highest reported mean), followed by "Dedicated long blocks," "Mentoring," "Editor corrections/services," and "English language support." Media related items are rated last.

Table 8.10. Mean Values and Standard Deviations for Types of Writing Supports

Types of Writing Support	Mean*	SD
1. Access to relevant literature	4.28	.91
2. Dedicated long blocks	3.73	1.23
3. Mentoring	3.72	1.21
4. Editor corrections/services	3.70	1.19
5. English language support	3.60	1.35
6. Writing workshops, courses, lectures	3.52	1.28
7. Training in supervising others	3.42	1.18
8. Training in working as part of an editorial board	3.38	1.19
9. Dedicated short blocks	3.37	1.17
10. Training in publishing	3.36	1.21
11. Reading circles	2.91	1.20
12. Tailored support in writing for mainstream	2.83	1.24
14. Communications/media skills training	2.61	1.30
13. Social media writing training	2.54	1.29

Range of values 1–5.

Tables 8.11 and 8.12 indicate participants' answers on institutional support for teaching. More specifically Table 8.11 shows frequencies and percentages for initial support, first year support, ongoing support and teaching qualifications. Table 8.12 indicates mean values and standard deviations for types of teaching supports and important factors regarding teaching development, in descending order. Student related items including "Feedback from students" and "Student performance/learning" are top ranked. Colleague-related items are also rated highly "Informal professional conversations" and "Feedback from colleagues." Interestingly, "Awards and recognitions" are ranked last.

Table 8.11. Frequencies and Percentages for Institutional Support for Teaching

Institutional Support		Frequency	Percent
Initial teacher training	Yes	68	27.1
	No	154	61.4
	Somewhat	29	11.6

Support during the first year	Yes	49	19.6
	No	167	66.8
	Somewhat	34	13.6
Ongoing Institutional Support	Yes	79	31.7
	No	99	39.8
	Somewhat	71	28.5
Formal teaching qualification	Yes	138	54.8
	No	79	31.3
	Somewhat	35	13.9

Table 8.12. Mean Values and Standard Deviations for Types of Teaching Supports

Types of Teaching Support	Mean*	SD
1. Feedback from students	4.28	.79
2. Student performance–student learning	3.92	1.14
3. Informal professional conversations	3.82	1.13
4. Feedback from colleagues	3.72	1.13
5. International teaching opportunities	3.63	1.38
6. Engaging with the scholarship of teaching and learning	3.53	1.30
7. Researching your teaching	3.51	1.35
8. Team-teaching (co-teaching) opportunities	3.45	1.29
9. Attending teaching and learning workshops	3.42	1.37
10. Mentoring other colleagues	3.38	1.24
11. Contributing to teaching and learning workshops	3.35	1.35
12. Awards and recognition	3.04	1.38

Range of values 1–5.

Table 8.13 shows mean values and standard deviations for professional learning supports. "Support on engaging in EU/international projects" and "Conference attendance" are reported as the strongest types of support, followed by "Disciplinary related research support," "Support on building collaborations and networks," and "Cross-disciplinary research support." "Financial training" is rated as the least useful."

Table 8.13. Mean Values and Standard Deviations for Types of Learning Supports

Types of Learning Supports	Mean*	SD
1. Support on engaging in EU/international projects	4.13	1.03
2. Conference/event attendance	4.00	1.00
3. Disciplinary related research support	3.99	1.03
4. Support on building collaborations and networks	3.96	1.06
5. Cross-disciplinary research support	3.87	1.08
6. Teaching and learning workshops	3.79	1.15
7. Project management	3.66	1.19
8. Teaching and learning programmes	3.59	1.21
9. People management	3.49	1.18
10. Time management	3.48	1.31
11. ICT (technology) training	3.45	1.26
12. Managing teams	3.45	1.17
13. Work-life balance support/training	3.43	1.31
14. Leadership training	3.38	1.25
15. Negotiating institutional systems and processes	3.26	1.27
16. Career planning	3.24	1.33
17. Recruiting staff	3.21	1.25
18. Financial training	3.18	1.27

Range of values 1–5

Table 8.14 shows participants' answers on the types of research support they find useful. Frequencies indicate the number of participants checking in the specific supports. As can be noted the largest number of the sample reported "Grant funding" (reported by 66.5% of the sample), followed closely by "Presenting research results and international events" (64.6% of the sample). "Opportunities to collaborate" and "Attending research-oriented events" were also checked by more than half of the sample. "Workshops/professional development" was the less relevant item checked by only 1/3 of the sample.

Table 8.15 shows mean values and standard deviations for participants' answers regarding continuous professional development (CDP). Items are ranked in descending order of relevance for CPD as reported by participants. The three top ranked factors are: Personal interest in further learning, Time, and Funding.

Table 8.14. Frequencies and Percentages of Research Supports

Research Supports	Frequency	Percent
1. Grant funding	175	66.5
2. Presenting research results at international events	170	64.6
3. Opportunities to collaborate	152	57.8
4. Attending research-oriented event	149	56.7
5. Flexibility to adjust commitment	120	45.6
6. Release time to conduct research	116	44.1
7. International professional development opportunities	109	41.4
8. Workshops/professional development	86	32.7

Table 8.15. Means and Standard Deviations for Factors relevant to CPD

Factors Related to CPD	Mean*	SD
1. Personal interest in further professional learning	4.41	.85
2. Time	4.21	1.00
3. Funding from my institution/university for CPD	3.69	1.33
4. A clear framework for continuing professional development	3.63	1.21
5. Institutional recognition of further professional learning	3.62	1.11
6. The availability of CPD opportunities in my institution/university	3.60	1.28
7. Institutional commitment to CPD for staff	3.47	1.29
8. Institutional requirement for CPD for staff	3.27	1.25

Range of values 1–5

Discussion of Findings

The higher education experience globally over 2020 and well into 2021 has been fraught with uncertainty, change, and challenges. One of the many effects of the sudden move to online/remote/blended teaching, learning, and assessment was the necessity for staff to extend and improve their digital capabilities and to engage in other pedagogy-related professional learning. The need for ongoing professional learning for all those who teach and research is unlikely to diminish in the near future not least where engagement in professional learning by the individual, and support for staff professional learning support by the institution, are indicators of ongoing commitment to the enhancement of T&L practice and research. In this discussion of findings, we suggest factors which might be considered in the provision of impactful professional learning.

The Self

Our findings suggest that the academic's character is central to success where the character refers both to professional disposition and individual practice. It reflects the fact that, as Sorcinelli suggests, "individual practice is the core site of learning" in the roles of writer, researcher, learner and teacher (in conversation, 2020). It echoes the Irish *National Professional Development Framework for all Staff Who Teach in Higher Education* (2016) which identifies "The Self" as Domain 1. In our data, certain personal and professional characteristics were overwhelmingly shared by our key informants. The patterns that predominate in the findings suggest that intrinsic motivation is at the core of academic behaviour, e.g., the most significant factor with regard to continuous professional development was "personal interest in further professional learning." The importance of the self which emerged in this work echoes Matheson's research into teaching excellence where, drawing on Parker's work (2014), she highlights the importance of personal attributes suggesting that "teaching excellence lies within the individual" (2019, p. 15). Similarly, it resonates with Harland and Wald's research where work with their participants suggested to them that "teaching quality depended first and foremost on intrinsic motivation and pride in the job" (2017, p. 427). In turn, it echoes King's work where writing in 2019, she builds on her own work published in 2004 about what CPD academics engage in; her title has shifted from the 2004 version, "Continuing Professional Development in Higher Education: What Do Academics Do?" to "Continuing Professional Development: What Do Award-Winning Academics Do?" in the 2019 article. In the latter she talks about researching "expert" teachers in higher education; we see links with our work with "stellar colleagues" here. She suggests that CPD might be defined as "a self-determined and purposeful process of evolution of teaching and learning approaches, informed by evidence gathered from a range of activities" (2019, p. 4). The centrality of the self echoes our findings as does the emphasis on change—"evolution." She also mentions the idea of "Artistry" in teaching, which is in harmony with the idea of the "craft of teaching" which emerged in our conversations for this chapter.

Community, Connection, and Collaboration

In addition to the significance of professional disposition, community, connection and collaboration matter to our key informants. Colleagues noted that community-related aspects such as partnerships, relationships, mobility, mentoring, professional conversations, etc. were important supports. The findings show that academics as researchers want to collaborate and that connectedness and relationships emerge as important in teaching also; three of the four most relevant supports for teaching involved interacting with others, either students or staff. The data suggest that our key informants value professional collaboration and conversations with colleagues, and meaningful feedback from students as part of professional learning. These findings resonate with the work of Roxå and Mårtensson who make connections between the individual work of the teacher, the microculture to which they belong, and the context in which they exist. They note that "academic teaching is an extremely context-dependent practice . . . Teaching is easier to perform for the individual teacher if the microculture to which he or she belongs supports learning about this practice through continuous adjustment to reality and through constructive sharing of new insights among colleagues" (2015, p. 202). In turn, there is potential to build on the importance that key informants placed on meaningful feedback from students towards the development of student partnership. O'Leary and Cui argue for such a "reconceptualisation" of teaching and learning in higher education, one which shifts "from a performative focus to one that foregrounds the importance of collaborative, educational inquiry to understand the situated realities of T & L" (2020, p. 153). They suggest that "meaningful improvements to the quality of T & L in HE require substantive collaboration between students and staff that provide opportunities for both to generate situated, reciprocal understanding of T & L in the context of their programmes" (2020, p. 153).

Context

While we have identified many similarities in terms of the responses from our key informants, one of the striking things about the key informants is the difference that we know exists in terms of context, particularly in terms of their institutional and national settings. We know from our own experience that there is variety across higher education provision in national settings. That variety appears to be amplified when one looks across Europe and to our near neighbours. It is certainly the case that the provision of centralised support varies greatly across our data and that any goals and aspirations we have about models of support need to be particularly mindful of context including policy, resources and infrastructure, but also values and principles. As Skelton notes, within the higher education professional setting there can be a clash of values, and this can occur at the micro, meso, and macro level. These "value conflicts" can lead to "personal and professional discomfort" but they can be "potent sites for professional development" (2012, p. 264). Because our work is situated, it is influenced by the context. Recognising the relational nature of higher education, Bass et al. (2019) take an "ecosystemic approach" to professional learning and educational development. Bass and colleagues suggest a "new learning compact" as a way "to strategically and effectively link change in individual practice with essential issues of community, institutional structure and systemic policy" (2019, p. 5). They suggest that "Transformational change requires an ecosystemic approach that links processes of individual change with institutional culture and structure, and individual institutions with networks and systems, through the involvement of external stakeholders and change initiatives" (2019, p. 4). Their framework is characterised by integrating strategy, a strong research base, a humane and respectful perspective, and a systems-thinking, inquiry- and action-focused approach (2019).

Our key informants had shared values which included collegiality, freedom, quality, ethics and integrity, respect, creativity, openness, and diversity. These values are ones which are often reflected in the strategic plans of higher education institutions. These values are also reflected in the characteristics and inclinations of our participants who display curiosity, optimism/positive attitude, freedom, imagination, determination/persistence, openness and problem solving, and a very strong desire to connect, share and collaborate. Our similarities emphasize the human factor of higher education which can be easily forgotten and/or neglected in the policies and strategies, the "KPIs" and the accountability and transparency measures. The similarities we see reinforce the utterly essential human component of higher education. We suggest that support for academics should recognise this human component in the importance of the self and should seek to tap into the well of intrinsic motivation that academic colleagues bring to their work. A strong inclusion of "bottom up" and collaborative approaches would be practical ways to enact this commitment.

Holistic Approach

In the field of educational development, since our Action began in 2016, other perspectives have begun to seep into the professional learning fabric and we see other researchers writing about the connections across all professional learning as "holistic academic development." This topic was addressed in the previously mentioned 2018 special edition of the *International Journal for Academic Development* where Sutherland notes that "Practitioners and researchers . . . could be reading and talking to each other a lot more, and working together more closely to provide holistic programmes of support and development for academics. Such programmes would address the *whole of the academic role*, the *whole* institution, and the *whole person*." (p. 265, emphasis in original). Austin and Sorcinelli had anticipated this move in 2013 when they observed that the profession of "faculty development" will require "new thinking about ideal structures for faculty development and ways of operating organizationally" as well as approaching its work "as collaborative, community work within and beyond the institution" (p. 96).

Based on our findings we suggest that a holistic approach to professional learning across writing, research, learning and teaching which considers character, community, and context; we propose this approach as a 3Cs Professional Learning Framework in the Action's final report (COST Action 15221, 2021). This approach is reflective of King's broader recommendations which note along with the necessity for an emphasis on the individual's CPD, the need for collaboration and interaction, and for alignment with "institutional structures and reward policies" (2019, p. 4). We assert that support for WRLT should aim to capitalise on the intrinsic motivation of staff and to strongly recognise, endorse and practically support community and collaborative approaches in and across these areas. We acknowledge that context matters and that identical provision, across higher education, nationally or indeed internationally would be neither desirable nor effective. Rather, provision should be context sensitive and reflective of the specific goals of the institutional learning community.

Conclusion

In this chapter, we have presented our findings about what personal (internal) and contextual (external) factors contribute to success for academic staff in writing, research, learning and teaching. These findings are part of the broader work of our COST Action around trying to identify the sorts of supports that might be useful for academics in terms of writing, research, learning and teaching, and the possible intersections between those supports. All the work across the Action has enabled us to explore the challenges that readers might recognise in their daily writing, research, learning, and practices. In this vein, as to professional development in the EHEA, we have discovered a distinctive and emerging "human factor" among our key informants.

The approach of our COST Action and the broader COST model itself, which supported the work communicated in this chapter, resonates with what we have learned in our research. Though COST as an organisation operates at a macro level, with a clear international dimension, it deliberately nurtures "bottom up" networks of colleagues who will work together to address a challenge while also learning and connecting. In many ways, the COST approach encapsulates what we have discovered matters in terms of supporting academics; it facilitates individual career development and learning, within community building and nurturing, in a context sensitive and supportive manner.

Higher education is expanding and changing, and as colleagues working in higher education we need, and want, to continue to learn and develop. Based on our research, we suggest starting with the people, as individuals and communities, who work in a particular context, and trying to identify, understand and offer that which could work best in their setting towards a "feasible utopia" (Barnett, 2019, p. 54). Such a human and humane approach might go some way to counteracting the dystopian facets of contemporary higher education including the frenetic pace, the competition, the burn out, the lack of support, publish or perish mentality, excessive accountability, etc. As part of the antidote to these everyday higher education challenges, professional learning ought to be nurturing and could echo the intentions captured in the *Slow Professor manifesto*: "to alleviate work stress, preserve humanistic education, and resist the corporate university" (Berg & Seeber, 2016, p. ix). We see the conversation as ongoing and we remain hopeful in the present and about the future.

Acknowledgments

This chapter is based upon collaborative work by COST Action 15221 members,[2] supported by COST (European Cooperation in Science and Technology).

We acknowledge the contribution of colleagues Chris Anson (North Carolina State University), Mary Deane Sorcinelli (University of Massachusetts, Amherst), Jessie Moore (Elon University), and Rachel Riedner (George Washington University) who helped us at various points along the Action's journey including participating in a conversation to better understand our findings as presented in this chapter.

References

Åkerlind, G. S. (2005). Academic growth and development - How do university academics experience it? *Higher Education, 50*(1), 1–32. https://doi.org/10.1007/s10734-004-6345-1.

Altbach, P. G., Reisberg, L. & Rumbley, L. E. (2009, July 5–8). *Trends in global higher education tracking an academic revolution* [Conference session]. UNESCO 2009 World Conference on Higher Education, Paris, France https://www.scirp.org/(S(351jmbntvnsjt1aadkposzje))/reference/ReferencesPapers.aspx?ReferenceID=1683701.

---

2   https://www.cost.eu/actions/CA15221/#tabs|Name:management-committee

Arum, R. & Roksa, J. (2011). *Academically adrift: Limited learning on college campuses.* University of Chicago Press.

Austin, A. E. & Sorcinelli, M. D. (2013). The future of faculty development: Where are we going? *New Directions for Teaching and Learning, 2013*(133), 85–97. https://doi.org/10.1002/tl.20048.

Bain, K. (2004). *What the best college teachers do.* Harvard University Press.

Barber, M., Summers, L. H., Donnelly, K. & Rizvi, S. (2013). *An avalanche is coming: Higher education and the revolution ahead.* Institute for Public Policy Research.

Barnett, R. (2000). University knowledge in an age of supercomplexity. *Higher Education, 40*(4), 409–422. https://doi.org/10.1023/a:1004159513741.

Barnett, R. (2012). Learning for an unknown future. *Higher Education Research & Development, 31*(1), 65–77. https://doi.org/10.1080/07294360.2012.642841.

Barnett, R. A. (2019). The thoughtful university: A feasible Utopia. *Beijing International Review of Education, 1*(1), 54–72. https://doi.org/10.1163/25902547-00101007.

Bass, R., Eynon, B. & Gambino, L. M. (2019). *The new learning compact: A framework for professional learning and educational change (Every learner everywhere).* https://www.everylearnereverywhere.org/wp-content/uploads/NewLearningCompact.pdf.

Berg, M. & Seeber, B. K. (2016). *The slow professor: Challenging the culture of speed in the academy.* University of Toronto Press.

Carmody, A. (2019). *Thematic analysis of focus group data in order to understand and map excellence in teaching, learning, research and writing at higher education: Report of short term scientific mission COST Action 15221.* COST Action 15221. https://www.maynoothuniversity.ie/sites/default/files/assets/document//Carmody%20STSM%20report%20.pdf.

Conole, G. (2013*). Designing for learning in an open world.* Springer https://doi.org/10.1007/978-1-4419-8517-0.

COST Action 15221. We ReLaTe (n.d., a). *Advancing effective institutional models towards cohesive teaching, learning, research and writing development.* Retrieved December 2, 2021, from https://www.werelate.eu.

COST Action 15221—We ReLaTe. (n.d. b). *About and partners.* Retrieved December 2, 2021, from https://www.werelate.eu/about-us/.

COST Action 15221. (2018). *Agreed criteria for the identification of key informants and subsequent identification of key informant group (list of criteria).* COST Action 15221. https://www.maynoothuniversity.ie/sites/default/files/assets/document//Criteria%20for%20selection%20of%20key%20informants.pdf.

COST Action 15221. (2021). *Final action dissemination. Report of COST Action 15221.* https://www.maynoothuniversity.ie/sites/default/files/assets/document//WeReLaTe%20Final%20Action%20Dissemination%20Report.pdf.

COST—European Cooperation in Science and Technology. (n.d.). *COST Actions.* Retrieved December 2, 2021, from https://www.cost.eu.

COST—European Cooperation in Science and Technology. (2016). *Memorandum of understanding for the implementation of "Advancing effective institutional models towards cohesive teaching, learning, research and writing development" (We ReLaTe) CA 15221.* https://www.cost.eu/actions/CA15221/#tabs|Name:overview.

European Commission. (2013). *Report to the European Commission on improving the quality of teaching and learning in Europe's higher education institutions.* https://op.europa.eu/en/publication-detail/-/publication/fbd4c2aa-aeb7-41ac-ab4c-a94feea9eb1f.

Geller, A. E. & Eodice, M. (Eds.). (2013). *Working with faculty writers.* Utah State University Press.

Giroux, H. A. (2010). Bare pedagogy and the scourge of neoliberalism: Rethinking higher education as a democratic public sphere. *The Educational Forum, 74*(3), 184–196. https://doi.org/10.1080/00131725.2010.483897.

Gunn, A. (2018). The UK Teaching Excellence Framework (TEF): The development of a new transparency tool. In A. Curaj, L. Deca & R. Pricopie (Eds.), *European higher education area: The impact of past and future policies* (pp. 505–526). Springer. https://doi.org/10.1007/978-3-319-77407-7_31.

Guri-Rosenblit, S., Šebková, H. & Teichler, U. (2007). Massification and diversity of higher education systems: Interplay of complex dimensions. *Higher Education Policy, 20*(4), 373–389. https://doi.org/10.1057/palgrave.hep.8300158.

Harland, T. & Wald, N. (2017). Vanilla teaching as a rational choice: The impact of research and compliance on teacher development. *Teaching in Higher Education, 23*(4), 419–434. https://doi.org/10.1080/13562517.2017.1395408.

King, H. (2004). Continuing professional development in higher education: What do academics do? *Educational Developments, 5*(4), 1–5. https://www.seda.ac.uk/resources/files/publications_25_Educational%20Dev%205.4.pdf.

King, H. (2019). Continuing professional development: What do award winning academics do? *Educational Developments, 20*(2), 1–5. https://uwe-repository.worktribe.com/output/2917962.

Kuh, G. D., Kinzie, J., Schuh, J. H. & Whitt, E. J. (2010). *Student success in college: Creating conditions that matter.* Jossey-Bass.

Laurillard, D. (2012). *Teaching as a design science: Building pedagogical patterns for learning and technology.* Routledge.

Lynch, K., Grummell, B. & Devine, D. (2012). *New managerialism in education: Gender, commercialisation and carelessness.* Palgrave Macmillan.

Matheson, R. (2019). In pursuit of teaching excellence: Outward and visible signs of inward and invisible grace. *Teaching in Higher Education, 25*(8), 909–925. https://doi.org/10.1080/13562517.2019.1604508.

Melonashi, E. (2020). *Short term scientific mission (STSM) Scientific Report: Quantitive Research Analysis COST Action: CA15221.* COST Action 15221. https://www.maynothuniversity.ie/sites/default/files/assets/document//Melonashi%202020.pdf.

National Forum for the Enhancement of Teaching and Learning in Higher Education. (2016). *National professional development framework for all staff who teach in higher education.* https://www.teachingandlearning.ie/publication/national-professional-development-framework-for-all-staff-who-teach-in-higher-education/.

Neave, G. (2014). Quality enhancement: A new step in a risky business? A few adumbrations on its prospect for higher education in Europe. In M. João Rosa

& A. Amaral (Eds.), *Quality assurance in higher education* (pp. 32–49). Palgrave Macmillan.

OECD. (2012). *Education indicators in focus*. OECD Publishing. https://www.oecd.org/education/50495363.pdf.

OECD. (2014). *Education at a glance 2014: OECD indicators*. OECD Publishing. http://dx.doi.org/10.1787/eag-2014-en.

O'Leary, M. & Cui, V. (2020). Reconceptualising teaching and learning in higher education: challenging neoliberal narratives of teaching excellence through collaborative observation. *Teaching in Higher Education, 25*(2), 141–156. https://doi.org/10.1080/13562517.2018.1543262.

Parker, P. (2014). Developing criteria and guidance for assessing teaching excellence. *Educational Developments, 15*(2), 11–14. Seda.

Pascarella E. T. & Terenzini P. T. (2005). *How college affects students: A third decade of research*. Jossey-Bass.

Roxå, T. & Mårtensson, K. (2015). Microcultures and informal learning: A heuristic guiding analysis of conditions for informal learning in local higher education workplaces. *International Journal for Academic Development, 20*(2), 193–205. https://doi.org/10.1080/1360144X.2015.1029929.

Shavit, Y., Arum, R. & Gamoran, A. (Eds). 2007. *Stratification in higher education: A comparative study*. Stanford University Press.

Skelton, A. (2012) Value conflicts in higher education teaching. *Teaching in Higher Education, 17*(3), 257–268. https://doi.org/10.1080/13562517.2011.611875.

Sorcinelli, M. D., Austin, A. E., Eddy, P. & Beach, A. (2006). *Creating the future of faculty development: Learning from the past, understanding the present*. Jossey-Bass Publications.

Stefani, L. (2011). Current perspectives on SOTL. *International Journal for the Scholarship of Teaching and Learning, 5*(1). https://doi.org/10.20429/ijsotl.2011.050102.

Sutherland, K. A. (2018). Holistic academic development: Is it time to think more broadly about the academic development project? *International Journal for Academic Development, 23*(4), 261–273. https://doi.org/10.1080/1360144X.2018.1524571.

Thaiss, C., Bräuer, G., Carlino, P., Ganobcsik-Williams, L. & Sinha, A. (Eds.). (2012). *Writing programs worldwide: Profiles of academic writing in many places*. The WAC Clearinghouse; Parlor Press. https://doi.org/10.37514/per-b.2012.0346.2.01.

Tight, M. (2017). Higher education journals: Their characteristics and contribution. *Higher Education Research & Development, 37*(3), 607–619. https://doi.org/10.1080/07294360.2017.1389858.

Tight, M. (2019). The neoliberal turn in higher education. *Higher Education Quarterly, 73*(3), 273–284. https://doi.org/10.1111/hequ.12197.

Torres, C. A. (2011). Public universities and the neoliberal common sense: Seven iconoclastic theses. *International Studies in Sociology of Education, 21*(3), 177–197. https://doi.org/10.1080/09620214.2011.616340.

Trowler, P., Saunders, M. & Bamber, V. (2012). *Tribes and territories in the 21st-century: Rethinking the significance of disciplines in higher education*. International Studies in Higher Education. Routledge.

Van Vught, F. A. & Ziegele, F. (2011). *Design and testing the feasibility of a multidimensional global university ranking: Final report*. Commissioned by the directorate general for education and culture of the European commission. CHERPA Network. http://www.ireg-observatory.org/pdf/u_multirank_final_report.pdf.

Wheeler, S. & Gerver, R., (2015). *Learning with "e"s: Educational theory and practice in the digital age*. Crown House Publishing.

Appendix 1: Partners in COST Action 15221

COST Countries

Albania	Hungary	Poland
Austria	Iceland	Portugal
Bosnia and Herzegovina	Ireland	Romania
Bulgaria	Israel	Serbia
Croatia	Italy	Slovakia
Cyprus	Latvia	Slovenia
Czech Republic	Lithuania	Spain
Denmark	Luxembourg	Sweden
Estonia	Malta	Turkey
France	Montenegro	United Kingdom
Germany	Netherlands	
Greece	North Macedonia	

COST Near Neighbour Countries

Ukraine	Morocco	Lebanon
Georgia	Belarus	Russian Federation

COST International Partner Countries

United States of America

9 Moments of Intersection, Rupture, Tension: Writing and Academic Disciplines in the Semiperiphery

Amy Zenger
AMERICAN UNIVERSITY OF BEIRUT, LEBANON

John Pill
LANCASTER UNIVERSITY, UK

This chapter focuses on the relationships between writing and academic disciplines in a space of academic practice in the semiperiphery, as conceptualized in world-systems analysis. Defined by its role in mediating between the core and the periphery in cultural, economic, or political domains, the semiperiphery acts as a conduit for centre goods and culture towards the periphery, and has also been credited with the potential to challenge core practices and thinking and to promote innovation. To investigate the value of a world-systems analysis approach for the study of academic writing, we bring it to bear on our reading of existing data from interviews with eight multilingual faculty members working at a long-established Middle East university that uses English as the medium of instruction. Analysis of their responses allowed us to interrogate the concept of the semiperiphery and identify how it may be experienced in the lives and scholarship of individuals. We adopt a world-systems perspective that situates European academic writing in a core location linked systemically to particular semiperipheral and peripheral locations of scholarly production and teaching. Our findings suggest that scholars are not affected to the same extent or in the same way by their situation in a semiperipheral context. Nevertheless, the concept of the semiperiphery is useful for articulating the potentials of the situation—particularly for the purpose of evaluating academic production by disclosing intellectual work that might otherwise go unrecognized—as well as for accounting for specific constraints. We illustrate a link between academic disciplines and global interrelationships, framing

> academic writing as a performance that can both enable participation in an academic field and work to contest disciplinary norms or boundaries.

Writing studies and language studies scholars have long been interested in the role writing plays in constituting academic disciplines. Histories of how academic disciplines developed (Bazerman & Paradis, 1991; Russell, 2002), models of how disciplinarity works (Flowerdew & Costley, 2017; Gere et al., 2015; Prior, 1998, 2009), and scholars' observations of how writing is called upon to enact the work of a discipline (Tusting & Barton, 2016) all inform writing programme design and approaches to teaching undergraduate and, more pertinently, graduate student writing. Gere et al. (2015) note a distinction between disciplines as epistemological forms, governing knowledge creation and dissemination, and disciplines as institutional forms, most often university departments, that exert power over disciplines in terms of employing and promoting scholars, maintaining curricula, and mentoring new scholars. Disciplines are also represented in dynamic terms, as complex networks that are open to interactions with other fields while also being anchored in their fundamental concepts and approaches (Prior, 1998, 2009; Thaiss & Zawacki, 2006). Tusting and Barton (2016) study how managerial strategies shape disciplinary writing practices of scholars in the UK. Similarly, in this chapter, we consider how sociohistorical factors shape the practices of writers in a semiperipheral context.

Our study derives from a project designed to promote conversations and develop local understandings about academic writing in one institution, a university in the Middle East at which English is the predominant medium of instruction and communication within a broader multilingual environment. By representing the work of successful multilingual scholars at this university in their own words, we aim, in the broader project, to highlight for students and faculty the strengths of multilingual writers as they navigate teaching, research, and publishing in their disciplines across languages, across sociopolitical contexts, and across academic and public audiences. In this chapter, we consider how individual experiences of scholars as reported to us appear to be shaped by or to engage with an assumed position of the institution within a core-periphery framework. The framework we use comes from world-systems analysis, which was first put forward in the 1970s by the sociologist Immanuel Wallerstein and has since been taken up by researchers in a wide number of fields (e.g., sociology, politics, economics; see Babones & Chase-Dunn, 2012). The approach proposes three fundamental categories, none of which is meaningful in and of itself, but all of which are significant because of their relationships to each other: core, periphery, and semiperiphery. Positing the university in our study as a semiperipheral space, we interrogate the concept of the semiperiphery as an analytical tool to help understand disciplinary writing and its teaching in this institution.

In the sections that follow, we present an overview of world-systems analysis, focusing on the category of the semiperiphery, describe the institutional context and our broader research project, offer evidence presented through individual interviews with faculty members, and discuss what we learn from considering our data through this lens.

World-Systems Analysis and the Semiperiphery

Immanuel Wallerstein characterizes world-systems analysis as a "knowledge revolution"—a challenge to the accepted ways that knowledge has been categorized (Wallerstein, 2012, p. 517). In the mid-twentieth century, he began developing his interpretive approach as a framework to coherently address his concerns, namely: "concern with the unit of analysis, concern with social temporalities, and concern with the barriers that had been erected between different social science disciplines" (Wallerstein, 2004, p. 16). Wallerstein's approach questions the boundaries of disciplinary formations that emerged in the nineteenth century and proliferated, especially the division that emerged between the arts and the sciences. Our current academic disciplines developed primarily in universities in Germany, France, the United Kingdom, and the United States, evolving within and closely tied to the long historical period associated with the development of the capitalist system. Rejecting nation-state borders as the primary spatial unit of analysis, the approach proposes instead a broader multi-state world-system to argue that features of core or periphery are not inherent, but rather derive from their positions within a system of political, economic, and sociocultural relationships. Wallerstein is careful to note that in this usage, world-system does not imply *the* world; rather it points to *a* world—a set of locations that are connected through and defined by systematic relationships (2012). As Wallerstein (2004) stresses, "In world-systems analysis, core-periphery is a *relational* concept, not a pair of terms that are reified, that is, have separate essential meanings" (p. 17). In temporal terms, drawing on the work of *annales* historians, world-systems analysis rejects the event as a unit of political and social analysis in favour of developments of much more extended duration—not so extended, however, as to become, in effect, universal laws.

Wallerstein's approach, like other core-periphery theories, allows him to address inequalities but also avoid representing nation-states and sociocultural phenomena in absolute terms. For example, he argues that underdevelopment must be understood "not as an original state, the responsibility for which lay within the countries that were underdeveloped, but as the consequence of historical capitalism" (Wallerstein, 2004, p. 12).

While the intervention represented by world-systems analysis can be readily understood as applicable to social and political disciplines, Wallerstein argues that this analytical approach is relevant for all domains of knowledge. Writing about the humanistic disciplines specifically, he says:

> The world in which we are living is, I contend, a capitalist world economy. It has its history, its structure, its contradictions, its prospects. I try to study this directly. Others study it implicitly. I think it might help us all if the latter reflected more openly on what it is they are really doing. . . . [All disciplines tell us about] the world in which we are living now. (2011, p. 226)

In research on writing, core-periphery studies take a broad, structural perspective of academic practices in order to understand forces that shape inequalities in the material resources available and in practices such as peer review for publication, criteria for promotion and tenure evaluations, and resources available for travel, research, and teaching. Studies adopting these perspectives have considered publication practices, language choice (English as a lingua franca as opposed to local languages), and rhetorical styles (Canagarajah, 2002; Lillis & Curry, 2010). Karen Bennett (2014) focuses on the idea of the semiperiphery for an edited collection about academic writing in Europe, specifically in areas she presents as semiperipheral in relation to other parts of Europe. In her introduction, Bennett notes that universities in the semiperiphery perform boundary work between the core or centre and the periphery, frequently acting as "buffer zones" and "conduits for knowledge flows emanating from the centre" to serve institutions and people in more peripheral locations (p. 3). Given that universities in the semiperiphery often depend on centre institutions for funding and serve to translate knowledge from the core to the periphery, they can be portrayed as derivative. Bennett counters this perception, however, by arguing that the semiperiphery is more aptly described as "a place of tension . . . effervescent with possibilities, allowing dominant attitudes to be challenged and new paradigms to arise in a way that would be unthinkable in centre countries" (2014, p. 7). She argues that the semiperiphery plays an important role in the global university system.

While Bennett's (2014) volume considers locations on the edges of Europe as semiperipheral, the current study moves beyond the continental border to the eastern coast of the Mediterranean Sea. Prompted by Bennett's claim for the value of semiperipheral contexts and aware of our own observation of creativity and dynamic tension in the stories related in our research data by academics at a university in Lebanon, we looked in our data specifically for reference to the concerns of the semiperiphery.

Context of the Study

The Syrian Protestant College was founded in Beirut in 1866 by missionaries from the United States. Initially the language used in teaching was Arabic but in the late 1870s English was chosen as the medium of instruction. The institution became the American University of Beirut (AUB) in 1920, when its proselytizing mission ended (Anderson, 2011). Women were accepted as students at AUB from 1922. The university now follows the American liberal arts model of higher education and is accredited in the United States by the Middle States Commission on Higher Education. The university's mission is "to provide excellence in education, to participate in the advancement of knowledge through research, and to serve the peoples of the Middle East and beyond" (American University of Beirut, 2019, p. 5). It is a private university with about 9,000 students representing 89 countries; 78 percent of the student body has Lebanese citizenship (American University of Beirut, 2019). The over 900 full-time faculty members are a similarly international group. Many AUB faculty members of Lebanese origin have earned postgraduate qualifications at North American or European universities and subsequently taken up academic posts at the university.

In a history of AUB, Anderson (2011) describes how the university "has stood at a vital intersection between a rapidly changing American missionary and educational project in the Middle East and a dynamic quest for Arab national identity and empowerment" (p. 2). The history sets out to show how students "used both of these American and Arab elements to help make the school not only an American institution but also one *of* the Arab world and *of* Beirut, as the very name, the American University of Beirut, indicates" (Anderson, 2011, p. 3). This perspective explicitly sets up the institution as mediating between educational and cultural worlds or, we suggest, as being situated in the semiperiphery. The civil war in Lebanon (1975–1990) had catastrophic effects for the country as a whole and the university, and the subsequent process of rebuilding has been gradual. Academic tenure, which was suspended during the war, is currently being reinstated, and AUB is actively seeking to raise its international standing as a research university. As our interviews show, these goals have an impact on faculty members, as the university looks towards the core and to matching the standards and expectations set by universities in the United States deemed to be comparable with

AUB concerning, for example, the types of research and publication that are valued in applications for promotion and tenure.[1]

The university expresses characteristics of its home country. Lebanon can be described as a multilingual society, where Arabic, the official language, is widely supplemented by English and French in everyday life. Patterns of language use are complex and vary according to domain. For example, Arabic is the preferred language of political discussion, while text messaging often uses a mixture of Lebanese Arabic, English, and Arabizi, that is, Arabic written using Latin script (Esseili, 2017). In the school system, the official requirement is that mathematics and science are taught in English or French while other subjects are taught in Arabic. (For discussion of the language use in science classes at Lebanese schools, see Salloum & BouJaoude, 2020.) Unofficially, further subjects are likely to be taught in English or French, particularly in private schools, thus reducing the amount of education students receive in Arabic (Orr & Annous, 2018). Lebanon's ties with the French language are demonstrated through its membership of the Organisation internationale de la francophonie (https://www.francophonie.org/).

Researchers writing about the current linguistic situation in Lebanon are likely to refer to the country's geographical location between the Middle East and Europe (the Western world) and to the historical relationships arising from this, from ancient Phoenician commerce around the Mediterranean Sea to the French mandate in the interwar period; they will also refer to economic and pragmatic reasons for Lebanese to know several languages, namely, to facilitate trade and to gain employment within and outside Lebanon (see, e.g., Esseili, 2017; Shaaban, 2017). Some scholars take a critical approach, for example, about the "linguistic imperialism" demonstrated in the growth of English as a medium of instruction in Lebanese schools (Orr & Annous, 2018).

In this section, we have presented a view of AUB as an institution and of its wider context in Lebanon. In our opinion, this view demonstrates characteristics of the semiperiphery: The name of the institution itself indicates its allegiances, first to an American model of higher education taught in English—a model drawn from a core country for use elsewhere (cf. other institutions named "American University" around the world), and second to Beirut, a city widely seen historically and in current times as a cultural and economic intersection between East and West. The mission of the "American

---

1   Our data were collected before the financial, economic, political and social crises in Lebanon in 2019–2020 and the explosion of 4 August 2020, which caused great damage to Beirut and her people. The full consequences of these major disruptions are not yet apparent.

University" to "serve the peoples of the Middle East" situates the institution in the mediating role ascribed to the semiperiphery. Having made the claim that AUB is a promising context for an investigation of the concept, we now proceed to see how individual faculty members at AUB represent themselves and their disciplines in terms of the constraints and affordances of the semiperiphery as posited by Bennett (2014).

Methodology

The aims of the research project were broader than may be apparent from the data presented in this chapter. We wanted to collect individual literacy narratives from multilingual faculty members at AUB to investigate their views on how they developed their own language and writing abilities to perform at a high level in their academic disciplines. We believed this would at the same time shed light on disciplinary and institutional writing practices. To share this insight, we aimed to report on the language learning and writing strategies of multilingual language users identified by the participants (the current paper is one part of this project) and to present these findings in an easily accessible format as a resource for reflection, discussion and (self-)development in the AUB academic community and beyond. Our specific intention was to create a website containing edited video clips drawn from the interviews with our participants along with notes to prompt viewers—undergraduates, graduate students and faculty members at AUB and elsewhere—to relate their own practices and goals to the views and experience shared by successful academics who they might recognize at the university and who perhaps had a similar background to their own.[2] Therefore, the study was not designed specifically to interrogate the notion of the semiperiphery. Nevertheless, when we were introduced to the concept in Bennett's (2014) edited volume, we anticipated that it would be productive to consider our data from this perspective.

Ethics approval for the study was given by the university. Members of the AUB faculty were invited to take part in the study as a convenience sample. We asked multilingual academics whose first language was not English and sought to represent a variety of disciplinary areas and a range of research and teaching experience in these disciplines. We also sought a gender balance. Participants had to agree to being video-recorded and to allow an edited version of this recording, including their name, to be published on a freely accessible web page. They would be able to review the proposed video clips and ask for revisions to be made before publication.

---

2   This project is still underway.

Data collection was carried out in the first six months of 2017. In preparatory small-group meetings involving two or three academics and then in individual video-recorded interviews lasting an hour or more, research participants were prompted to reflect on three broad topics: the nature of writing in their academic discipline, their experiences as a multilingual scholar, and their approaches to teaching writing. As we did not want participants to feel constrained in what they spoke about, an indicative set of prompts was provided in advance of the interview rather than a more structured protocol. The interviews with our eight participants were completed in English. Transcripts were subsequently prepared and then studied and annotated by the two researchers iteratively to establish themes in the dataset.

Scholar Interviews

We met with and interviewed eight scholars, working a range of fields: comparative literature, linguistics, ecosystems management, systems management, sociology, anthropology, biology, and education. Our participants had worked at AUB for between four and 25 years when the interviews were recorded. In this paper, we focus on interviews with four of these participants. These interviews included topics that we see as relating to issues of the semiperiphery. Content from the interviews with the other four participants is not presented, because it is not directly pertinent to our argument. However, these interviews do of course indicate that issues of the semiperiphery are not what immediately comes to mind for all academics working in our research context. In the discussion section, we consider why the contributions of the four other interviewees covered different ground. To reiterate an important point, our data were not collected originally with the intention of exploring the concept of the semiperiphery; absence in the data of content relevant to this concept is consequently unremarkable, indicating the personal nature of the interviews and the participant-led methodology employed. On these grounds, we have chosen also to present our data for each interviewee in turn rather than thematically with interviewee comments as illustration. An overarching finding in this paper is that the semiperiphery appears differently in the stories of individuals, and we believe the structure used here captures better this personal manifestation.

Saouma BouJaoude

Saouma BouJaoude was educated in Lebanon and the United States. He was a science major as an undergraduate at AUB and is now a professor in the university's department of education. His research considers how science is taught to children at school. BouJaoude indicates that he is aware of his location on a core-periphery continuum and that he seeks to exploit this: "AUB wants me to write in English and I want to be promoted."[3] He finds the requirement to publish in English in international journals can be managed by being strategic and finding a niche. In talking about his work, he also exemplifies how those away from the perceived centre may be well placed to see differences in the traditions and behaviours of the core and therefore able to benefit from their broader perspective on the discipline.

In his interview, one of the main topics he discusses are strategies to get published and the need to be pragmatic: "since AUB wants me to publish in high-quality journals in English, therefore I have to do it . . . It can be done if you put your mind to it." BouJaoude explains the problem as he sees it and how he deals with it:

> There are a lot of issues that are mature in the USA or in the UK—they have been studied and studied and studied. Whatever you do here [in Lebanon] is not going to be innovative enough to be published in a journal. You have to find a niche—a niche, which is really interesting to journals, meaningful to you, and innovative. I think this is how I describe my own decisions to do certain kinds of research here to be able to meet the requirements of the university. I started doing things related to evolution, and the reason for that is because this is a context that is different than the USA and Europe, in that we have Muslims and Christians, and therefore you can look at how students think about evolution in a very different context, but it's useful for journals in the West, because, more and more, they have diverse populations . . . So, this is an area that I decided to take and then, from there on I looked at how I can introduce language as a factor in the studies that I do, because I thought it's very useful to Lebanon, but at the same time it's giving a very different perspective. Teaching science in a multilingual context is very different from teaching science in a monolingual context.

As well as finding a topical niche—in his case, religion and cultural aspects of science education—and explicitly considering issues of language

---

3   Because interview transcripts are not accessible to our readers, we do not mention page numbers or line numbers in our citations, but simply refer to the interview transcript as a whole. See the previous footnote.

use in science classrooms, both of which are novel and interesting from a core perspective as well as having potential impact on local teaching practice in Lebanon, BouJaoude also reports seeking a methodological niche as a way to make his research attractive for publication. He gives an example of research that involved collecting quantitative and qualitative data independently from the same class of students to investigate whether the two approaches produced compatible findings.

Another major topic in BouJaoude's interview concerns his recognition of distinct cultural perspectives on research and research traditions in the discipline of education. He is aware of practices and expectations varying in different contexts, which might not be so apparent to "insiders," that is, scholars working in the core who take for granted that their "mainstream" views are ubiquitous. As a first example, BouJaoude sees his disciplinary perspective (in science education) as "Anglo-Saxon, whether it's UK [or] the US." He comments on previous collaboration with colleagues at the Université Saint-Joseph, the oldest French-oriented university in Beirut, founded in 1870, and how he found the French traditions in his field to be very different: "Even the theoretical frameworks of the French system are very different. The literature in the science education is very different." BouJaoude gives an example from a project with the Lebanese Ministry of Education to develop a trilingual (Arabic-English-French) glossary of pedagogic terminology: the French term *transposition didactique*—"how you change the science of the scientist to science that is taught in the classroom" is not found in English. He states that "the English tradition of science education is very different from France and Germany—the theories they research, sometimes there is a crossover, but it's different." He also refers to research indicating that scholars in the discipline read different journals in Europe and in the United States.

As a second, broader reflection of differences between educational traditions, BouJaoude shares his opinion on the writing skills of AUB students, noting that students "who have been in good French schools [i.e., Lebanese schools where French is the first foreign language] do much better in writing than those who come from good English schools." He attributes this variation to a lack of focus on writing in many of the schools teaching science in English (in Lebanon), where science knowledge is more often checked using multiple-choice questions than through student writing. BouJaoude discusses an area of research around *writing to learn* in science education: "when you're writing, you're expressing your ideas and communicating to an audience . . . The process of writing is essential in the writing of science—science is all about critiquing and defending arguments." The processes involved in writing promote reflection and the development of metacognitive skills to critique one's text. He explains how the French-oriented education system uses an approach he terms "analysis of documents" (*commentaire de texte*), where the teacher gives students "a document that describes something scientific and they have to analyse it and relate ideas to it" in writing. He sees experience in doing this task to give French-educated students an advantage over English-educated students.

The third example of disciplinary difference comes through BouJaoude's experience of educational consultancy work in various countries in the Middle East and North Africa. He is aware of a need to mediate between academic traditions, between the core and periphery. In terms of academic production, he notes that writing in the English and French research traditions is quite similar when compared to Arabic practice, with its more formulaic approach and literature reviews with "no integration of the research articles to come up with a gap so that you can address it." The discipline of science education itself is hardly visible in the Arab context, with few publications in any language. BouJaoude believes the prevailing view is that science research must be positivist and quantitative, which is not the case for many studies in science education, his field of expertise.

This insight into various expressions of disciplinary difference is more likely obtained by an outside observer trying to understand core-focused practices and traditions in order to engage with them. BouJaoude comments during his interview, "You had to find ways of making this meaningful."

Sari Hanafi

Sari Hanafi is a professor of sociology who studied engineering at Damascus University, before deciding to study sociology. He obtained his doctorate in sociology from a French programme in Cairo. His areas of research include migration issues, transitional justice, and the sociology of knowledge. His work has led him to conduct scholarship in Arabic, French, and English, making significant contributions in all these languages.

As a scholar whose research interests include knowledge production, Hanafi articulates his consciousness of his semiperipheral location as a scholar very clearly. During his interview, he recounts how this evolved over time and informs decisions he has made as a researcher, editor, and teacher. He strongly emphasizes the importance of making knowledge accessible for diverse audiences. This principle can entail translation, which in his account is a generative intellectual project in itself. He also advocates teaching disciplinary courses to graduate students in Arabic as well as English, recognizing the need to theorize in each language. Furthermore, Hanafi extends his willingness to engage in controversy to interventions in disciplines themselves, for example by expanding the boundaries of the literature or by challenging a core conceptualization.

Hanafi argues that "You need to publish in language accessible to people." "Social science need always to ask ourselves as scholars I mean 'knowledge for what, for whom?'" he says. In his own field, it is important to translate scholarship into Arabic because "you don't want to downplay language, vernacular language into just a fieldwork, I mean just a kind informational articles, while theory [is] kept to be taken from those who write in English or French." This is a matter that the scholarly community is not addressing enough, in his view. When he surveyed the publications produced by all faculty members at AUB over a period of three years, he found that only two out of 270 books were published in Arabic.

The process that Hanafi calls "arabizing" social science entails advocacy, translation, and instruction. As a professor, he tells his students "The whole [of] social science is to delay your value judgment . . . to [a] maximum. So, I would say the same, that handling different languages . . . is definitely an enabler of this sense of humanism, relativism, multiculturalism. That things can be said, done in different ways, I think is so enabling and refreshing and inviting for critical thinking." He advocates including elective courses in the curriculum in which students are taught social science in Arabic, so that they are not limited to learning to theorize and communicate in English.

Translation, usually from English into Arabic, requires sophistication to be able to follow the arguments precisely and at the same time use the style, terminology, and form of Arabic academic sociology. Sometimes, the translation must also navigate political consequences in the real world, as the following account about Palestinian refugee camps in Lebanon shows:

> I work on different modes of governance of refugee camps and . . . I heard a very harsh criticism . . . from popular committees but also from a high-rank man in police who came to talk and he told me "If you ever use the word 'governance' in a refugee camp, I put you in the prison—Palestinians can administrate their camps but governance is something related to sovereignty, so we Lebanese we govern the camps, but they administrate the camps." . . . This guy still think[s] that "governance" only about "government" . . . and "government" related to sovereignty. So, we changed . . . the first version was "hawkama," which is "governance" of the camps, and the second version of

> this report ... when it was published as [an] article, I changed it to "administrating camps"—"idaret al-moukhayamat" ... just to appease the criticism of what I wrote.

In the examples he presents, Hanafi suggests translation as an important element in the production of knowledge and in performing what would in world-systems terms be identified as mediation within the system.

Hanafi's insights into writing and disciplinarity were often hard-won through experience as he navigated across disciplinary traditions and linguistic boundaries. His account of his own enculturation into academic publication is punctuated by sometimes painful experiences of being schooled by reviewers, editors, or mentors into conforming to different linguistic and disciplinary expectations. He recalls how an early mentor in sociology told him, "Look you are very stingy in words and this is the problem of your education, background as a civil engineer ... so I want to liberate you from this." From this interaction he gained the understanding that "social science need[s] really to handle complexity of social phenomena, and complexity cannot be handled by 'yes,' 'no'." On a different occasion, a colleague removed "all the metaphors" in a presentation Hanafi had written in Arabic, explaining that they "were not scientific language." It was many years before Hanafi questioned the advice of his respected colleague and recognized that "it's a kind of symbolic violence when we say 'no, it's a fact, it's zero/one'." In another experience Hanafi shares with beginning writers, the editor of a collection contacted him about his contribution, and her first comment was: "I will take all your footnotes and put them inside of the text and take your text and put it in the footnote." She told him, "Your footnote is so important, and your text is so boring!" Hanafi says, "She noticed that every time I want to say something interesting, if you like, I got hesitant and I want to extrapolate ... so I put it in the footnote."

Hanafi also notes that in many universities in the Arab world, students may complete a degree without having received guidance or instruction in academic writing. As editor of *Idafat: The Arab Journal of Sociology*, Hanafi grew so tired of receiving submissions with structural and stylistic weaknesses that he created a writer's guide in Arabic, drawing upon his own experiences of learning to write academic texts in sociology. He published "Common Mistakes in Sociological Writing" (2014) as an editorial and, after posting it on the website https://www.academia.edu/, he noted that it has been downloaded many times. The piece encourages scholars in the Arab world to feel confident in publishing.

At times, Hanafi has encountered tensions related more to disciplinary bodies of shared knowledge or biases in a field, rather than languages per se. "This sometimes bring headache," he notes, "but really this is how I see science progress—I mean with controversies." For example, one of his efforts to publish an article in an American journal was not successful because it was based on literature central to European scholarship but failed also to mention authors on the subject who were more well-known in the United States. Hanafi also notes that "We never say sufficiently that academia in the West can also bear its political biases." As evidence of this, he recounts his experience of publishing an article critical of the way that Human Rights Watch reported rights violations in Palestine. After being reviewed by two English language journals, each of which circulated it to several referees, the article was rejected. It was eventually published in French and in Arabic but has never appeared in English. For Hanafi, this is "a pity" because the audience that needed to hear his criticism became less likely to hear it. He is committed to diversifying his audiences even to the extent of courting controversy.

While recognizing that disciplines originated historically in colonialist enterprises, Hanafi considers attempts to decolonize knowledge by directly rejecting core disciplinary traditions a trend that "had led nowhere." He aspires to follow the wisdom of Abd al-Qahir al-Jurjani, an Iranian linguist of the tenth century, who believed that "language has a lot of potentiality [in] resolving problems." As Hanafi explains al-Jurjani's ideas:

> You keep interpreting the sacred books . . . and the language will enable you more and more to understand social actors, what kind of meanings they put for . . . their actions. The meanings go beyond the vocabulary you have. So, stretch your language . . . and language will end up by bridging. . . . This way, I keep the social science immune from too much normativity . . . and the language will do the miracle of bridging.

Finally, for Hanafi, "writing is part of the research method." "It's not something you do once your field work is over," he says, "not once you say 'look the scientific part is done' and now it just a kind of dull translation of factual things you observed, you quantified et cetera into a language that is accessible to public or 'jargon-al' for your peers."

Sirène Harb

Sirène Harb grew up in Lebanon during the civil war, studying at AUB before going to the United States to earn her doctorate. Her academic field is American and comparative literature. In her interview she tells her personal story, reflecting on her development as a writer in three languages and as an academic. This educational and professional history makes it clear that Harb inhabits the semiperiphery. She is conscious of disciplinary and institutional pressure affecting what and how she writes and recognizes a tension between her individual goals and externally imposed requirements: she asks, "Why am I putting so much effort for something that has no guaranteed result?" This feeling is familiar to many academics, but we suggest that it is a particular feature of the semiperiphery if scholars in this context are sensitive to their situation, as Harb is, having awareness of the acceptability of the range of options available as well as of the obligation to conform to assumed norms of the core. Harb's experience of being educated and becoming an academic in a semiperipheral context—multilingual and culturally diverse—makes her valuable as a teacher and academic mentor, to nurture others growing up in the same context.

On the topic of tensions between compliance and creativity, Harb recounts two childhood memories which anticipate her experience as an academic. She grew up using Arabic at home and French at school; she enjoyed reading and writing poetry. When she showed examples of her poetry in French to her schoolteachers, she was told they didn't rhyme: "for them this was the most important thing, and I saw with one of them, she had divided the verses into like stressed, unstressed syllables." Harb now sees the criticism as an "early insight into the difficulties also that I will be facing as a writer who does not necessarily want to follow these commonly accepted rules, except when they make sense to them."

Her second account concerns practicing *analyse de texte* at school, a task Harb enjoyed: "very often I could get away with not answering it the way it should be . . . by justifying why is it that it would be more important or more interesting to look at it in a different way." However, as end-of-school exams approached, she was instructed to keep to what was expected in order to pass. Harb presents this imposition positively, as a realization that she must take account of her audience, "the imagined examiner . . . a projected figure."

Now, as an academic writer, Harb writes literary criticism, enjoying its challenges "up to a certain point." She notes how disciplinary expectations are moving away from a primary focus on the text towards theory and context. She teaches her students that academic writing is an intervention in an ongoing conversation but is conscious how growing specialization and the variety of analytical tools available make any intervention increasingly difficult for novices, and for herself. Harb states, "the challenge is really about negotiating the boundaries of what you know is wanted from you and what you want to really put in . . . a piece of analysis", which reflects her reported childhood experiences. She contends that "we cannot make it work if we have to stop at every term that we use and say 'oh but I have to qualify'" and asks "what's the margin that I have? how much can I negotiate?"

In her interview, Harb notes that she sometimes questions why she writes "except that this is part of the requirements of the profession" and indicates that her creativity is limited by these constraints. She explains how the imagined voice of the reviewer or reader can affect this obligation to be a productive writer—the consequences of what this voice says "could be very positive but also extremely debilitating", leading to the loss of one's voice in the disciplinary conversation and, potentially, even to the loss of one's job: "there is no place of safety . . . [without] tenure or . . . a certain system that would allow for productivity to take its time." Harb feels that institutional requirements often do not align smoothly with the creative path: "you start projects, but they don't materialize in the way . . . that's institutionally readable or legible."

Such tension—recognizable to all academics—is brought into sharp focus viewed through the lens of the semiperiphery. An individual's creativity seems dampened due to inflexibility imposed from elsewhere, and the scholar must learn how to deal with this dilemma. A positive consequence of this experience is that the scholar is then well placed to help others deal with similar challenges. Harb came late to English, as a medium of her education and then as an academic discipline in English literature. In her interview, she reflects on how she has learned to do what she does. Being able to reflect in this way allows her to draw on her own experience to help others following a similar educational path. Again, this is not a feature exclusively of those in the semiperiphery; however, the context can be seen to promote a capacity for reflection in some of its inhabitants, including Harb, which allows them to serve effectively as educators and mediators in their situation.

Through the biography in her interview, we can reflect on Harb's relationship with English as a language and subject of study through her education in Lebanon, posited as a location in the semiperiphery. She first experienced English in school as a second foreign language (after French). She describes first engaging with writing in English in the communication skills programme when she entered AUB as an undergraduate majoring in biology, which was planned to provide a "day job" to support her creative writing. She appreciated the structured and clear approach to writing that was taught: "I really loved the straightforwardness of the English texts that I was reading." English writing is an object of study for Harb—"a relationship with ideas"—in contrast with her personal, instinctive connection with writing in other languages. She chose to study English (rather than French) literature to avoid losing the intimacy of her relationship with French while also recognizing a "freedom to speak [which] can say much more than one would expect it to" through studying texts in a new language.

Coming to teach English writing skills to Lebanese students during her career, Harb draws on her experience of consciously learning how to write in terms of processes (e.g., free writing) and labels (e.g., topic sentences), encouraging her students to "observe how you build knowledge personally also, your process of knowledge building", as she did. The approach has received positive feedback and indicates the importance of students seeing how their teacher succeeded on an educational and developmental journey that they recognize as like their own. Harb also talks with her literature students about how they might be able to intervene in the academic conversation by starting from their own experience. She reminds them that "this author himself herself, they were in your shoes some time ago." This capacity for self-reflection and empathy makes Harb a valuable educator in a context where she shares the background of many students.

Harb is working out the challenges of her discipline on a daily basis. She is consequently well-placed to educate and support students at AUB. What concerns her is the possibly limited extent of her employing institution's recognition of the need for such "local" expertise, while it prioritizes the emulation of characteristics of the core.

Salma Talhouk

Salma Talhouk is a professor in the department of landscape and ecosystems management. Her research has moved from purely scientific investigations to a more social science approach to studying ecology and landscape. In Lebanese schools, she was educated in French, Arabic, and English. During her doctoral training in landscape horticulture, which she undertook in the United States, Talhouk specialized in molecular fingerprinting.

In her account of her work as a scientist engaged in her community, Talhouk shows that she has been led to wrestle with her disciplinary identities and to invent or adopt unfamiliar modes of researching and writing. Her literate abilities in French, English, and Arabic have all been necessary to the new directions her academic work has taken, deployed according to the needs of the work.

When Talhouk returned to Lebanon to take up an academic position, she set up a laboratory and continued her scientific research. She reports experiencing a turning point in her work in mid-career:

> I felt like I had to make a decision about my life, not my work, which is that I know I can do the research and publish, but at the same time, I know that it's useless for the country. Because, for example, I would collect different olive trees or pistachio trees and I will do the molecular fingerprinting, but then I know that these trees are going to be destroyed and cut because of the social set-up.

She dismantled her laboratory and sought to continue her work in innovative directions. She recognized that her action represented a risk in terms of her academic career: "In spite of the fact that we have promotion and tenure pressure and all these things, I decided to go with my gut feeling." She says, "As an academician, I feel that our duty is to serve the society."

Reflecting on the deep specialization that is encouraged and rewarded in academic fields, Talhouk comments, "If you look historically about people, they tell you 'he used to be a physician, and a plant expert, and a poet, and a painter, and this and that' and it was not strange to do many things. Now, it's strange to do many things, and this is . . . it doesn't work in developing countries *not* to do many things." She observes that "it's sad that people have to fit you into a discipline, because when you are in a developing country at least, you just respond to what's around you, and you do what needs to be done."

Since moving away from strict laboratory investigation, Talhouk's work has taken two main directions. On one hand, she has invested her energies in a range of projects that address the general public on matters related to the environment. She established an academic centre for nature conservation research and communication to sponsor projects. One project sponsored by the centre she describes as "participatory mapping" of biodiversity, where "people can do a self-assessment in their own villages", a process completed by 80 villages to date. Her work in this direction also includes several publications. She has written a children's book in Arabic called *The ABCs of Nature* (2017). Another book project she developed, *Trees of Lebanon* (Talhouk et al., 2014), is a bilingual illustrated guide to local trees. This project is unique in that the trees are described and named from the perspective of the knowledge and language of nature of the region. Talhouk's aim was to foster people's sense of connection with nature and encourage their investment in reforestation projects. She had noted that "if they don't feel that these trees are part of their history or their heritage, why would they connect?" In the book, she "tried to find, to create the story that links us. And it wasn't easy, because all the information is produced in Europe and the US."

Her work has also turned towards new kinds of academic research, disseminated through conferences and academic publication. She studies "people and their perception and attitude towards nature and conservation." As her work moves away from pure science towards sociological studies, she says "I'm like still a student in this other field that I have decided to go into, which I don't know what it is." Her previous training did not prepare her in the methods she needs to follow, or in how to write about her findings. She often feels that her work is "between the cracks" of different disciplines. "It's starting to shift, but it's very difficult," she says.

Her approach to conservation is also critical of practices that are currently in place. For example, reforestation projects, which she suggests should be managed by rural inhabitants themselves, are actually "run by NGOs. Millions of dollars. Proposals. And funding. I don't know what. And media. If I donate, I want to see the tree, I want to see the forest, the billboards, et cetera. And it's like going against what I think it should be."

Language occupies an important dimension of her current research, as she seeks to name places and refer to nature in the terms that reflect connections of local populations with nature. Discussing nature reserves, she says they often have names understandable to an international scientific community, but "before it wasn't like this. It was an area, a place. It had a name . . . sometimes it had the name of (the plant) [but] sometimes it had like 'the Valley of the Mosquitoes'—it was a *place*."

> The issue is that when you think about the connection of people with nature, the language also is a major issue, because if you say "biodiversity" it's a common thing: "biodiversity." People say it. But in Arabic, it sounds very scientific. And then "nature" you can say "nature" or "environment"—it's different. I felt that maybe what I want is to ask people, "what do you call that?" and see what they call it. And then I use what they call it. . . . [In] one of the surveys I did . . . I asked them "where is nature?" So, a lot of them said "in the olive groves." So, for them, cultivated terraces are nature. So, this is rural (nature). We cannot say that nature is only the protected areas.

Talhouk chafes at how academic work is evaluated. In her own experience, the evidence-based projects she works on do not fit easily into conventional measures of academic production. She notes:

> It's really intriguing that it takes much more effort to relay information to the general public but there is no way that it is

> evaluated. It looks like outreach, service. It's not looked at as anything that is important, but I am doing it all the time . . . I feel this is serving the society.

Discussion and Conclusion

Our aim in this study has been to pose questions about how we conceptualize writing in the disciplines when viewed from the perspective of world-systems analysis. We have sought to illustrate how some scholars' work is specifically shaped by their own sense of semiperipheral location. Those who recognize semiperipheral characteristics in their location may gain particular insight into how the core operates and be well placed to recognize behaviours and assumptions in the core that otherwise remain tacit. This sensitivity may cause them to challenge such behaviours and assumptions; it may also make them astute teachers and academic mentors for new scholars joining their context.

For the four other academics who participated in our original project, but are not presented in our analysis, the tensions we attribute to semiperipheral location are not evident in their interview responses, and we must consider why this is so. As noted, our data were not collected with the intention of investigating our participants' relationships with their working context, assuming it to be in the semiperiphery. While general topics were suggested to participants, they were not asked to respond on set themes, and the scope of the interview was unconstrained. Each interview therefore followed its own path. We cannot know whether an interviewee who did not talk about issues that relate to the semiperiphery would never do so; indeed, they may have strong opinions that simply went unexpressed during the interview. Based on our existing data, these four other participants do not view themselves as in a different situation from others in their discipline, wherever they may be based. They recognize that there may be some drawbacks to working at an institution in the semiperiphery, but these do not have a fundamental impact on what they can achieve. For example, the scientist recognizes practical limitations, such as needing government permission to import special laboratory supplies, but is able to work around such problems without compromising her research with international collaborators.

The four scholars whose interviews we did not represent in this chapter are connected globally and work globally, each seeing their own field of study as a shared, international endeavour. Their academic training was within this network, and they continue to engage with the core regardless of physical location. Two participants in particular, a linguist and an anthropologist, also recognize that working at AUB ideally situates them to undertake the particular research and teaching they are most interested in. Their working context provides access to data that they use to contribute to a global disciplinary conversation. This is different from the relationship described by Salma Talhouk, where the work of an academic researcher in "a developing country" cannot resemble a colleague's work in a core context, because scholars outside core contexts must "do what needs to be done." She asserts a fundamentally different position for herself in relation to a broader discipline. Although it was materially possible for her to conduct the same research that a scientist in "the Midwest" conducts, to do so made no sense to her. Similarly, Sari Hanafi's research challenges both basic disciplinary assumptions in his field and conditions of social research in this region. To explain this range of evidence, we return to the principles of world-systems analysis, which state that categories of core, periphery, and semiperiphery are not territorial locations and are not static; instead, they are formed by relations across locations. Based on this principle, it is likely that scholars in the same institution or nation will experience a particular location differently: for some it will have characteristics attributed to the semiperiphery and for others it will operate like an institution in the core.

Bringing the interview data into focus through the lens of the semiperiphery discloses how a scholar's sense of their relationship with their discipline may play a significant role in intellectual understanding, scholarly production, and participation. It allows the semiperiphery to be characterized in the way articulated by Bennett (2014), as "a place of tension . . . effervescent with possibilities, allowing dominant attitudes to be challenged and new paradigms to arise" (p. 7). Much core-periphery literature has focused on material conditions and issues around the language of knowledge production for publication, although researchers may also indicate that they recognize some of the broader disparities that a world-systems analysis perspective has foregrounded in our own study (e.g., and somewhat controversially, Hyland, 2016). However, the experiences related by our participants show how a semiperiphery context can also represent challenges to core disciplinary assumptions, disciplinary boundaries, or institutional practices, especially related to scholar evaluation.

As teachers of academic writing who work with students and faculty members in many fields, we are led to conceptualize disciplinarity and the roles writing plays in creating and sharing different areas of knowledge. Like the work of Gere et al. (2015) and Tusting and Barton (2016), our analysis in this paper urges us to be conscious of the variations within and across disciplines, and to understand disciplinary practices as shaped by a complex of factors including material and socio-political ones. The ruptures and tensions we have highlighted in our interview data are played out at the level of disciplinarity. These scholars' accounts strongly reaffirm the centrality of writing in performing disciplinary knowledge. At the same time, however, writing is also represented as a site for contesting what are often deeply rooted configurations, for working out tensions within a discipline, and for challenging the values and approaches of that discipline.

Wallerstein (2016) insists on framing world-systems analysis as an analytical approach, not a theory with the sense of closure a theory implies. He prefers his approach to serve as a means to continue probing the complex relationships between the social, the cultural, and the political domains that have been difficult to link together, assigned as they are to their own disciplinary spaces. The interconnections and interdependencies between core, periphery and semiperiphery posited by world-systems analysis suggest that disciplinary work in any location can be queried through this approach. This framing suggests questions that may be useful for all teachers of academic writing and scholars to consider. We have drawn these from our initial engagement, through this paper, with some concepts from world-systems analysis in the field of academic and disciplinary writing:

- How do I see myself situated in core-periphery terms? Would this look different from someone else's perspective? How do I present myself to those I teach and mentor?
- Have I considered my academic role in terms of my relationships with core and periphery and with a globalized academia?
- Where do I look for exemplars, good practice and professional expectations?
- To what extent am I aware of tension between institutional or disciplinary expectations and my own goals or the goals of my students?
- What affordances does my working context give me that I might contest core expectations and assumptions?

Naturally, each of us will respond differently to these questions depending on our professional context and perspective, and no claim is made of there being "correct answers." The views of the four scholars presented in this paper indicate some of the many dimensions along which we might place ourselves with our own responses. Sirène Harb questions what is currently valued in her discipline while concurrently working to help her students join that same disciplinary conversation. Saouma BouJaoude consciously aligns his research to appeal to institutional and disciplinary orientations towards the core. Salma Talhouk challenges the conventional focus of academic effort and production, as she seeks to situate her work and create local impact. Sari Hanafi does not shy away from controversy as he pushes disciplinary boundaries, skillfully adapting his writing to reach non-academic audiences. While the complexity and contradiction of these positions might be seen as symptomatic of a particularly complicated, and sometimes testing, semiperipheral context, we should not be surprised if our own reflections on the questions set provoke similarly challenging and critical perspectives, whether we locate our work in a core, peripheral, or semiperipheral situation.

Acknowledgments

We are indebted to our eight research participants and colleagues for their expert insight, generosity, and patience. We are grateful for funding for this project through a Scholarship of Teaching and Learning grant from the Center for Teaching and Learning at the American University of Beirut (2016–2017).

References

American University of Beirut. (2019). *American University of Beirut: Facts and figures 2019*. https://www.aub.edu.lb/AboutUs/Documents/Facts-Figures-2019.pdf.

Anderson, B. S. (2011). *The American University of Beirut: Arab nationalism and liberal education*. University of Texas Pr is envisaged is an ess.

Babones, S. J. & Chase-Dunn, C. (Eds.). (2012). *The Routledge handbook of world-systems analysis*. Routledge.

Bazerman, C. & Paradis, J. (Eds.). (1991). *Textual dynamics of the professions: Historical and contemporary studies of writing in professional communities*. University of Wisconsin Press.

Bennett, K. (Ed.). (2014). *The semiperiphery of academic writing*. Palgrave Macmillan.

Canagarajah, A. S. (2002). *A geopolitics of academic writing*. Pittsburgh University Press.

Esseili, F. (2017). A sociolinguistic profile of English in Lebanon. *World Englishes, 36*(4), 684–704. https://doi.org/10.1111/weng.12262.

Flowerdew, J. & Costley, T. (Eds.). (2017). *Discipline-specific writing: Theory into practice*. Routledge.

Gere, A. R., Swofford, S. C., Silver, N. & Pugh, M. (2015). Interrogating disciplines/disciplinarity in WAC/WID: An institutional study. *College Composition and Communication, 67*(2), 243–266. https://www.jstor.org/stable/24633857.

Hanafi, S. (2014). Al-Akhta' al-sha'i`a fi kitabat makalat al-baḥth al-ijtima`i [Common mistakes in sociological writing]. *Idafat: The Arab Journal of Sociology, 26–27*, 6–11.

Hyland, K. (2016). Academic publishing and the myth of linguistic injustice. *Journal of Second Language Writing, 31*, 58–69. https://doi.org/10.1016/j.jslw.2016.01.005.

Lillis, T. & Curry, M. J. (2010). *Academic writing in a global context: The politics and practices of publishing in English*. Routledge.

Orr, M. & Annous, S. (2018). There is no alternative! Student perceptions of learning in a second language in Lebanon. *Journal of Language and Education, 4*(1), 79–91. https://doi.org/10.17323/2411-7390-2018-4-1-79-91.

Prior, P. A. (1998). *Writing/disciplinarity: A sociohistorical account of literate activity in the academy*. Routledge.

Russell, D. R. (2002). *Writing in the academic disciplines: A curricular history* (2nd ed.). Southern Illinois University Press.

Salloum, S. & BouJaoude, S. (2020). Language in teaching and learning science in diverse Lebanese multilingual classrooms: Interactions and perspectives. *International Journal of Science Education, 42*(14), 2331–2363. https://doi.org/10.1080/09500693.2019.1648909.

Shaaban, K. (2017). The ongoing rivalry between English and French in Lebanon. In A. Gebril (Ed.), *Applied linguistics in the Middle East and North Africa* (pp. 161–182). John Benjamins.

Talhouk, S. N. (2017). *Alif ba' al-tabi`a* [The ABCs of nature]. Arab Scientific Publishers.

Talhouk, S. N., Yazbek, M. M., Sleem, K., Sarkissian, A. J., Al-Zein, M. S. & Abou Eid, S. (2014). *Ashjar Lobnan* [Trees of Lebanon]. Nature Conservation Center, American University of Beirut.

Thaiss, C. & Zawacki, T. M. (2006). *Engaged writers and dynamic disciplines: Research on the academic writing life*. Boynton/Cook Publishers.

Tusting, K. & Barton, D. (2016). Writing disciplines: Producing disciplinary knowledge in the context of contemporary higher education. *Ibérica: Revista de la Asociación Europea de Lenguas para Fines Específicos, 32*, 15–34. http://www.aelfe.org/documents/32_01_IBERICA.pdf.

Wallerstein, I. (2004). *World-systems analysis: An introduction*. Duke University Press.

Wallerstein, I. (2011) Thinking about the humanities. In D. Palumbo-Lui, B. Robbins & N. Tanoukhi (Eds.), *Immanuel Wallerstein and the problem of the world: System, scale, culture* (pp. 223–226). Duke University Press. https://doi.org/10.1215/9780822393344-011.

Wallerstein, I. (2012). Conclusion: World-systems analysis as a knowledge movement. In S. J. Babones & C. Chase-Dunn (Eds.), *The Routledge handbook of world-systems analysis* (pp. 515–521). Routledge. https://doi.org/10.4324/9780203863428.ch15_7.

Wallerstein, I. (2016). The itinerary of world-systems analysis; or, how to resist becoming a theory. In I. Wallerstein, C. A. Aguirre Rojas & C. Lemert (Eds.), *Uncertain worlds: World-systems analysis in changing times* (pp. 195–217). Routledge.

Part Two. Reflections on an EATAW Outlook: Observations from Colleagues with Overlapping Interests

Towards the closing stages of the production process, when the nine chapters were shared in late versions, we asked a handful of colleagues to offer a reflection on the perspectives the chapters offer. As collection editors, we asked Djuddah Leijen, the chair of the association, to comment; we asked for a post-script from Emma Dafouz as one of the keynotes at the conference; we asked our researcher colleagues on the EARLY SIG Writing group for their reflections on the possible overlap and mutual interests; for similar reasons we also asked Robert Wilkinson, chair of Integrating Content and Language in Higher Education (iclhe.org) to offer a perspective; and reaching further abroad, we asked Elaine Espindola from the Latin American Association of Writing Studies in Higher Education and Professional Contexts (ALES) to comment on the work of two similar associations continents apart.

10 EATAW as a First-Year College Composition Course

Djuddah Leijen
EATAW Chair
University of Tartu

There are three main avenues I wish to take when presenting my reflection on this collection. All three of these avenues represent, in part, the interest I maintain with our EATAW community, my main interest as an academic in the field of writing research, and my dedication to the teaching of writing in my institution.

With some degree of bias (but with a high degree of honesty, primarily acquired throughout the years being a member of the EATAW community and being an elected official on the board of EATAW) EATAW is an incredibly exciting organization and community to be part of. To get some sense why I think so, I strongly recommend you read Erin Zimmerman's chapter which drives home a much more objective account which reflects my personal bias. Erin does so by synthesizing 12 EATAW voices. A few of these voices were there right from the beginning. Other voices entered the organization a little later, such as my own. Being part of these voices, represented in Erin's article, and understanding that my voice is a relatively new voice, I am humbled that many of the founders of EATAW are still active participants in our community today, inspiring newcomers and frequent visitors who bring with them an incredible insight in the ever-growing complexity which is the teaching of academic writing and the research of academic writing in the context of Europe. Reflecting on my own development, I know that in 2009, when I first attended EATAW, I felt that I was finally in the company of people and colleagues who would make sense and simplified the teaching of writing, only to realize, that the complexity grew the deeper I dove. Neither the word simplified here nor complexity are words which have a negative connotation when it comes to what we do. The complex role of writing just is, as Machura, Melonashi et al., and Zenger and Pill highlight in their chapters. Overall, this collection represents the growing complexity of what we do and who we are. EATAW has, over the years I have participated as member of the community and as an elected representative on the board, diversified. EATAW, as have other organizations which centralize writing, has managed to build a following and a voice for those who are stranded on diverse European islands when it comes to the teaching of writing and the research of writing. As many of you know, and as became clear in the last Keynote address of Dylan Dryer at the EATAW conference in Ostrava 2021, Europe does not have a discipline which is called writing, as they do in the US. Writing lives in many different areas where we are, and in many different languages and many different cultures. Given my own personal growth within the organization, but also as a researcher and instructor of writing, I embrace this complexity, and welcome the diversity of these messages represented in this collection.

As I highlighted earlier, three papers in this collection provide a clear demonstration of the complex environment we reside in. Machura's paper investigates superdiversity at a German University; Melonashi et al. reporting on the challenges European institutions of higher education face through the COST action, We ReLaTe; and Zenger and Pill, demonstrating how we may be able to better understand the challenges highlighted by the former studies through the lens of world-systems to better understand the connectivity between the complex structures we operate in. Superdiversity is represented by student populations, with different social economic backgrounds, and social cultural backgrounds, linguistic backgrounds operating in different disciplines. Many of us work in these environments. I applaud Machura for placing superdiversity central in her work, primarily, knowing full well, that investigating any group of students results in these diversities to be factors we should be taking into consideration when drawing our inferences. As Zimmerman highlights through her conversations with EATAW voices, Europe does not have a unified approach to teaching and learning writing as they do in the US. Most countries in Europe do not have anything which closely resembles first year composition courses. As a result, it is a huge challenge for all of us. There is no common denominator we can fall back on. As such, superdiversity is what we have, and will continue to create.

Melonashi et al.'s chapter on the incredible work COST action We ReLaTe undertook to better understand what kind of institutional support models there are in European institutions of higher education. Where do we place writing, teaching, learning and research? Who is responsible to teach, support or even develop these competences? And more important, who are the stakeholders, where do they come from, and when we ask stellar colleagues in these countries, where and how did they pick up on these skills? Reading through the accounts of their research, it becomes clear there has not been a winning institutional formula in the European context. This might primarily be as there does not seem to be a general standard, and from their findings, stellar scholars find their way through a more bottom up, personal network building approach. It highlights the need for European organizations and networks and projects as essential to build and foster these skills. However, Zenger and Pill's study, reporting on the conversations had with scholars in higher education institutions, describes the scholars' understandings of academic writing in their institutions and how this operates across institutional boundaries. As in Melonashi et al.'s study, there is evidence of networked bottom-up perspectives, but Zenger and Pill also conclude that there are also scholars who do not present these perspectives. It should be noted, however, that these perspectives were not in the European context. From the perspective of EATAW, complexity and diversity is part of our responsibility to support and bring scholars together not only once every two years during our conference but continuously as a community.

Teaching writing is a passion of mine, and surely for many of you who are reading this collection. This is what brought me to EATAW and will keep me engaged with EATAW. The previously mentioned papers have demonstrated the complexities, but the following three papers highlight why EATAW is so important when it comes to navigating these complexities as instructors of writing, specifically in our context. Castelló's study, for me as an instructor of writing for doctoral students, emphasizes that the teaching of writing is not (only) about teaching writing, but it is about approaching writing through personal discovery and raising awareness. This may well be attributed to the fact that, again, in the European context, there are no writing and composition courses which all students take at the beginning of their higher education journey. As a result, students have to go through the journey of understanding themselves as a writer, who they are writing for, and how that is achieved in the text. The time students find out, is when they are confronted with a writing assignment. Doctoral students end up in the deep end, where writing is their prime outlet for research results. We know this, but how many of our colleagues at our institutions know this? How many times do we need to convince others that writing is not about language alone, and writing is about becoming a writer? Castelló's studies are instrumental for those working with doctoral students and in research intensive programs.

Evident also in Ankersborg and Pogner's research, teaching writing is not always about teaching writing. In their study, they investigated the role of supervision as an intervention to support and develop students writing skills. When we do not teach writing directly, what role does a pedagogical intervention such as supervision, more specifically student-centered supervision, have on students learning of writing? According to Ankersborg and Pogner, such supervision empowers students to become more much aware the writing process has in their personal development as writers. When these skills and such revelations are fostered during the early years of higher education students, the better a non-uniformed centralized first year composition course can support the diversity we operate in. In other words, studies such as these highlight that in the European context, we may find strength in alternative ways of teaching writing. First year composition courses, as some of us long for in some of our institutions, might actually not be a beneficial pedagogical model. Given the diversities of languages, cultures, institutional contexts, etc. Our models are supported in our lack of direct teaching of writing and more in the ways we support our complexities to foster students' individual and personal awareness of what writing is and means in their contexts. For some it might live in a small cultural and linguistic context, for others, one which operates and is influenced by the global stage of writing and research, as also highlighted by Zenger and Pill.

Dengscherz' reporting of 17 case studies further highlights of situational variation in the modeling of writing processes. This paper attempts to make visible the complexities we do not see. Not to sound too repetitive, but writing contexts differ, languages, cultures, and institutional models differ. Writing process models have given us a glimpse into the complex system of writing. When agglomerating all our EATAW contributions, we see all sorts of contributions poking holes and filling holes that many of the models cannot model or have not modeled extensively yet. Which brings me to the two remaining papers in this collection, which both address the latest challenge we are all facing in light of the COVID-19 pandemic, and how technology interrupts and adds multiple complexities to everything we do. Both Anson and Head caution us when we apply any technological tool. For many of us, in the last months, it has been a savior and a curse. It has required many of us to rethink, quickly, how we can transform everything we know and have done with technological tools which will support us in the process of teaching and supporting students in the process of learning to write. As readers of this conference collection, you are invested in the teaching of writing, and I encourage you to read Anson's and Head's work. They are challenging us to think and rethink the role technology plays in our new normal.

We're still in the middle of this crisis and in some ways, as an elected EATAW board member, I am looking forward to the challenges that lie ahead for us as an organization. The take-away message for me, and one which I share with my colleagues on the board, is that we need to broaden our scope of support to our members. After 20 years, EATAW stands for something in all our individual complex contexts. We can, perhaps, be the first-year composition course, for instructors and institutions. In other words, we are a representative voice reflected in our studies and combined knowledge. Too valuable to be shared once every two years. If one thing what the new normal has taught us, we can come together much more often. We can share our knowledge through online platforms. We do find each other's voices. We just need to make it easier and more accessible.

11 A Reflective Post-Script of Academic Writing in Times of Internationalization, Interdisciplinarity and Multilingualism

Emma Dafouz
COMPLUTENSE UNIVERSITY OF MADRID

As a researcher working in the field of English applied linguistics for nearly thirty years now, academic writing has accompanied me throughout all my professional life. First, as a novice writer learning to accommodate my ideas to the conventions of the academic register, and, later as a lecturer, teaching students how to do the same effectively. However, in the space of time that separates my current students from myself, academic writing practices, pedagogies and research have changed noticeably in order to adjust to the global times. Luckily, such a change is faithfully reflected in this volume, where the different contributions weave a multifaceted landscape of academic writing—a landscape which, as the book accurately shows, is probably more international, interdisciplinary and multilingual than ever before. Against this background, the following lines intend to be a brief and personal reflection of four inter-related challenges that, in my view as a keynote speaker at the 2019 EATAW Conference and as a non-Anglophone scholar, lie ahead academic writing research and pedagogy, two decades into the twenty-first century.

A first challenge, indeed addressed in this timely edited book, concerns the unfolding of teaching and learning paradigms related to "social participation, identity and learner experience" (Hyland, 2012, p. 30). From such a socio-constructivist perspective, the importance of language in the building of knowledge and of disciplinary identity is foregrounded as is too attention to students' subject knowledge, interests and perceptions. In this light, further research which adopts an ethnographic, participant-oriented and longitudinal approach to the practices surrounding student academic writing, both in class and extramurally, is always welcome. This emic viewpoint will help to unveil the super-diversified profile of our learners, enable us to draw on their theoretical frameworks and their system of beliefs, and ultimately, round our understanding of such participants, as well as of the texts they produce and the communities they belong to.

A second challenge, closely connected to the first, refers to the growing presence of students in internationalized higher education institutions where English is largely used as the medium of instruction (EMI). In these settings, learners are expected to produce their academic texts in English (usually as a foreign language) but are often not supported in the writing processes. This discrepancy between what is demanded from students and supplied by (content) lecturers is an area that, as I pointed out in my keynote, should be investigated more broadly. Lecturers need to realize that academic writing in EMI is not simply about mastering disciplinary English but also, and perhaps most importantly, about co-constructing disciplinary literacies. In other words, the difficulty, as content-experts largely believe, does not lie exclusively in the native vs. non-native (English) distinction, but also in the novice vs. experienced writer variable. Thus, the acquisition of disciplinary knowledge involves an encounter with a new and dominant literacy which, for the student—but the content lecturer as well—entails a true shift in the epistemological perspectives and literacy practices followed. In this regard, an interdisciplinary view of academic writing in EMI that envisages the close collaboration of content and language experts and, concurrently, provides systemic institutional support needs to be actively fostered. Such cooperation, moreover, has shown to develop more disciplinary-sensitive and self-aware writers who are better able to construct not only appropriate texts but also more robust authorial selves (Wingate, 2015).

The third challenge stems directly from the second above, as it addresses how to counterbalance the increasing presence of EMI programs in (higher) education with the use and value of other natural languages. While in the oral mode a shift to acknowledging a more multilingual approach to teaching and learning has gradually gained space with the construct of translanguaging (see García & Wei, 2014) and with the view of translanguaging practices as episodes for pedagogical scaffolding and learning (see Paulsrud et al., 2021), in the case of academic writing the orthodoxy seems to be mainly monolingual (i.e., English-only). There are, however, recent moves that view languages in a much more dynamic and multilingual fashion, whereby the mixing of multilingual repertoires in academic settings is envisaged as an opportunity to broaden or deepen knowledge rather than as a source of interference (see for e.g., Palfreyman & van Der Walt, 2017). In this sense, a challenging task for researchers and practitioners will be to examine how multilingual written practices, ranging from informal student use of different languages, to pedagogical, institutional or disciplinary strategies leveraging multilingual resources, can be used to support learners and lecturers in the construction of their respective pluriliteracies (see Meyer et al., 2018). In doing so, a fourth challenge will be to explore which extant rhetorical models will be prioritized, discarded, or perhaps which new models will emerge as a result of academic writing in English taking place increasingly beyond non-Anglophone settings. Thus, research, into the intersecting or blended academic norms that learners have been found to produce in EMI and multilingual scenarios, and which combine national rhetorical models with Anglo-Saxon or Western patterns (see Brown, 2017) will be another interesting source of inquiry.

To close this short reflection, and as stated at the beginning of this piece, research, practice and pedagogies in academic writing have indeed come a long way to adjust to this new globally connected and growing digitalized world. In this setting, Gustafsson's and Eriksson's topical edited volume is the living proof that truly exciting and innovative studies—which address how international, interdisciplinary and multilingual experiences impact academic writing—are conducted across the four corners of the world. I am confident that the diverse cases portrayed in this book will inspire further research and engage participants from different disciplinary areas in unearthing other unchartered areas of academic writing.

References

Brown, H. (2017). Cooperation and collaboration in undergraduate EMI: Adapting EAP to the emergence of blended academic norms and practices in a Japanese university. In J. Valcke & R. Wilkinson (Eds.), *Integrating content and language in higher education: Perspectives on professional practice* (pp. 151–166). Peter Lang.

García, O. & Wei, L. (2014). *Translanguaging*. Palgrave Macmillan UK. https://doi.org/10.1057/9781137385765.

Hyland, K. (2012). "The past is the future with the lights on": Reflections on AELFE's 20th birthday. *Ibérica, 24*, 29–42.

Meyer, O., Imhof, M., Coyle, D. & Banerjee, M. (2018). Positive learning and pluriliteracies. In O. Zlatkin-Troitschanskaia, G. Wittum & A. Dengel (Eds.), *Positive learning in the age of information* (pp. 235–265). Springer.

Palfreyman, D. & Van der Walt, C. (Eds.). (2017). *Academic biliteracies: Multilingual repertoires in higher education*. Multilingual Matters.

Paulsrud, B., Tian, Z. & Toth, J. (Eds.). (2021). *English-medium instruction and translanguaging*. Multilingual Matters.

Wingate, U. (2015). *Academic literacy and student diversity*. Multilingual Matters.

12 A Reflection on Academic Writing: The Perspective of a Group of European Writing Researchers

Nina Vandermeulen
UMEÅ UNIVERSITY

Catherine Meulemans
UNIVERSITY OF ANTWERP

Lise Paesen
KdG UNIVERSITY OF APPLIED SCIENCES AND ARTS

Teresa Limpo
UNIVERSITY OF PORTO

In addition to being writing researchers, a common feature of the authors of this chapter is that they all belong to the Special Interest Group (SIG) on Writing. SIG Writing is a multidisciplinary organization promoting research on writing and providing a forum for exchange of ideas and collaboration. The organization was founded in 1988 as the 12th Special Interest Group of the European Association for Research on Learning and Instruction (EARLI). Through a biannual conference (SIG Writing conference), publications (Journal of Writing Research and the Studies in Writing book series), and several national writing initiatives, SIG Writing aims to promote collaboration between writing researchers from various countries and from various disciplines. SIG Writing members carry out research on a variety of writing related topics from theoretical, empirical and practice-based perspectives. One of the topics that is rather well represented within the SIG Writing community is academic writing. When going over the contributions of the past SIG Writing conferences, it seems that about fifteen percent of the total contributions targets themes related to academic writing.

In this reflection, we will touch upon a few academic writing related topics present in recent research of SIG Writing members and in this way, we will draw parallels with the European Association for the Teaching of Academic

Writing (EATAW). Firstly, we reflect on the importance of writing process studies, both from a social and a cognitive point of view. Secondly, we look into writing beliefs and writer identity, which is a main topic in academic writing studies. Thirdly, we present a short reflection on the growing interest for a specific type of academic writing, namely, writing based on sources.

Writing Processes

From primary school to university, writing primarily receives attention through the actual texts that are written (i.e., the end product): students' scores are based on the texts they produce and not on *how* they produce the texts (Vandermeulen, 2020). However, in recent years, writing processes and the relationship between them and their resulting texts seem to gain more coverage. The attention to writing processes in this book is therefore much appreciated. Dengscherz' chapter proposes the PROSIMS writing process model that looks at the influence of individual and situational factors on the writing situations that shape the writing process. This approach also takes into account the interrelations between writing activities and a large number of factors, such as task requirements and writers' strategies, providing a powerful example of how to look at writing processes from a social perspective. In her chapter, Castelló proposes an original and interesting addition to this social perspective, by also considering the ways in which reviewers help to shape a text.

This social approach aligns with the pedagogical focus of EATAW research but contrasts with the rather cognitive approach, very common among SIG Writing members (Galbraith & Baaijen, 2019; Limpo, 2018; Olive, 2014; Paesen & Leijten, 2019). While the social approach adopts a macro perspective and usually studies how the writing context influences texts from one version to the next, the cognitive approach tends to adopt a more micro approach concerned with the writing processes, for example by looking at the moment-to-moment production of a text. Typically, researchers opt to follow the text formation closely, using synchronous software to record keystrokes (e.g., Inputlog, Leijten & Van Waes, 2013; ScriptLog, Frid et al., 2014) or handwriting movements (e.g., Eye and Pen, Alamargot et al., 2006). When combined with other methods such as eye tracking, the writing process patterns give insight into several cognitive processes (i.e., planning, translating, reviewing, and transcription) (Wengelin et al., 2009).

Castelló briefly mentions the additional use of keystroke logging and screen capture software for one case study and thus provides an example of how the EATAW and SIG Writing perspectives can complement and reinforce each other. In future research, we would like to encourage bringing together the social nature and the cognitive aspect of writing. For example, studies focusing on language disabilities (e.g., dyslexia) would benefit from looking at the writing process from a cognitive point of view combined with a practice-oriented component. This would address the need to both understand certain language problems as well as to provide practical solutions for addressing them. It would be particularly helpful for university writing centers that offer support to undergraduates with language disabilities.

Writing Beliefs and Writer Identity

Besides an attention to academic writing products and processes, studies in writing also focus on the personal and social settings of writing. Writing beliefs and writer identity were two of the related and recurrent themes within research on academic writing of the last SIG Writing conferences. It is very encouraging to see the shared interest of EATAW and SIG Writing on this topic. The chapters provided by Dengscherz and Machura show a nice variety in studies with a focus on writing beliefs. Dengscherz presents a writing process model that considers individual variation in writing processes by taking into account attitudes, self-perception, motivation and beliefs. This study presents a more theoretical perspective, though one with implications for a more practical approach. Machura presents a pedagogically oriented approach. She presents an intervention study that resulted in substantial changes in participants' writing beliefs and attitudes.

Studies presented at SIG Writing conferences or published within Journal of Writing Research have focused on the link between writers' beliefs on writing and the strategies or approaches they adopt during the writing process when writing an academic text (Cuevas et al., 2018; Hewitt, 2018). Consequently, writing beliefs also influence the quality of the final text (Galbraith, 2018; Neely, 2014). Intervention studies to promote academic writing such as the ones by Wischgoll and Klingsieck (2018) and Strobl (2014) tested the effect of strategy instruction on text quality and writing beliefs (including writing approaches, strategies, and self-efficacy). These studies provide evidence for the beneficial impact of interventions targeting undergraduate students' writing beliefs. In the future, more intervention studies could be set up, based on insights from the various theoretically oriented studies, as a deeper understanding of the connection between writing beliefs, writing processes and text quality brings to light important elements that can be targeted in writing instruction on academic writing.

In addition to writing beliefs, there is also a representative body of work on the writer's identity in this collection. Castelló's chapter highlights the importance of acknowledging other voices while differentiating a personal voice in developing an academic writer identity. In addition, the work of Ankersborg and Pogner recognizes the importance of students becoming aware of their learner and writer identity as part of a student-supervisor model for thesis writing. Also within the SIG Writing community, there is a research interest for writer identity. For example, a symposium bringing together work of Donahue, Maguire, and Jeffery (Spelman, 2014) mapped the development of writer identity in settings of the transition from secondary education to higher education, meanwhile taking into account a wide personal and social context. An interesting niche within writer identity research focuses on writer identity of professional academic writers, such as doctoral and postdoctoral researchers (Rubin, 2018; Skakni, 2018). Insights from these studies could be very valuable to shape writing training sessions as part of universities' doctoral programs.

Source-based Writing

We would like to reflect on a specific type of academic writing, namely, source-based writing, sometimes also referred to as synthesis writing. Source-based writing is gaining attention in recent writing research as it is a fundamental skill in upper-secondary and higher education. Writing a text that integrates the content of multiple sources involves a complex interplay of reading and writing activities, and thus poses a challenge for students. Intensive writing training sessions such as the ones proposed by Machura in this book, are most valuable to support students in developing their source-based writing skills. This study is a great example of an evidence-based intervention with a pedagogical aim.

Within SIG Writing, two main areas of source-based writing research can be distinguished: a theoretically and a pedagogically oriented approach. Escorcia (2018), Leijten et al. (2019), and Vandermeulen et al. (2020) mapped synthesis writing processes, focusing on reading and writing strategies and the use of sources during writing. These types of studies provide theoretical insights into source-based writing, which in their turn can give input to more educationally focused studies and implementations. Intervention studies—both online (Luna et al., 2020; Strobl, 2014;) and offline (Cuevas et al., 2018; Raedts & Rijlaarsdam, 2012)—aimed to improve students' writing. They showed the positive effect of instructional methods such as explicit strategy instruction, guided exercises, graphic organizers, and video modeling on the students' synthesis text quality.

Conclusion

When going through EATAW's work, the organization's goal of making the link between research and practice definitely catches the eye. Academic research having an impact on academic practice might seem obvious, but in day-to-day practice, it is far from evident. Though educators in higher education generally show a positive attitude towards evidence-based practice, they also find it challenging and point to the need for more support in bridging the gap from research to practice (Diery et al., 2020). EATAW's mission to connect the teachers and scholars of academic writing is thus extremely valuable. This is well illustrated in the present book volume of EATAW, which provides a comprehensive perspective on current studies focusing on the teaching of academic writing from multiple viewpoints.

In this contribution, we highlighted three recurrent themes in academic writing research from our perspective as researchers within the SIG Writing community. Though the research within the SIG Writing organization covers a wide range of topics, studies on academic writing are well represented at the biannual conferences, as illustrated above. While reflecting on writing processes, writing beliefs, and source-based writing within the field of academic writing, we drew some parallels between the work of EATAW and SIG Writing that may stimulate collaborative works between the two organizations.

Despite the increasing amount of research focusing on teaching academic writing, there are still many avenues that can be taken for that joint research in the future. The three academic writing related subtopics that we highlighted in this reflection point to possible directions for that. Combining various perspectives like a product and a process approach provides valuable insights that will lead to a deeper understanding of academic writing. Additionally, there is the attention to writer-related characteristics such as writing beliefs and writer identity that adds to the teaching of academic writing. Our third subtopic, namely source-based writing, constitutes an example of a complex academic writing task in upper-secondary and higher education for which students need support. With changing student populations, varying university agendas, and shifts in teaching modes, there will be a need to continue developing and adapting evidence-based practice. A recent example calling for more research and a bridge to practice is the rise of remote teaching.

We believe combining perspectives of different fields and various methodological approaches, which complement each other, is fundamental to gaining relevant insights into both theory and practice of academic writing. We do hope this chapter was another step forward to that end.

References

Alamargot, D., Chesnet, D., Dansac, C. & Ros, C. (2006). Eye and pen: A new device for studying reading during writing. *Behavior Research Methods, 38*(2), 287–299. https://doi.org/10.3758/BF03192780.

Cuevas, I., Mateos M. & Martín, E. (2018, August 29–31). *Teaching to write argumentative synthesis collaboratively in higher education* [Paper presentation]. SIG Writing Conference, Antwerp, Belgium.

Diery, A., Vogel, F., Knogler, M. & Seidel, T. (2020). Evidence-based practice in higher education: Teacher educators' attitudes, challenges, and uses. *Frontiers in Education, 5*. https://doi.org/10.3389/feduc.2020.00062.

Escorcia, D. (2018, August 29–31). *Writing and reading strategies when producing texts in higher education* [Paper presentation]. SIG Writing Conference, Antwerp, Belgium.

Frid, J., Johansson, V., Johansson, R. & Wengelin, Å. (2014, February 19–22). *Developing a keystroke logging program into a writing experiment environment* [Paper presentation]. WRAB Conference, Paris, France.

Galbraith, D. (2018, August 29–31). *Identifying writing beliefs* [Paper presentation]. SIG Writing Conference, Antwerp, Belgium.

Galbraith, D. & Baaijen, V. M. (2019). Aligning keystrokes with cognitive processes in writing. In E. Lindgren & K. Sullivan (Eds.), *Observing writing. Insights from keystroke logging and handwriting* (pp. 306–325). Brill. https://doi.org/10.1163/9789004392526_015.

Hewitt, C. (2018, August 26–28). *Not writing from the heart: Exploring the relationship between students' beliefs about academic writing and the approaches they adopt* [Paper presentation]. SIG Writing Research School, Ghent, Belgium.

Leijten, M. & Van Waes, L. (2013). Keystroke logging in writing research: Using inputlog to analyze and visualize writing processes. *Written Communication, 30*(3), 358–392. https://doi.org/10.1177/0741088313491692.

Leijten, M., Van Waes, L., Schrijver, I., Bernolet, S. & Vangehuchten, L. (2019). Mapping master's students' use of external sources in source-based writing in L1 and L2. *Studies in Second Language Acquisition, 41*(3), 555–582. https://doi.org/10.1017/S0272263119000251.

Limpo, T. (2018). Development of a short measure of writing apprehension: Validity evidence and association with writing frequency, process, and performance. *Learning & Instruction, 58*, 115–125. https://doi.org/10.1016/j.learninstruc.2019.101272.

Luna, M., Villalón, R., Mateos, M. & Martín, E. (2020). Improving university argumentative writing through online training. *Journal of Writing Research, 12*(1), 233–262. https://doi.org/10.17239/jowr-2020.12.01.08.

Neely, M. E. (2014). Epistemological and writing beliefs in a first-year college writing course: Exploring shifts across a semester and relationships with argument quality. *Journal of Writing Research, 6*(2), 141–170. https://doi.org/10.17239/jowr-2014.06.02.3.

Olive, T. (2014). Toward a parallel and cascading model of the writing system: A review of research on writing processes coordination. *Journal of Writing Research, 6*(2), 141–171. https://doi.org/10.17239/jowr-2014.06.02.4.

Paesen, L. & Leijten, M. (2019). Name agreement and naming latencies for typed picture naming in aging adults. *Clinical Linguistics and Phonetics, 33*(10–11), 930–948. https://doi.org/10.1080/02699206.2019.1590734.

Raedts, M. & Rijlaarsdam, G. (2012, July 10–13). *Influence of writing instruction and cognitive skills on undergraduate students' academic writing* [Paper presentation]. SIG Writing Conference, Porto, Portugal.

Rubin, H. (2018, August 29–31). *Academics' plurilingual voice: Fostering creativity in writing* [Paper presentation]. SIG Writing Conference, Antwerp, Belgium.

Skakni, I. (2018, August 29–31). *Early career researchers and academic writing: A love-hate relationship?* [Paper presentation]. SIG Writing Conference, Antwerp, Belgium.

Spelman, K. (2014, August 27–29). *Transitions in writing: Perspectives from academic and social contexts* [Symposium]. SIG Writing Conference, Amsterdam, Netherlands.

Strobl, C. (2014, August 27–29). *The effect of online collaboration of individual academic writing development in a foreign language: Discussing a discrepancy between analysis results of writing process and product* [Paper presentation]. SIG Writing Conference, Amsterdam, Netherlands.

Vandermeulen, N., Van Steendam, E., van den Broek, B. & Rijlaarsdam, G. (2020). In search of an effective source use pattern for writing argumentative and informative synthesis texts. *Reading and Writing, 33*(2), 239–266. https://doi.org/10.1007/s11145-019-09958-3.

Wengelin, Å., Torrance, M., Holmqvist, K., Simpson, S., Galbraith, D., Johansson, V. & Johansson, R. (2009). Combined eyetracking and keystroke-logging methods for studying cognitive processes in text production. *Behavior Research Methods, 41*(2), 337–351. https://doi.org/10.3758/BRM.41.2.337.

Wischgoll, A. & Klingsieck, K. (2018, August 29–31). *Effects of (meta)cognitive strategy instruction on self-efficacy, writing beliefs, and text quality* [Paper presentation]. SIG Writing Conference, Antwerp.

13 Reflections: An Evolving Academic Writer

Robert Wilkinson
MAASTRICHT UNIVERSITY, NETHERLANDS

How do you become an academic writer? We are not born with the skill of writing. It is a learned competence—learned usually at school—and academic writing is acquired, to varying degrees, after entry into the academy (or university). An academic writer ranges from the starter student constructing their first piece of writing to the experienced faculty member producing for professional publication. Competence is complex, forged gradually and moderated by personal disposition, previous experiences of writing and its reception, conceptions of the target readership, context, discipline, belongingness to a community, among many other factors. The authors of the collected papers in this book attest to the complexity of the issues engrained in the process of acquiring and maintaining the status of academic writer.

The authors indeed stimulate me to reflect on the question: how I acquired (a degree of) academic writing competence, and how over half a century of personal involvement in academia has shaped or interacted with themes raised by the authors, taking the position of the reflective practitioner (see Anson, this volume). I acquired a basis of academic writing competence at university (like most students), and that basis is likely to have forged my writing style which probably remains very similar today, though I have not compared writings to verify this. Hartley et al. (2001), however, note how their writing styles remained constant over forty years despite changing writing technologies.

Twenty years ago, I attended the first EATAW conference in Groningen (see Zimmerman, this volume) and recall with much pleasure intense discussion with the many delegates and, for me, it represented my first encounter with experts from dedicated writing centres. This broadened my outlook immediately since my work was more specifically dedicated to writing integrated in the disciplines (see Björk et al., 2003, pp. 11-12). I had volunteered to "teach" writing for publication to academic economists in 1984 and this then opened the door to like-minded courses for a range of health science and biomedical disciplines in the years following. The courses were heavily based on evidence from published articles in the disciplines in question. The pedagogical approach may have been similar, but the strong focus on (intended) meaning and the close peer-group analysis of participants' writings entailed that up to three-quarters of the time was devoted to disciplinary content ("Do I need to elaborate this point?" "How should I convey that to my disciplinary peers?" "Do I need to provide additional evidence for this claim?"). The high degree of disciplinary coherence and understanding among health science academics and biomedical academics generated a collegiate atmosphere for peer discussion, especially in courses for Ph.D. students aiming to write for publication that started at the same time. Yet it was in the very first group of economists that I encountered challenges to this disciplinary approach. Economists come in all shapes and sizes: I had not realized that my motley crew of labor economists, social economists, financial economists, econometricians, macro-economists, economists of the firm, even one evolutionary economist, shared neither the same expectations nor the same conceptions of how writing was in their specific disciplines. My approach faltered. The striking absence of an expected (degree of) homogeneity between the economics disciplines was even more dramatic when I worked in law, where the academics would use highly suggestive legal argument to undermine the propositions in the writing of other law academics with whom they disagreed. I was unable to distinguish play-acting from reality.

My homogeneous approach faltered again, years later, but less dramatically, when the customized Ph.D. courses for health sciences and biomedical sciences were combined. Again, conceptions of the target writing did not concur, but the basic genre principles, that is the IMRD article structure (e.g., Swales & Feak, 2004), still largely applied because of the shared "reservoir of understandings" in these disciplines (Hyland, 2004, p. 71). The course programme which was designed in the 1980s remained essentially unchanged (except for the relevant example publications which differed according to the participants' research fields) and was not unlike that presented by Glasman-Deal (2010). The writing course still continues, as a blended programme, focused on the IMRD, notwithstanding the critique of such formalist academic writing which constrains perspectives on the construction of knowledge (see Labaree, 2020).

I stress the disciplinary differences (as emphasized in Machura, this volume, and Castelló, this volume) because I have been fortunate to work both in academia and in industry where the range of genres demanded may well exceed that in academia. Machura's contribution highlights the contrast between academic writing and workplace writing, and Castelló stresses the difference between writing for processes of education (academic) and for the disciplinary community (writing with one's peers as both source and target readers). This leads me back to how I began to write "academically" (as distinct from academic writing).

My first experience of writing "academically" was in Paris in 1967-1968 when I was ostensibly studying French. My experiences in Paris during that momentous year gave me a deep insight into the relationship between education and society, as well as a few bruises. At the time I did not think of myself as a writer. Two practical tasks stood out and both helped me understand what it meant to write not just "for the teacher" but also for external readers (for example, of newspapers, magazines, exhibition brochures, and "engagés"). The first task concerned summary writing: the teacher would choose a longish text (usually on a cultural or social issue of that particular day) and read it aloud at near normal speed. This was usually 15-20 minutes. We the students had to take notes and then construct a written summary for a specified readership without ever seeing the original text. At first I found it an extremely demanding task, which required intensive listening for a relatively long period, a need to keep in mind the intended readership (i.e., be selective), take notes, and then construct a summary of what I would consider the relevant information (and pay attention to structure, style, grammar, spelling, etc.).

The second task was the traditional "explication de texte," a method widely used for the analysis of literary and other texts (see Mermier & Boilly-Widmer, 1993; Perret, 2020; also Aldridge et al. (1963) for a brief explanation in English of the approach; the strong French tradition is referred to in Zenger & Pill, this volume). Barthes (1963), in particular, considers the "explication de texte" a "critique of language," embedded essentially in a certain type of culture that he characterizes as "national" and "French," appropriate for the study of the "classics," but not so for works of "modernité" such as Beckett or the products of mass culture (p. 170). "Explication de texte" required my fellow students and me to engage in close reading and detailed commenting on texts from the level of the word, through phrase and sentence, to the whole. The approach demanded a fine appreciation of metaphor and allusion and I recall learning how metaphors shape the reader's interpretation. As Derrida (1967, p. 30) states, "La métaphore n'est jamais innocente. Elle oriente la recherche et fixe les résultats." This seems most apt in that Derrida has science, particularly biology, in mind. While not explicitly adopting a Derridean approach, my fellow students and I learned (slowly) to view texts as part of a system: form or structure was not separable from meaning nor from prior and subsequent texts. (For a more extensive elaboration of Derrida's conception of "écriture," see Johnson (1993). Zenger and Pill, this volume, also use a systems approach but rather differently.) The practice of both tasks, week-in week-out for six months, succeeded in enabling me to construct "academic" texts that were embedded in a national educational culture that subsequently served me well at university.

Guidance in academic writing at university in the late 1960s and early 1970s was not something that students expected nor that teachers felt a need to provide, unlike the extensive support reported in different contexts in, for example, the chapters by Machura, Dengscherz, and Ankersborg and Pogner, this volume. Guidance in my case came through feedback and comments on the papers submitted—and we had to submit a lot of albeit short papers (about four every week)—but these comments did not always translate from one paper to the next, as demonstrated by my erraticism. However, then I had only hazy ideas of academic writing let alone research writing (as emphasized by Castelló, this volume). I began to familiarize myself with the resources available in the small department library at the Université de la Sorbonne Nouvelle–Paris III where I was then working (e.g., works of W. S. Allen, A. N. Hornby, and especially W. F. Mackey's *Language teaching analysis* (1965), among others), and later the work of John Swales and Mackay and Mountford's *English for Specific Purposes* (1978). Although my career over the subsequent decade did involve providing support for beginning student writers (as well as professionals), my help was often limited to language guidance and text structure as if the structure was a fixed uncontestable entity which could not be resisted.

During the 1990s, as the number of English-medium programmes expanded at Dutch and European universities, the need to provide academic writing support for both domestic and international students strengthened. Initially I and others saw this in the context of content and language integrated learning (CLIL) since the language concerned could be the L1 or any of the instructional languages used (see Hellekjaer & Wilkinson, 2001, who emphasize the need for collaboration between subject experts and language specialists in this form of instruction, an issue highlighted by several authors in this volume). The scope of collaboration at this time is shown in the example of a bilingual (Dutch and English) arts and culture writing programme that I was involved with (see Wilkinson, 2001), where, over four semesters, students wrote four research-based semester papers. Three were in Dutch and the fourth in English. There were no non-Dutch-speaking students on the programme at that time, international students being limited to Belgians from Dutch-speaking Flanders. Much use was made of the L1 and multilingual sources (a point emphasized in the chapters by Zimmerman, Machura, and Dengscherz, this volume). Regrettably, the growth of EMI programmes has led to the progressive reduction of Dutch programmes at the faculty concerned, though not the principles of collaboration behind the writing development programme as John Harbord intimates (see Zimmerman, this volume).

These concerns with rapid change in higher education and with content and language integration, whatever the language, underpinned the origins of the ICLHE (Integrating Content and Language in Higher Education) conferences from 2003 and the founding of the ICLHE Association in 2016—an organization that is younger than EATAW. Like EATAW, ICLHE has been concerned with any instructional language, at least in principle. Unlike EATAW, ICLHE does not limit its concerns to a single competence, academic writing literacy. Yet the themes addressed by the authors of this volume are also reflected in publications emerging from ICLHE, especially aspects of professional development (see Melonashi et al., this volume) which have recurred throughout ICLHE publications (see especially Valcke & Wilkinson, 2017; and Dimova & Kling, 2020). The impact of technology and its appropriateness (chapters by Head and Anson, this volume) has, however, only been marginally addressed by the ICLHE community (the 2019 Castelló conference being an exception, publications forthcoming), even though all content and language integrated programmes today depend, to some extent, on various electronic technologies for their success.

One key motivator for me in academic writing was the extent to which I could imagine the local perspective and the potential readers. Zenger and Pill's interviewees strongly emphasized how it was necessary to relate writing to their local context (Lebanon) and that what might be appropriate in the core (western Europe) would not necessarily fit locally. It was a lesson I encountered early in my writing journey when writing my undergraduate thesis on a highly contentious ecological question concerning salt marshes in France. Rather than my home university, my target readers were the local salt panners and environmentalists involved. In a way, writing for a "real" readership ought to come naturally to an academic writer, adding as it does dimensions to the nature of the self (see Melonashi et al., this volume). But as Reinertsen and Thomas (2019) affirm, "we write to de-comfort ourselves" (p. 3). In this Foucauldian approach, writing opens up a path to creating and adding to one's identity, as student, teacher, and researcher, in transdisciplinary, multilingual and transcultural contexts.

Acknowledgment

I am grateful to experienced colleagues in Paris in the 1970s who helped me acquire an understanding of academic writing when I had to teach students to write academic papers (in literature studies), as well as to the salt panners and environmentalists of the Presqu'île Guérandaise (France) who taught me the value of writing for a real context. Much credit is also due subsequently to my mentors at Edinburgh during the same decade: Bill Cousin, Leslie Dickinson and John Swan.

References

Aldridge, A. O., Meriwether, J. B. & Fleischmann, W. B. (1963). Symposium on "Explication de texte." *Books Abroad, 37*(3), 261–270.

Barthes, R. (1963). Oeuvre de masse et explication de texte. *Communications, 2*, 170–172.

Björk, L., Bräuer, G., Rienecker, L. & Stray Jörgensen, P. (2003). Teaching academic writing in European higher education: An introduction. In L. Björk, G. Bräuer, L. Rienecker & P. Stray Jörgensen (Eds.), *Teaching academic writing in European higher education* (pp. 1–15). Kluwer Academic Publishers.

Derrida, J. (1967). *L'écriture et la différence*. Editions du Seuil.

Dimova, S. & Kling, J. (Eds.) (2020). *Integrating content and language in multilingual universities*. Springer.

Glasman-Deal, H. (2010). *Science research writing*. Imperial College Press.

Hartley, J., Howe, M. & McKeachie, W. (2001). Writing through time: Longitudinal studies of the effect of new technology on writing. *British Journal of Educational Technology, 32*(2), 141–151.

Hellekjaer, G. O. & Wilkinson, R. (2001). Content and language integrated learning (CLIL) in higher education: An issue raising workshop. In F. Mayer (Ed.), *Languages for special purposes: Perspectives for the new millennium*. Vol. 1 (pp. 398–408). Gunter Narr.

Hyland, K. (2004). *Disciplinary discourses. Social interactions in academic writing*. Pearson Education.

Johnson, C. (1993). *System and writing in the philosophy of Jacques Derrida*. Cambridge University Press.

Labaree, D. F. (2020). Turtles all the way: Academic writing as formalism. *Journal of the Philosophy of Education, 54*(3), 679–693.

Mackey, W. F. (1965). *Language teaching analysis*. Longman.

Mackay, R. & Mountford, A. (Eds.). (1978). *English for specific purposes*. Longman.

Mermier, G. R. & Boilly-Widmer, Y. (1993). *Explication de texte. Théorie et pratique*. Edward Mellon Press.

Perret, L. (2020). L'explication de texte et ses avatars: Des exercices en tension dans les programmes. *Pratiques*, 187–188. https://doi.org/10.4000/pratiques.8812.

Reinertsen, A. B. & Thomas, L. M. (2019). Stepping into the flow . . . lif/ve decomforting academic writing: Smooth and striated spaces for being becoming performances. In L. M. Thomas & A. B. Reinertsen (Eds.), *Academic writing and identity constructions* (pp. 1–11). Palgrave Macmillan.

Swales, J. & Feak, C. (2004). *Academic writing for graduate students* (2nd ed.). University of Michigan Press.

Valcke, J. & Wilkinson, R. (Eds.). (2017). *Integrating content and language in higher education: Perspectives on professional practice*. Peter Lang.

Wilkinson, R. (2001). Merging content and language: Developing domain-specific writing skills in an arts and culture programme. In F. Luttikhuizen (Ed.), *V congrés internacional sobre llengües per a finalitats específiques: The language of international communication* (pp. 368–376). Universitat de Barcelona.

14 Intersection and Challenges in the Teaching of Academic Writing: Voices from Europe and Latin America

Elaine Espindola
Universidade Federal da Paraíba

It has been two decades since the establishment of the European Association for the Teaching of Academic Writing (EATAW) marked by the 10th Conference of its association in 2019. Since then, the world of Academic Writing has been facing dramatic changes but at the same time remains rather the same. This is to say that even though the abundancy of new technologies has been growing rapidly, bringing new models for the teaching of writing in general, experience in this realm of interaction is still lacking. If twenty years ago traditional methods, such as teachers being the holders of all knowledge and transmitting it to students was sufficient, this is no longer the case today. Students that enter higher education in the present days are those who were born immersed in the benefits and challenges arising from technology, and so education has had to shape and adapt to accompany the developments of these new natives.

Such exposition to the many different social media starts to build up a larger heterogeneous academic community, these communities are human institutions with actions and understandings influenced by personal and interpersonal relationships, as well as institutional and sociocultural issues that are associated with broad areas of knowledge (Hyland, 2009). Much of the content available in these contexts is usually produced and consumed in a foreign language, at least when it comes to Latin America. The consumption of this material in another language might bring problems to the writing in both first and foreign languages and English as the medium of instruction (EMI) is hardly a reality to this side of the world. Donahue (2018) says that today we face a highly diversified student population in higher education due to many factors. Building writing courses tailored to the "new" studentship is becoming even more problematic as disciplines have typical characteristics and must be understood based on specific knowledge, methodologies and practices shared by the members of a given community (Bathia, 2004).

As a consequence, Contexts of Culture and Situation (Halliday & Matthiessen, 2014) need to be taken into account when writing models are conceptualized as the ways of thinking, constructing and consuming knowledge in places where professional practices are negotiated and give rise to interdisciplinary discourses. In this manner, the term discipline can be used to describe and differentiate knowledge, institutional structures, researchers, and students in the educational setting as the term encompasses norms, specific epistemologies, its typical goals, and the practices that are carried out to achieve these specific goals. Nonetheless, a question that urgently needs to be answered, and has many faces to it, is: In this post- (if one can say that) pandemic period, what have teachers and professors and the other professionals involved in education learned in terms of what needs to be done for central and peripherical educational contexts to enhance their teaching practices in different international educational settings?

I will, in this piece of writing, attempt to reflect on an answer to this question trying to bring together the European context represented by the nine chapters of this collection of papers from the 2019 Conference of the European Association for the Teaching of Academic Writing and the Latin American context represented by the Latin American Association of Writing Studies in Higher Education and Professional Contexts (ALES), as I am currently a steering committee member of this association and the chair of the III ALES Conference.

In the context of the nine chapters of this collection, authors agree on the fact that writing needs to be seen as more than an assessment tool, but as a learning tool that guides students in examining, organizing, analyzing and synthesizing ideas. The studies that are presented in these chapters reflect on the tools and skills needed to aid higher education students in the development of academic writing as a set of abilities not taught as a recipe or a formula, but as a repertoire of communication strategies. However, one cannot leave aside the fact that any type of communication is construed within contexts of use. Taken into consideration the interconnectedness of this globalized and opulent world we live in, I would like to bring Bauman's (2001) concept of "liquid modernity" into this reflection. According to him, it is possible to see remarkable changes in the educational scenario in the production, distribution, acquisition, assimilation, and use of knowledge. Students are no longer passive; they have become part of knowledge construction well pointed in Castelló's and in Anson's papers. If we move down to the Latin American context, research has shown, in the ALES context, as for instance Navarro (2019), that we need to feed students with content, but also with critical thinking, capable of revising models that are currently unable to cope with dialoguing in the present scenario. In this sense, Parodi (2008) points out to the importance of finding ways to reach robust results based on large international corpora as a way of linguistically describing discourse variation among languages to develop an overview of similarities, and most importantly, differences across languages, disciplines and the institutions and workplaces where these discourses are realized.

As writing is permeated by many activity systems and the act of writing runs through both individual and collective spheres, academic writing is an achievement to be developed as a result of comprehensive practice shown in the papers presented in this collection and the collection entitled *Escrita na Universidade: Panoramas e Desafios na América Latina* (Pereira, 2018). Both of these volumes look at academic writing as an interactional dimension, motivated by its contexts and users, thus, studies that look at continuities, complementarities, and similarities can be seen as a concrete contribution to a common space for academic writing studies in higher education. Focusing, then, on the discovery of new knowledge and the development of teaching and research, perhaps it is time to globally collect theoretical and practical contributions which might lead to the reflection on the various aspects that can characterize and differentiate how academic genres in this new technological era are produced and maintained by social practices as this is the way members of the academic world interact with each other.

An interesting initiative is a global project put out by a group of scholars from many different countries worldwide looking at metaphors during COVID-19 and how this may shape language use around the world for years to come. The project is entitled Covid Metaphors Project and it is set to help scholars understand the dimension of shared human efforts to deal with the pandemic and its consequences. The main idea is to develop a global corpus that will contribute to an international description of the increased global awareness of the human dimensions and communication demands of healthcare. The researchers of the project believe that by putting together researchers from different areas of expertise, namely, academics, clinicians, caregivers, and people from business and the industry, it is possible to document and explore experiences to connect peripheral and central countries exploring fields and methodologies in healthcare communication as a way of collaborating to healthcare delivery.[1] I would like to argue that by giving attention to social issues such as healthcare and bringing it back to the classroom, we are able to increase writing proficiency in these institutions. Thus, the genres instantiated at workplaces may be used as materials for teaching writing tools

---

1   More information may be retrieved from: https://hedra.eu.

appropriate for learning and examining as well as analyzing the functions of language so as to communicate knowledge in an academic paper. As may be seen, then, teaching how to write is a central issue in the many curricular disciplines and as research universities become more international in focus, there is a need to strengthen teaching and learning cross-culturally across all levels and disciplines in higher education.

According to Bauman (2001), since the beginning of times knowledge has been evaluated based on the ability one has to "faithfully" represent reality. In this knowledge intensive society, the world that surrounds us, and writing being one of the spheres, is in constant change and it challenges the representation one has of current knowledge. With the fierce growth of technology, there is a need for constant innovation when it comes to the teaching of writing, and teaching in general, so that writing is not held back and thus fragmenting knowledge. The ease of accessing information has put down many obstacles in research that make us unconsciously ignore distances. Hence, as the world is being transformed, we need to develop skills and techniques necessary for the teaching of writing that is truly meaningful with the use of digital technologies in higher education. However, there is a twist to all of this, the distances that become invisible to teachers, researchers and educators cannot push aside the classroom the human component (Melonashi et al., in this volume) of interpersonal relations that are meaningful to knowledge construction and exchange of experience between individuals.

It seems, then, that both European and Latin American contexts are undergoing similar transformations and academic writing does not stay behind. As one can say, in any side of the globe, it is clear that people in general are writing more, even though, this amount of writing cannot be evaluated in terms of its quality. I would like, then, to conclude with a call for potential dialogue and collaboration across EATAW and ALES as sites where we are able to address current imperatives in the teaching of academic writing. By tying the world together through literate participation, it is possible to advance writing competence that allows us to share knowledge and research together.

References

Bauman, Z. (2001) *Modernidade líquida.* Jorge Zahar.
Bhatia, V. K. (2004). *Worlds of written discourse: A genre-based view.* Continuum.
Donahue, C. (2018). "We are the 'other'": The future of exchanges between writing and language studies. *Across the Disciplines, 15*(3), 130–143. https://doi.org/10.37514/ATD-J.2018.15.3.17.

Halliday, M. A. K. & Matthiessen, C. M. I. (2014). *An introduction to functional grammar*. Routledge.
Hyland, K. (2009). *Academic discourse*. Continuum.
Navarro, F. (2019). Aportes para una didáctica de la escritura académica basada en géneros discursivos. *DELTA Documentação de Estudos em Lingüística Teórica e Aplicada, 32*, 1–32.
Parodi, G. (2008). *Academic genres and genres. Discursive access to know and do*. Editions University of Valparaiso.
Pereira, R. C. M. (2018). *Escrita na Universidade: panoramas e desafios na América Latina*. João Pessoa.

§ Contributors

Vibeke Ankersborg is senior advisor and part-time Lecturer at Copenhagen Business School and an expert on master's thesis writing and supervision. Her research focuses on learning and study conditions for master's thesis students. In addition to research, she initiates and implements initiatives at the organizational level, which are designed to improve master's thesis students' conditions. Over the years, she has counseled more than 6,000 individual master's thesis students. She has previously published on writing retreats for master's thesis students as well as on methodology, including problem-oriented project work. In addition, she has 25 years of teaching experience in philosophy of science and methodology at Danish universities.

Chris M. Anson is Distinguished University Professor and Director of the Campus Writing and Speaking Program at North Carolina State University. He has published extensively in the field of writing studies and has spoken and consulted widely across the US and in several dozen other countries. He is past chair of the Conference on College Composition and Communication and past president of the Council of Writing Program Administrators, and currently serves as vice chair of the International Society for the Advancement of Writing Research. His professional summary can be found at www.ansonica.net.

Montserrat Castelló is Professor of Educational Psychology and Director of the Research Institute on Psychology, Learning and Development (Re-Psy) at Universitat Ramon Llull in Barcelona, Spain. She was vice-dean of research and doctoral studies at the Graduate School of Psychology and Educational Sciences. Her research interests include early career researcher writing and identity development.

Emma Dafouz is Associate Professor in the Department of English Studies at Complutense University of Madrid. Her research deals with understanding the roles of language in education, and particularly, in English-medium higher education. She served as advisor for curricular internationalization at her university from 2014 to 2019. At present, she is chair of the Spanish regional group of ICLHE.

Sabine Dengscherz is Researcher and Lecturer at the University of Vienna (Centre for Translation Studies and German Department). After her studies of German philology, communication and Hungarian philology, she has been teaching at universities and other tertiary institutions in Russia, Hungary, Austria, and Germany. Lately, she was head of the research project PROSIMS, funded by the Austrian Science Fund FWF. She has published

Contributors

several books and articles and holds a "venia" for transcultural communication and multilingualism.

Paul Donovan is Emeritus Associate Professor at the School of Business, Maynooth University since 2009. He has, during that time served also as Head of School and Director of Teaching and Learning. He was previously Registrar and Head of Management Development at Irish Management Institute (IMI) specialising in management development where he delivered hundreds of management development programmes to thousands of participants across the globe. His research interests include effective teaching in higher education and learning transfer in corporate education.

Başak Ercan works as an instructor of English at Akdeniz University. She has a degree in English language teaching (ELT). She completed her master degree on educational management, supervision and planning. Currently, she is pursuing her Ph.D. degree in educational management at the University of Latvia. Her research interests include ELT, higher education learning environments, and professional development.

Andreas Eriksson is Associate Professor of Academic Writing and Communication in the Disciplines at Chalmers University of Technology. He is currently also the head of division of the Division for Language and Communication in the Department of Communication and Learning in Science. His main research interests are within the fields of writing research, writing pedagogy and the integration of content and language in higher education (ICLHE). He has been an active member of the EATAW community since 2009. He has also served as a reviewer for *Journal of Academic Writing* and guest edited a special issue for the journal.

Elaine Espindola holds a B.A. in English and Portuguese language teaching (UNOESC/CHAPECÓ) and holds both an M.A. and Ph.D. in linguistics from the Universidade Federal de Santa Catarina (2005, 2010, respectively). She has undertaken postdoctoral fellowship at the Hong Kong Polytechnic University focusing on systemic functional linguistics and multimodality under the supervision of Professor Christian Matthiessen. Currently, she is Assistant Professor at the Universidade Federal de Paraíba (UFPB) and the Director of International Academic Mobility. She is the coordinator of the research group Investigative Professional Contexts; Systemic-Functional Linguistics and a member of the HEDRA and SAL (Systemics, Environments, and Languages) research groups. Her research interests are devoted to professional discourse studies, textual analysis, and applied linguistics.

Alison Farrell established the University Writing Centre in Maynooth University in 2011. She is the founding chair of the Educational Developers in Ireland Network (EDIN) and the Irish Network for the Enhancement of Writing (INEW). She was management committee (MC) chair of the European COST Action WeReLaTe. She is currently seconded to Ireland's National Forum for the Enhancement of Teaching and Learning in Higher Education as Senior Lead for Sectoral Engagement. Her research interests include academic writing, collaboration, professional development, and policy and power in higher education.

Magnus Gustafsson is Associate Professor of Academic Writing and Communication in the Disciplines at the Department of Communication and Learning in Science at Chalmers University of Technology. His main research interests are within the fields of writing studies, integration of content and language, and higher education pedagogy. He is an EATAW member since 2007, chaired the association from 2011 to 2017, and is the current treasurer. He is a co-editor of the *Journal of Academic Writing*. He is also a series editor at the WAC Clearinghouse for international Exchanges on the Study of Writing.

Karen J. Head is Executive Director of the Naugle CommLab at the Georgia Institute of Technology, and Professor and Associate Chair of the School of Literature, Media, and Communication. Since 2006, she has been a visiting scholar at Technische-Universität-Dortmund, where she helped establish one of the first writing centers in Germany. Her book, *Disrupt This!: MOOCs and the Promises of Technology*, explores the rhetoric surrounding higher education and arguments about technological disruption, especially the utopian view that technology answers all problems. She is the author of several books of poetry and editor of the international poetry journal *Atlanta Review*.

Djuddah A. J. Leijen is Lecturer at the College of Foreign Languages and Cultures, and Head of the Centre for Academic Writing and Communication at the University of Tartu, Estonia. He leads an interdisciplinary course on communicating science with a dedicate crew of Ph.D. students and staff. His research interests include intercultural rhetoric, Ph.D. writing, web-based peer review systems, writing research methodologies, and using machine learning as an integrated method to evaluate writing products and processes.

Teresa Limpo is Assistant Professor at the University of Porto and co-coordinator of the SIG Writing. In the past decade, she has conducted research on the cognitive and motivational processes involved in writing and developed evidence-based interventions to promote this academic skill in school-aged children. Recently, she has been exploring the role that general-domain factors (e.g., mindfulness, executive functioning, socio-emotional learning) play in writing achievement and, ultimately, students' success inside and outside the school.

Ina Alexandra Machura teaches discipline-specific courses in English linguistics for undergraduate students as well as interdisciplinary writing-intensive courses for graduate and doctoral students in the social and life sciences, cooperating with lecturers from various departments in team-teaching partnerships. In her Ph.D. project, she investigated undergraduate and graduate students' multilingual writing knowledge development, with a focus on the role of translanguaging strategies in EFL source-based writing processes. In her current research, she investigates the importance of modeling and cognitive apprenticeship for writing knowledge transfer.

Erika Melonashi is Associate Professor at Wisdom University College in Tirana, where she serves as Dean of the Faculty of Economics and Social Sciences. She holds a Ph.D. in psychology and her research interests lie within the sub-disciplines of social, health and developmental psychology. She has been actively involved in quality assurance processes in higher education, as external evaluation expert for the Agency of Quality Assurance in Higher Education in Albania. She is a member of the Commission for Continuous Education, in the Albanian Order of Psychologists. She was Management Committee member of the European COST Action WeReLaTe, representing Albania.

Catherine Meulemans is a doctoral researcher at the University of Antwerp. She explores written sentence production in healthy aging adults and cognitively impaired adults by using keystroke logging. With her findings, she aims to contribute to the detection of language change in the earliest stages of Alzheimer's disease on the basis of writing processes.

Sonia Oliver del Olmo has a degree in Anglo-German philology (University of Barcelona, 1992) and a Ph.D. in translation and interpretation (University Pompeu Fabra, 2004). She is Lecturer in the Department of English and German Philology in the Autonomous University of Barcelona (UAB), Spain, where she teaches English for academic purposes (EAP) and advanced academic abilities in the master's program. Her research interests include intercultural studies, academic writing, critical discourse analysis (CDA) and English L2. She is currently the academic exchange coordinator (Faculty of Arts and Humanities) and Head of Unit (Faculty of Education Sciences) in the UAB.

Lise Paesen is a doctoral researcher at the University of Antwerp and L2 English lecturer at Karel De Grote University of Applied Sciences and Arts. She specializes in linguistic changes in healthy aging based on narrative writing tasks and the development of a new clinical tool for the evaluation of written spontaneous speech in healthy aging adults and adults with a cognitive impairment.

John Pill is Lecturer in the department of linguistics and English language at Lancaster University in the UK. Previously, he spent three years as Assistant Professor in the English department at the American University of Beirut, Lebanon. He completed his doctoral studies in language testing at the University of Melbourne, Australia. His research interests include specific-purpose language assessment and the consequences of language testing. More generally, he is interested in discourse communities and how newcomers gain access to them in language terms. He studies English in healthcare and academic contexts.

Karl-Heinz Pogner holds a Ph.D. from Odense University, Denmark. He has researched and lectured at Odense University and the Southern Denmark Business School in Sønderborg, Denmark. In 1998, he joined the Department of Intercultural Communication and Management (now Department of Management, Society, and Communication), Copenhagen Business School, as associate professor. He was one of the founding parents and academic program director of the BSc and MSc study programs, "Business Administration and Organizational Communication," and is one of the founders of the "ComCaseCompetition" (https://www.facebook.com/comcasecompetition/) and of K1: Association of Professional Communicators (https://k1kommunikationsforening.dk/)—as well as a founding member of the European Literacy Network (http://www.is1401eln.eu/en/). His primary interests in research, publication, and teaching are in the areas of academic literacy, text production, writing in the workplace, organizational communication, media and communication, co-creation, and urban governance.

Nina Vandermeulen is a post-doctoral researcher at Umeå University. In September 2021, she defended her dissertation on source-based writing and process-oriented feedback at the University of Antwerp. She focuses on writing process patterns in source-based writing using keystroke logging, and she develops intervention studies to give feedback based on keystroke logging data and comparison with exemplars.

Robert Wilkinson is a visiting research fellow in the Department of Philosophy at Maastricht University (Netherlands) and conducts research on English-medium instruction (EMI) and multilingualism. For three decades, he taught academic and professional writing to students and academic and non-academic staff, mainly at the Language Centre of the same university, as well as running writing courses for industrial and commercial firms and governmental and inter-governmental organizations. Previously he worked in France, Czechoslovakia, and Scotland. He is currently chair of the ICLHE Association.

Amy Zenger is Associate Professor of Rhetoric and Composition at the American University of Beirut, where she also directs the writing center. Lately, she has been thinking about (and occasionally writing about) transnational writing program administration and on turning to visual and spatial disciplines to think about writing. Originally from Portland, Oregon, in the

US, she has lived in Beirut since 2004. She noted, "I so much enjoyed the EATAW 2019 conference and am pleased to have written this chapter with my colleague, John Pill, and to have it be included in this collection."

Erin Zimmerman is Director of the Writing Center at the University of Nevada, Las Vegas. She first attended an EATAW Conference in 2013 in Budapest while still a graduate student. In 2017, while employed at the American University of Beirut, she joined the EATAW Board and served as membership secretary for four years, where she learned a lot and fell in love with the organization and its membership. She looks forward to (at least) 20 more years with EATAW.

www.ingramcontent.com/pod-product-compliance
Lightning Source LLC
Chambersburg PA
CBHW071230070526
44583CB00017B/2114